CITY, ECONOMY AND SOCIETY:
A COMPARATIVE READER

CITY, ECONOMY AND SOCIETY:

A COMPARATIVE READER

EDITED BY ALLAN COCHRANE, CHRIS HAMNETT AND LINDA McDOWELL

Harper and Row, Publishers *in association with* The Open University Press

Harper & Row, Publishers
London

Cambridge
Hagerstown
Philadelphia
New York

San Francisco
Mexico City
Sao Paulo
Sydney

Harper and Row Ltd
28 Tavistock Street
London WC2E 7PN

British Library Cataloguing in Publication Data

City, economy and society
  1. City planning – Addresses, essays, lectures
  I. Cochrane, Allan   II. Hamnett, Chris
  III. McDowell, Linda
  307.7′6   HT151

  ISBN 0-06-318205-X
  ISBN 0-06-318206-8 Pbk

Typeset by Inforum Ltd, Portsmouth
Printed and bound by The Pitman Press, Bath

Open University Course Team

Melanie Bayley
Andrew Blowers
Christopher Brook
Giles Clarke
Allan Cochrane
Mary Geffen
Chris Hamnett
Linda McDowell
Jerry Millard
Stephen Potter
Enid Sheward
Paul Smith
Eleanor Thompson
Graham Turner

Other contributors

Mike Bateman
Bob Colenutt
Peter Daniels
Patrick Dunleavy
Anne Jones
Camilla Lambert
John Lambert
Bill Lever
Martin Loney
Rosemary Mellor
Ken Newton
Chris Pickvance
John Raine
Eric Reade
Peter Saunders
Nigel Spence
Ray Thomas
Bob Wilson

Contents

Section VI   The Power of Planning   173

Section VII   State Intervention   203

Preface

This edited Reader has been conceived and produced primarily to accompany the Open University course *Urban Change and Conflict*. It is accompanied by a sister Reader *Urban Change and Conflict: An Interdisciplinary Reader* which also relates to the *Urban Change and Conflict* course. Both the course and its associated eight 50-minute TV programmes possess a similar structure and organizing theme to that embodied in the Readers. The overall theme is that of the relationship between market processes and their social consequences, planning and state intervention as they relate to urban change and conflict. Our central concern is to address the question of how far market forces constitute the primary determinant of urban structure and change. Equally we are concerned to enquire how far planning and other forms of state intervention serve to constrain, modify or replace the operation of market forces as they relate to urban areas. Finally, the relationship between planning and other types of state intervention in the spheres of housing, transport, education and employment, to take just four examples, is of importance in its own right.

In the course itself, these issues are approached within a predominantly, but by no means exclusively, British context, the stress being on the theoretical and conceptual questions involved. The course Reader *Urban Change and Conflict : An Interdisciplinary Reader* primarily serves to present the set readings associated with the course in a coherent and structured form. By contrast, this Reader, along with the related TV programmes, attempts to tackle the question of the relationship between the market, planning and the state in an explicitly comparative perspective. The types, nature and problems of comparative analysis are discussed in the Introduction, and all that needs to be said here is that our choice of the three cities of Vancouver, Birmingham and Cracow reflects our desire to contrast the market–state intervention polarity in three different social contexts; namely, a relatively *laissez-faire* economy, a mixed economy and a centrally planned command economy. This enables a clearer assessment to be made of the power of planning and state intervention *vis à vis* market forces than would be possible in a single country or in countries with a similar mode of economic organization.

This then is the overall theme of the book and it explains both the choice of the three different types of economy and society and, incidentally, the title selected for the Reader, for we have explicitly adopted the view that cities must be located in their social, economic and political context if they are to be adequately understood, let alone compared, however loosely. Where the internal structure and organization of the Reader is concerned, this follows on from the broad theme already outlined.

The first section on the 'images' of the three cities and their historical background is specifically designed to convey both an overall impression of certain key aspects of the three cities and an understanding of some of the central features of their historical development. Inevitably, as in all books of this kind, they are highly selective but that is unavoidable and it would be worse in our view to adopt even the loosely comparative approach taken in this book, let alone a more rigorous one, without attempting to fill in at least some aspect of both the historical background and the dominant characteristics of the three cities. This is all the more so, given that Cracow consists of an almost perfectly preserved medieval city centre, linked to a post-war socialist industrial new town, whereas Birmingham is essentially a product of the nineteenth-century Victorian era of urban–industrial growth, and Vancouver is largely a product of the twentieth century and can be said to exhibit the characteristics allegedly associated with the 'post-industrial city'. The historical dimension then is almost as important as the economic one.

The second section of the Reader, entitled 'The Impact of Urban Growth', seeks to locate the cities in their regional context, showing both how they have grown and the causes and consequences of that growth. The third section is more narrowly focused; entitled 'City Centre Development and Change', it is concerned with the *determinants* of the changing patterns of urban land use. Nowhere are these more clearly shown than in the central areas of cities where land is scarce, stakes are high and the pressures for development (and the associated conflicts) most intense. Both the second and third sections of the Reader are concerned more with market forces than with planning, the fourth and fifth sections dealing more with the consequences or outputs of the allocation mechanisms. In the fourth section entitled 'Housing, Class and Space', the focus is, as the title suggests, on the relationships between class structure, the housing market and residential differentiation. The fifth section 'Local Government and Politics' is designed to serve both as a bridge to subsequent sections on planning and the state and as a culmination of preceding sections. It views urban political activity throughout local government structure, as an outcome of the conflicts over scarce resources such as land, housing, environment and the pattern of facility distribution. Insofar as spatial or land use planning seeks to exert an influence over the pattern of urban land uses, the question addressed in the sixth section, 'The Power of Planning', is the extent to which planning can and does in fact exert some control over the pattern of land uses and land use change. Finally, the issue of 'State Intervention' is discussed in Section VII. Although the issues vary, from housing in Canada to housing and education in Poland and inner-city employment policy in Britain, the theme is the same.

As will be apparent from the table of contents, not all the articles specifically address the city in question. Whilst we have endeavoured to ensure a city-specific focus wherever possible, some articles are inevitably broader in scope. Finally, it will be seen that whilst each section has at least one article relating to each city, some sections have two or even three articles on one city. We have followed this policy both where the articles merited inclusion and where it was necessary to include more than one per city to ensure appropriate coverage of the important issues.

Given the diversity of the literature on each of the cities in the three countries, there is a considerable degree of variation in the articles in terms of level, focus, methodology, degree of analysis, style, etc. Some of the Polish material in particular is both descriptive and rather stilted, but given the relative paucity of English-language literature on Eastern Europe this is almost inevitable. We hope nonetheless that the effort to put together and bring out a Reader examining a number of specific themes in three carefully chosen cities will have proved worthwhile both in terms of the greater accessibility of the material to the Reader and the greater level of understanding afforded regarding the workings of the three cities in question. The structure of the Reader should make it easy to use the material either on a comparative theme by theme basis or on a city-specific basis.

Finally, we should like to thank all those who helped us make the completion of this Reader possible, who put up with our failings and often did the most unpleasant work. In particular, thanks are due to Enid Sheward who suffered with us, to the editorial and production staff, John Taylor, Giles Clark and Melanie Bayley, and to our secretaries, Eve Hussey, Maureen Adams and Pat Cooke who somehow coped with all the extra work.

Allan Cochrane
Chris Hamnett
Linda McDowell

Introduction

Comparative urban enquiry

If the nineteenth century is commonly known as the century of industrial revolution, the twentieth century might equally well be dubbed the century of urban revolution. In the last 50 years, the world's urban population has more than quadrupled. This average figure covers a range of variation, of course, from a less than threefold increase in the urban population in the developed economies of the Western world to much higher rates elsewhere. In both Latin America and Africa, for example, the rate of increase was eightfold over the same period. The movement of population from rural to urban areas, however, from the land into industrial and service employment in cities that has been observable in the West since the nineteenth century is now a virtually universal phenomenon. Progressively, more and more of the world is becoming urbanized.

Table 1. The world's largest cities in 1960–61.

	Population (thousands)
New York – north-eastern New Jersey	14 759
Tokyo – Yokohama	13 628
London	11 547
Rhine – Ruhr	10 419
Moscow	7884
Paris	7810
Osaka – Kobe	7608
Shanghai	6900
Chicago – north-western Indiana	6794
Buenos Aires	6763
Los Angeles – Long Beach	6743
Calcutta	6243
Peking	5420
Mexico City	4816
Bombay	4698
Rio de Janeiro	4692
Sao Paulo	4369
Philadelphia	4343
Berlin	4154
Randstadt – Holland	3937
Detroit	3762
Leningrad	3579
Cairo	3500
Hong Kong	3133

Source: Hall P 1966 *The World Cities* (London: Weidenfeld and Nicolson) p11.

A high proportion of twentieth-century urban growth has been in the largest cities of the world. In 1966 Professor Peter Hall (1966) dubbed this trend the 'metropolitan explosion'. By the early 1960s he found that there were already 24 metropolitan centres in the world each with a population of over three million: these are listed in table 1. It is clear that these large metropoli are not solely a feature of the most economically advanced nations of the world but, as the table shows, they include cities in less developed parts of the world, in both capitalist and in state socialist societies, in democracies and in dictatorships, in societies where the rural–urban population movement is relatively free, and in others where it is controlled by the state.

As world urbanization accelerates questions such as why do cities grow, how and when the majority of the population became urban dwellers and what the consequences are of urbanization, assume increasing urgency as many cities in the world are facing problems of urban overcrowding, unemployment, poor housing and political unrest. From the perspective of the advanced industrial West, the answers to questions such as these lie mainly in the large-scale changes in the structure of society and the economy that took place during the nineteenth century. The intellectual basis not only of many urban social theories but also of much of urban policy and state intervention in the advanced capitalist societies is derived from these nineteenth-century changes. There is a marked tendency among Western scholars to extrapolate directly from the experience of Britain and North America in particular, and to assume that there will be a repetition of the urban experience of the West in countries in other parts of the world as modernization and industrialization take place. However, it is by no means apparent that urbanization is a general phenomenon explicable by reference to the same set of processes and so amenable to universal explanation in whatever context it takes place.

The assumption that societies that are experiencing urban growth at present are merely at an earlier stage of a process through which the advanced industrial economies have already passed fits into a more general argument known as the technological convergence thesis. Briefly, it is argued that the social structure of industrial–urban societies adjusts to the needs of the economy. Corporate organization and state intervention in the market lead to increasing similarities in the class structure, the occupational distribution of rewards, in the use of market principles of pricing and efficiency, in the structure and internal organization of urban areas in industrial and industrializing societies. The more determined adherents of this thesis believe that these similarities develop from the limited possibilities of adapting to large-scale technological industrialism despite differences in the timing of industrialization, in the histories, traditions, languages and institutions of societies. Despite differences in the key institutions and economic methods of one country and another, similarities in what they do, rather than what they say they do, develop over the years. Thus, the significance of ideology in the determination of socio-economic and political structures is denied. The logic of industrialism — that specific social and economic forms are prerequisites for efficient functioning — results in increasing convergence between industrial–urban societies. The most explicit development of the convergence thesis was by Clark Kerr and his associates in their book *Industrialism and Industrial Man*, first published in 1962, in which they outlined the key features of the 'pluralistic industrialism' towards which all industrial societies would converge. Greatest attention was focused on aspects of social structure and on the development and growth of state intervention in the economy and in the broad area of social welfare.

The convergence thesis has stimulated research in two main areas: firstly, occupational stratification and class inequality; and secondly, state intervention in social welfare; and both adherents and critics of the thesis have manipulated the available cross-national data — on income inequalities, rates of social mobility, levels of social expenditure, age and type of welfare programmes — to prove or disprove its contentions. The area of urban and regional development and questions about the rate and scale of urbanization *per se* were not specifically tackled by Kerr *et al*. However, a number of writers in this field have either explicitly or implicitly relied on the idea of convergence and technological determinism. Williamson (1965), for example, in a statistical study of 24 countries relating the level of economic development to regional and urban–rural inequalities, believed he had identified a universal trend. His thesis was that in the early stages of industrialization and urbanization, spatial income inequalities between regions increased before levelling off again with higher levels of economic growth. He assumed that all countries could be meaningfully aligned along a single dimension of 'successful' development — basically the path taken in the industrial West. Similarly, Hawley (1971) considered that:

The regions and nations of the world are being absorbed into an expanding world economy. As one society after another has yielded to the superior economic and political power of an industrialized market economy, it has been thrust along a path towards drastic internal reorganization. For it could not remain in its traditional path and at the same time participate in a highly rationalized network of interregional relations. *Participation in the world economy has demanded of every society the adoption of a* new technological regime [editor's emphasis], a reorientation of resources, a fundamental reconstitution and realignment of social units, and a broad-scale redistribution of its population. Urbanization is a more or less localized manifestation of this region-wide or multi-regional transformation . . . Although urbanization begins in very different cultural contexts, in each instance the land soon begins to reproduce phases and patterns that have occurred in other times and places. The convergence tendency penetrates surface features such as spatial arrangements — though even these are not as arbitrary as an uncritical view might lead one to suspect. (pp 311–12)

Some countries, however, have attempted, in their official statements at least, to challenge the supposed inevitability of the Western pattern. Tanzania, for example, has formulated a development programme that has the aim of minimizing regional inequalities by spreading industrial and urban investment throughout the country. Similarly, China has adopted various policies to reduce urban–rural differences.

Other authors, in the development of typologies of urban growth identifying stages through which countries pass, have also, although less explicitly than Hawley, transferred the experience of the industrial West to other settings. An early contribution to comparative urban studies by Hoselitz (1960, Chapter 7; original publication dated 1953), linking urbanization to economic development, was marred by his assumption of the universal nature of capitalism. Similarly Redfield and Singer (1954) assumed a unilateral transition from pre-industrial to industrial cities under the eventual global domination of industrial capitalism. Reissman (1964), a decade later, developed a four-stage model of urbanization and although he was at pains to point out that 'some societies will stop short, are retarded so to speak at one or another stage', his very terminology seems to imply that the fourth stage is both more advanced and more desirable. Another decade passed before Friedmann (1973), an urban planner, presented a systems model of urban development, linking urbanization to economic growth and assuming a progressive development of a single system of cities within nation states, based again on the extrapolation of observable trends in the advanced industrial economies of the West to other societies.

Comparative urban studies is, however, a relatively recent development and as work has proceeded in recent years, the basic assumptions of these stage models have been subjected to severe criticism. The need to investigate the specific historical nature of urban development under a range of economic systems has been recognized (McGee 1971, Harvey 1973) and the presupposition of a universal urban process challenged. Brian Berry, for example, when approached to write a book under the already decided title *The Human Consequences of Urbanization* (1974), felt compelled to subtitle his work 'divergent paths in the urban experience of the twentieth century'. Similarly, Hugh Stretton (1978), in a comparison of urban planning in affluent and poor capitalist and non-capitalist societies, argued thus:

Historical experience seems to be steadily reducing the number of simple generalizations which hold in this field. Here for example are some negative conclusions from the last twenty or thirty years' experience, where positive regularities (and therefore simple scientific models) were once looked for . . . [although] there is some increase in the rate of urbanization over most of the world, its rate and its forms vary, and new variations keep appearing. Some urban growth is chiefly by migration, some is chiefly by natural increase; some nations have a faster natural increase in the country, some in the town, others similar rates all over. Cities grow in diverse spatial and social patterns; development models derived from one country's experience rarely fit another's, and models derived from one period of growth rarely fit growth at other dates. Cities with apparently similar political and economic systems can have different architecture, life styles, crime rates, accident rates, and different cleanliness or pollution. (pp 93–4)

Stretton, however, seems almost to have moved from one extreme — the explicit or implicit belief that universal generalizations are possible (what is known as a nomothetic approach) — to another, and seems to be implying that generalizations about urban development are not possible at all as each country's experience is virtually unique (the idiographic approach). This does not necessarily invalidate comparative enquiry. At the very least, comparisons may illuminate or give fresh insight into the study of urban processes in the familiar context of the researcher's own society. There is, however, an intermediate approach to comparative urban enquiry based on the belief that it is possible to develop a range of *limited generalizations* about urban development that may be tested by a careful selection of specific countries to compare. Those collections of urban case studies whose only feature in common is their location in a 'foreign' setting are just as unacceptable as grand assumptions about universal urban processes.

This brings us directly to the question of the logic of comparative enquiry and the methods to be adopted. The comparative method may be described in general terms as a study of the extent of similarities or difference among a wide variety of units that are assumed to have at least one characteristic in common — in this case the characteristic of being urban. The aim is to move beyond a description of the similarities or differences between the units to the establishment of causal relationships, or at least similar chains of historical events, underlying the characteristics which the units allegedly share. Within this general statement a number of approaches to comparative urban development might be adopted. One immediately obvious approach is to compare cities in different societies at the same period in time — cross-national or cross-cultural comparisons. Other types of comparison are also useful; for example, cities within one society might be compared at different periods of time, to establish for example generalizations about the interrelationships between city, economy and society over time. Similarly, cities within one society at the same period of time may be compared, contrasting, for example, patterns of social class segregation, income inequalities, extent of suburbanization or women's participation in the labour market. The method to be adopted will depend on the purpose of the enquiry and is most likely to be successful if the initial selection is guided, if not by theory, at least by a set of testable hypotheses about the expected relationships between urban development and other social and economic processes.

In this Reader, the approach adopted is the first of the three possibilities outlined above. The historical development, regional relationships, internal structure, political conflicts and planning policies of three cities in different societies will be compared for one historical period. The aim is to establish links between urbanization, industrialization or level of economic development and official state ideologies.

An initial criterion was to choose for comparison societies which all had relatively well established urban–industrial economies, but which industrialized at different periods of history under different conditions. Although urbanization is increasing almost universally, it is widely accepted that there are two distinct trends to this phenomenon, distinguished by the interrelationships between urbanization and industrialization. In relatively advanced industrial societies, current urban growth is associated with economic growth and a productive sector characterized by sophisticated technological developments and an organized transportation network. In less advanced societies, rapid urban growth often takes place despite limited economic expansion and a poorly developed urban infrastructure and communications network. Growth in the urban population takes place at a faster rate than industrialization, unemployment is often endemic in the growing towns, and a high proportion of the urban proletariat are unable to gain access to adequate shelter and other services. This discontinuity between the rate of urbanization and industrialization has been labelled over-urbanization.

In contradiction to this trend, Konrad and Szelenyi (1977), East European urban sociologists, have identified a process of under-urbanization in state socialist societies, where the relationship between industrialization and urbanization is reversed. In this case, state investment in industrial expansion proceeds at a faster rate than investment in the urban infrastructure. Employment opportunities in urban areas, for example, increase at a more rapid rate than housing and thus overcrowding and homelessness, subletting, temporary shelter or daily long-distance rural–urban commuting where urban migration is strictly controlled, results. Thus similar problems of urban overcrowding and fierce competition for limited services may result from diametrically opposed relationships between industrialization and urbanization in the Eastern bloc and in third world countries. The 'under-urbanization' identified by Konrad and Szelenyi in Hungary, in Czechoslovakia, in the GDR and also to some extent in Romania and Poland (approximately 50 000 people a day commute into Cracow to work, for example, from the surrounding rural areas) is, however, more similar to the conditions of nineteenth and early twentieth-century urbanization in the Western economies where the rate of industrialization also outstripped the rate of urbanization and the provision of adequate urban services. In the latter case this occurred because of the lack of state intervention rather than national economic planning and investment controls as in present-day state socialist societies.

Because our aim is to compare and contrast urban processes and problems in societies that are relatively similar in terms of their present level of industrialization and urbanization, those states exhibiting marked degrees of both under- and over-urbanization were immediately excluded from consideration. Similarly, only countries that are relatively advanced in terms of the shift in the economy from a predominantly rural to an industrial commercial base were considered for selection. A further basis for comparison was then introduced in order to examine the hypothesis of the convergence theorists that it is industrial–technological organization *per se* that leads to increasing similarities between societies, whatever the official state ideology and system of production and distribution. Thus three societies which broadly span the range from a capitalist system based on the ideology of the market, a mixed economy based on assertions of limited state intervention to a command economy based on the ideological principles of socialism were selected for study. The three societies chosen were, respectively, Canada, Great Britain and Poland, and within these countries, attention is focused in detail in the succeeding readings on the three cities of Vancouver, Birmingham and Cracow–Nowa Huta. Brief outlines of the relevant characteristics of the three cities are included in the introduction to Section I of the Reader.

As is usual in the selection of case-study areas, which in this case were not only to be subjected to written analysis but also are the object of eight television programmes, purely theoretical criteria of selection had to be tempered by more practical considerations. The societies had to be open to access by Western researchers, obviously a limiting factor in the case of the selection of a state socialist society. Poland was chosen from a range of East European societies not only because of its level of industrial development, but also because access was relatively easy and because contacts had already been established there during the production of an earlier Open University course. At the opposite end of the political spectrum, either the United States of America or Canada was an obvious choice, although it might be argued that the general movement towards the right, accompanied by a rhetoric of 'rolling back state intervention' in a number of West European economies, not least in Great Britain, in the recent past made the choice less obvious than it might have been in earlier decades. Indeed, events in Poland during 1980 and 1981, particularly the challenge posed by the independent trade union movement *Solidarity* to the centralized economic control of the state, might also be seen to be reducing the original distinctions between the three countries. In the event, Canada was chosen as the 'free-market' economy as there was a Canadian academic on the course team during 1979 with first-hand knowledge of Canadian urban development.

The choice of Great Britain needs less justification for a Reader and, particularly, a course designed predominantly for an English-speaking audience. The context of British industrialization and urban development will be familiar, to a greater or lesser extent, to many readers. Of the three countries, Britain is the most thoroughly urbanized. Over 90% of the population live in towns or cities, compared with 76.6% (1971) in Canada and 56% in Poland. Each country, however, is dominated by a small number of urban areas in which a relatively substantial proportion of the total population live. In Great Britain, a third of the total population of 55.8 million (in mid-1978) lived in the seven major conurbations of Greater London, central Clydeside, Merseyside, south-east Lancashire, Tyneside, the West Midlands and West Yorkshire. In Canada 55% of the total population of 23.7 million (in 1979) lived in the 22 major cities including the provincial capitals. In Poland, there are nine major cities, in which almost a fifth of the total population of 34.5 million (in 1976) live. The cities are, in descending order of size, Warsaw, Łódź, Cracow, Wroclaw, Poznań, Gdańsk, Szczecin, Katowice and Bydgoszcz. In all three countries, the industrial sector of the economy is a major employer of the working population, which accounts for just under half the total population in all three societies. However, as might be expected from the period of initial industrialization, the agricultural sector remains a far more important employer in Poland than in the other two countries. In the mid-1970s, of the total employees, manufacturing accounted for 35% in Great Britain, 19.8% in Canada and 28% in Poland, whereas agriculture was respectively 3%, 8.3% and 31%. There is, however, still large-scale movement from agriculture into both manufacturing and service employment in Poland, often in association with rural–urban migration.

In the selection of the particular cities to be studied, the only criterion was that none should be the capital city, in order to eliminate additional complicating influences on their urban growth and structure. Although the majority of papers in this Reader focus exclusively on the three cities Birmingham, Cracow and Vancouver, the intention in their selection was to illustrate and compare particular sets of general urban processes within different contexts rather than to produce complete descriptions of the cities *per se*. Thus, in the section on political conflicts and urban social protest, for example, the case studies were chosen to illustrate general points about the mobilization of the urban population rather than to be the most important or most representative example of local or community action in each of the three cities.

Linda McDowell

References

Berry BJL 1974 *The Human Consequences of Urbanization* (London: Macmillan)

Friedmann J 1973 *Urbanization, Planning and National Development* ch. 4 (Beverley Hills: Sage)

Hall P 1966 *The World Cities* (London: Weidenfeld and Nicolson) p7

Harvey D 1973 *Social Justice and the City* (London: Arnold)

Hawley AH 1971 *Urban Society: an Ecological Approach* (New York: Ronald Press)

Hoselitz BF 1960 *Sociological Aspects of Economic Growth* (Glencoe, Illinois: Free Press)

Kerr C *et al* 1962 *Industrialism and Industrial Man* (London: Heinemann)

Konrad G and Szelenyi I 1977 Social conflicts of under-urbanization, ch. 8 in *Captive Cities* ed M Harloe (London: Wiley)

McGee T G 1971 *The Urbanization Process in the Third World: Explanations in Search of a Theory* (London: Bell)

Redfield R and Singer M 1954 The cultural role of cities *Economic Development and Cultural Change* 3 pp53–73

Reissman L 1964 *The Urban Process* (New York: Macmillan)

Stretton H 1978 *Urban Planning in Rich and Poor Countries* (London: Oxford University Press)

Williamson J G 1965 Regional inequality and the process of national development: a description of patterns *Economic Development and Cultural Change* 13 pp3–45

1 The Growth of Birmingham, 1800–1950

by M J Wise and P O'N Thorpe

Three main periods may be discerned in the growth of Birmingham as an industrial and commercial centre since the close of the eighteenth century. During the earliest of these, which occupied the first 60 years of the nineteenth century, occurred far-reaching changes in the regional pattern of the town and the development of those areas which remain today as the central industrial districts.[1] The second period was characterized by the migration of industry to the outskirts of what was then the built-up area and the growth of a number of new industrial districts at a distance of two to three miles from the town centre. The most recent phase of development, during the last 40 years, has seen the evolution of a new series of industrial areas at a radius of, generally, four or five miles from the city centre and the development, between and around them, of extensive housing estates.

The evolution of the central districts, 1800–60

By the early years of the nineteenth century Birmingham had fully emerged as the leading industrial and commercial centre on the Birmingham Plateau. The population of the town which had been some 70 000 in 1801 continued to increase remarkably and was well over 130 000 by 1831 and over 300 000[2] by 1861. Birmingham grew rapidly outwards and the early nineteenth century saw the further extension of building estates over the wide belt of fields and gardens which surrounded the town.

The growth of industry

The period 1800–60 was one of general industrial progress in an increasing variety of metal trades. Especially important were the four staple manufactures of guns, jewellery, buttons and brass products.

By the commencement of the century, the gun trade was already highly developed and the increased demand for fire-arms resulting from the Napoleonic Wars was reflected in the expansion of the trade. Throughout the first half of the century, the trade remained subdivided into many branches carried on by 'small masters' in workshops in or behind their own houses. The majority of masters resided in the district around St Mary's Church, immediately to the north of the town, and by 1800 a high degree of localization in this quarter had become a marked characteristic of the trade.

Whereas the gun trade had been fully developed in Birmingham by 1800, the jewellery trade was, as yet, in its infancy. The first years of the century were years of rapid progress. By 1845 the jewellery trade alone employed 3700 persons, while there were 5300 toymakers, many of whom were engaged in making the cheaper forms of jewellery. As the trade grew in size and in the range of its products, subdivision of process became a general rule. In this respect the gun and jewellery trades were comparable, and in both the typical manufacturer was the 'small master, often working in his own house, with his wife and children to help him.'[1] As the trade progressed, the small houses in districts near the centre of the town proved inadequate in size and manufacturers removed to larger and better class buildings in new estates on the fringe of Birmingham. Due, partly, to the intensive subdivision of the trade, a high degree of localization was characteristic, and, at periods of expansion, the centre of localization tended to shift in conformity with movements of manufacturers to larger premises on newly built estates.

The manufacture of metal buttons declined in rela-

Source: M J Wise (ed) 1970 *Birmingham and its Regional Setting: A Scientific Survey*, County Historical Reprints pp213–28. By permission of the British Association for the Advancement of Science.

building has been undertaken primarily under the aegis of the state and as in Nowa Huta the main housing form has been high-rise apartment blocks, leading to a visual impression of greater uniformity than in either of the other two cities.

In the six readings that make up the first section of this Reader, the historical development and 'image' of the three cities is discussed in more detail. Wise and Thorpe distinguish three important periods in Birmingham's development since 1800 and link the expansion of the city to the growth and change of its industrial structure. Despite growing variety in its industrial structure during the nineteenth and twentieth centuries, Birmingham has remained very dependent on a range of metal and related industries, from the gun trade of the earliest years of industrial development to its present-day reliance on the car trade and associated trades. In this respect, it exhibits certain similarities with the two other cities, both of which also developed from a primary reliance on a small range of industries. In Vancouver, exploitation of the natural timber resources formed the basis of timber-processing plants, whereas in Cracow–Nowa Huta, iron and steel processing and a range of associated metallurgical industries have been the basis for industrial growth. In Vancouver, despite the limitations imposed by its physical location at the mouth of the River Fraser, Hardwick emphasises a similar process of peripheral expansion as Wise and Thorpe document in Birmingham. In both cities, urban growth was relatively unconstrained by land-use controls and planning policies, whereas in the Cracow region the development of Nowa Huta was a deliberate planned expansion, a consequence of national economic planning policy rather than the product of local decisions. This is not, of course, to deny the links between national economic processes and local developments in capitalist societies, but to point out the contrasts between the circumstances under which the location of particular urban developments is decided in different settings and at different periods of time. Urban growth and industrial development at the present time in Great Britain, for example, are subject to far greater constraints than during the nineteenth century when a large proportion of Birmingham's growth took place.

In the second three of the six readings, the specific influence of the prevailing ideology on urban development in each of the three cities is considered and some of the then-current social responses are indicated. Briggs emphasises the conflicts between economic individualism and civic pride: the former leading to appalling conditions of health, disease, overcrowding and lack of amenities; the latter to the erection of visible monuments to progress in a flamboyant urban architecture but also legislation to curb the worst excesses and to improve living standards. In the extract on Vancouver, Ley focuses on more recent developments in documenting the significance of a new liberal ideology based on various and somewhat contradictory strands — from consumerism, the environmental movement, youth culture and student politics, and culminating nationally in Trudeau's election as Prime Minister and locally in the foundation of TEAM (The Electors' Action Movement) a municipal reform party dominated by relatively youthful liberal professionals. In this extract, the idea and implications of a 'livable' city are explored. In a later extract in the Reader, the political influence of TEAM is subjected to closer scrutiny.

In the third extract, from French and Hamilton's book *The Socialist City*, the question of the impact of socialist theory on urban structure is tackled. Unlike Birmingham and Vancouver, which both reflect the principles of capitalist organization (albeit at different historical periods), the major expansion of Cracow took place under centrally planned state control, with a high degree of intervention in such matters as land ownership, industrial location and housing policy, rents, wages and prices. Rather than examining the particular growth of Cracow, French and Hamilton take examples from a range of cities in order to answer the question of whether there are distinct spatial differences between capitalist and socialist cities because of the greater degree of state control in societies aspiring to socialist goals. Their answer is a qualified yes, and in the succeeding sections of this Reader some of the differences in the specific areas of regional relations, land use, housing, politics and planning will be examined.

Linda McDowell

Section I
Historical Development, Images and Ideology

Introduction

The three cities of Birmingham, Cracow and Vancouver are today important industrial and commercial centres within their national system of cities. Birmingham is the second largest city in Britain, with a population of just over a million in the city itself and a further four million in the surrounding West Midlands region. Vancouver is the principal city of British Columbia, ranking third in Canada as a whole after Toronto and Montreal. In 1976, the population within the city boundaries reached almost half a million; in the metropolitan region as a whole it was 1.2 million. Cracow, with the industrial new town of Nowa Huta, is the third city in Poland in terms of population, and the fifth largest urban industrial agglomeration. In 1976 it had a population of almost three quarters of a million.

These cities are, however, products of very different ages and social and historical circumstances. Birmingham is an archetypal nineteenth-century industrial city, primarily a product of Victorian enterprise, expansion and civic pride although the site had been occupied for centuries beforehand. It experienced an enormous population increase in the mid-nineteenth century and the legacy of the industry and housing developed in this period is a visible part of the urban environment today. Vancouver, on the other hand, developed into a metropolitan centre during the second half of the twentieth century from its origins in the late nineteenth century as a port and western terminus of two trans-Canadian railroads with an employment structure dominated by lumber. The city is now dominated by white-collar public administration and service employment which generated an office building boom in the city centre or downtown area in the 1970s. Residential building has also been rapid in recent decades. In the city itself there has been immigration of single

people, especially young adults, whereas families with children tend to live in suburban developments in the metropolitan region. Vancouver's combination of an attractive natural location within easy reach of both the mountains and the ocean with their associated leisure opportunities, service-dominated employment structure and relatively high income levels is in marked contrast to Birmingham. Whereas Birmingham has been labelled an archetypal industrial city, Vancouver might be designated a post-industrial city. Indeed, in the extract on Vancouver included in this section, Ley chooses just this term to describe the city.

The site of Cracow in Poland, like Birmingham, but unlike Vancouver, has also been occupied for centuries. Indeed, Cracow is one of the oldest European cities and the medieval, Gothic and Renaissance buildings still standing in the central area are an important tourist attraction. Until the twentieth century, however, the population remained small — only 85 000 at the beginning of the century. Rapid urban expansion and population growth did not take off until the post-war period with the designation in 1949 of a site at Nowa Huta, five miles east of the city centre, as the location for an integrated iron and steel works. The city's boundaries were extended to include the new town that was built to house the workers attracted from surrounding rural areas. Development was rapid and Nowa Huta has in effect become a huge working-class suburb of Cracow where over 200 000 people are housed in predominantly high-rise apartment blocks. The photographs in the text of the extract by Kortus and Vlassenbroeck give an impression of Nowa Huta's housing. The built environment of Cracow itself is somewhat varied. In addition to the medieval core, there is an inner zone of nineteenth-century building, which is, however, being redeveloped in part. Post-war

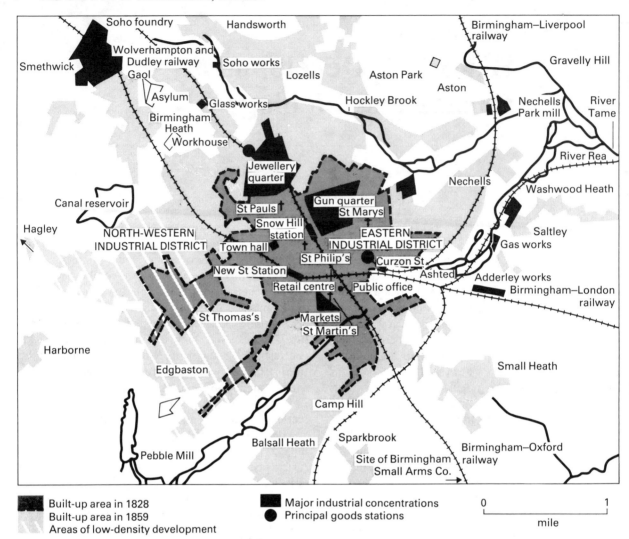

Soho foundry Handsworth Birmingham–Liverpool railway

Wolverhampton and Dudley railway Soho works Gravelly Hill

Smethwick Gaol Lozells Aston Park Aston Nechells Park mill River Tame

Asylum Glass works Hockley Brook

Birmingham Heath Workhouse

Jewellery quarter Nechells River Rea

Washwood Heath

Canal reservoir St Pauls Gun quarter St Marys

Hagley Snow Hill station EASTERN INDUSTRIAL DISTRICT Saltley Gas works

NORTH-WESTERN INDUSTRIAL DISTRICT Town hall St Philip's Curzon St.

New St Station Retail centre Public office Ashted Adderley works

St Thomas's Markets St Martin's Birmingham–London railway

Harborne Small Heath

Edgbaston Camp Hill

Balsall Heath Sparkbrook Birmingham–Oxford railway

Pebble Mill Site of Birmingham Small Arms Co.

Built-up area in 1828 Major industrial concentrations 0   1
Built-up area in 1859 Principal goods stations mile
Areas of low-density development

Figure 1.1 The regional pattern of Birmingham in 1859 (based on a map by Charles Henry Blood 1859).

tive importance during the first half of the century in competition with newer branches of the trade, which included the production of covered buttons and pearl, ivory, bone and glass buttons. The button trade as a whole, however, maintained its position of importance in Birmingham and in 1865 employed no less than 6000 persons (some two-thirds of whom were women and children). Though a number of large factories existed in 1865, the typical Birmingham system of manufacture by small masters still persisted, and the practice of employing outworkers, as in the gun and jewellery trades, was still general.

The brass trade, which had grown rapidly in Birmingham during the last quarter of the eighteenth century, had reached, by the early nineteenth century, the status of a staple trade. Rapid expansion took place in the early nineteenth century as a result of the demand for brass products for engineering and for domestic purposes. The brass trade quickly became subdivided into a number of branches whose products ranged from cabinet and plumbers' brass foundry to brass wire, lamps, gas fittings and naval brass foundry. An increase in the demand for rolled brass was met by the establishment of numerous rolling mills, with power provided by steam engines.[1] Railway developments led to large increases in the demand for brass tubes, while the brass bedstead trade emerged as a particularly important branch.

Contemporary observers attributed the success of the brass trades in Birmingham to the existence of a large labour force, skilled in metal working. Before 1825 the trade was carried on entirely in 'small workshops, low roofed and imperfectly lighted . . . for the most part situated in back courts.' In the second quarter of the century, the average size of firm increased and the building of new, larger factories became general. By 1850 the Birmingham brass trades were distributed throughout the town but were especially characteristic of the industrial areas north and north-west of the town and of the north-eastern and eastern industrial districts (figure 1.1).

Though the four trades of guns, jewellery, buttons and brass were the main they were by no means the only manufactures of Birmingham during this period. As time went by the industries of the town became more diverse. They included the manufacture of edge tools, fire irons, hinges, fenders, grates and light iron castings. Engineering developed rapidly, while the leather trades, which had been a principal manufacture of Birmingham 300 years earlier, continued as a trade of some local importance.

Birmingham grew also as a centre providing services for a widening region. Commercial links with the Black Country were close, and with the development of that great industrial district, Birmingham's prosperity as a financial and trading centre grew also. Associations of manufacturers from the whole of the 'hardware district' centred their activities in Birmingham. The town maintained its earlier function of marketing the products of the Black Country and the numbers of factors and merchants increased year by year. In 1849, out of eight leading banking houses represented in the town, six were Birmingham-owned and managed. The markets served an increasingly wide district; wholesale and retail merchants multiplied. Birmingham became a centre of amenities, providing theatres, gardens and other entertainments for town and countryside.

The railways
Of great importance was the entry into the town of the railways. Early railways, including the Grand Junction Railway (opened in 1837) and the London–Birmingham Railway (1838) terminated on the eastern outskirts of Birmingham in the Rea Valley at Duddeston. This was the nearest point to the town centre to which the railway could be brought without involving tunnelling or the demolition of property. For the London–Bir-

mingham railway, a terminus was erected at Curzon Street, Duddeston, although this was too remote from the real centre of Birmingham to remain for long as the main centre for passenger traffic. Proposals for extending the main streets of Birmingham to this station were considered, but after a few years Curzon Street was left to become only a centre of the heavy goods traffic for the growing town.

No opposition was offered to the final entry of the railways. By the early 1850s Birmingham had become the centre of a network of railways, and two main stations (at New Street and Snow Hill) had been constructed within the town centre. New Street station was approached at both ends by tunnels, and its construction necessitated the clearance of a part of one of the worst slum areas of Birmingham, including King Street, Peck Lane, the Froggery and many other courts and alleys. In the centre of the town, the increase in wealth and prosperity was reflected in the growth of public buildings and the extension of the retail shopping area. Building density increased steadily and vacant plots were seized upon for the erection of shops and warehouses.

Social conditions
The rapid growth of Birmingham in size and population was far from matched by improvements in sanitation and public health services. Despite this, Birmingham enjoyed, in comparison with other large industrial centres, the reputation of a comparatively healthy town. Observers and investigators during the nineteenth century compared Birmingham favourably with London, the Black Country and the industrial centres of the north of England. This was due, in part, to the comparative prosperity enjoyed by the craftsmen and small masters of Birmingham, particularly in the gun and jewellery trades.

Within the town itself, however, conditions were far from ideal. Although there were no cellar dwellings, many streets were narrow and the state of the poorer-class houses was reported as 'much neglected'. The main streets possessed underground drainage, but open sewers lay in front of the houses in the Bordesley and Deritend districts. Bordesley and Summer Lane were built chiefly of back-to-back houses and there were many 'close courts.' The habit of 'keeping pigs in the courts and houses of the poor' was said to be productive of great evil. This was not surprising, since the pig population of the borough in 1845 was no less than 3210.[1]

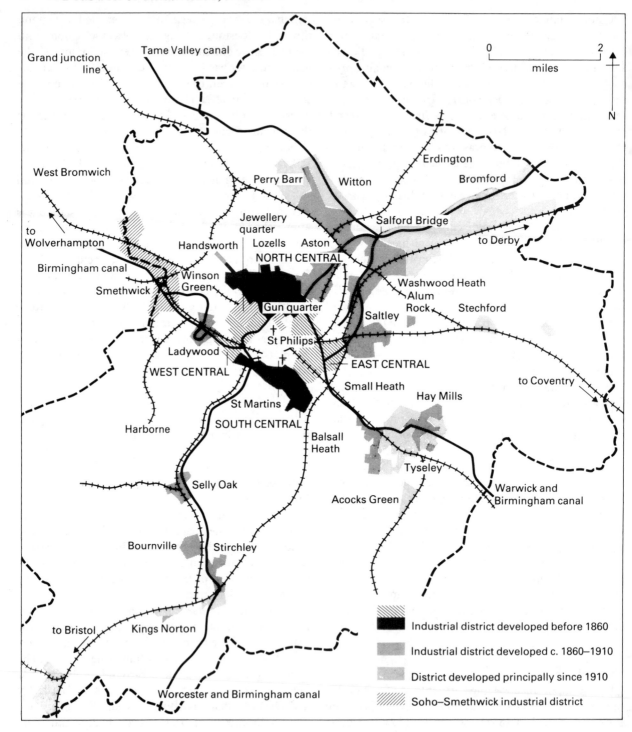

Figure 1.2 The modern industrial pattern of Birmingham.

The expansion of Birmingham 1860–1914

Changes in the industrial pattern

The principal features of the industrial pattern of Birmingham in 1860 are summarized in figure 1.1. By this time the gun and jewellery quarters were almost fully evolved, and the general pattern of the present central industrial districts had been determined. The factors influencing industrial location now began to change, with the gradual growth of 'pockets' of industry on the fringes of Birmingham at a distance of up to two or three miles from the centre of the town. The causes of this change in the industrial pattern may be seen to lie partly in developments in industrial organization. Prior to about 1860, a principal characteristic of industrial Birmingham had been the 'large number of small masters employing a few workmen' in the various trades. Normal dwelling houses provided adequate accommodation for this type of enterprise. Although some workshops of this type continue to thrive to the present day, by 1860 the activities of many of them had begun to be absorbed by larger factories. The factory system was associated with developments in the gun trade, and the large-scale production of military arms was begun by a number of companies on the eastern fringe of Birmingham. New industries introduced during this period included the manufacture of cycles, electrical apparatus and motor cars[2] and these too were accommodated in large factories built on the fringe of Birmingham.

The principal changes in the industrial pattern may be seen clearly in figure 1.2. Four main directions of growth appeared. To the north-west an industrial district developed along the banks of the Birmingham canal, beyond Ladywood. Here, in addition to the good rail and canal facilities, the barren waste of Birmingham Heath offered cheap sites for industrial concerns. Proximity to the Black Country was an added attraction and the district grew as predominantly a metal-working centre.

New industrial districts grew alongside the canal and railway at Selly Oak, Bournville and Stirchley to the south-west and south of the town centre. Selly Oak and Stirchley were primarily interested in metal working. On the other hand, Bournville became the home of the famous cocoa and chocolate factory of the Cadbury Brothers who removed from the town centre in 1879. Around the factory was developed the celebrated 'village' of Bournville, one of the first practical experiments in planning 'garden cities.' A long tongue of industrial development stretched south-eastwards along the Warwick Canal and the Birmingham–Oxford railway. The largest single factory was that of the Birmingham Small Arms Company, established at Small Heath in 1861.

The most important of all the industrial changes of this period took place to the north-east. Two tongues of industry spread outwards in this direction. The northernmost followed the line of the Fazeley canal to Aston; the southern tongue utilized available cheap land in the Rea valley, hitherto undeveloped on account of its liability to flood. This tongue was also well served by transport facilities, particularly by the main Birmingham–Derby line which followed the valleys of the Rea and Tame to the north-east. Factories in this tongue included large railway wagon and motor works, in addition to the gas works which were grouped at Saltley and Nechells. The Saltley district forms, to the present day, the most unsightly of all the industrial areas of the city.

At Salford Bridge, near Aston, the two tongues met, and thence industry spread out to the east and north-west along the Tame Valley. Like much of the Rea Valley, the low-lying land there remained unsuitable for housing development and was available cheaply for industrial use. The valley was used already by the Tame Valley and Fazeley Canals, as well at by main railway lines. The Grand Junction line passed to the north-west through Perry Barr to Bescot and Walsall, and the main Derby line followed the valley to the east. The establishment of a large works at Witton 'for the manufacture of cartridges and fog signals' was noted in the census report of 1871. Perhaps the most important single development was the erection at Witton of the works of the General Electric Company in 1901. Witton became the chief centre of the local electric trade at this time.

Suburban development

Around and between these industrial areas grew new suburbs; as early as 1859 Small Heath, Saltley, Aston, Lozells and other districts had begun to grow. Suburbs erected during this period remain easily recognizable by reason of the well defined, regular, rectangular street pattern and the long monotonous rows of uniform terraced houses. A wide belt of districts of this type arose, extending from Perry Barr and Aston in the north, through Saltley and Small Heath in the east of Birmingham, to Sparkbrook and Selly Oak in the south. Terraced houses represented, also, the first major additions to such outlying village centres as Erdington, Stechford, Yardley and Harborne.

Changes in the central districts

The period was marked also by great changes in the regional structure of the central districts. The new centre of civic administration was now firmly established, and the clearance of many acres of squalid slum and industrial property was begun. The most spectacular of all the improvements to the town centre was the completion of the celebrated Corporation Street scheme, with which the name of Joseph Chamberlain is justly associated. In 1875 a committee of inquiry had reported upon the state of property in the district through which the street was to be cut. They found 'narrow streets, houses without back doors or windows, situated both in and out of courts; confined yards, courts opening at one end only, and this small and narrow; the impossibility in many cases of providing sufficient privy accommodation; houses and shopping so dilapidated as to be in imminent danger of falling, and incapable of proper repair.' The new street was begun in 1878 and completed in 1882. Leases of property were granted, to revert to the corporation after 75 years. 'This,' declared Mr Chamberlain, 'will make Birmingham the richest borough in the country sixty or seventy years hence.'

The general state of Birmingham at the close of this period was examined carefully in a report to the city council in 1914.[3] Despite the rapid suburban development many of the evils resulting from an earlier lack of planning remained. The division of the town into central and suburban districts was recognized. Around the public buildings and the retail and commercial centres lay a 'jumble of mean streets, huddled terraces, dark, insanitary and badly lit courts' which housed the unskilled labourers of the city. Most of the dwellings were unfit for habitation. 200 000 people were still housed in 43 366 dwellings of the back-to-back type, already long condemned as injurious to health. In the six worst wards 51–76% of the houses were of this type. Over 42 000 houses had no separate water supply, no sinks and no drains and over 58 000 no separate sanitary facilities. Despite the great increase in extent of the town, the rate of building had failed to keep pace with the increase in population. Factories and houses were inextricably mixed in the widespread slum districts.

Though many of the evil features of the central districts were repeated in the suburbs erected after 1860, the terraced houses in general represented a limited advance in convenience and sanitation. The planning of the drab streets and houses, however, still left very much to be desired. Few open spaces were provided. Perhaps the greatest advance was a social one — in the new suburbs, factory and home were separate. The factories and suburbs were built, however, with little regard to the general layout of the city. Birmingham sprawled across the countryside. Life was concentrated on the main roads. Along the roads radiating from the city were built the shops and offices serving the new suburbs. These remain to form a major planning problem today.

Recent changes in the regional pattern

The latest stage in the growth of Birmingham has been a time of industrial progress and prosperity in, particularly, the motor car and allied trades. The results of this prosperity are to be seen in the development of a further series of industrial districts located, generally, at a radius of three to five miles from the city centre. The location of these districts has been influenced by many factors. Control has been exerted under town planning schemes, one result of which has been the virtual exclusion of industry from growing residential areas as, for instance, the Harborne and Quinton suburbs to the west of Birmingham. The demand for increased floor space for modern factories has prompted location on the fringes of Birmingham at points where cheap land and good communications were available, such as that of the present BL plant at Longbridge. The Longbridge factory, developed from the derelict premises of a former printing works, covered some 2½ acres by 1906. As a result largely of post-1914 extensions, the factory site now extends over more than 100 acres and around it has grown the modern suburb of Northfield.

Perhaps the most striking feature of the modern industrial pattern is the almost complete industrialization of the valley of the Tame through the city from Perry Barr in the north-west to Bromford and Castle Bromwich in the east. On the wide floodplain of the Tame many large factories have been erected, a particularly important example of which is the motor tyre and rubber factory at Fort Dunlop, which lies between the main Birmingham–Derby railway and the Fazely canal. The main roads of the district are lined with small modern factories, producing, in many cases, parts and accessories for the motor and allied trades.

The second principal feature of Birmingham's growth since the 1914–18 war has been a spectacular growth of the built-up area to north, east and south. The outward flood of building has submerged many of the older village centres, including Yardley, King's Norton and Northfield, which prior to 1914 remained separated from Birmingham. These districts have been transformed from semi-rural centres into almost uniformly built-up areas, with building patterns which, resulting from lower-density standards and open layouts, are far less rigid, but no less distinctive, than those of an earlier age.

The results of the activities of modern speculative builders and of the corporation of Birmingham are now to be seen in a wide belt of predominantly semi-detached modern housing, some two to three miles wide, which extends from Kingstanding in the north, through Erdington, Ward End, Stechford, Yardley, Acocks Green and Hall Green to Harborne and Quinton in west Birmingham, and in which the extensive intricate geometrical designs of the corporation estates contrast with the simpler, linear layouts of the speculative builders.

Birmingham continues to prosper and to grow, and as each year passes the industrial basis of the city becomes more diverse. Birmingham manufacturers have for centuries possessed the secret of modifying their products to suit the changing demands of the market. At a comparatively early stage of development Birmingham possessed marked local geographical advantages of site and position relative to the South Staffordshire coalfield. With a long history of industrial prosperity the city has become the heart of a great industrial district and the hub of a network of communications. From an unimportant village in the centre of uninviting plateau country has grown a city of a million inhabitants. Birmingham today exercises three functions. The city is, firstly, a major industrial centre; secondly, the commerical capital of the Birmingham–Black Country conurbation. Birmingham provides, thirdly, a growing range of services for a large and widening region.

[This article was originally published at the beginning of the 1970s. Since then the economic recession which has affected the peripheral areas of Britain so badly has also begun to affect the previously prosperous West Midlands region. The decline in the engineering and car industries, in particular, have increased the rate of unemployment in the city. Birmingham's industrial expansion can no longer be guaranteed. (Eds)]

Notes

[1] *Parliamentary Papers* 1845 **18** Appendix 1, pp3–4.

[2] For details see G C Allen 1929 *The Industrial Development of Birmingham and the Black Country 1860–1927* (London: Cass) p291 *et seq.*

[3] See the summary in *When We Build Again* 1941 (Birmingham: Bournville Village Trust) p14 *et seq.*

2 The Growth of Vancouver: From Resource Town to Urban Region

by W Hardwick

The core city

The resource town

The frontier resource towns on Burrard Inlet that preceded Vancouver clung to the waterfront, imperceptibly intruding on the west coast forest environment. Buildings were hewn from the local cedars and Douglas fir, and their placement was as irregular as could be expected from the diverse group of residents who occupied the area. Seamen, loggers, frontier merchants, Americans, Scots, Indians and Englishmen had gravitated to Burrard Inlet, one of the more remote frontiers of the nineteenth century, and provided the labour force for a marginal forest industry.

Had the process common to other areas on the coast persisted, then, once the logs were gone, the people would have moved on to the next inlet of the sea where resources abounded, and would have founded a new settlement. The forest would again have taken over Burrard Inlet and the marks of man's settlement would rot into the forest floor. That was not be be. The choice of Burrard Inlet as the western terminus of the Canadian Pacific Railway dramatically altered the destiny of the region. The city of Vancouver was founded in 1886 to become the port for western Canada.

The terminal city

In the nineteenth century, the city of Vancouver grew slowly, centring on the piers, mills, and railroad facilities along Burrard Inlet and False Creek. Frame housing was erected on a rigidly surveyed grid of streets. By 1890, just four years after the incorporation

of the city, an electric street railway system had been installed. This not only provided inter-urban connections between Vancouver and New Westminster, its rival on the Fraser River 13 miles to the east, but also constituted an embryonic radial transportation system, opening an area of some three miles in radius to urban residence. Even in those years, substantial brick and stone commercial buildings had sprung up on major streets.

The coincidental development of the street railway system with that of the city itself meant that neither inner-city tenements within walking distance of major work places, nor residences over shops, such as were found in eastern American or European cities, became part of Vancouver's tradition or heritage. Workers could and did seek out small plots of land and built detached houses, small or large depending on their income and social standing. This easy availability of land suited the goals of most newcomers who saw Vancouver and British Columbia as a land to exploit for individual opportunity. The forest that still stood was cleared. In contrast with the 1860s, man's works began to dominate the landscape around Burrard Inlet. But rapid growth took place only after 1905 with 100 000 persons coming in seven years.

In the years 1905–13 subdivision resulted in the expansion of the city to encompass much of the peninsula between Burrard Inlet and the Fraser River, a distance of six miles, while the street railways of north Vancouver were connected by ferry to the core of Vancouver. The new suburbs of the day were segregated: the élite to the south, the middle-class to the west, workers to the east, while ethnic groups crammed into the margins of the core. The core itself attracted buildings of strong design, symbolizing the entrepreneurial

Source: W Hardwick 1974 *Vancouver* (New York: Collier-Macmillan) pp 3–21; 80–2.

dominance over the region. In general, the pace of land subdivision in these decades exceeded the growth of population. Many subdivisions, particularly in east and south Vancouver had plank roads, no sewers, and inadequate local water systems. The direction of development reflected speculator interest, sometimes associated with streetcar expansion. The Fairview belt line, for example, was to have been financed in 1890 in part by sale of 68 lots to be granted the Westminster and Vancouver Tramway Company by the Canadian Pacific Railway.

The radial pattern of land uses focusing upon a primate downtown became firmly established in the 1920s and, once organized, persisted into the 1930s and was carried over into the 1940s. Countervailing tendencies that might have evolved did not do so because of the characteristics of the 1930s and 1940s. The thirties suffered the privation of the depression and the forties, the exigencies of war and its aftermath. Neither decade enjoyed high capital investment levels in any but essential and strategic facilities. The extended transportation network and the residential, commercial, and industrial dispersal of early decades of this century ensured that development in the 1930s and 1940s would be largely a case of filling in an established pattern, rather than the evolution of new patterns intrinsic to the dynamics of new growth. The tendency to accept the predetermined pattern was reinforced by the strength of the central city concept that prevailed in much of the professional urban thinking throughout most of North America during these decades, and by the fact that it was incorporated into civic by-laws in 1931.

The role of the marketplace was critical, but the role of government was minor in moulding the form and structure of the city. With the physical expansion of urban activities during the 1920s, and the need for improved public services brought on by increased densities, a change in the scale of government became necessary. The population had spread far beyond the limited boundaries of Vancouver city as incorporated in 1886. To deal with the new realities, Vancouver amalgamated with its two southern neighbours, Point Grey and South Vancouver, in 1929. With that, the effectively occupied urban area fell under one political jurisdiction. Civic government was now competing with the private entrepreneur as a major determinant of urban growth.

The persistence of the core city

Population expansion in the post-World War II period might have suggested the need to 'leap-frog' over the old suburbs into the southern and eastern farmlands, thus demonstrating the car-oriented sprawl so characteristic of many North American cities. However, several factors postponed that event until the 1960s. The process of infilling land within the city, particularly in South Vancouver, was important. The opening of Lions Gate Bridge across the First Narrows of Burrard Inlet in 1938 further contributed to the stability of the core-focused urban pattern. When post-war population expansion took place, this bridge offered, particularly for middle- and higher-income families, a route to housing sites on the foothills of North and West Vancouver as close to the core as many built-up neighbourhoods in Vancouver city. The subdivision in the north provided a reserve of land which helped to hold down land prices throughout the region.

Although the North Shore has been looked upon by many as an 'outer suburb', the functional links between it and the core suggest that West Vancouver and the western parts of North Vancouver are as much a part of the core-oriented system as the older parts of Vancouver city. Nevertheless, the physical separation of these municipalities from Vancouver by Burrard Inlet, and the general affluence of the population, have permitted local governments to service those areas without calling on central city resources. No amalgamation plans have been made.

About 1960, fundamental changes in the patterns of residence, commerce and industry began to influence land uses in greater Vancouver and break down the core-focused radial city known to three generations of Vancouverites. Increased mobility and greater affluence permitted urban dwellers to penetrate new areas once protected by isolation — a process that could threaten the natural west coast environment. Furthermore, important changes in values and attitudes of resident and immigrant alike have become recognizable. These pressures, of course, were recognized in the private sector and by thousands of individuals. Major governmental institutions, however, did not appear to comprehend the pace of change, and only reluctantly adapted to new situations. Only the advisory Lower Mainland Regional Planning Board and some professionals and academics sounded warnings. In fact, local government continued as if nothing much had changed until the Province intervened by creating the Greater Vancouver Regional District. Traditional assumptions about community values continued to be used by local administrative/political leadership; the result was confrontation on an increasing scale — and a challenge at the polls.

Although the founding generations had come to British Columbia seeking a land of opportunity, and one in which resource exploitation was an important component, second-generation residents and many more recent immigrants have seen the region as a quality environment second to none in Canada — an environment that should be protected and enhanced. This conflict in images of the region is manifest in hundreds of ways, ranging from issues of mining in provincial parks to the preservation of waterfront for public use in the cities. The contrasting values can be recognized by noting that first-generation residents built homes on promontories with no windows toward the view, and permitted warehouses to be built on other amenity sites. For present residents, however, the same sites command high prices, and marginal industries and warehouses in central locations are being replaced by parks, hotels and apartments. Each new activity is making full use of Vancouver's comparative advantage — its natural amenities.

Although concern for the environment has in the past been a minority view, the enhancement of the public environment may now be becoming a majority view. This change has also had a major impact on public policy in the region.

Greater Vancouver

Its functional components and physical site
Metropolitan Vancouver occupies lands that surround the mouth of the Fraser River, a river which drains a good proportion of British Columbia and provides natural transportation routes from the interior. The land comprises three basic physiographic divisions: the coastal mountains and their foothills to the north; several discontinuous uplands composed of various materials of glacial origin; and the flood plains of the Fraser River and its delta to the south. To the west lies Georgia Strait, the body of water that separates Vancouver Island from the mainland. To the south, the forty-ninth parallel marks the boundary between Canada and the United States.

The mountain backdrop is the most prominent feature of the city, and is highlighted on postcards and embedded in the public consciousness. One need never lose a sense of direction when 4000- to 5000-foot mountains block the northern horizon. But the mountains are more than a natural compass point. Along with the sea to the west they are visual proof that the wilderness still lives — that the city lies in stark contrast to the adjacent environment of isolation, quiet and mystery. True, this wilderness is penetrated by hikers and skiers, but to most it represents the wall that separates Vancouver from the rest of the continent.

Early settlement
European settlement on Burrard Inlet began when a sawmill was built at Moodyville on the north shore. This mill was followed by a second mill at Hastings, near the present Gastown. Exports of lumber started in 1864. A resort on tidewater at the northern end of the Douglas Road was built for New Westminster. Reflecting the origins of its residents, it was appropriately called New Brighton.

By 1870, two of the three groups that would shape the destiny of Greater Vancouver were already resident in the region. These were the British colonial officials and engineers, possessing distinctly Victorian values and senses of propriety, and a ragtag collection of miners, seamen and foresters — the group that has been called the 'British Columbians.' A third group, the eastern Canadians, arrived with the CPR in 1886, as CPR managers, as entrepreneurs, and as professionals who came to establish themselves in the terminal city by the Sunset Sea.

Places in the Vancouver region

These founding groups, and many that have followed, have given names and character to many places within Greater Vancouver. These places have changed function often as population has increased and relative locations have changed. Some are of current importance, while others date from the past and evoke feelings and reactions from residents. Some familiarity with the place names is important for an understanding of the changing urban geography of the region. They are described briefly in the following paragraphs, incorporating a 'core–ring' urban model (Hardwick 1971). The core system comprises the downtown and the radially organized suburbs that surround it. The peripheral system comprises a dozen or more centres, originally independent, which have been drawn into the Vancouver-centred region.

The core system
Downtown Vancouver and its adjacent port, industrial

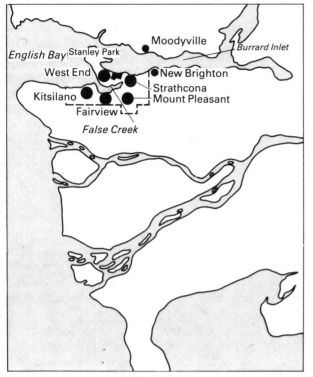

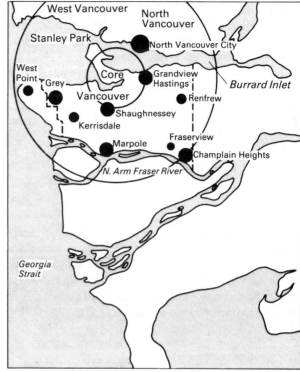

Figure 2.1 The inner city: core areas of present high-density development in Vancouver. The broken line indicates the extent of the city in 1901.

Figure 2.2 The old suburbs of Vancouver.

and high-density residential areas occupy an area of about two miles in radius. This comprises what was the total city of the 1890s. It is the area of the major centre of work in the region, with 91 000 workers, 11.2 million square feet of commercial offices, 6.1 million square feet of retail space, 7.7 million square feet of industrial space, 3.1 million square feet of hotels and entertainment facilities, and 1.7 million square feet of public buildings (1970). To the west, a high-density, high-rise apartment district, the West End, houses some 35 000 people (see figure 2.1). From here many residents may as conveniently walk to work as to the English Bay beaches and Stanley Park. To the north, the Burrard Inlet waterfront is variously used for hotels, railyards, and coastal and deep-sea docks. The portions of the harbour adjoining downtown are experiencing competition between traditional port and industrial uses and amenity activities such as hotels, marinas, parks and restaurants. To the east lies Strathcona, an old inner-city neighbourhood of frame homes once adjacent to the Hastings mill and the home of the 'British Columbians', now largely occupied by people

of Chinese origin. To the south lies False Creek, an inlet of the sea once surrounded by sawmills, but more recently by obsolete industry. False Creek, like much of the margin of the city centre comprises a zone of land-use transition and is ripe for redevelopment. Overlooking the water to the south lie Kitsilano, Fairview and Mount Pleasant, turn of the century, single-family neighbourhoods quickly being redeveloped into rooming house and apartment districts (see figure 2.2).

South-west of the inner city lie the neighbourhoods of Shaughnessey, Kerrisdale, Dunbar and West Point Grey. Collectively they made up the old municipality of Point Grey, an area settled after 1900, but most intensively during the 1920s. Shaughnessey is a high-income, residential area, while the adjoining areas are basically middle-income neighbourhoods. Marpole in the south was a market and mill town on the Fraser River.

South-east of the inner city was the old municipality of South Vancouver, now substantial, established 'blue collar' neighbourhoods. Early settlement was encouraged by the inter-urban railway line that joined Vancouver with New Westminster. Later, as streetcar lines were built southwards, the whole municipality was subdivided into small lots, only a small number of which were occupied by the 1920s. By 1950, only the south-east corner of the area was undeveloped. It became the Champlain Heights subdivision of the 1970s. Along the northern arm of the Fraser River, a string of sawmills and light industrial plants are large employers.

Directly east of the inner city is East Vancouver. In the north, the residential areas are cut off from the harbour by railways, industrial plants, grain elevators, and the piers themselves. Grandview, an inner neighbourhood, has a high percentage of Italian immigrant population. In the Hastings Townsite area, well established communities surround Hastings Park, the exhibition site, coliseum, stadium and racetrack that abuts New Brighton Park, which was founded in the 1860s. Renfrew to the south has a high proportion of subsidized housing built immediately after World War II.

On the north side of Burrard Inlet 100 000 persons occupy the North Shore. The city of North Vancouver and downtown Vancouver, connected for 70 years by a Burrard Inlet ferry, have similar development histories.

After the construction of the Lions Gate Bridge in 1938, West Vancouver, with its élite British properties subdivision, and North Vancouver district's western sections became prime suburbs; they function very much as the Point Grey and South Vancouver areas do, *vis à vis* the core. In the east, toward Deep Cove, land is yet to be developed. Behind the North Shore, the mountains rise 4000–5000 feet and provide summer and winter recreational areas.

The peripheral ring

There are many pre-existing centres that are being drawn into the growing Vancouver-centred region. Among these are New Westminster, Bridgeport, Port Moody, Steveston and White Rock. New Westminster, we have noted, was founded in 1858 as the first capital of the mainland British colony of British Columbia. Although the capital was soon moved, the city continued to function as an administrative, industrial and market town. Today, with a population of 42 000, it acts as the centre for some 200 000 people and has not been distinctly eclipsed by its younger but larger sister city, Vancouver.

Directly south of Vancouver on the delta lands of the Fraser River is the municipality of Richmond and western portions of Delta. Across the river from Vancouver are industrial areas as well as the small agricultural holdings of an area settled after the inter-urban railway arrived in 1905. On the western half of Richmond, focusing upon Richmond Square, are large tracts of suburban housing, most of which have been built in the past 20 years. On the tip of the island is the old fishing town of Steveston and, on adjoining Sea Island, the international airport is expanding. The whole eastern portion of Lulu Island remains largely a dairy-farming region while along the main channel of the Fraser River extensive industrial sites are being developed. Immediately to the south, Ladner, an old service town, is ringed by new subdivision while further south on an upland, Tsawwassen houses some 15 000 persons. Off the coast, the Roberts Bank port is newly established. The inter-urban areas remain farmland.

South of New Westminster lies the municipality of Surrey, and adjacent areas of North Delta and White Rock. Once exclusively an agricultural and logging area, urban settlement has intensified, particularly at various nodes in large sprawling municipalities. The

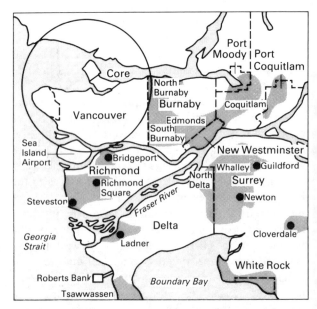

Figure 2.3 The ring of Vancouver. The broken line indicates the municipal boundaries; shading denotes continuous urban areas.

northern parts are connected by bridge and by the 401 Freeway to New Westminster and Vancouver, while in the south the 499 Freeway connects with Richmond and the west side of Vancouver. Although rapidly being filled in with urban land uses, 76 300 acres of the ring were set aside in October 1973 as agricultural reserves. Of this, some 2500 acres were designated as industrial land (see figure 2.3).

East of Vancouver and north of New Westminster lie the municipalities of Burnaby, Coquitlam, Port Coquitlam and Port Moody. Burnaby, with over 100 000 residents, does not have a conventional core-oriented urban form. The north is a natural extension of the Hastings East area of Vancouver, while Burnaby South was an extension of South Vancouver along Kingsway and the British Columbia Electric Railway inter-urban line. In the south-east, the Edmonds area is related closely to New Westminster. Each sub-area is separated by the central Burnaby Lake depression. The Coquitlam area is experiencing very rapid growth as old neighbourhoods are leap-frogged by those developers searching for new lands to subdivide.

At the present time, although the primary area of commuting is contained within the areas described above, all parts of the Greater Vancouver Regional District and additional areas are under pressure from continued population growth, and a fight for control over green space and farmland is taking place there.

Reference

Hardwick W G 1971 Vancouver: the emergence of a 'core-ring' urban pattern, in *Geographical Approaches to Canadian Problems* ed R L Gentilcore (Toronto: Prentice-Hall).

3 The Growth of Cracow and Nowa Huta

by N J G Pounds†, K Dziewoński‡, B Kortus*
and W Vlassenbroeck*

Cracow and Nowa Huta: a brief introduction

Cracow

The expansion of the city limits to include the new industrial township of Nowa Huta, five miles to the east, has brought Cracow into third place among the cities of Poland, with a population of about 525 000. Cracow grew up during the early Middle Ages on the north bank of the Vistula, a small river navigable only by the smallest river craft. Its nucleus was the limestone bluff on which the Wawel fortress was built. In 1305 this became the seat of the Polish kings and the capital of Poland. Within its walls was built the gothic cathedral of the bishops of Cracow, and in the sixteenth century much of the fortress was rebuilt in the Renaissance style which we see today. The medieval city — its walls now replaced by parks and gardens, known as the *Planty* — grew up to the north of the Wawel in two stages, first the Slav city close to the fortress, and then the planned German city beyond. At the centre of the latter lies the town square *Rynek Główny*, in which during the sixteenth century the city merchants built the Cloth Hall, or *Sukienice*. Cracow was for much of its history more a commercial than an industrial city. It lay where the ancient trade routes from Silesia and Moravia converged and then continued eastward along the loess belt to Lwów and the Ukraine. At the time of the partitions it had passed into the possession of Austria. From 1815 until 1846 it was a penurious 'free city', but was thereafter again placed under the ineffective rule of Austria. Its economic growth was discouraged in consequence, and Cracow remained merely a small town with a great past, until in 1918 it again became part of an independent Poland. At the beginning of the century its population was only 85 000. It was the finest historical monument in Poland, but it contributed little to the country's industrial future. Its industrial undertakings were small, and had grown up in spite rather than because of the policy of the Austrian government. They included a few metallurgical and engineering works and some textile, foodstuffs and other consumer goods industries; even in 1945 Cracow remained one of the least industrialized and most bourgeois of Polish cities.

This was one of the reasons among many which led to the location on the eastern outskirts of the city of the integrated Lenin steelworks of Nowa Huta, and the extension of the city's boundaries to enclose this working-class suburb of at least 100 000. The character of Cracow has been changed; about half its industrial employment is now in iron and steel, and the old Cracow residents lament the changed character of this once conservative and middle-class city.

Nowa Huta

Nowa Huta was founded in 1949 on a river terrace almost a mile to the north of the Vistula and five miles east of Cracow. A new town of immense, characterless apartment blocks was built nearby, and quickly filled with workers drawn in from the overcrowded farms of Galicia. Coal comes from Upper Silesia and Moravia; iron ore from the USSR, and limestone flux from the

Sources:

†N J G Pounds 1969 *Eastern Europe* (London: Longman) pp358–9.

‡K Dziewoński 1943 The plan of Cracow *Town Planning Rev.* pp29–37.

*B Kortus and W Vlassenbroeck 1979 A new industrial town and the steel plant in Cracow–Nowa Huta (Poland) *De Aardrijkskunde* **4** pp347–58.

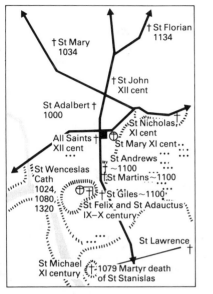

The pre-location town (reconstruction)

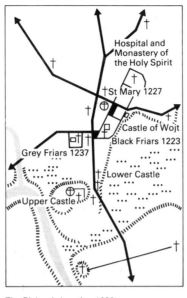

The Bishop's location 1223
(reconstruction)

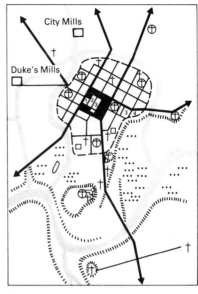

The Duke's location 1257
(reconstruction)

1. Town Hall   2. Clothiers and other Halls   3. Food Market   4. Castle of Wojt   ··· Jewish Settlement   † Churches   ➔ Routes through city

Figure 3.1   The early development of Cracow.

nearby Jura. The possibility of river navigation, undoubtedly a factor in choosing this site, has not been realized. The Vistula remains a river of uncertain value, and dock basins at the works and a canal linking them to the river have yet to be constructed. The reasons for locating the plant here appear to have been overwhelmingly political — to proletarianize the city of Cracow — and social, to provide employment in a heavily overpopulated part of the country. Writing of the factors which influenced the placement of the town of Nowa Huta, Renata Siemieńska (1969) noted that the intention was

... to create a large new and strong socialist urban working class society, which would in time influence the development of the social structure and social relations in an old and extraordinarily staid population such as existed in Cracow.

Before considering the development of Nowa Huta in more detail, the medieval origins of Cracow and its later growth and development are outlined. In the central core, at least, something of the old character of Cracow remains. The medieval buildings are now a noted tourist attraction.

The origin, design and evolution of Cracow

Medieval origins
Cracow is a masterpiece of an unknown medieval town planner. It has an unusual proportion of architecturally good buildings of all styles, and, except for the Tartar invasion in the twelfth century, has been fortunate in war. An analysis of its plan shows not only organic development, but also a consciously planned, balanced city. It clearly demonstrates, in its spatial design, the relation between people and environment.

Although the site was settled at a very early date, apart from some short remarks in Arabian and other chronicles, the first certain facts about the history of the town itself are established by church sites and buildings together with corresponding ecclesiastical documents. Cracow emerges there as an already large road settlement, at a well defended river crossing on an important commercial route from western and southern Europe to the Ukraine, the Black Sea and the Caucasus. The town is already the seat of political and ecclesiastical potentates. The number and size of its churches clearly indicate its importance (see figure 3.1). Christianity was brought probably first by the Slavonic apostles, Cyrilus and Methodius, and afterwards directly from Rome. The fight of Pope Gregory VII for the celibacy of the clergy and the right of investiture is reflected in the struggle between the King and the Bishop (the Castle and the Church) which was tragically ended in the martyr's death of Bishop Stanislas (1079), and finally resolved in the future political unification of the country. His canonization as the first Polish saint became a symbol of the reconstructed state. This struggle brought out the duality, the internal dialectic, in the development of the city. The existence and the competition of several centres is, from this time on, characteristic of Cracow through the ages.

Early in the fourteenth century during political struggles for the unification of the country (divided in the twelfth century according to hereditary laws and customs) the city, already rich and important, rebelled against the King, and was besieged and captured. The punishment was severe; the hereditary *wójt* (chief magistrate) and his partisans were beheaded, his office abolished or rather taken over by the King, and the political independence of the city was lost. The influence of this event on the layout was deep and significant. First, the city walls were partly demolished and left open towards the royal castle. Secondly, the King Ladislas Lokietek and later his son Casimir the Great started a deliberate policy of weakening the city by the creation of other settlements alongside the old one. These were the cities of New Cracow, Kleparz, Stradom and, most successful of all, of Casimir. In this way the multi-nucleus character of Cracow was further advanced. All these cities followed the usual medieval plan (rectangular blocks with a square market place containing the town hall, the church being separate although in close proximity).

Later growth

The fifteenth and sixteenth centuries were the epoch of the greatest growth and importance of the city, as the capital of the group of states governed by the Jagellons, comprising Poland, Lithuania, the Ukraine, Bohemia, the whole of Silesia, Prussia and Pomerania, Hungary, and a large part of Yugoslavia.

Cracow University was then at its best, being an exponent of the Christian and humanistic theory of the political federation of nations, against the Teutonic Knights of the Cross theory of the state ruled by force; a stronghold of supporters of the councils (Basle, Constance, Florence) in their fight for church reform and for supremacy; and a centre of humanistic and mathematical sciences. Cracow became the centre of the new Renaissance culture north of the Alps.

In the plan this period was marked by the introduction of Renaissance city houses with arcaded courtyards and by suburban villas. In the royal castle and in the new churches the triumphant new architectural style was introduced. Among others the church of SS

Peter and Paul was built according to the strict rules established by Vignola in *Il Gesu*.

The city was also an important and rich commerical centre. In the sixteenth century the growing Turkish state closed to European merchants all but the Cracow road to the East. At the same time Poland temporarily became the granary of Europe and the Wisla (Vistula) the main inland waterway for the transport of grain, with Gdańsk (Danzig) at the mouth of the river and Cracow at the beginning of the navigable part. The merchants of Cracow became rich and influential. Men like Boner and Decius were among the leading statesmen of the last Jagellons, but the dominant rural culture of the nation was irrepressible. All the important families like Bethmans, Solomons, Montelupis, Morstzyns and others quickly acquired large estates, or married into the landed gentry, and moved from the city to the country.

By the end of the sixteenth century the problem of enlarging the city became inevitable, and could not be ignored. But King Sigismond III, shaping his policies on the Renaissance ideal of a prince, preferred to move the capital to Warsaw. Cracow slowly became a residential town and an education centre. The Swedish wars caused it to decline even further, although several important churches were erected, typically closing the vista of a street, a change from the medieval planning. The end of the eighteenth century brought a change for the better; the reorganization of the university by Hugo Kollataj (later the chief Jacobin in Poland) and a renaissance in the social and political life in the city exerting most influence on its development. The three consecutive divisions of Poland, and the Napoleonic wars, have influenced the evolution of Cracow, which became a frontier town.

At the beginning of the nineteenth century the city walls were demolished, but at the last moment a small part was saved from destruction. In place of the old fortifications a park was created, called *Planty* (the plantations). Some churches were also demolished, an additional market place was established by the clearance of a block of houses and a theatre was built on the site of the medieval hospital. Finally, by the demolition of the town hall (with the exception of the tower) and part of the market hall, the main market place changed its character from a built-up area to an open space. The town hall was transferred to an old palace in the oldest square.

All these changes were on the whole quite satisfactory, making a successful modern business centre out of the rational and organic medieval city. In this respect Cracow is a unique example of medieval planning, still keeping its original character in spite of the change of conditions and function. At the end of the 1940s however, the establishment of an iron and steel plant at Nowa Huta initiated a number of changes in the character of Cracow.

The development of Nowa Huta

Location

In the middle of 1949 the construction of a new iron foundry, the Lenin steelworks, began. Out of more than ten locations considered, the one near Cracow was selected due to such factors as the proximity of Upper Silesian coal, its position on the Cracow–Przemyśl–USSR railway line by which coal (from Upper Silesia) and iron ore (from Krivoy Rog, USSR) are supplied and large reserves of manpower. In addition, Cracow's scientific institutions, especially the Mining and Metallurgical Academy/Technical University, could provide qualified personnel and research facilities. The proximity of the large cultural centre of Cracow was also an important factor from the point of view of the provision of social facilities for migrant workers.

The first blast furnace was put into operation in 1954 and the production of steel began in 1955. According to the initial plan the total output of steel was to be 1.5 million tons and this capacity was reached by the steelworks in 1960. Economies of scale were the main fac-

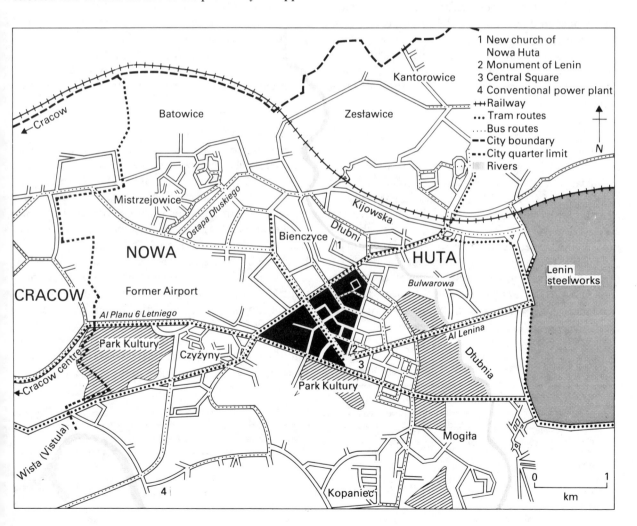

Figure 3.2 Nowa Huta and the Lenin steelworks.

tors in the further development of the combine. In 1978 the foundry produced 6.8 million tons of steel (38% of the total production of Poland), and the number of employees was 40 000 (table 3.1).

Population structure

Contemporaneous with the construction of the steel-works, a new town called Nowa Huta was built around Mogila village 10km east of Cracow (figure 3.2). In 1951 this town was incorporated as a new district of the city of Cracow. The population of Nowa Huta was planned to be 100 000, but owing to the development of the combine and other industrial plants, the housing project increased faster than expected (table 3.2).

The population of the district consists almost entirely of immigrants, born in formerly overpopulated regions of central and southern Poland, especially from rural areas (60%). Its demographic structure is typical of an immigrant population, i.e. youthful with a high birth rate and a preponderance of men over women. These features are very different from those of other Cracow districts (tables 3.3–3.6).

Housing

In 1970 Nowa Huta district had an industrial character; for instance manufacturing industry and construction employed 77.5% of the labour force, while the services were underdeveloped. As regards the tertiary sector, Nowa Huta had only basic services, without those of the quaternary sector, but the situation is improving gradually. The main service centre of the district is under construction, as well as two universities (Polytechnic University and the Physical Training Academy). A department of the Mining and Metallurgical Academy is affiliated to the steelworks.

Table 3.1. The development of the Lenin steelworks.

Year	Employment	Production of steel (1000 tons)
1950	733	—
1955	16 090	324
1960	17 700	1627
1965	24 331	2651
1970	30 886	4572
1975	—	6612
1978	about 40 000	6800

Table 3.2. Development of the population of Nowa Huta.

Year	Population	Development (1950=100)	% of Nowa Huta in the total population of Cracow
1950	18 800	100.0	5.5
1955	82 200	436.2	19.5
1960	104 300	536.4	21.0
1965	129 200	685.6	24.5
1970	161 400	850.6	27.3
1975	204 600	1 085.6	30.0
1977	217 100	1 151.0	32.8

The oldest housing estates of the district were built in 1950. Changes in architectural style are reflected in building forms, as well as land use structures. There are five main avenues (figure 3.2) dividing the central part of the district into sectors (figure 3.3), limited in the north-west by Kocmyrzowska Street, in the north-east by Bulwarowa Street, and in the south by the edge of an escarpment of the upper terrace of the Vistula River valley. The oldest estates of this unit, built in 1951–54 (Góralj and Krakowiaków) have rather low buildings, with 2–4 floors (figure 3.4). The built-up areas occupy only a third of that of open space. Service industries seldom occupy ground floors.

The next style of estate, built in 1954–56, was similar to that of old Cracow. The buildings were longer and higher, surrounding open spaces with lawns, trees, creches and children's homes; shops and other services were often located on the ground-floors of apartment blocks. The best examples are the estates Teatralne, Urocze and Zgody, especially those around the Place Centralny. The built-up areas and land used by transport occupy a greater proportion of land than do open spaces (figure 3.5).

The buildings of the third phase (1956–60) were built in a simpler style and stand separately to provide more light. There are services in the special low build-

Table 3.3. Age structure (in %).

Age groups	Nowa Huta		Cracow	
	1960	1970	1960	1970
A. 0–15	35.9	26.7	27.6	19.8
B. over 60	3.2	4.6	9.6	12.9
A/B	11.2	5.8	2.8	1.5

Figure 3.3 The main avenue of Nowa Huta and the Lenin memorial.

Figure 3.4 An example of one of the older housing estates in Nowa Huta with its many open areas.

Figure 3.5 An example of the type of housing in Nowa Huta built in 1954–56.

Figure 3.6 High-rise blocks of flats in Bienczyce, Nowa Huta.

Table 3.4. Sex structure (in %).

Year	Sex	Nowa Huta	Cracow
1955	M	54.5	—
	F	45.5	—
1960	M	53.7	47.3
	F	46.3	52.7
1970	M	52.8	47.7
	F	47.2	52.3
1977	M	51.8	47.5
	F	48.2	52.5

Table 3.5. Birth rate (live births per 1000 population).

Year	Nowa Huta	Cracow
1970	12.6	5.3
1977	—	7.4

Table 3.6. Employment structure (%) in 1970 (private sector excluded).

Sectors of national economy	Nowa Huta	Cracow
Industry	53.2	37.7
Construction	24.3	19.9
Agriculture	—	0.6
Transport	3.5	7.9
Commerce	5.3	8.5
Education, science, culture	4.4	10.5
Health service	3.6	5.4
Municipal services, administration, etc.	5.7	9.5

ings (pavilions). In the typical estates of this period, the buildings occupy 10–15% and open spaces 50–60% of the land. The youngest estates situated to the north and west of the centre of the district are very different (figure 3.6). These are the groups of high-rise blocks on the edge of Miechów Upland (Krzesławicke Hills) and at Biénczyce and Mistrezjowice. An area of open space between Nowa Huta and Cracow has now been almost filled in with new housing estates (on the former airport) and the Park Kultury.

The areas outside the urban part of Nowa Huta are still rural in character; about 45% of the land area is given over to agriculture, which has recently had to become more intensive due to increased demand, even though it has lost a large area covered by fertile loess soils. Wheat, potatoes and vegetables are typical crops produced on Nowa Huta farms.

Finally, some other interesting features can be seen from the map of the Cracow region. The conventional thermal power plant (see 4 on figure 3.2) located on the Vistula River produces electricity solely for the Cracow agglomeration, rather than for the Lenin steelworks. The distance between the steelworks and the residential areas of Nowa Huta is only about 1600 metres, so that a green belt is planned for the Dłubnia Valley between the two areas. All the new housing estates are easily accessible by public transport (trams and buses).

Reference

Siemieńska R 1969 *Nowe Zycie w Nowym Miescie* (Warsaw) p18

4 Images and Ideology: Birmingham, an Industrial City

by A Briggs

The idea and development of the Victorian city

The impact of changing transport technology
The Victorians began to interest themselves in cities in the late 1830s and early 1840s when it was impossible to avoid investigation of urgent urban problems. They were horrified and fascinated by the large industrial cities which seemed to stand for what a writer in 1840 called 'a system of life constructed on a wholly new principle'.[1] Both Blue Books and novels demonstrated the horror and the fascination. So did the reports of religious and charitable agencies and the surveys of provincial statistical societies. Newspapers and periodicals also provide an indispensable record of contemporary opinions.

The period of Victorian urban development falls between the coming of the railway and the coming of the automobile. The railway linked the new cities together and made their growth possible: like the cities themselves, it was a symbol of 'improvement'. As Emerson put it, 'railroad iron is a magician's rod in its power to evoke the sleeping energies of land and water'. Railways were also often believed, like cities, to be symbols of 'democracy', in Dr Arnold's words 'destroying feudality for ever'. The first impetus to build them came largely from groups of active businessmen in the great cities, like the 'Liverpool Party', for example, who were responsible for the building of Crewe.[2] The first railways encouraged the concentration of urban populations. Some new towns, like Barrow-in-Furness, owed their dynamism to railway interests and to men like James Ramsden, appointed Locomotive Superintendent of the Furness Railway in 1846.[3] Some older towns without railways withered away, like

Courcy in Trollope's *Doctor Thorne* (1858).

Transport was also important in determining the chronology of Victorian urban development. Railway building led to drastic changes, usually in the poorer parts of the cities. Slums were pulled down without much care being given to the rehousing of the slum dwellers. 'We occasionally sweep away the wretched dens, hidden in back courts and alleys, where the poor are smothered: but far too rarely do we make provision for them,' Charles Knight complained in his study of London.[4] More specifically Manby Smith in his *Curiosities of London Life* (1853) wrote of 'the deep gorge of a railway cutting, which has ploughed its way right through the centre of the market-gardens, and burrowing beneath the carriage-road, and knocking a thousand houses out of its path, pursues its circuitous course to the city'.[5]

If railways were symbols of progress, all too often the railway embankment became a symbol of the ruthless terror of the mid-Victorian city: it reappeared in Charles Booth's massive survey of London life as a frontier hemming in secluded groups of suspicious neighbours who hated intruders from outside. The building of local and suburban railway lines helped to determine the main lines of suburban growth. The first local passenger service to be authorized in London was started between Tooley Street, Southend and Deptford in 1836: the first workman's fare was introduced in London by the Metropolitan Railway Company in 1864 and on a section of the Stockton and Darlington Railway in the north of England as early as 1852. The Cheap Trains Act of 1883, which compelled the railway companies to offer workman's fares as and when required by the Board of Trade, was deliberately designed for 'further encouraging the migration of the working classes into the suburbs' in order to relieve housing congestion in the central areas.[6]

Source: Reproduced by permission of the Hamlyn Publishing Group Limited, from *Victorian Cities* by Asa Briggs (Lord).

Trams served the same purpose. First introduced in Birkenhead in 1860 by the American engineer George Francis Train, they were of enormous importance, particularly in the provincial cities. After the Tramways Act of 1870 gave local authorities the option to buy out private tramways by compulsory purchase after 21 years of operation, Birmingham, Glasgow, Portsmouth, Plymouth and London were quick to take advantage of the new facilities. By the end of Queen Victoria's reign 61 local authorities owned tramways and 89 undertakings were managed by private enterprise.[7] Richard Hoggart has described trams as 'the gondolas of the people'.[8] They certainly brought new areas of the city within access of working men by reducing the time taken to get to work. They also made it possible to get to the football grounds and to the holiday firework displays and galas in the public parks. Their introduction was a local landmark in all the provincial cities: battles between the protagonists of different systems of operation and of different structures of ownership enlivened late-Victorian local government.

Social conditions

The cities of the Victorians are the cities of the railway and tramway age, of the age of steam and of gas, of a society sometimes restless, sometimes complacent, moving, often fumblingly and falteringly, towards greater democracy. The building of cities was a characteristic Victorian achievement, impressive in scale but limited in vision, creating new opportunities but also providing massive new problems. Perhaps their outstanding feature was hidden from public view — their hidden network of pipes and drains and sewers, one of the biggest technical and social achievements of the age, a sanitary 'system' more comprehensive than the transport system. Yet their surface world was fragmented, intricate, cluttered, eclectic and noisy, the unplanned product of a private enterprise economy developing within an older traditional society.

To the early twentieth-century critic of Victorianism the cities seemed as unsatisfactory as Victorian people: to a later generation they have acquired a charm and romance of their own. It is fascinating to compare H G Wells with John Betjeman. To Wells the cities were even more grim when they were considered as wholes than when they were judged by their component parts. 'It is only because the thing was spread over a hundred years and not concentrated into a few weeks', he wrote in his *Autobiography*, 'that history fails to realize what sustained disaster, how much massacre, degeneration and disablement of lives was due to the housing of people in the nineteenth century.' Betjeman found interest and excitement, above all enjoyment, in at least some of the houses and in many of the public buildings which Wells would have condemned.

Quite apart from changes in taste or differing individual capacities for enjoyment, we are by now far enough away from Victorianism to understand its various expressions more sympathetically while at the same time retaining our freedom to criticize. We can and should criticize the appalling living conditions in Victorian cities, the absence of amenities, the brutal degradation of natural environment and the inability to plan and often even to conceive of the city as a whole. There is truth in Lewis Mumford's remark that 'the new industrial city had many lessons to teach; but for the urbanist its chief lesson was in what to avoid'. At the same time we realize also that in a very different twentieth-century society we are often just as hard pressed as the Victorians were to make cities attractive and inspiring. The story of twentieth-century local government has not been a story of 'ever-onward progress', as the Victorians hoped it would be. The appearance of cities has been spoilt by 'subtopian' horrors which the Victorians could not have foreseen. Year by year we are pulling down the older parts of the our cities — Victorian and pre-Victorian — with a savage and undiscriminating abandon which will not earn us the gratitude of posterity.

The worst aspects of nineteenth-century urban growth are reasonably well known. The great industrial cities came into existence on the new economic foundations laid in the eighteenth century with the growth in population and the expansion of industry. The pressure of rapidly increasing numbers of people and the social consequences of the introduction of new industrial techniques and new ways of organizing work involved a sharp break with the past. The fact that the new techniques were introduced by private enterprise and that the work was organized for other people not by them largely determined the reaction to the break.

The industrial city was bound to be a place of problems. Economic individualism and common civic purpose were difficult to reconcile. The priority of industrial discipline in shaping all human relations was bound to make other aspects of life seem secondary. A high rate of industrial investment might mean not only a low rate of consumption and a paucity of social investment but a total indifference to social costs.

The 'Sanitary Idea'

It was not until after the 1870s that health conditions in the poorer parts of the cities began to improve. The inquiries of the late 1860s and 1870s, backed by advances in medical science, were more productive of results than the noisier inquiries and the better publicized legislation of the 1840s, when the 'Sanitary Idea' was inspiring poets, moralists and artists as well as philanthropists and administrators.

Belated public interest in housing and constant interest — fluctuating in intensity and range of appeal — in the 'Sanitary Idea' characterized the Victorian city, which was the locus and focus of all theories and policies of environmental control. The theories and the policies had to be backed by statistics and to be fought for by dedicated men. As late as 1869, when professional and administrative skills were greatly superior to those of 1848, the language of some of the pioneers of the Sanitary Commission echoed that of the pioneers of the Public Health Act of 1848. 'Our present machinery', Dr John Snow told the Social Science Congress in Bristol, 'must be greatly enlarged, radically altered, and endowed with new powers', above all with the power of 'doing away with that form of liberty to which some communities cling, the sacred power to poison to death not only themselves but their neighbours.'[9]

Lack of general concern for social costs was related to the pressures not only of urbanization but of industrialization. The city offered external economies to the businessman: it was all too easy to forget that the economies entailed social costs as well. In the new industrial society belief in private property survived as the foundation of the whole social system. The belief was sustained by the law. It had also shaped eighteenth- and early nineteenth-century schemes of improvement. When Victorian legislation was passed which tampered with the rights of private property, it was always contentious and difficult to implement. A Nuisance Removal Act, for instance, had been passed as early as 1846 and there was further legislation in 1855, 1860, 1863 and 1866, yet nuisances remained unchecked and prominent in all the cities. Sir John Simon, the great sanitary reformer who took over where Chadwick left off, claimed in 1868 that disease resulting from non-application or sluggish application of the nuisance laws accounted for a quarter of the entire mortality of the country.[10]

Throughout the Victorian age the most effective argument for sanitary reform was that it would actually save money in the long run, not squander it. 'Civic economy' was a branch of political economy. As the *British and Foreign Medico-Chirurgical Review* put it in the 1840s, 'one broad principle may be safely enunciated in respect of sanitary economics — that it costs more money to create disease than to prevent it; and there is not a single structural arrangement chargeable with the production of disease which is not also in itself an extravagance'.[11]

The early advocates of the 'Sanitary Idea' were usually amateurs, men like Chadwick himself, who 'seized on an abuse with the tenacity of a bulldog' and believed that he was battling against Fate itself, or Charles Kingsley, who identified sanitary reform with the will of God. The moral strength of Victorianism often lay in its reliance on amateurs rather than on professionals to get things done. At the same time, delay in implementing legislation was made worse by the tardiness of the Victorians to develop the necessary skills for managing growing cities — civil engineering skills, for example, and medical skills. The noisy opposition to Chadwick made the most of his self-confident dogmatism, his eagerness to provide non-expert answers to highly complex technical problems. Simon, by contrast, was distinguished not only for his moderation of temperament but for his greater willingness to accept expert advice when it could be made available. Yet he too reached an impasse. It is difficult to avoid the conclusion that if half the technical skill applied to industry had been applied to the Victorian cities, their record would have been very different. As it was, Victorian cities were places where problems often overwhelmed people.

Even when a labour movement developed (and as it developed it was very slow to develop the demand for improved health and housing), even when working hours were cut, even when social investment increased, even when attempts at planning were made, and even when engineering and medical skills improved, as they did in the last phases of Queen Victoria's reign, the city remained a centre of problems. Far more remained to be done than had been done. Some of the changes within cities were the product of conscious municipal policy. Most changes, however, were the result of a multitude of single decisions, public and private: inevitably there had to be bargains and compromises. The general plan of the Victorian city continued to express all this. At the end of the reign the cities remained confused and complicated, a patchwork of private properties, developed separately with little sense of common plan, a jumble of sites and buildings with few formal frontiers, a bewildering variety of heights and eye-levels, a social disorder with districts of deprivation and ostentation, and every architectural style, past and present, to add to the confusion. It is not surprising that George Bernard Shaw suggested that all British cities, like all Indian villages, would have to be pulled down and built again if people were to live in an environment worthy of them.

The two sides of urban growth

This, however, is only one side of the picture, the side which impressed the young H G Wells. The sheer magnitude of Victorian urban problems directed attention to issues about which people had hitherto been silent. The growth of the new industrial city meant that people took a closer look at the problems both of the old market town and of the village. It was true, as one of the great Blue Books of the 1840s put it, that 'more filth, worse physical suffering and moral disorder than Howard describes as affecting the prisoners, are to be found among the cellar population of the working people of Liverpool, Manchester, or Leeds and in large portions of the Metropolis',[12] but factual knowledge of these conditions and the conscience and drive to do something about them influenced pre-Victorian towns like Exeter and Norwich which had hitherto pushed their urban problems into the background. 'The discovery of the laws of public health,' the Registrar-General noted in 1871, 'the determination of the conditions of cleanliness, manners, water supply, food, exercise, isolation, medicine, most favourable to life in one city, in one country, is a boon to every city, to every country, for all can profit by the experience.'[13]

Social conditions in the new communities encouraged both the amassing of facts and the airing of viewpoints. However great the resistance, there was persistent pressure to control social change. Victorian cities were not the 'insensate' ant-heaps which find a place in Mumford's pages. At their worst they were always more than 'mere man-heaps, machine warrens, not organs of human association'.[14] They were never mere collections of individuals, some weak, some strong. They had large numbers of voluntary organizations, covering a far wider range of specialized interests than was possible either in the village or the small town. They were more free of aristocratic 'influence'. They allowed room for middle-class initiative and for greater independence and greater organization of the 'lower ranks of society' than did smaller places: by the end of the century, both independence and organization were

being reflected in new policies and in genuine transfers of power. Moreover, the cities possessed in their newspapers what were often extremely effective propaganda agencies focusing attention on local issues and through competitive rivalry stimulating the development of articulate opinions. 'In the forums of the public press,' one nineteenth-century writer put it, 'we see the forms of all the greater and lesser associations into which society at large has wrought itself.'[15] At their best, the cities created genuine municipal pride and followed new and bold courses of action.

The two sides of the picture must be taken together in assessing Victorian experience. There was alarming waste and confusion before there were signs of effective control, but the speed of urban development and the energy which lay behind it impress posterity even more than they impressed contemporaries.

The people of the twentieth century, able to draw more easily on expert skills, have had to wrestle with complex urban problems bequeathed by the Victorians — health, housing, education and traffic, for example; at the same time they are still relying (and this in itself is a part of 'the plight of the contemporary city') on the vast accumulation of social capital which the Victorians raised, usually by voluntary or by municipal effort. Much of the effort went into church building — this reflected Victorian concern for the future of religion in an urban environment[16] — but particularly in the last 25 years of Queen Victoria's reign there was a huge development of public offices, hospitals, schools, sewage farms and water works. The Victorian phase in city development cannot be ignored even as a visible factor in the present. It obtrudes in every provincial city and in London itself, although it is now being destroyed in the name of 'progress', a cause which was used by the Victorians themselves to sanctify much of their own destruction.

It is this side of the Victorian city that Betjeman understood and appreciated. He recognized that the right approach to a Victorian city is from the railway station, that 'the best guide books are the old ones published in the last century', that the 'restorations' of the Victorians revealed their mood and purpose as plainly as their new buildings, that the symbolism outside and within the Victorian public buildings is in its way as interesting (and as dated) as medieval symbolism, that both the variety and the individuality of private middle-class houses merit sensitive and discriminating attention, that to understand the detail of the cities is more important than seeking to generalize about the general effect of the whole.

Your sense of the whole depended, of course, on your own place in it. G M Young emphasized that this was true of Victorian people. 'Suppose you fall asleep tonight and wake up in 1860. What is the first thing you would notice?' There is no single answer. It would depend on where you woke up.[17] Suppose you arrived at a Victorian railway station, the key building of the age, your impression of the city world beyond the waiting room and the new station hotel would be determined not only by your mood or your company, but as likely as not by the direction in which you first decided to go. Very quickly, within a few yards of the station, you might find yourself among the workshops and warehouses 'on the wrong side of the track'. For miles beyond there might stretch more workshops and more warehouses, gas works and breweries, long rows of ugly working-class houses in brick or stone, with occasional churches and chapels, institutes and clubs, dingy public houses and small corner shops, cemeteries and rubbish-heaps. You would pass through what Engels called those 'separate territories, assigned to poverty', where, 'removed from the sight of the happier class, poverty may struggle along as it can'. If you were more fortunate, you might move instead towards the crowded 'city centre' with its covered market, its busy exchanges, its restored (?) parish church, its massive 'city chapels', its imposing town hall, its cluster of banks, its theatres and its public houses, the newest of them gleaming with rich mahogany, engraved glass and polished brass. It says much for the Victorians that despite these varieties of urban condition, they were occasionally able to create a general shared enthusiasm for the city as such, an enthusiasm which transcended the facts and consciousness of social class. Yet it was an enthusiasm which the collective achievement of the city often did far too little to justify.

The spatial spread of cities

The growth of suburbia

There were, of course, great changes within the cities during the Victorian period, particularly as they grew in size. Sprawling expansion at the outskirts was accompanied by a decline in the population of the central parts of the city and by a redrawing of social boundaries in the huge areas between the centre and the periphery. As the houses were pulled down, shops, factories, warehouses, banks and offices took their place. Railway building itself led to much large-scale clearance. The process went further during the 1880s and 1890s, when the great provincial cities acquired central 'layouts' which in many cases did not alter substantially until the 1950s. There were marked changes, however, in possession. Family shops gave way to chain shops and large department stores. W H Smith & Sons, directly dependent on the railway, began to build their network in the 1850s, and department stores, which also had their origins in this decade, began to flourish both in London and the provinces in the 1880s and 1890s; 30 years later the music halls gave way to cinemas and the trams to buses. Formerly 'desirable residences' near the city centre, in the 'middle ring' and at the city end of the radial routes leading out to the suburbs often passed into the hands of people from lower-income groups. The houses might remain, but whole districts of what has been called 'the blighted belt' could change in social character.

On the outskirts of every city undeveloped land was turned into suburbia. In the early part of Queen Victoria's reign this term did not necessarily suggest 'superior' properties. The 'industrial suburbs' of Hunslet and Holbeck near Leeds had much the same kind of reputation as the *faubourgs* of medieval cities where artisans, who could not find or could not afford accommodation within the city, lived and worked. They were often more unhealthy than the 'city centres': this was as true of the suburbs of nineteenth-century Sydney as of those of Elizabethan London. As the nineteenth century went by, however, the term 'suburbia' became increasingly associated with flight from the worst parts of the city. It had been used in this sense in the Manchester and Birmingham of the 1790s. Stress was laid on the superior amenities, including 'the pure breath of Heaven', which could be found outside the smoke and noise of the city. Builders were natural propagandists, selling without too much difficulty when times were good the 'detached villas of pleasing and picturesque appearance' which they said would become 'the seats of families of distinction'.

The title of 'city' however, was a coveted badge of status and the idea of a city, moreover, whatever its legal and administrative definition in this country, had deeper and more universal undertones. It was enriched by the knowledge that there had been great cities in the past and the belief that there could be even greater cities in the future. The sense of the city, never as strong in England as in certain other parts of the world, was nonetheless strong enough to qualify and extend simpler notions of the autonomy of private enterprise and the priority of individual interest. It carried with it a sense of 'dignity', if only a latent sense. In active form, it could stir voluntary bodies, influence the programme of political parties, and inspire mayors, aldermen and councillors.

The social context

Environment and architecture

The Victorians reacted quite deliberately and with no regrets against what they considered to be the dull, monotonous, uniform architecture of Georgian England. Later Victorians revelled in the ransacking of old styles. They identified Georgian architecture not only with formal dullness but with lack of imaginative inventiveness, and once they had fought out inconclusively their own famous 'battle of styles' between the Greek and the Gothic, they allowed for a limited amount of specialization (Gothic for churches, classical or Renaissance motifs on public buildings) or settled down to a comfortable eclecticism.

The eclecticism was displayed, often ostentatiously, not only in individual Victorian buildings but in Victorian city streets. There were some Victorians, a minority, who wanted a style of their own, with a sensible and imaginative use of new materials, just as there were Victorians who wanted to plan towns on formal eighteenth-century lines. The majority, however, liked a diversity or a blending of styles. Just because they lived in an age which had abandoned the rule of taste, they took immense pains to educate people in taste or to use one of their favourite verbs, to 'elevate' taste. They liked 'imposing' buildings with 'pretensions'. They loved symbolism. They were seldom afraid of exuberance. Individuality and status-seeking were both expressed in their villas: their banks and shops became more and more ornate and decorated as the century went by. Even mills, warehouses and docks, which retained a dignified and still handsome functionalism throughout the early years of the industrial revolution, became places to decorate as well as to use. Their churches might be in many styles, for they ceased to be dominated by rules as to which style was appropriate for which kinds of building. Their town halls were the subjects of lively and sometimes exciting debate.

There was an effort, whatever may be thought of its results. Many Victorian buildings were appalling: others have withstood the test of time. Mid-twentieth-century reaction against 'bare' functionalism has encouraged a revision of judgment concerning a number of Victorian buildings. The detail of the buildings deserves a closer examination than it has often received, and greater imaginative power is needed than is usually applied to envisage the colours and even the general appearance of buildings now begrimed in industrial soot. Victorian architecture in Australia — and even in India — has suffered less in this last respect, and it is far easier to appreciate the appearance of a Victorian town in twentieth-century Ballarat, where there is some superb Victorian architecture, than in twentieth-century Middlesbrough.

'Culture'

The willingness to express hopes and fears in buildings, and not to pay too much attention to what experts said ought to be admired or condemned, was a general feature of the Victorian approach to 'culture'. The culture of the mind also remained less specialized and more open to amateur influences than the culture of the twentieth century.

The mechanics' institutes were nineteenth-century inventions, products of the age of improvements, and were subsequently transported round the English-speaking world. The literary and philosophical societies almost all had pre-Victorian foundations. The mechanics institutes stood for the diffusion of knowledge among all classes, particularly among the skilled artisans: the literary and philosophical societies were proud of their role as the local cultural élite. Their presence or absence in the nineteenth-century cities (or the date when they came into existence) was of considerable cultural and civic importance. Manchester's society came into existence in 1781, Newcastle's in 1793, Liverpool's in 1812. Leeds founded its society in 1819, Sheffield three years later. It was to the Sheffield Society that Sorby, who was also a patron of university extension, gave much devoted service. There was no such society in nineteenth-century Birmingham — the famous Lunar Society founded in 1766 had passed out of existence — and this may account in part at least for the intensely political flavour of the 'civic gospel' as it was preached in Birmingham.

Library facilities, the existence of clubs and reading rooms, the growth of musical societies and statistical societies, the blossoming and withering of local periodicals, some of the first of them concerned specifically with local theatres, the local pull of national cultural bodies like the National Society for the Promotion of Social Science, must all be taken into account in examining the cultural life of a Victorian city.

The rise of a national system of cities

During the 1890s, however, the pull of London tightened. Local newspapers began to lose ground to national newspapers. National advertising began to increase greatly in scope and scale. The same branded goods began to be offered in shops in all parts of the country. Neither the aesthete nor the expert was as much at home in the provinces as he was in the huge metropolis. Political and economic trends began to depend less on local social and market forces and more on national pressures from the centre. It was then, as the same kind of working-class houses were being built in the same kind of suburbs under the building by-laws of the 1875 Public Health Act, that cities began to be more alike — and not in the early years of the industrial revolution.

World War I and the rise of the mass communications system of the twentieth century completed the process. Whereas the word 'masses' was first used in the nineteenth century to describe the mysterious working-class population of the great new industrial cities, it began to be used increasingly during the twentieth century in a national context. It came to mean first the London crowd and then the faceless millions who could be manipulated from a single cultural centre. There is room for intensive research on the 1890s, one of the least studied decades of recent British history. It is clear from what has already been written, however, that it was not merely the coming of the automobile nor even the death of Queen Victoria which brought the age of Victorian cities to an end.

References and Notes

[1] *Bentley's Miscellany* 1840 vol. VII.

[2] The story of the struggle of the 'Liverpool Party' with groups based on Manchester and Birmingham is told in W H Chaloner 1950 *The Social and Economic Development of Crewe* ch. 1.

[3] Ramsden's career is discussed in J D Marshall 1958 *Furness and the Industrial Revolution*.

[4] C Knight, *London* (1841–4), vol. IV, p254. See also H J Dyos 1957 'Some Social Costs of Railway Building in London' in *Journal of Transport History*, vol. III. It was not only railways which created such problems. When the St Katherine's Dock was built in the late 1820s, some 800 houses were destroyed and 11 000 people turned out into the streets (see R Sinclair 1950 *East London* p245).

[5] C Manby Smith 1853 *Curiosities of London Life* p361.

[6] S A Pope 1906 *The Cheap Trains Act* p15.

[7] Cmd 305 1900 *Joint Select Committee on Municipal Trading*.

[8] R Hoggart 1957 *The Uses of Literacy* p120.

[9] *The Times* 5 October 1869. *The Times*, which had asked in 1848 for a 'bettish and personal opposition [to the Public Health Bill] just enough to quicken Lord Morpeth's energies', noted in 1849 that while apathy was still the main problem, 'the stage of universal consent has never been reached'.

[10] See the important article by E P Hennock 1957 'Urban Sanitary Reform a Generation before Chadwick' in *Economic History Review* vol. X, and *Eleventh Annual Report of the Medical Officer to the Privy Council* (1868). For Simon's work, which points forward to the twentieth century, see R Lambert 1963 *Sir John Simon and English Social Administration*.

[11] For the attitudes of the 1840s, see my lecture 'Public Opinion and Public Health in the Age of Chadwick' *Chadwick Lecture* 1946.

[12] *Report on the Sanitary Conditions of the Labouring Population* 1842 p60.

[13] Quoted in H Jephson 1907 *The Sanitary Evolution of London* p100.

[14] L Mumford, *The Culture of Cities* (1938 edn) p148. The remark is repeated in *The City in History* (1961) p450. The same view is expressed in G M Trevelyan 1952 *Illustrated English Social History* vol. IV p118. 'The modern city, in the unplanned swamp of its increase, lacks form and feature; it is a deadening cage for the human spirit.' See also J L and B Hammond 1917 *The Town Labourer*, especially Chapter III, and *The Age of the Chartists* (1930).

[15] R Vaughan 1843 *The Age of Great Cities, or Modern Society Viewed in its Relation to Intelligence, Morals and Religion* p278.

[16] See M H Port 1961 *Six Hundred New Churches* for early Victorian development; and G Kitson Clark 1962 *The Making of Victorian England*.

[17] See *Victorian People* p13 (Pelican edition).

5 Vancouver: A Post-industrial City

by D Ley

In the late 1960s in Vancouver a new ideology of urban development was in the making. Urban strategy seemed to be passing from an emphasis on growth to a concern with the quality of life; the new liberalism was to be recognized less by its production schedules than by its consumption styles. These changes were not of course unique to Vancouver, but were felt to a greater or lesser extent in every major city in North America. But in some metropolitan areas the livable city ideology was expressed more forcibly and successfully than in others.

In Vancouver, a post-industrial west coast city where employment is dominated by service and administrative occupations, the liberal professional community, aided by a system of civic elections, was influential enough to exercise both economic and political power. The cultural hegemony of the liberal community was reflected not only in the market place but also in public policy.

The post-industrial thesis

The changes in urban policy associated with the livable city ideology were associated with shifts at the economic, the political, and the socio-cultural levels of society, so that an understanding of the emerging urban landscape requires a prior grasp of wide-ranging processes of change in society itself. Such an examination will also place the Vancouver case study in its more general theoretical context.

It is helpful as a starting point to consider the insights of two significant theorists of modern Western society, Daniel Bell and Jürgen Habermas. Such a liaison might

Source: D Ley 1980 Liberal ideology and the post-industrial city *Annals of the Association of American Geographers* **70**(2) pp238–58.

at first seem unlikely, for Bell is often interpreted as a conservative thinker and Habermas as a radial. Post-industrial society is Bell's term (1973, 1976) implicating at least partially a technological phase blurring ideological distinctions, where technology rather than the mode of production is a major force shaping society. Habermas (1970, 1971, 1975), in contrast, speaks of an advanced capitalist society, so that the distinction between broadly capitalist and socialist nations remains of some importance. But apart from the obvious differences there is also a deeper complementarity in their positions. Both see a decisive transition between nineteenth- and late twentieth-century society, between the industrial period (or period of early capitalism) and post-industrialism (late capitalism), so that modes of thought originating in the nineteenth century no longer fit the changed circumstances of the present era.

In the economy, a major break with nineteenth-century society has been the declining role of unskilled labour in the production process and the growing importance of technology, not only in the factory but also in service industries and administration. Habermas reviews the epistemological consequences of the ascendancy of technology, equating it with the rise of technical solutions and positivist science. As significant are the empirical consequences. Technology has become a dominant force in production; rather than the factory, university and research establishments are emerging as leading institutions. Theoretical knowledge has acquired a privileged status: 'In capitalist society the axial institution has been private property and in the post-industrial society it is the centrality of theoretical knowledge (Bell 1973).

The rapid development of technology and technical management and problem-solving have brought about a remarkable transformation of the labour force this

Table 5.1. Framework of major societal relations.

	Industrial era (early capitalism)	Post-industrial era (advanced capitalism)
Economy	Production; manufacturing; blue-collar occupations	Centrality of technology; services; white-collar occupations
Politics	*Laissez-faire*; alliances with entrepreneurs; business control	Intervention and regulation; plural interests and multiple criteria; power moving to professionals
Culture	Growth ethic; belief in progress; centrality of work	Rise of an amenity ethic; role of the aesthetic; centrality of consumption
	The industrial city	*The post-industrial city*

Source: Developed in part from Bell (1973) and Habermas (1970, 1975).

century. The proportion of white-collar workers in the United States has risen from 18% in 1900, to 37% in 1950, and to 49% by 1974. Blue-collar employment amounted to 35% of the workforce in 1974, about the same level as in 1900, although the proportion has been declining since 1950. Government forecasts anticipate that from 1968 to 1980 the gap will widen further as new job creation will favour white-collar occupations by a ratio of five to two. The job categories showing the most pronounced growth (about twice the national rate) have been professional and technical occupations, which numbered less than a million workers in 1890 but over 12 million in 1974 (Bell 1976). In relative terms even more dramatic trends are under way in Canada. While the national labour force expanded by 8.5% from 1971 to 1975, white-collar employment increased by 26%. Among the major white-collar categories, the increase was most marked in professional and technical occupations which grew by 33%, and managerial and administrative positions which rose by 65% (*Canada Year Book 1976–77*).[1] In recent years a large new cohort of highly paid white-collar workers has been added to the labour force. By 1975 this privileged cohort accounted for 20–25% of all workers in both Canada and the United States. One worker in seven in each country was in a professional or technical occupation, part of a privileged, quaternary labour force.

There is an important subjective corollary to the numerical increase of senior white collar employees and professionals. These occupations enjoy the highest social prestige, whether the assessment is derived from the indicators of income and education or from perceived job rankings held by the public at large (Treiman 1977). In Canada both objective and subjective

assessments have revealed that the highest prestige occupations are the senior white-collar posts (Blishen 1967, Pineo and Porter 1967). Among these high-status positions, professionals are favoured over owners, managers and administrators: 'Professional occupations ranked highly, particularly physician, university professor, county court judge and lawyer' (Pineo and Porter 1967). We might expect, therefore, that these professional occupations will contain a disproportionate share of a post-industrial state's taste-makers and opinion leaders; as we will see, this expectation is borne out emphatically by their leadership role in Vancouver's urban reform movement.

A second corollary of the employment shift in the post-industrial state is the economic transition from a goods-producing to a service-producing society. Over 70% of the non-agricultural jobs in the United States were service-related by 1977, while less than 30% were goods-related, a reversal of the proportions in 1900 (*Statistical Abstracts of the US* 1977). In the post-industrial city the office tower rather than the factory chimney dominates the downtown skyline.

A large number of these services are public rather than private; the different tiers of government employ about 16% of the US workforce, while the state's purchases amount to more than 20% of the nation's GNP. This active role of government is a second feature distinguishing post-industrial from industrial societies (table 5.1).

Whereas in the nineteenth century government promoted entrepreneurial interests either actively or else indirectly, under post-industrialism state intervention has become forceful while its objectives are social, ecological and even aesthetic as well as economic. Decision-making and the allocation of resources is now referred to the political arena and not only to the market place. Goal achievement for a particular interest group has become an exercise in political lobbying and not simply the execution of market power. As Bell has noted, 'We have become a communal society, in which many groups now seek to establish their social rights — their claims on society — through the political process' (Bell 1973). The politicization of varied interest groups is challenging the formerly firm hold of the business lobby on political decision-making: power is being diffused among a range of lobbyists, accelerated by programmes which require consultation and participation among a plurality of legitimate interests. The single-minded commitment to efficiency, technical rationality, and economic development is tempered and in some instances overturned amid the competing claims of different 'public interests'.

At the socio-cultural level, Habermas continually raises the necessity of preserving the personal world of values and meaning against the onslaught of the rational, bureaucratic and secular world view. But during the 1960s a considerable cultural counter-offensive gained momentum. This movement was popularized by the counter-culture even though its roots lay much deeper, and its effects have infiltrated mainstream society to the extent of institutionalization in new legislation in some areas, notably environmental protection. In contrast to the rational world view it challenges, the cultural resurgence is characterized by its promotion of alternative values which emphasize the realm of experience, man's emotional, spiritual, and aesthetic nature. There is an insistence that the realm of meaning and the quality of experience are central concerns.

The assault on Cartesian rationalism and its political and technological apparatus has encouraged a liberation of the senses to occur. In the original counter-culture Habermas observed how 'The lifestyle of protest is defined by sensuous and sensual qualities' (Habermas 1970). Bell concurs that 'The search for the modern was a search for the heightening of experience in all dimensions,' but he takes the assessment further in positing the emergence of hedonism as a lifestyle: 'The cultural, if not moral, justification of capitalism has become hedonism, the idea of pleasure as a way of life' (Bell 1976).

The sensuous and aesthetic philosophy released by the counter-culture has been appropriated in various forms by the growing numbers of North America's leisure class. Shorter working hours, earlier retirement and rising real wealth have diverted attention from basic needs to what Maslow identified as the higher need of self-actualization (Maslow 1970). Even work itself is being redefined; a Canadian survey found that 30% of those interviewed placed self-fulfilment over conventional forms of job satisfaction as their major employment goal. Of all occupational groups, professionals expressed the greatest consensus on the primacy of the goal of self-fulfilment. A second poll, on Canadian attitudes to the value of education, showed that lifestyle satisfaction was rated as of equal significance to economic advancement. But in British Columbia more than 60% of residents placed lifestyle satisfaction in first place, while less than 25% gave primacy to economic success. The aesthetic lifestyle is becoming its own justification. At the same time these traits are not uniformly distributed; there is a geography of the post-industrial society.

Although it has been possible here to give no more than an outline of a post-industrial theory of society, we may see from this framework the appearance of a theoretically significant group of actors. Senior white-collar workers in professional, technical and administrative occupations account for over 20% of North America's workforce and form a theoretical counterpoint to nineteenth-century notions of capital and labour; as a class in emergence they have received considerable theoretical attention and would seem to have the capacity to become a politically significant group. This cadre encompasses the outer limits of a nation's intellectuals; as a group they are highly educated and many have postgraduate training. Their younger members in particular exhibit a high degree of social if not political liberalism, and have plural life goals, placing a higher premium on self-fulfilment as a major career objective than any other occupational category. With a secure economic base, they represent the present-day counterparts of Veblen's leisure class, displaying the canons of good taste, intent upon the aesthetic (Veblen 1953; see also Diggins 1977). Their lifestyle is commonly consumption and status oriented in the pursuit of self-actualization, while their prestige is considerable and in many ways they are national opinion leaders. They are sensitive to amenity and social cachet in the places they adopt; an industrial landscape is anathema to them. It was from the ranks of this emergent élite that Pierre Trudeau was drawn.

Vancouver: a post-industrial city

The post-industrial thesis has been developed prim-

Table 5.2.   British Columbia employment index by industry, 1962–76.

	Forestry/ mining	Manufacturing/ construction/ transport	Trade/finance	Services	Public administration	All non-agricultural employment
1962	100	100	100	100	100	100
1964	101	110	112	113	103	110
1966	112	126	126	140	111	127
1968	113	125	140	162	128	136
1970	121	129	151	183	138	147
1972	118	144	175	194	145	161
1974	135	162	204	220	171	184
1976	131	161	205	239	204	190

Source: Developed from data in Statistics Canada, *Estimates of Employees by Province and Industry*, Catalogue 72-516 (Ottawa, 1978).

arily by sociologists and as such it is not locationally specific. Clearly it might fit circumstances more closely in San Francisco or London than in Cleveland or Glasgow. This section will examine several aspects of the geography of Vancouver which suggests that the model presents some useful categories for examining social change and urban development within the city since the late 1960s.

A service economy

The articulation of an urban reform movement among professionals in the late 1960s needs to be seen against several contexts, the first of which was the occupational transformation of the British Columbia labour force (table 5.2). During the period under review the workforce nearly doubled; the largest single period of job expansion was from 1972 to 1974, coinciding significantly with the peak of the development boom and the virtual doubling of house prices in Greater Vancouver. Particularly notable was the differential between categories in job creation. Despite British Columbia's reputation as a frontier economy, the primary and blue-collar categories added new jobs at a rate much below the provincial average, while white-collar categories considerably exceeded the average. By 1976 over 60% of non-agricultural jobs fell in predominantly white-collar categories; the rather different classification by occupation indicated (in June 1978) a non-manual share of 65% of all jobs, the highest provincial level in Canada. Such detailed information is not available for Vancouver except for the census years. Since the metropolitan area accounted for over 50% of the province's labour force in 1971, however, it provides the major contribution to the provincial trends. The city of Vancouver, with almost one-quarter of provin-

cial jobs in 1971, is over-represented in the fastest-growing categories of trade and finance, and services; already in 1971 70% of the city's jobs were in white-collar categories. Between the 1951 and 1971 census the proportion of the city's labour force engaged in services and public administration increased by more than half.

It is more difficult to establish trends in occupational rather than industrial categories because of changing definitions between census periods. It is certain, however, that within the city of Vancouver all white-collar employment categories increased both absolutely and relatively from 1951 to 1971. Professional and technical employees probably doubled in number and by 1971 included one employee in seven; in contrast residents in blue-collar occupations declined slightly overall, and by 8% in relative terms. It seems certain that these trends have accelerated since 1971 with the office boom adding 3000 jobs per year downtown alone between 1968 and 1975. The downtown construction boom was of remarkable extent for the city's size and rapidly created a high-rise skyline of offices and apartments. Between 1967 and 1977 downtown office space doubled to 14 million square feet; 8000 new jobs a year were added in Vancouver from 1971 to 1975 (40% of the metropolitan total) and 75% of these were generated by new office construction. The white-collar proportion was much higher, and, including hotels, retailing and public service facilities, was probably not less than 90% of new jobs created.

The rising real wealth of western North America

A second and related contextual factor is Vancouver's location within the rapid growth region of western North America. In the United States the distinction between the growth states of the west and south and the slow (or zero) growth states of the north and east has been suggested as the major feature of the nation's regional geography in the 1970s (Sternlieb and Hughes 1975). An east–west distinction is equally marked in Canada, where population growth in British Columbia and Alberta has been increasing at twice the national rate since 1966. These provinces also lead the nation in average weekly earnings; in 1976 the national level of $228 contrasted with $237 in Alberta and $260 in British Columbia. These trends are accurately summarized in the housing market. In the western United States (as defined by the US Census), housing costs were 50% higher than the national average in 1978, while in Canada, Vancouver, Calgary, and Edmonton have consistently figured (with Toronto) as the four metropolitan areas with the most expensive housing.

In 1976 a survey suggested that the mean household income in Vancouver was $14 600, or 70% above the level in 1972; even discounting inflation, this represented a real gain of 17%. Almost a quarter of the city's households earned in excess of $20 000 a year in 1976; even in constant 1976 dollars this represented an increase of over 12 000 households in the top income category over 1972. Another feature of this population cohort is revealed by demographic data. Although the city lost population from 1971 to 1976, it experienced a net increase of households as large families left Vancouver to be replaced by one- or two-person households. Indeed, despite a decrease of 20% in children under 14 years, there was a gain of 5% in the age group 25–44 years, the age range that might ordinarily be expected to include younger children. One persuasive inference is that conventional households with children and a single wage-earner were being displaced by one- or two-person households without children and with both spouses working. Support for this contention is provided by the construction of over 5000 condominium units in inner-city Vancouver between 1970 and 1976. A survey of condominium households in Greater Vancouver and Victoria conducted in 1977 showed that 70% of households contained no children, that in half of them household heads were aged under 40 years, that a quarter of households earned over $24 000 and that the dominant employment categories were professional and managerial occupations.

The west coast culture realm
Within the post-industrial cities employees in quaternary occupations are emerging as a new élite and, as such, the new taste-makers. In Vancouver an added context is the city's setting within the west coast cultural realm which has assumed a cultural hegemony in the development and diffusion of social movements and lifestyles. Meinig regards southern California as 'a leisure society . . . the chief source-region of a new American life-style which has been expanding and elaborating for more than fifty years, featuring a relaxed enjoyment of each day in casual indoor–outdoor living, with an accent upon individual gratification, physical health, and pleasant exercise' (Meinig 1979). More recently, San Francisco has been suggested as a new centre of lifestyle innovation; over the past 20 years it has been the headquarters of the ecology movement and various human potential societies.

Vancouver has been an intimate part of the west coast cultural realm for 50 years. California house styles have provided a major contribution to the city's landscape, while the headquarters of the Greenpeace Foundation make Vancouver a significant northern member of 'ecotopia'. An abiding popular image has linked Vancouver with San Francisco more than with any other city and it is not difficult to find substantial lifestyle associations. One suggestive indicator is provided by the Canadian sales of *Gourmet*, a magazine published in New York with the subtitle 'the magazine of good living', and a message of consumption with style. *Gourmet* readership is at a high level in California, and among the ten Canadian provinces there are also marked geographic differentials in the monthly sales of the more than 50 000 copies, with the highest relative sales occurring in British Columbia, followed by Ontario and Alberta. Assuming that purchase of *Gourmet* intimates a distinctive set of values toward consumption, then proportionately those values are held most widely in British Columbia. The sales index has much higher values in metropolitan centres. Vancouver with less than 2% of the national population in 1976 contained almost 5% of Canadian *Gourmet* subscribers.

These attitudes are reflected in the recent emergence of informal associations and a vigorous retail sector serving a leisure-seeking and consumption-oriented lifestyle. A marked transition of store types has occurred in many neighbourhoods in response to the changing clientele. In Kitsilano, an inner-city neighbourhood with beaches, and mountain and ocean views, the main shopping street has been 'making a comeback as a recreation and shopping area for the upwardly mobile condominium set. Trendy restaurants, clothes shops and other specialty stores are springing up like mushrooms after a spring rain.' The canons of good taste have extended especially to cuisine, as the city has experienced a rapid increase in specialty restaurants; directories indicate that the diversity of ethnic restaurants has expanded fourfold since 1961. Vancouver now claims more restaurants per capita than any other city in North America. Veblenian man has indeed triumphed!

References

Bell D 1973 *The Coming of Post-Industrial Society* (New York: Basic Books) pp115, 364

—— 1976 *The Cultural Contradictions of Capitalism* (New York: Basic Books) pp 118–21

Blishen B 1967 A socio-economic index for occupations in Canada *Canadian Review of Sociology and Anthropology* **4**

Canada Year Book 1976–77 1977 (Ottawa: Ministry of Supply and Services)

Diggins J 1977 Reification and the cultural hegemony of capitalism: the perspective of Marx and Veblen *Social Research* **44** pp 354–83

Gottmann J 1978 The mutation of the American city: a review of the comparative metropolitan analysis project *Geographical Review* **68** pp201–8

Habermas J 1970 *Toward a Rational Society* (Boston: Beacon Press) p 33

—— 1971 *Knowledge and Human Interests* (Boston: Beacon Press)

—— 1975 *Legitimation Crisis* (Boston: Beacon Press)

Maslow A 1970 *Motivation and Personality* (New York: Harper and Row)

Meinig D W (ed) 1979 Symbolic landscapes: models of American community, in *The Interpretation of Ordinary Landscapes: Geographical Essays* (New York: Oxford University Press) pp164–92

Pineo P and Porter W 1967 Occupational prestige in Canada *Canadian Review of Sociology and Anthropology* **4** pp24–40

Statistical Abstracts of the United States 1977 (Washington, DC: US Dept of Commerce)

Sternlieb G and Hughes J (eds) 1975 *Post-Industrial America: Metropolitan Decline and Inter-Regional Job Shifts* (New Brunswick, NJ: Rutgers University Press)

Treiman D 1977 *Occupational Prestige in Comparative Perspective* (New York: Academic Press)

Veblen T 1953 *The Theory of the Leisure Class* (New York: New American Library)

Note

[1] These groups represent the so-called quaternary occupations, regarded by some writers as symptomatic of advanced urbanism (see Gottmann 1978).

6   Is There a Socialist City?

by R A French and F E I Hamilton

The pre-socialist situation

The basic question here is whether or not the socialist city is fundamentally different from the city in what may be called, for lack of a better term, capitalist societies. The cities of Eastern Europe and the Soviet Union exist within societies which are organized on Marxist, not capitalist, premises, which aspire to socialist goals, which apply socialist theory in their actions and mechanisms. All these societies, excepting only Yugoslavia today, operate planned economies where, whatever the degree of centralization in decision-making, the ultimate decisions on priorities, on capital investment, on targets for sectoral and spatial patterns of growth and change, and on means for achieving these targets, are taken by state organizations, primarily by the central organs of government and party. The very high order of control vested in the state over such matters as land ownership, land use, the degree and direction of industrialization, capital investment in all sectors, and at all levels of the economy, rents, wages, prices and even (in certain periods and in certain places) movements of population, means that the state has a power to determine the pace and the form of urban development far greater than that wielded by any Western government, central or local. Has the exercise of this formidable power during three decades, or even during six, created an urban form which is a distinct, special phenomenon, more or less sharply differentiated from the capitalist or market-economy form? The authors contend that the answer to such a question is definitely 'yes' — but with certain qualifications.

As one might expect, there are significant differences in the geography of towns, not only between 'socialism' and 'capitalism', but also between the various socialist countries themselves — for good historical, social,

economic and even political reasons. To start with, the processes of urbanization have differed. The advent of socialism in Eastern Europe inherited a variety of situations. None of the countries in the late 1940s was as little urbanized as the USSR had been in 1917, although the southern group of Romania, Bulgaria, Yugoslavia and Albania was only slightly more so. Already Czechoslovakia had 44% of its citizens in urban areas, while the German Democratic Republic (GDR) was the most urbanized, with 67.6%, although that proportion represented a drop from the pre-war level of 72.2%. Indeed the GDR alone has experienced little new city growth since 1950. In Poland there has been relatively rapid urban growth since 1950. 39% of the population lived in towns and cities at that date; by 1975 this percentage had risen to 55. Bulgaria has made the most remarkable strides, with the share of its urban population rising from 24.7 to 59.3%. Although only the GDR, Czechoslovakia and Bulgaria now have levels of urbanization presently comparable to that in the USSR, where 62% of the population live in urban areas, the slowing rate of growth in the late 1960s and 1970s has affected the other East European countries also, although Hungary is an exception.

The degree of urbanization at the time of the socialist acquisition of government power and the subsequent pace and character of urban change have affected what has been achieved. Of course, in each country urban development became subject to the responsibilities of various planners. Everywhere the broad aims of planners have been the same — to create an optimum living environment where enhanced productivity, social justice and maximum satisfaction of the inhabitants would be attained. But in every case, the planners have had to start from given 'inherited' situations, to take into consideration the legacies of the pre-socialist era.

Medieval street plans, buildings of historic, architectural and national sentimental value, environmentally undesirable industries, slums and other substandard

Source: R A French and F E I Hamilton (eds) 1979 *The Socialist City* (New York: Wiley) pp3–9; 11–12; 14–20.

housing, overcrowded accommodation, and the lack of amenity or open space are just some of the key problems that capitalism bequeathed to socialism in Soviet and East European cities. The extent to which such problems existed or were eliminated, modified, or worsened by war and Nazi occupation, and the extent to which their preservation or removal was deliberately sought, became major variables in urban planning decisions. The Poles placed the reconstruction of the historic cores of their largest and most war-destroyed cities among their highest priorites in the rebuilding of Warsaw (Stare Miasto, Krakowskie Przedmieście and Nowy Świat) and Gdańsk (Główne Miasto) after 1945, although in many smaller towns it was simpler to clear away the rubble and build anew, as in Elblag, Nysa and Kołobrzeg.

Nevertheless, the greater the existing fixed capital of buildings and infrastructure and the more objects for conservation, the harder it has been for planners to make a wholly socialist imprint. The initial challenge facing government and planners, therefore, was how to compromise satisfactorily between revolutionizing the fuedal or capitalistic society fossilized in stone while sustaining also pride in national heritage and devoting the utmost resources to ambitious plans for economic development and 'socialist transformation'. Indeed, all major cities of the pre-socialist period, and many smaller ones, retain a very substantial element of their past — e.g. Leningrad, Prague, Łódź, Cracow and Budapest. Is one justified in calling these 'socialist cities'? Perhaps it is more appropriate to term them 'socialized cities', for, against the background of highly inert fixed capital, some signs of change are overt. Street names and monuments of past imperial, religious, and capitalist personalities have been replaced by those of revolutionaries, socialist events and symbols, war victims and heroes. Except for some private handicraft concerns, which often flourish in East European (but not Soviet) cities, shops no longer bear family names, but carry signs starkly describing their functions: 'dairy', 'hairdresser', 'electrical products' or 'supermarket'. Those offering specialized services requiring specific identity, like restaurants, cinemas or hotels, have individual names. Among cinemas in Gdańsk, for example, are the 'Fairy Tale', 'Dolphin', 'Leningrad', 'Friendship', 'Heather' and 'Tram Driver', while among those in Irkutsk are the 'Pioneer', 'Peace', 'Seagull', 'Komsomol' and 'Screen'. Other changes are deeper — less visible — as the fabric of the pre-socialist city became subject to functional adaptation to the needs and ideals of the new society, its ownership was nationalized, and its inter-organizational and inter-personal relationships were modified. People in such cities, brought up on old behaviour patterns and attitudes, had to attempt to adapt to change.

New towns

In each country, however, many — though not all — towns have expanded, and industrial and other investors and city councils have constructed new housing districts on planned lines. Wholly new towns have been developed in every country, untrammelled by the past and embodying solely socialist designs. In all, almost 1200 have been built, more than 1100 of them in the USSR, since the late 1920s. It is thus in the new towns that one might seek a true realization of socialist ideals. At present, such a search would prove to be partly in vain. Always a greater or lesser gap has existed between theory and practice. In part this was an inevitable consequence of World War II, and in the USSR also of World War I and the Civil War. Serious population loss and damage to industrial and urban property had to be made good, and rapidly, with little short-term regard to desirable yet longer-term objectives. Even more so, the heavy emphasis on a forced pace of industrialization which has characterized all the socialist countries for most, if not all, of their existence, has meant that only limited capital, manpower, and effort could be diverted into other sectors of the national economies, including housing and town planning. Backing the weight given to industrialization is the pre-eminent influence of the industrial ministries which generally succeed in carrying their point when conflicts of interest arise with city authorities. In consequence, what has been done has frequently not been in accord with ideals, theories, and optimum goals, but rather has taken the form of swift, inexpensive and loosely controlled expediences. In recent years, however, particularly in the 1970s, these hampering factors have lost some weight, their place being supplanted in part by greater attention to the aspirations of the citizens themselves. For the first time, through questionnaire surveys and public participation in discussion, the inhabitants of towns in socialist countries are being asked for their opinions on shortcomings and their wishes for the future. Much of this debate is vented through city or local newspapers and sooner or later will inevitably influence the application of theory to an increasing extent.

Throughout the socialist period theories have been

propounded about the role of the town and how this should be reflected in its form and appearance. Urban living has always been, and still is, seen as the highest form of socialist life — the town is the place where socialist consciousness can best develop the necessary environment for achieving the perfection of a socialist society. Eventually a minimum settlement size of 1000, or preferably 2000, inhabitants is envisaged. Such centres would form the lowest ranks in an ordered, planned hierarchy of settlements which would form a 'unified settlement system': in this, centres of services and functions appropriate to each level in the hierarchy would be rationally and regularly distributed — though varying regionally in density — throughout the country. By the year 2000, it is estimated that 72.3% of East Europeans and 76.5% of Soviet citizens will be encompassed by the urban systems of these countries.

Within each urban place, or city, there is to be an equally rational, planned, spatial ordering of its functions. Industry and residence should be physically separated from each other by green, or isolation, belts, yet located in sufficient proximity to each other to minimize the journey to work. Service functions should be distributed rationally, too, with daily needs met by local facilities within each residential neighbourhood, weekly requirements satisfied by establishments sited in a district service centre (usually located to serve between four and ten neighbourhoods) and less frequent needs provided for by specialized services in the city centre (Hamilton 1976, 1978). Such a nested hierarchy is based on the premise that, for comfortable living in a socialist society, all citizens should have equal access with minimal outlays of journey time and effort, whether on foot or by public transport, to all the material, cultural and welfare goods and services that they require.

Neighbourhood planning

Although communal living has not developed and now seems unlikely ever to do so in either the USSR or Eastern Europe, the physical format of the micro-district, or residential neighbourhood, has become the basic unit of new housing construction throughout the socialist countries. In practice the micro-districts have not always been provided either immediately or fully with the optimum range of services. Even more usually, they are grouped into large, sometimes huge, residential complexes without close spatial links with any specific industries or job markets. Quite often their

inhabitants are employed over the whole urban area. This is particularly the case in larger cities where the variety of job opportunities and wage rates encourages higher labour turnover. One might cite as an example some staff of Cracow University who live in or near Nowa Huta, the new satellite town to the east of Cracow and adjoining what, for the past 25 years, has been Poland's largest steel plant. Thus minimization of the journey to work becomes often an ideal, especially once cities pass the quarter-million mark in population. Nevertheless, the micro-district is one major element of socialist urban planning which in the past two decades has been translated into bricks and concrete.

Optimum city size

Less successful have been the concepts of optimum city size. Originally, it was fashionable among planners to think of towns of from 50 000 to 100 000 inhabitants as of optimal size. Beyond that, growth in any one place, it was thought, had to be 'hived off' into new towns located at some distance, rather in the manner depicted by Ebenezer Howard for his evolving system of garden cities. From the very beginning, however, this was hopelessly unrealistic, requiring as it did the restriction of growth in larger towns. It ignored a whole series of economic processes which in reality bolstered growth in larger towns: the priority given to rapid industrialization in large-scale integrated plants, which required plentiful labour and skills; the multiplier effects of establishing new industries; the attraction of migrants to bigger towns, with better amenities, more especially the capitals; and those with industrial employment offering higher wages than are on offer in rural areas. Thus theoreticians have steadily conceded ground over optimum size, first up to 100 000, then 200 000 to 300 000 inhabitants (Bater 1977), although to a degree this reflects an increase in economies of scale accruing from prefabricated construction methods. Yet the growth of cities has continued to run ahead, despite efforts to control in-migration to the largest cities such as Moscow, Sofia and Warsaw. Ever greater proportions of Soviet and East European populations live in the cities of largest size. By the 1970s, therefore, 'optimum size' had become a dead letter among socialist planners, although some writers still pay it lip service. Even so, the debate surrounding this issue has proved of value, at least insofar as it raised the question of costs of urban infrastructure, welfare provision, and growth to a position in the forefront of the criteria that planners have applied to shape the internal spatial design and organization of socialist cities in general.

Planners are now supplementing controls on in-migration by devising ways of organizing effective linkages between 'clustered' or 'grouped' towns, which they term agglomerations. Much recent East European and Soviet research has been investigating the functional structures and dynamics of all types of urban agglomerations, with a view to improving their management. In itself, this reflects increased urbanization and city size in all countries, yet it also mirrors everywhere the growing complexities of inter-city interaction and integration, within and across regional and national boundaries, as factories proliferate along lengthening chains of manufacture on an increasingly CMEA-wide[1] basis, as the tertiary and quaternary sectors enter a phase of accelerated growth, and, in consequence, as transport flows multiply and intensify. No less, though, it also expresses the impact of scientific progress on planning organization and on planning strategies, because the advent of systems analysis has baldly exposed — most sharply in the functionally complex arena of the urban agglomeration — the inadequacies of the past and continuing dominance of 'productive sector' planning decisions. Significant, too, is the growing tendency to approach urban problems from the 'human' viewpoint, by treating agglomerations as key labour market structures and key components of social planning in the national planning system.

City regional planning experiments should integrate national economic and spatial–social planning for the agglomeration. In Poland, the reorganization of local administrative regions in 1975 has been implemented with this objective partly in mind. However, two further reasons are suggested as to why city regional planning must be made to work. Although highly practical, both express existing problems in realizing a socialist manifesto for the city. First, the use of 'administrative measures' to restrict city growth, that is the use of the residence passport to prevent entry by would-be migrants into the largest cities, has not operated satisfactorily, whether it be Moscow, Warsaw, Budapest or Sverdlovsk, and in any case is increasingly frowned upon as governments become more liberal. Instead, planners advocate action on two levels to regulate city growth: a national spatial policy framework within which national economic decisions must ensure more effective steering of growth away from the biggest and most densely populated agglomerations and into other agglomerations; and on the lower level vast improvements of infrastructure, amenities and the aesthetic appearance of smaller towns to make them more attractive to industry and workers. To date Poland is the only country to have designed, in 1972, a national spatial development plan, while only certain agglomerations (usually capital city regions in other East European countries and in the USSR, together with Leningrad and Sverdlovsk–Nizhniy Tagil) have had detailed plans drawn up for them. Other agglomerations await integrated socio-economic plans. Second, a continuing and often thorny problem in many agglomerations, especially in the Soviet Union, results from the priorities for heavy industrialization, that is the limited supply of jobs for women, while often there is a surplus of jobs for men. The planning approaches outlined should be applied to ensure the location of growth in lighter industries, research and services among agglomerations and among places within agglomerations to absorb labour surpluses; otherwise the 'right to work' and the 'right to equal opportunity' lose some of their meaning.

The urban environment

The sharing of the foregoing theoretical concepts and actual planning strategies by planners in the various socialist countries, and the similar problems of translating theory into practice, have brought about a certain degree of uniformity in cities throughout the Soviet Union and Eastern Europe. The casual visitor may well be conscious of the differences between one town and another, from Mecklenburg to Mongolia and from the Adriatic to the Arctic, but this is because his experience is mainly of central areas where the historical, cultural and religious differences remain most strikingly apparent. The cores of Prague, Gdańsk, Łódź, Split, Plovdiv, Craiova, Moscow, Leningrad, Bukhara and Irkutsk are classic examples of the variety. Soon the visitor, in exploring, begins to find resemblances: architectural styles recur; the heavy and grandiose 'Stalinesque' architecture of early skyscrapers in Moscow, like the Ukraina Hotel or University, is reproduced in the Palace of Culture and Science in Warsaw, and in key buildings in Bucharest and Sofia. Blocks of flats of the same period appear virtually indistinguishable, whether at the Kaluga Gates in Moscow, on the

---

[1] Council for Mutual Economic Aid or Assistance, or COMECON: this is equivalent to the European Economic Community, but for the communist countries.

Miners' Prospekt in Prokop'yevsk, in Mokotów in Warsaw, along Karl-Marx-Allee in Berlin, or in central Nowa Huta, Eisenhüttenstadt, Havířov, Dunaújvaros or Dimitrovgrad. Even more widespread are the pre-fabricated five-storey blocks of the 1960s and high-rise towers of the 1970s. Everywhere the apartment blocks are grouped in neighbourhoods of closely similar lay-outs. Indeed, if one were transported into any residential area built since World War II in the socialist countries, it would be easier at first glance to tell when it was constructed than to determine in which country it was. The uniformity extends equally to the street furniture — the heroic statuary, the white-on-red slogans, the central square as a ceremonial focus, the kiosk selling newspapers, or the *kvas* vending machines.

Yet national culture and tradition express themselves in nuances of modern architectural design, and also in the persistence of customs, traditional behaviour, music and drama. Decorative designs which surmount the walls of the Palace of Culture in Warsaw were copied from the medieval Cloth Hall (*Sukienice*) in Cracow. 'Central European' red-tiled gable roofs and shopping arcades in Eisenhüttenstadt or the Czechoslovakian new town of Havířov, the 'Romanian' tower in the new centre of Vaslui, and the Uzbek 'filigree' concrete designs on the Lenin Museum in Tashkent, all these are intended to testify to socialism as a mode of national and cultural expression and development. An immediate impact on the first-time visitor from Western countries anywhere in socialist Europe is made by the lower order of service provision, the fewer shops or petrol stations, and the more thinly stocked shelves, especially when one travels away from the capital cities. Yet important differences do exist, too, with their roots in historic cultural legacies and response to local environment, for whereas in the USSR the visitor will search far and wide for a coffee house for refreshment, in Polish cities cafés are as thick on the ground as are bars in Paris; in Yugoslav cities the *slastičarne* are as frequent as the ice-cream parlours in Italy or the cake shops in Vienna, and in Bosnian or Serbian towns the barber is as common as in Istanbul. In general, to date, however, it is only when going to the cinema, participating in sports, or travelling on public transport outside rush hours that the visitor may find better provision in the socialist city than in almost any developed, capitalist city.

Social and spatial segregation

Far more subtle, less visible to the casual visitor, are the greater uniformities of spatial distribution within the socialist city that form the major subject for discussion in this paper. Urban areas created since the 1940s all share a much more even spread of industry than is common in the capitalist city, where firms seek out wedges of cheap land close to good transport facilities. Such evenness, however, is combined with a physical separation of factory from dependent housing by trees and open spaces. Everywhere, social segregation of the socialist city by *sectors* is absent or very greatly diminished, although in each city there is a tendency for some social segregation by apartment *building* to be found. In part, relative homogeneity of the occupational composition of the work force in industrial cities facilitates such uniformity. Nevertheless, in *any* city the low, largely nominal and relatively uniform rents for state-owned apartments mean that no part of the city is barred to any inhabitant or migrant on the grounds of cost, income, status, or race. Indeed, one may suggest that in the larger, polyfunctional cities that embrace the entire range of occupations, potential seg-regation can or could occur from application of the criterion of minimizing journeys to work; this could be between administrative, scientific or welfare sector employees working in city centres or in particular 'wedges' of the city (as in southwest Moscow) and the manual employees operating machines in factories, working on construction sites or driving transport vehicles from depots in outer city areas or other 'wedges' (as in eastern or western Moscow). Such seg-regation can be, and is, diminished substantially by trading off social mixing in the micro-districts and housing blocks for more and longer-distance commuting on public transport at nominal flat-rate fares. These fares, very low to the individual, represent higher transport infrastructure and operating costs to the city. These problems, however, become geographically enlarged as socialist planning, in seeking to avoid the conurbation, creates the urban agglomeration. Thus it is in the agglomeration that planned initial specializa-tion on particular activities, whether industry, tour-ism, or research, among the satellite and new towns creates *inter-city* social differentiation, not only among the smaller cities but between them and the major polyfunctional centre of the agglomeration. That is also why the agglomeration is also an object of growing social concern among planners.

Whatever the differences and similarities between

socialist and capitalist towns, any account must be limited to a moment of time. In neither form is the situation static. Planners modify their theories, and at least their immediate aims, as realities force themselves to their attention. Some Western observers see a convergence of the two forms and believe that the differences reflect different stages of urbanization, or merely the circumstances of post-war austerity, and that the socialist city is now becoming more and more like its capitalist counterpart. There is much, at least superficially, which might tend to support such a view. Standards of living have been gradually but steadily rising, although economic circumstances in the mid-1970s appear to have slowed this progress in some socialist countries as a result of food deficits and growing sensitivity to inflation on the world market. In particular, the increase in car ownership is making the street scene, at least in larger cities in the socialist countries, resemble more closely that in the West. Problems long familiar to the Western planner — traffic congestion, parking, air pollution from exhausts, garage facilities — are increasingly preoccupying their socialist counterparts. Mobility and recreation patterns among individuals are being changed by the car as they have been in Western Europe and North America. As yet, however, the predominance — and hence the relative efficiency — of public transport has not been impaired to any significant extent, but no longer can authorities in the socialist countries set their face against a car-owning society, as Khrushchev did in more than one public utterance.

Rising living standards, however, go hand in hand with changes in social status. Differences in income in the socialist city are still substantial and there are signs that they may be increasing, rather than decreasing, social stratification, particularly as opportunities to work and to travel abroad open up. If circumstances in the early years of socialism have largely prevented such social stratification acquiring any significant spatial dimension, might the future not see at least a degree of occupational segregation? Segregation can be observed in Warsaw, but it is neither marked now nor likely to become so. The availability of free welfare services in socialist countries, notably health and education, is general and in itself is rarely a spatial variable. Even when consumer goods and services are scarce (as has widely been the case in the past and is still so in certain instances), this has not significantly affected patterns of residence of various groups. Rather it has increased cross-town journeys in search of such services and

goods. The increasing provision for such needs will reduce any future possibility of social segregation on grounds of better access to services, especially for the less mobile sections of society.

Furthermore, emphasis which has been given since the 1960s to cost-effectiveness in all aspects of socialist economic management has made some planning decisions appear to resemble more and more those of capitalist enterprise. It has been argued frequently, even by central ministries, for example, that it is more efficient to locate new industries in existing cities, where pools of labour, skills and markets are available, than to go on creating new towns on green-field sites. The new Khromotron plant manufacturing colour television tubes was built in Moscow itself; and not in Siberia or even in the outer areas of Moscow *oblast*, for excellent practical reasons — the existence of a major electronics industry, skilled labour, a large market, and the transportability of the product. Much the same could be said for the development of the Polish vehicles industries in Warsaw and Upper Silesia. Nor, it can be argued, is convergence on one side only. The period since World War II has seen the growth of planning, government intervention, and developmental controls in Western societies. The need for planning permission to alter land uses in cities or to erect buildings can greatly circumscribe the actions of private enterprise. Centrally taken decisions, at least in Western Europe, can be enforced by the issue or refusal of development certificates, permission and financial provision to proceed with hospital, education or housing programmes. Problems of Western urban areas, such as the redevelopment or revitalization of the inner cities, may not be resolved as yet, but they are now regarded as the responsibility of local and national public authorities, problems which can now more rarely be left to the uncertain consequences of untrammelled action by private enterprise.

Conclusions

All this said, fundamental differences remain and, in all probability, will remain. Above all, decision-making affecting the capitalist and the socialist cities operates in quite distinct socio-economic and political contexts. State intervention and control in Western countries is aimed at, and can only hope to achieve, the amelioration of the inadequacies of the existing system because planning has to operate within limits imposed by private ownership of land and buildings, private control of investment, and the greater freedom of choice and action possessed by the individual, even when such action may not be in the best public interest. The inner-city problem is a classic case in point. Governments, at least in Britain, have encouraged industries to move from inner cities, especially London, without analysing the long-term consequences which are now all too apparent; little in the way of systematic *economic* planning has been able sensibly and acceptably to fill the void. While differences in national growth rates are a significant variable here, it is nevertheless true that the same process of industrial out-movement from inner areas of socialist cities has not left a crisis, partly because the process so far has been slight, partly because people have been moved with their jobs (and in any case there has not been the same 'flight to the suburbs'), and partly because new employment opportunities have become available in the centre as administration, research, welfare and service provision have increased in scale.

The complexities of the situation are formidable, however, and while change in the socialist city can also be less smooth than desirable and planning is more piecemeal than is often suspected, nevertheless the existence of a much higher degree of planning in socialist countries permits reductions in uncertainties and encourages more inter-sector and city–region–nation coordination. Above all, planning is set on course towards clearly prescribed long-term objectives. The socialist planner has greater freedom from the constraints set in Western or developing world cities either by capitalist enterprise and market forces or by the public planning enquiry which has yet to become a feature of socialist city life. However, it is misleading to correlate the introduction of market socialism with the market economy in the capitalistic sense, since the former is a means of achieving economies, subject to many of the same economic–scientific variables as in a capitalist system, but within a totally different framework of ownership relations and social objectives. Thus, with much land ownership (though not all) vested in state organizations, a land-value surface as understood in the West simply does not exist; socialist planners' evaluations of land are not based on the same criteria. In consequence the patterns of urban land use are markedly different, save where these are relics of the capitalist period of development. Many models of urban development, which have been devised primarily in North America — but also in Western Europe — cannot readily be applied in the socialist context. To the socialist planner indeed they are, or may be, irrelevant. It is suggested that such models are attempts to analyse the processes of the past and to understand the resulting spatial patterns of the present, at best to extrapolate to the future. Socialist urban models are of what is intended, blueprints for a planned future.

'Utopia' is always over the horizon. Between future ideals and present reality a gap remains. To attempt to bridge it in practice, however, national governments have encouraged the councils of the larger socialist cities to devise long-term master plans. The Moscow plan for the 1990s is a classic example of the way in which such master plans seek to attain socialist city planning objectives within the framework of modern aspirations and technology (Hamilton 1976). Moscow is not at all alone. Master plans are the practical blueprints for the future socialist city.

Nevertheless, the gaps in our knowledge and understanding remain, too. Thus there is a need for more research on the socialist city, in particular for detailed studies of functional structure and actual land-use patterns, of spatial organization and circulation within the city, and of distributions and behaviour patterns of various ethnic, social and occupational groups. The growth of sociological research and urban studies in general in the socialist countries will surely provide greater quantities of material which the urban geographer can use. One cannot doubt that there is much to be gained, positively learned, from further work. Planners, economists, geographers and sociologists in the socialist countries take great interest in the research methodology and findings of Western scientists and practitioners. To return that interest will provide us with object lessons, new ideas, and perhaps some solutions to current and future problems. Undoubtedly we can learn from the study of socialist experience.

References

Bater J H 1977 Soviet town planning: theory and practice in the 1970s *Progress in Human Geography* **1**(2) pp177–207

Hamilton F E I 1976 *The Moscow City Region* (London: Oxford University Press)

——1978 The East European and Soviet city *Geographical Magazine* May pp511–16

Section II
The Impact of Urban Growth

Introduction

Cities are not like Topsy, they do not just grow. The origins of cities, their growth, change and, in some cases, decline, all have their causes and consequences whether they be at the local, regional or national level. It is therefore essential to locate cities in both a temporal and spatial context if they are to be properly understood. If cities are abstracted from their wider context, be it social, historical or regional, there is a very real danger that they will be reified, treated as independent entities and analysed as if they existed in a vacuum. This is quite clearly both unrealistic and undesirable and accordingly, just as Section I of the Reader dealt with the historical dimension of cities, this section attempts within the confines of the articles selected to set cities within their regional framework.

The examination of urban–rural relationships is important for a number of reasons. Links between most cities and their regional hinterland have developed over time. These links are economic, political and social. Cities act not just as administrative or market centres — although these functions are important — but also as centres of innovation and of political power. There is a continuing debate as to whether cities have had a symbiotic or a predatory relationship with their rural hinterlands, and although it is not our intention to enter into that debate here, it should be stated that there has always been a strong mutual dependency relationship between cities and their surrounding regions. Historically, very few cities have grown solely or even largely by virtue of internal population growth. They have grown (or in some cases survived) by a continuing inflow of rural migrants either seeking economic improvement, or relief from adverse economic and social conditions in the rural areas. More recently, as the pace of urbanization has reached its peak in Western industrial economies, there has occurred substantial out-migration from cities, resulting in either relative or absolute decentralization.

This process has manifested itself first in the growth of suburbs and secondly in the growth of 'urbanized villages' and increased rates of rural–urban commuting. Although said by some to reflect household preferences for lower density, or more environmentally attractive residential areas, the process has not been without its problems. First, it has tended to deplete the population and tax base of the older core cities. Secondly, it has resulted in a high rate of agricultural land consumption as well as serving to generate considerable costs for new facility provision. Thirdly, it has generally resulted in a greater level of residential social segregation; and finally, it has generated considerable transport problems and costs, stemming from higher car ownership rates, lower public transport provision, greater commuting costs and the costs of new road and motorway construction. As a result urban growth has frequently led to considerable conflict between cities and their surrounding areas as these areas have sought to resist what they see as urban imperialism and encroachment, and as the cities have faced what they may perceive to be conservative rural areas determined to attempt to stem the inevitable pressures for change and development.

Our three cities collectively exemplify all these different aspects of urban–regional relationships, although not all are present in each city or in our selected readings. Looking first at Vancouver, the article by McCann examines the causes of Vancouver's rise from a small fishing village of 100 people to the most important city on Canada's Pacific coast in just 30 years. The three decades between 1886 and the outbreak of war in 1914 saw Canada transformed as the cities became the centres of the new industrialism, of migration and of progress. McCann's thesis is that 'the measure of progress was the growth performance of individual cities, and growth depended largely upon a city's ability to gain control of a resource hinterland', and he suggests in his introduction that the success of many Canadian cities in their early years corresponds to the role they performed within a regional staple economy. McCann summarizes the dramatic change in Vancouver's position as follows:

On the eve of 1886, before the Canadian Pacific Railway had arrived in Vancouver, the capital city of Victoria stood alone as the only metropolis on Canada's Pacific coast; it controlled the province's trade, communication networks, industrial activity and financial concerns. But by 1914 Vancouver had usurped all these roles. In less than two decades Vancouver emerged as the focal point of the regional space economy.

Vancouver was indeed 'born of the railway', as McCann so accurately and graphically puts it. Vancouver would not exist today as we know it if it were not for the Canadian Pacific Railway who chose Vancouver as their continental rail head. From that base the resources of British Columbia, particularly its timber, were exploited and it is the relationship between resource exploitation and the growth of contemporary Vancouver as a corporate office centre that is the basis of Roger Hayter's article. As Hayter puts it: 'To a large extent Vancouver's corporate head office, research and development, trading and manufacturing functions are orientated towards the harvesting, conversion and export of the provincial timber resource.'

As Hayter indicates, the growth in the forest product industries of British Columbia has been extremely rapid since the 1950s, and during this period as companies increased both the size and the geographical area of their operations, they split their head offices from their processing and manufacturing operations, relocating the offices in downtown Vancouver. Such a central location has freed decision-makers from the details of day-to-day manufacturing operations, provided them with better access to government, financial and legal services, a larger pool of executive and clerical labour, a centralized point of provincial, national and international air access, as well as permitting the easier centralized coordination of province-wide corporate activities. Vancouver has increasingly become the decision-making centre of the industry and the expansion of corporate headquarters has provided both an expanding source of employment and income growth and has, in turn, generated considerable multiplier effects in the areas of research and development, legal, financial and marketing services. As such Vancouver has come to dominate and control its provincial hinterland and has become, as Hayter puts it, 'a metropolis in

the pattern of forestry exploitation'.

The situation in Cracow is, not unexpectedly, very different. Although the third city in Poland in terms of population after Warsaw and Łódź, and the fifth largest urban–industrial agglomeration after Upper Silesia, Warsaw, Łódź and Gdansk, Cracow performs a very different function from that of Vancouver, which is Canada's third largest city after Toronto and Montreal. First, as Kortus points out in his paper, despite its medieval origins, industrial Cracow is relatively young compared to Warsaw or Łódź, having developed mainly after World War II as a result of the development of the Skawina aluminium smelter and the Lenin steelworks at Nowa Huta. Prior to the war Cracow was mainly a historical centre of education and science with little industry. In the 40 years between 1931 and 1970 the percentage of Cracow's population who worked in industry rose from 33 to 57%, the numbers employed in this sector increasing fourfold from 30 000 to 120 000 and its population doubling to 586 000. No other city in Poland with the exception of Warsaw has undergone such rapid growth.

Cracow has certain similarities to Vancouver however, notably in its dependence on a single industry — timber processing in Vancouver and iron and steel in Cracow. The Lenin steelworks employs 26% of total industrial employment and produces 46% by value of industrial production. Metallurgy has become the dominant industrial sector of Cracow displacing the pre-war dominance of machinery production (31% of employment), food processing (28%) and chemicals (10%). Nonetheless, Cracow has retained its importance as a university and industrial research centre, employing 16 000 in this sector in 1970. Its historical legacy is also such as to make it the largest tourist centre in Poland. Significantly, Cracow's rapid growth has resulted in a substantial labour deficit and some 30 000 people commute daily from the surrounding rural areas to the city. This is the second highest number of commuters after Warsaw, and this phenomenon should not be confused with Western-style suburbanization and its resultant commuting. It is quite different in kind, being more a product of 'under-urbanization', and it illustrates the dominance of rural–urban migration in post-war Poland.

This theme is taken up in Iwanicka-Lyra's article. As she points out, Poland has experienced massive migratory movements during and after the two World Wars as a result of evacuation, displacement and repatriation. The shifts in Poland's boundaries as a result of the two World Wars has resulted in very considerable movements of population, not least in rural–urban migration. This results partly from the greater population losses suffered by the large cities, particularly from Warsaw which was 90% destroyed and reduced to 20 000 people in 1945; Poland lost some six million people out of a total pre-war population of 34 million. This loss, mainly to the Nazi death camps, was proportionately the largest of any country involved in the war. Considerable rural–urban migration had been occurring in the inter-war period, reflecting the relative level of Poland's economic development and the overwhelming dominance of the rural population in what was still predominantly an agricultural country. From 1946 to 1950 however, rural–urban migration was 170% of the increase of urban population. Even by 1950 however, only 38% of Poland's population was urban compared with 52% in 1970, and rural–urban migration has remained a major component of post-war urbanization.

In the Cracow area rural–urban migrants came from the overpopulated rural hinterland which had long since been a source of migrants — many to the United States in the early twentieth century. The construction of Nowa Huta attracted migrants from all over the country, however, and, as indicated above, Cracow still suffers a considerable labour deficit. This has been overcome, as elsewhere in parts of Eastern Europe by the rise of so-called 'worker-peasants', that is to say, elements of the rural agricultural population living around large employment centres who work their small farms in the evenings and weekends and commute to work in the urban centres by day. They are helped in this by other members of their families who either help work the land or, in the case of older people, help look after the grandchildren during the day, particularly if both husband and wife work in the towns. As Galeski makes clear in his paper, the growth of the worker-peasant phenomenon has resulted in considerable rural social change, some villages increasingly becoming residential areas for an essentially urban population.

The contrast with the more well known form of Western suburbanization and population decentralization is considerable. As Rugman and Green indicate in the introduction to their paper on Birmingham, fundamental changes in the size, distribution and structure of the population of the West Midlands conurbation and region have occurred since 1950: 'Population growth, faster than in any other conurbation or region

in Great Britain during the 1950s, has slowed, stabilized and recently changed to decline.' Whereas the earlier growth took place in Birmingham and Coventry and their hinterlands, there has been an increasing tendency towards population decentralization, with the major growth zone being in the periphery of the region. This growth has been associated with differential out-migration from the inner areas of the younger age and higher socio-economic groups, resulting in a greater degree of social class segregation across the region. These developments are not restricted to Birmingham, the trend in all the major British conurbations being for the out-movement of population from the declining older urban centres. This demographic change is inextricably linked with social and economic change, and the spatial expression of these changes is restructuring the relationship between city and region as well as changing the nature of the demands upon the housing market.

The nature of the developments outlined by Rugman and Green have major consequences for planning policy and attempts to contain the outward growth of the conurbations by green belt policies, and similar pressures have been generated by Vancouver's rapid growth. In British Columbia, an attempt has been made to control the rate of scarce agricultural land consumption for housing and industry by the establishment of a British Columbia Land Commission and agricultural land reserves. These have come under very similar pressures to those found in the green belt around Birmingham. In Cracow by contrast, the problem is, as indicated in the articles, not one of Western-style suburbanization, but rather one of rural–urban commuting by worker-peasants which is only likely to be resolved by the consolidation of small land holdings into fewer larger holdings and a permanent move to the city by elements of the rural population.

From the articles by McCann and Hayter on the economic basis of the rapid growth of Vancouver to the major regional metropolis of British Columbia, through the articles on Poland which highlight the continuing role of rural–urban migration in urbanization, to the more familiar pattern of decentralization in Birmingham, all the readings highlight the importance and centrality of an understanding of urban–rural relations and conflicts for an understanding of the city.

Chris Hamnett

Urban Growth in a Staple Economy: The Emergence of Vancouver as a Regional Metropolis, 1886–1914

by L D McCann

The decades between 1886 and 1914 were marked by critical events in the progress of Canadian urban development. Canada became a 'nation transformed' during these years, and the city played a vital role in the process of nation building (Brown and Cook 1974). Reacting to changing technological and socio-economic impulses, Canadian cities embraced the new industrialism and became the focal points for newly arrived immigrants, embryonic industries, and the expanding railway network which was binding the country together. The city had become a symbol of progress. The measure of progress was the growth performance of individual cities, and growth depended largely upon a city's ability to gain control of a resource hinterland. The inability to do so forced many cities to experience low rates of growth, if not to stagnate. Indeed, the essential well-being of many Canadian cities in these formative years can be equated satisfactorily with the role they performed within a regional staple economy.

On the eve of 1886, before the Canadian Pacific Railway had arrived in Vancouver, the capital city of Victoria stood alone as the only metropolis on Canada's Pacific coast; it controlled the province's trade, communication networks, industrial activity and financial concerns. But by 1914 Vancouver had usurped all of these roles in its quest for regional metropolitan status. The terminal city, born of the railway, exploited its symbiotic relationship with the adjoining hinterland; it

Source: L J Evenden (ed) 1978 *Vancouver: Western Metropolis*, *Western Geographical Series* Vol. 16 (University of Victoria, British Columbia) Ch. 2.

became directly involved in extracting and processing resources, in importing supplies and exporting staple commodities, and in servicing the diverse financial and transportation needs of the province. In less than two decades, Vancouver emerged as the focal point of the regional space economy. This paper examines the ways in which Vancouver achieved status as the province's regional metropolis.

It does so from the perspective of a theoretical consideration of the nature of urban growth in a staple economy. But before introducing this perspective, it is essential to outline the context of the changing socio-economic milieu of British Columbia at the turn of the century, thereby setting the stage for interpreting Vancouver's rise to prominence. This discussion will also serve to establish the underlying theoretical premise that the emergence of an urban system in a frontier region is related directly to the expansion of a staple economy.

British Columbia at the turn of the century: economy and society in transition

The initial development of a frontier economy is critically dependent upon the inflow of capital, labour and entrepreneurship, as well as extra-regional market conditions. Indeed, in British Columbia during its pioneer phase of development before World War I, economic growth was hindered until external demand prices rose and until productive technology and a newly constructed transportation network made it economically feasible to exploit the province's vast resource inventory. Despite the widespread financial crisis of

Table 7.1. Urbanization and economic development in British Columbia, 1891–1911.

	1891	1911
Total population	98 173	392 480
Total urban population[a]	41 823	196 638
Percentage of population urban	42.6	50.1
Total urban places	4	18
Employment by sector[b]		
Agriculture	8309	24 442
Extractive sector		
Forestry	1119	11 831
Mining	4688	15 569
Fishing	3798	4580
Manufacturing sector		
Wood products	1135	14 730
Fish canning	1388	4184
Other manufacturing	4388	14 995
Construction	2341	24 094
Service sector		
Transportation and utilities	3918	30 536
Wholesale and retail trades	3900	22 736
Services	11 514	38 111
Total employment	46 798	205 908

[a]Urban population comprises the population living in incorporated cities, towns and villages of 1 000 or more people.

[b]Employment data have been adjusted to maintain comparability among industries over time.

Sources: *Census of Canada 1891,* I, Table 7; *Census of Canada 1911*, VI, Table 7; and *Census of Canada 1921*, I, Table 12.

1893–97, these improvements had been introduced early in the twentieth century, by which time substantial amounts of capital, labour and business expertise had also been mobilized (Howay *et al* 1942). These scarce factors of production came primarily from Great Britain, United States and eastern Canada; their impact was immediate. As shown by labour force statistics of the period, however crude an index of economic growth these data may be judged, considerable expansion took place in the provincial economy between 1891 and 1911 (table 7.1). Employment in the staple industries increased dramatically. By the eve of World War I the economic base of the province was firmly established in the products of the mines, the fisheries and forests, and, to a lesser extent, agriculture.

Economic theory further suggests that other sectors of a frontier economy will remain weakly developed until capital which has been derived from, or attracted to, the success of the export base stimulates these sectors. The provincial staples did provide such a base for secondary and tertiary activities in this pioneer period. By attracting primary resource workers and their families, the staple economy was soon supported by a cluster of city-based manufacturers, trades and services, and by a network of urban organizations providing necessary financial and social capital. This multiplier process was most apparent in the tertiary sector. Wholesale, financial and transportation firms, essential for servicing the needs of the resource hinterland, as well as for supporting the import and export trading function, made appreciable gains. But the structure of secondary manufacturing remained poorly diversified. The limited size of the local market is commonly cited to explain this situation.

These economic advances quite naturally forced changes in the social make-up of British Columbia. Population increased fourfold between 1891 and 1911, rising from 98 173 to 392 480, as a surge of new immigrants sought their places in an emerging urban-based society (table 7.1). By 1911, just over half of the province's population (50.1%) lived in places of 1000 or more people; this share had increased by 8% since 1891, and almost 30% since 1881. Besides adjustments in the urbanization level, there were other fundamental social changes. The new arrivals came with a broader base of job skills and from a wider range in the class spectrum than their earlier colonial counterparts. Their ethnic origins were also more diverse, thus complementing the traditional but still dominant British element. But of particular significance was the fact that this surge of immigrants brought to the province a new business acumen based on national corporate enterprise which would quickly erode the existing community-oriented pattern. British Columbia had thus reverted to its pre-gold rush form of economic organization, a form dominated by corporate rather than individual enterprise; it had once again become the 'company province' (Robin 1972).

This pioneer era of progress is portrayed vividly on the settled landscape. The essential development between 1886 and 1914 was the emergence of core–periphery organizational design as the governing principle of the regional space economy (Robinson and Hardwick 1973). Urban places in the Georgia Strait region constituted the core; resource centres in the

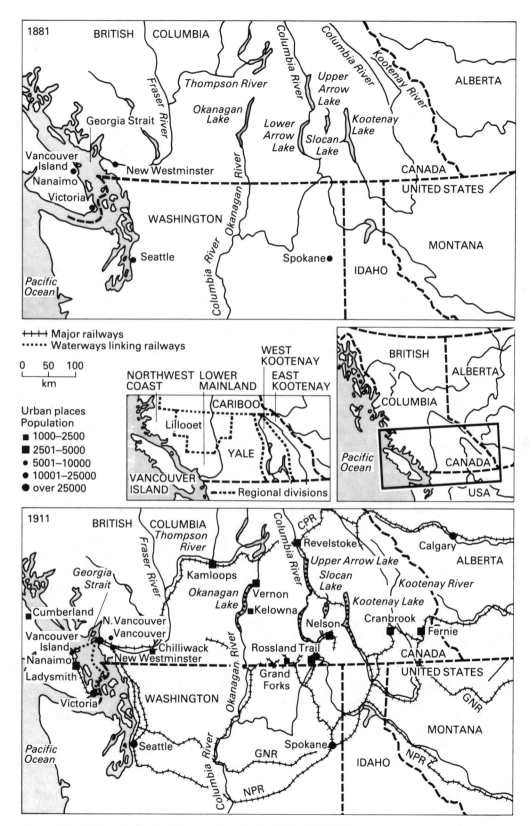

Figure 7.1 Urban places in Western Canada in 1881 and 1911.

interior comprised a weakly articulated peripheral system (figure 7.1). The economic base of most of these resource towns (10 of the province's 18 urban places in 1911) rested almost entirely on mining enterprises. Nelson, Rossland and Fernie, the major mining towns of the period, lay in the mineral-rich Kootenay district. Cumberland and Ladysmith sat astride coal seams on Vancouver Island. Numerous other mining communities whose small size precluded an urban definition were located throughout the valleys of the Yale, Lillooet and Cariboo districts. Here too could be found several agricultural service centres (Vernon, Kelowna and Chilliwack) and transportation nodes (Kamloops). But none of these places could compare in size or functional importance with the coastal cities. Geographic situation had laid the basis for their more prosperous and diversified economies; and this initial advantage was further enhanced by a vigorous programme of railroad building which sought to integrate the emerging urban system. By the close of the pioneer era, however, this programme was only partially completed across southern British Columbia;[2] and the coastal cities were losing valuable trade with the interior because American competitors, chiefly Seattle and Spokane, had direct access into the Kootenays over the Northern Pacific and Great Northern rail routes (figure 7.1). Still, economic advantages coincidental with the integrating force of the growing provincial railway network had given the coastal cities, particularly Vancouver, the impetus to control the regional space economy.

Urban growth in a staple economy

There has been little attempt to examine the relationship between economic development and urbanization in Canada from a specific Canadian perspective.[3] Even the scholarly contribution of J M S Careless on metropolitanism is related more to creating an historiography than to achieving an understanding of the actual process of urban growth (Careless 1954). In those few cases where urban growth has been an explicit research theme, the usual procedure has been to adopt a model developed for a non-Canadian situation and then to test its applicability in the Canadian context.

More recently developed models, in particular the promising work of the American, A R Pred, have yet to be applied to Canadian cities. But it is doubtful whether these models would satisfactorily explain the precise pattern of Canadian city growth. According to

Pred (1973), the initial and critical stimulus for urban growth comes either from the expansion of the wholesale-trading complex, in the case of the mercantile city (1790–1840), or from the establishment of large-scale manufacturing, in the case of the industrial city (1860–1910) (Pred 1965, 1966). The mercantile model is associated with an export-based interpretation of regional economic development, and intuitively is applicable for explaining the emergence of port cities in Canada's Atlantic provinces and along the St Lawrence River system. By contrast, urban–industrial growth is associated with the sectoral model of internally induced development which may be relevant for interpreting recent urbanization trends in southern Ontario and Quebec (Spelt 1972).[4] But it can be argued that in many regions across Canada, initial and even sustained economic growth has been dependent upon an extra-regional demand for staple commodities. This has certainly been the pattern in British Columbia. Thus, the mix of stimuli inducing urban growth in a staple economy will be different from those outlined in the Pred models; it will be related explicitly to the types of interaction carried out by a city acting as an intermediary between its resource hinterland and its external markets. Over time, the wholesale-trading complex and manufacturing enterprise need not be mutually exclusive.

A model of urban growth in a staple economy

Quite clearly, a model depicting urban growth in a staple economy does not constitute a general theory of urban growth, but it is applicable to that atypical situation in which urbanization in a frontier region is associated with economic development based on the export of staple commodities. At the highest level of abstraction, there must be at least two regions: the margin or periphery, which is the source of staple commodities (those raw materials or resource-intensive goods occupying a central position in the region's exports); and the centre or core, which creates the demand for staple commodities and supplies capital, labour, technology and entrepreneurship, the factors of production which are so essential for the initial growth and sustained development of the margin. In the initial stage of the margin's development, infant settlements or colonial outposts — 'vassals of metropolitan powers elsewhere' (Stelter 1975) will emerge to function as the intermediaries which handle the in-migration of these factors of production and the processing and outflow of staple commodities.

Agglomeration economies create the need for such settlements (Isard 1975), and the siting of the colonial outpost represents a rational locational decision based primarily on a consideration of transfer economies, particularly those associated with accessibility to staple resources and to markets (Stabler 1968). Depending upon the type and distribution of resources found within the margin, the colonial outpost will function predominantly as a resource town, as a central place, as a trans-shipment point, or, in those situations where location favours diversification, as a multi-functional settlement. The functional profile of these outposts will therefore be distinguished by resource processing, by trading and related business activities, and by transportation services.

One or a combination of these functions will act as the stimulus for the initial growth of the colonial outpost. This basic or city-forming function will set in motion a multiplier-accelerator mechanism. Because it is axiomatic that, in a market-oriented economy, a business unit will be sited where the costs incurred by the enterprise are as small as possible for servicing the market in which the product is sold, then at the very least, non-basic residentiary activities which provide goods and services solely for the local population will be established.[5] Although most goods and services will be imported from the centre during the initial development of a frontier region, it is clearly uneconomical to import all goods and services. In its fullest expression, the growth-inducing stimulus could encourage still other residentiary activities to locate in the colonial outpost either to support or to use the output from a staple-dependent industry.

With sustained economic development, a system of cities with hierarchical properties will form in the margin. The development of this urban system implies that at least one colonial outpost will emerge as a regional metropolis. This largest city will probably function as the principal point of entry for factors of production emanating from the centre and as a major manufacturing and trans-shipment point for the staple commodities which comprise the margin's export base. These functions suggest that the regional metropolis should be a port city located at the edge of the margin and connected to the resource hinterland by railroads. Advantages attributable to agglomeration and transfer economies act as the locational impetus for prominence in these trading, transportation and manufacturing activities. But in addition to these functions, by definition, the metropolis will also house the headquarters of the principal financial and related business enterprises in the margin. It is this additional feature, nurtured by external economies, which distinguishes the metropolis from other cities.

The rise to regional metropolitan status also can be understood from the perspective of a circular and cumulative feedback process model. As in the case of the colonial outpost, the mix of growth-inducing stimuli is related to the intermediary role played by the regional metropolis in serving both margin and centre. These stimuli set in motion the multiplier-accelerator process, spawning locationally favoured industrial and commercial developments based on forward, backward and final demand linkages. Through similar processes, financial institutions will gradually assume greater importance in the economic base of the regional metropolis. When this position is reached, and coincidental with the continuing role of the centre, the metropolis will now serve as a major source of capital, labour, technical innovations and entrepreneurship for development within the margin, it may even export these production factors back to the centre. This will take place because it is reasonable to expect that local entrepreneurs will emerge over time to challenge external business organizations. With functional dominance achieved, the regional space economy of the margin will focus on the metropolis.

Differential urban growth in a staple economy
The existence of a settlement hierarchy in the margin implies that there is differential growth among the cities of the emerging urban system. The reasons which account for the prosperity of one city and the demise of another have been assessed by many scholars, and most succinctly by Pred (1965, pp173–85): transport and route developments; the accumulation of agglomeration economies; entrepreneurial behaviour, particularly combination practices, oligopolistic competition and inhibiting traditions; and initial advantages in the guise of site and situation, relative accessibility, labour and capital availability, and factor immobility lead to the growth of certain cities at the expense of others. There is little reason to doubt that these same factors, acting in unison or separately, would not account for differential urban growth in a frontier region based on staple production.

But of special significance in a staple economy is the importance attached to the resource base as a differentiating factor. Beyond this, it is essential to recognize that the pattern of urban growth in a frontier region is

Table 7.2.   The changing economy of Vancouver, 1891–1911.

	1891 Employment			1911 Employment		
Industrial sector	No.	%	L.Q.[a]	No.	%	L.Q.
Primary sector	n.a.[b]			1985	3.8	
Manufacturing sector						
Wood products	825	14.5	6.00	2764	5.5	0.78
Fish canning	300	5.3	1.82	183	0.4	0.17
Other manufacturing	579	10.2	1.08	6016	11.9	1.65
Construction	860	15.2	3.02	8916	17.6	1.50
Service sector						
Transportation and utilities	1179	20.9	2.49	5298	10.5	0.71
Wholesale and retail trade	1101	19.2	2.32	11 054	21.9	2.06
Services	839	14.7	0.59	14 332	28.4	1.21
Total employment	5708			50 548		

[a]L.Q. is the location quotient of each industrial group. It is defined as the percentage of the city labour force in a given industry divided by the percentage in that industry of the provincial labour force. The measure is used here to indicate the concentration of individual industries in the Vancouver economy; no assumptions about the exporting of goods or services are made. For a discussion of this measure see Isard *et al* (1960).

[b]Data are not available.

Sources: Vancouver Board of Trade, *Annual Report 1891* pp40–41; *Census of Canada 1911*, VI, Table 6.

largely dependent upon the contextual environment created by external events in the centre. The number and sizes of urban places, and certainly the timing of urban development, is critically related to the demand for staple commodities and to the supply of scarce factors of production, which in turn are influenced by social, political and economic conditions inherent in the centre.

The model of urban growth in a staple economy outlined here is admittedly descriptive and generalized; nevertheless, it does provide a conceptual tool against which Vancouver's rise to regional metropolitan status can be gauged.

From colonial outpost to regional metropolis: Vancouver's changing economy, 1886–1914

There is little doubt that by 1914 Vancouver had attained status as British Columbia's regional metropolis. Reviewing the city's growth performance to this date, Vancouver's ardent boosters could point proudly to appreciable statistical gains in key sectors of their economy. From an estimated 300 people in 1881, the population had surged to total 100 401 in 1911 (MacDonald 1970). Victoria, the closest competitor, could counter with only 31 660. On the eve of World War I, Vancouver controlled nearly one-third of the export trade (the Kootenay mining towns shared much of the remainder) and two-thirds of the import trade. Manufacturing output stood at just over $15 million — a leading provincial share — and in the financial sphere, Vancouver's chartered banks cleared nearly three times the amount exchanged in Victoria. In every area of metropolitan influence, Vancouver held dominance over its provincial rivals.

In the course of attaining regional leadership, the urban economy of Vancouver was altered substantially both in structure and in scale. This is shown very clearly in table 7.2, which isolates employment changes in key sectors of the economy between 1891 and 1911.

The 1891 data must be judged as crude estimates only, but they nevertheless point to the stimuli which were to propel Vancouver beyond its role as a colonial outpost: resource processing, transportation, and trading functions — the essential intermediary roles of cities in a staple economy — stand out as basic, growth-inducing industries. The immediate physical environment provided the basis for these developments: nearby staple resources (the forests and fisheries) and a deep-sea harbour created a decided initial advantage. Dominating the business community at this time was the Canadian Pacific Railway Company. It managed widespread interests not only in rail and water transportation, but also in resource processing, in real estate and finance, and in the import–export trade.

Despite this impressive base, Vancouver still relied heavily on external sources for many of its goods and services, particularly for scarce production factors. This fact is demonstrated by the lower location quotients attached to certain service and manufacturing industries (table 7.2). If these were not obtained directly from extra-regional suppliers, then they came to Vancouver via distributors in Victoria. By 1891 the capital city had acquired, chiefly through its business connections with San Francisco and London, leading status as an entrepôt manufacturing and wholesaling centre. In a similar way, it managed much of the export trade in staple commodities, including Vancouver Island coal, the Pacific salmon fishery, the pelagic seal industry, and a limited agricultural surplus. Moreover, it still handled the distribution of financial capital in the province; it supplied limited domestic funds acquired through the earlier gold trade and managed the inflow of foreign capital through the locally based Bank of British Columbia and the Bank of British North America.

Vancouver's deficiencies in the make-up of its secondary and tertiary sectors were largely overcome by 1911 when it had become apparent that spread effects had taken place around the export base (table 7.2). Although resource processing and transportation had diminished in relative importance, absolute gains in these spheres had been experienced; and Vancouver still outdistanced its nearest industrial competitors. The city's improved position in other forms of secondary manufacturing, in trading activities (particularly wholesaling), and in service industries (especially financing) attests to the fact that Vancouver had assumed, through the accumulation of various agglomeration economies, a polarizing position in the regional space economy. The transfer economies associated with Vancouver's position as Canada's major break-in-bulk centre between rail and water on the Pacific coast are obvious. For example, because most of the lumber produced in the coastal forest industry at this time went by rail to the newly settled Prairie provinces, Vancouver became a preferred location for sawmilling operations (Hardwick 1963). Coincidentally, economies of scale were introduced into these operations when various processing innovations were adopted by local sawmillers. Not so obvious, but compounding these initial advantages, were the preferential freight tariffs arranged by the Canadian Pacific to ensure that Vancouver monopolized the import–export trade. Victoria and New Westminster — and later Prince Rupert — could not compete against these advantages, however hard they tried, however imaginative their schemes. As a direct consequence, Vancouver was clearly favoured as a location for those manufacturing, transportation and trading services linked directly to the export base. The business directories and censuses of the period record the advance of these residentiary activities: machinists, tug boat firms, tin can manufacturers, and diverse other operations appear in increasing numbers over time. Backward linkages were the most pronounced residentiary developments; forward linkages tended to be restricted to the lumber industry.

It is commonly assumed, therefore, and with certain justification, that a singular event — the arrival of the first transcontinental train on the west coast in 1886 — fostered Vancouver's rise to regional metropolitan status (Morley 1961). But the abruptness with which Vancouver beat out its competitors in so short a time span should not be attributed solely to the appearance of the Canadian Pacific. The railway inevitably would have sealed the transition, but Vancouver's swift rise to prominence was hastened by several external forces which affected the basis of the staple economy, and acted upon the essential stimuli for urban growth.

The most obvious and directly felt influence at the time was the depression of 1893 to 1897. Its financial repercussions ran throughout the provincial economy, hitting particularly hard at the Victoria business establishment. Until this recessionary period, the Victoria banking community, through the locally based Bank of British Columbia, had been in the vanguard in supporting provincial businessmen when they forayed into the resource hinterland. But the Bank fared poorly during these five depression years. Soon afterwards its English directors sold their interests to the Canadian Bank of Commerce which had stationed its western offices in Vancouver in 1895. Several other eastern Canadian banking and financial institutions had also chosen Vancouver for their headquarters, compounding Victoria's losses. In this way, through a shift in the spatial direction of capital flows, Vancouver acquired provincial pre-eminence in financial affairs; the foundation of the metropolitan definition had been completed.

Less obviously, but more importantly, Vancouver reaped the benefits from the increased complexity of society and economy characteristic of British Columbia in the decades immediately preceding World War I. The old industrial order, dominated by community-minded businesses, gave way to the new industrialism, marked by complex technologies and organizational systems — the emerging hallmark of Vancouver. Indeed, new corporate strategies were required to ensure success in the staple economy. Increased capitalization is a measure of this need, and company formation data record this trend. Preliminary examination of newly collected information on this aspect of British Columbia's economic development indicates that the spatial destination of entrepreneurship played a decisive role in Vancouver's development. By the close of the 1890s, a majority of extra-provincial and foreign companies doing business in British Columbia were establishing offices in Vancouver. Eastern Canadian firms had always favoured Vancouver since its incorporation; British firms, on the other hand, maintained their long-standing links with Victoria well into the 1890s, but coinciding with Victoria's loss of financial leadership, this pattern was broken in 1897. American companies almost invariably located in the Kootenays. Most were mining companies based in Spokane, the centre of the adjacent mining frontier, and if the concept of economic shadow is applied, this diffusion pattern is entirely logical. Despite this deviation, Vancouver had attracted nearly two-thirds of the 1716 extra-provincial and foreign companies which had migrated to the province by the eve of World War I. It also headquartered just over half of the province's 3422 local companies. These entrepreneurs were also foraying into all sectors of the economy and into all districts of the resource hinterland. Some used domestic capital derived from the export base, but most in this group raised risk capital for investment in staple and residentiary industries by borrowing from banks or by promoting their stocks on external trading exchanges, particularly in Toronto and in London. The need for local

flotation facilities led to the creation of the Vancouver Stock Exchange in 1907.

Very clearly, new corporate industrialism was instrumental in winning the upper hand for Vancouver. To complement these aggregate trends, several specific examples can be cited. The salmon canning industry, once administered from Victoria, was reorganized by 1902 in a series of mergers and relocated on the mainland. Reid has argued that the mergers were motivated by expected profits from the exploitation of market power achieved by restricting competition, rather than by expected profits from the achievement of internal economies of large-scale production (Reid 1975). He does not discuss in depth the locational underpinnings of this spatial shift in control; but it can be argued that urbanization economies associated with the trading, manufacturing and banking linkages already in existence in Vancouver at the time of the mergers were instrumental in bringing about the shift in locational concentration. As evidence of these economies, by 1901 Vancouver housed 42% of the province's wholesaling firms, 39% of its residentiary manufacturers, and 31% of its financial establishments. But the decisive corporate triumph which spelled the demise of competing cities was manoeuvred by the Canadian Pacific. Their Empress ships had dominated international traffic since 1891, so that when they bought control of the Victoria-based Canadian Pacific Navigation Company in 1901, Vancouver had an almost complete monopoly of international as well as coastal transportation. Until this date, the Victoria firm had been the largest steamship company in operation in British Columbia.

Conclusions

Vancouver's rise to prominence as a symbol of the new industrialism is undeniably related to the expansion of the provincial staple economy and to the intermediary role the city performed within the regional space economy. Metropolitan status had been decisively won by the eve of World War I. This achievement can be interpreted from the perspective of a staple model of urban growth: Vancouver controlled the in-migration of scarce production factors through its network of banking and business organizations and it engaged extensively in processing and exporting a variety of staple commodities. But by the close of the pioneer era, Vancouver's full growth potential had not been realized. For example, because a fully integrated railway network had not been completed, it was both difficult and costly to service the interior, particularly the Kootenays. Problems of this nature had been largely overcome by the 1970s; the most pronounced stimuli for development in this city of over a million people are now related to Vancouver's role as an amenity and administrative centre. Whether this recent trend can be interpreted from the perspective of the staple model of urban growth is unknown; it certainly warrants consideration. It is nevertheless clear that in the period down to at least 1914, the relationship between urbanization and staple economic development deserves careful attention in the interpretation of Canada's urban past.

References

Brown R C and Cook R 1974 *Canada 1896–1921: A Nation Transformed* (Toronto: McClelland and Stewart) pp98–107

Careless J M S 1954 Frontierism, metropolitanism and Canadian history *Canadian Historical Review* 35(1) pp 1–21

Hardwick W G 1963 Geography of the forest industry of coastal British Columbia (Vancouver: Tantalus) *Occasional Papers in Geography No. 5*

Howay F W, Sage W N and Angus H F (eds) 1942 *British Columbia and the United States* (Toronto: Ryerson Press)

Isard W 1975 *Introduction to Regional Science* (Englewood Cliffs, NJ: Prentice-Hall) pp80–156

Isard W *et al* 1960 *Methods of Regional Analysis* (Cambridge, Mass: MIT Press) pp123–6

MacDonald N 1970 Population growth and change in Seattle and Vancouver, 1880–1960 *Pacific Historical Review* 39

Morley A 1961 *Vancouver: From Milltown to Metropolis* (Vancouver: Mitchell Press) pp58–78

North D C 1955 Location theory and regional economic growth *Journal of Political Economy* 58 pp243–58

Pred A R 1965 Industrialization, initial advantage, and American metropolitan growth *Geographical Review* 55 pp158–85. Reprinted in *The Spatial Dynamics of U.S. Urban Industrial Growth, 1800–1914* 1966 (Cambridge, Mass: MIT Press) pp12–85

——1973 *Urban Growth and the Circulation of Information: The United States System of Cities, 1790–1840* (Cambridge, Mass: MIT Press)

Reid, D J 1975 Company Mergers in the Fraser River Salmon Canning Industry 1885–1902 *Canadian Historical Reivew* 56, pp282–302

Robin M 1972 *The Rush for Spoils: The Company Province, 1871–1933* (Toronto: McClelland and Stewart)

Robinson J L and Hardwick W G 1973 *British Columbia: One Hundred Years of Geographical Change* (Vancouver: Talonbooks)

Simmons J W 1974 *Canada as an Urban System: A Conceptual Framework* (Toronto: University of Toronto, Centre for Urban and Community Studies) *Research Paper No. 62*

Spelt J 1972 *Urban Development in South Central Ontario* (Toronto: McClelland and Stewart).

Stabler J C 1968 Exports and evolution: the process of regional change *Land Economics* 44 pp11–23

Stelter G A 1975 The urban frontier in Canadian history, in *Cities in the West* ed A R McCormack and I MacPherson (Ottawa: National Museum of Man History Division) *Paper No. 10*

Notes

[1] I would like to thank Geoff Lester and his staff in the Cartography Division, Department of Geography, University of Alberta, for preparing the maps which accompany this paper.

[2] 'In 1903 . . . the total provincial mileage of railways was about 1650 miles. Between 1903 and 1909 that mileage was increased by 400–500 miles . . . There will probably be at the end of 1915 about 5000 miles of railway in operation, with at least 1000 or more under construction or provided for, or 6000 miles in all' (see Howay 1942, p177).

For a discussion of the attempts to interpret this relationship see Simmons (1974).

[4] Spelt provides a detailed chronology of the relationship between manufacturing and urban growth over the period 1881–1951.

[5] The term 'residentiary' is used to designate secondary and tertiary industries which locate in urban areas to serve the local or regional market (see North 1955).

8 Forestry in British Columbia: A Resource Basis of Vancouver's Dominance

by R Hayter

Since the latter part of the nineteenth century, the expansion of forest product commodities, notably lumber, plywood, newsprint, pulp and paperboard, has contributed significantly to the economic base of British Columbia and has been intimately associated with the emergence of Vancouver as a metropolis. While other staples including minerals, fish, agricultural produce and energy have also been, and remain, important to the development of the provincial and Vancouver urban region economies, forest products have exercised the most pervasive influence on the political and spatial economies of British Columbia: to a large extent Vancouver's corporate head office, research and development, trading and manufacturing functions are oriented towards the harvesting, conversion and export of the provincial timber resource.

This paper is concerned with the extent to which Vancouver behaves as a metropolis in the pattern of forestry exploitation. Initially, the manner in which the organization of the forestry sector contributes to Vancouver–hinterland interdependencies is outlined and Vancouver's contemporary functions in the execution of forest product operations are examined. The second part of the paper then focuses upon the size, scope and autonomy of the forest industry's decision-makers in order to assess the extent of Vancouver's control over longer-term policies and plans influencing spatial patterns of forest product development.

Source: L J Evenden (ed) 1978 *Vancouver: Western Metropolis, Western Geographical Series* **16** (University of Victoria, British Columbia) Ch. 6.

Forest products and the metropolis–hinterland framework of British Columbia

The establishment of ties between hinterland staple exports and metropolitan decision-making, financial and marketing functions has been a noted dimension of Canadian regional economic development (Careless 1954). With reference to the spatial structure of British Columbia, for example, Robinson and Hardwick (1968) and Denike and Leigh (1972) argued the relevance of the metropolis–hinterland framework largely on the basis of the rapidly developing 'interdependencies' of the post-war period between Vancouver and dispersed patterns of staple production in the rest of the province. These studies were mainly concerned with the macro-spatial organization of the provincial economy, however, and not with the specific institutional bases of metropolis–hinterland relationships or with the role of the provincial urban network within an increasingly integrated national and international economic hierarchy. In this latter regard, the evolution, organization and structure of multi-plant, multi-product enterprises provide in many sectors causal links in explanations of regional settlement hierarchies and in the patterns of metropolitan specializations and inter-metropolitan rivalries over hinterlands (Pred 1974). To a considerable extent, the forestry basis of Vancouver's urban status derives from the industrial and geographical expansion of large integrated forest corporations and it is to the question of the corporate organization of the forest industries, and its relationship to Vancouver's role as a metropolitan centre, that attention must be given.

Historical aspects

Vancouver's experience in relation to forestry exploitation is distinguished by its early and continuing importance as a staple processing as well as a control and service centre. Indeed, export-oriented sawmilling on Burrard Inlet pre-dated both the establishment of the city itself and the arrival of the Canadian Pacific Railway (CPR) (Hardwick 1961). The CPR and later the Panama Canal, certainly improved Vancouver's relative location as an export point. From the end of the nineteenth century to 1939, notable wood-processing expansions were concentrated, with few exceptions, at Port Alberni, and in the Vancouver and New Westminster areas (Hardwick 1963). This concentration was encouraged by capital inertia, accessibility to labour, developing external economies and by innovations in the water transportation of logs which enabled Vancouver's raw material hinterland to be extended throughout the south-western littoral. The establishment of pulp and paper mills on sites where water power was available constituted the most important dispersal of log-converting activity in the coastal industry, although ownership ties to Vancouver were present. In the interior, the lumber industry, originally developed to serve local mining and railway needs, and to a limited extent Prairie agriculture, remained at a small scale and largely independent of coastal developments. By the 1940s Vancouver was clearly the single most important centre in the forest product industries of British Columbia. Even at that time corporate ownership was complex, reflecting the varied sources of capital and expertise upon which the industry had been built. However, a number of aggressive, growth-oriented enterprises, exemplified by the MacMillan Export Company, had emerged as large, relatively specialized producers with some degree of control over raw material supplies.

Trends since 1950

Growth in the forest product industries has been extremely rapid since 1950 (table 8.1) and has been implemented predominantly by large firms pursuing strategies of vertical and horizontal integration rather than by cooperative integration between specialized firms (Hayter 1976). During the 1950s the spatial pattern of development continued to emphasize the coastal littoral, and the construction of pulp and paper mills at Port Alberni, Prince Rupert, Harmac, Elk Falls and Crofton were the result. Also during this period several of the larger firms moved their head offices from sites

Table 8.1. Production levels and rates of growth of selected forest product commodities in British Columbia, 1950–1970.

Commodity	Quantity 1950	Quantity 1970	Growth p.a. (%)	Share GNP (%) 1950	Share GNP (%) 1970
Newsprint (000ton)	383	1394	7.3	7.3	16.2
Kraft pulp (000ton)	159	3101	16.3	15.1	46.2
Paperboard (000ton)	116	526	8.0	15.0	28.6
Lumber (MFBM)†	3364	7697	51.3	69.4	69.4
Softwood Plywood (M.Sq.Ft.)‡	250	1698	10.3	96.5	90.3

† Million foot board measure.
‡ Million square feet, ⅛″ base.
Source: *Statistics Canada* and Canadian Pulp and Paper Association.

adjacent to manufacturing operations to new downtown Vancouver locations, a move which confirmed Vancouver as the industry's decision-making centre.

From a longer-term perspective, the significance of the locational split between head office and manufacturing functions indicated that the larger firms had reached a size that required entrepreneurial adaptations to coordinate operations of increasing complexity, had separated ownership from management functions and, in so doing, had created the necessary centralized organizational capacities for further expansion. For Vancouver, corporate head offices have provided an important source of expanding employment opportunities and income growth and generated considerable multiplier effects, especially through the attraction of ancillary research and development, and through financial, consulting, legal and marketing services.

In the early 1960s the coastal firms began to look for growth opportunities elsewhere, including the provincial interior, as a result of approaching exhaustion of available timber resources in the south-western littoral. These corporate expansions have contributed significantly to the evolving Vancouver–interior interdependencies of the post-war period, especially through the supply of business services and corporate coordinating mechanisms on the one hand, and by the rail movement to Vancouver terminals of export commodities on the other. In day to day operations, except for the occasional shipment of chips and logs to coastal mills, the coastal and interior industries have remained essentially distinct entities serving (somewhat) different markets, utilizing different timber resources and functioning within different environmental conditions. This does complicate any interpretation of the metropolis–hinterland dichotomy with respect to the spatial structure of the British Columbia forest product economy. Certainly, the interior forests cannot be regarded as under the same degree of control by Vancouver decision-makers as the coastal forestry resource.

In the mid-1960s Kerr suggested that Vancouver was verging upon metropolitan status, a view which is supported by the activities of the forest product sector (Kerr 1968). By then several multi-region, multi-product Vancouver-based corporations had emerged as among the most geographically and industrially diversified forest product enterprises in the nation, thus

(a)

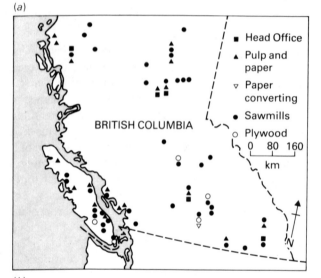

(b)

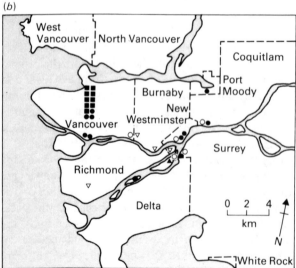

Figure 8.1 Selected facilities of major integrated forest product corporations (a) in British Columbia, and (b) in Vancouver (1975).

extending Vancouver's sphere of influence throughout the interior and into most Canadian provinces. At least one of these enterprises has recently embarked upon a multinational expansion strategy. The size and importance of the industry had also been sufficient to attract an expanding capital goods sector, research and development establishments and other related services, most of which have been concentrated in the Vancouver urban region. In recent years, some of these 'spin-off' developments have also become international in scope. By the early 1970s, the forestry industry had dispersed throughout the province and was to a significant degree controlled by integrated corporate oligopolies whose head offices, in most cases, are located in Vancouver (figure 8.1). This view of the industry does exclude hundreds of small firms, especially sawmills, and a few large firms such as Evans Forest Products and Scott Paper, which remain, in their British Columbian operations, relatively specialized. The firms shown here, however, dominate the production of forest products, manufacturing all the newsprint, most of the pulp and paperboard and over half of the lumber and plywood output of the province. The distribution of their facilities is, therefore, a reasonable representation of overall industry-wide patterns. Clearly, the scope and behaviour of these firms provide the key to assessing Vancouver's metropolitan status as regards the pattern of forestry exploitation.

Vancouver's roles in the pattern of forestry exploitation in British Columbia

Within the context of the contemporary spatial organization of provincial forestry exploitation, the Vancouver urban region performs important manufacturing, distribution and control functions, each of which exerts an influence upon metropolis–hinterland relationships.

Manufacturing and distribution functions

Although declining relative to other manufacturers, forest products in 1971 still accounted directly for 26.7% of the manufacturing employment in the Vancouver metropolitan area (table 8.2). The sawmilling industry, however, has been experiencing relatively slow employment growth, mainly as a result of substitution of capital for labour and from the closure of smaller facilities. Even so, export-oriented lumber and plywood mills remain the principal manufacturing components of the urban region's economic base. With

Table 8.2. Employment levels in forest product manufacturing, 1961 and 1971.

	Vancouver metropolitan area		Rest of British Columbia	
	1961	1971	1961	1971
Wood industries	14 422	16 210 (20.6%)	26 420	28 755 (36.8%)
(Sawmills/planing mills)	(9096)	(9335)	(22 363)	(24 235)
(Veneer/plywood mills)	(3461)	(4445)	(1666)	(3410)
Paper and allied industries	3727	4635 (5.9%)	8818	13 155 (16.8%)
Total wood industries and paper allied industries	18 149	20 845	35 238	41 910
Total manufactures	57 455	78 770 (100%)	55 564	78 150 (100%)

Source: *Statistics Canada.*

respect to markets, Vancouver's lumber mill production is mainly for international distribution. Two organizations dominate the international marketing of wood products, and have done so since the late 1930s when their rivalry reached cut-throat proportions: these are, namely, MacMillan Bloedel and Seabord, an exclusive export agency for several British Columbia producers. With access to large and diversified volumes of wood products, these organizations realize economies of scale in transportation and in the provision of centralized (that is, Vancouver-based) marketing information, research and development, quality control and sales promotion services.

A considerable degree of functional interdependence has developed between Vancouver's processing plants and the coastal hinterland (Hardwick 1961). These linkages include: the selective movement of logs harvested on Vancouver Island, the Queen Charlottes and the mainland either directly or via centralized sorting grounds, such as Howe Sound, to Vancouver area manufacturers, including the few paper converters which manufacture their own pulp, such as Scott Paper in New Westminster; the flow of pulp, paper and paperboard from large hinterland producers to Lower Mainland plants for conversion; and the shipment of large quantities of chips, bark and sawdust from Vancouver's wood processing plants to pulp and paper mills as inputs to processing and for fuel. The organization of these linkages is strongly influenced by the policies of large companies which have emphasized internal control of input–output needs.

Head office functions

All the major integrated companies with traditional ties to the coastal industry have established head offices within the financial district of Vancouver. Indeed, with extremely few exceptions, virtually the entire coastal industry is directed from head offices located somewhere in the metropolitan area. For the large firms, downtown locations offer particular advantages, especially with regard to personal (face to face) communication, whether this involves the negotiation of contracts, exchanging information, speculating on developments, utilizing a wide variety of specialized financial, legal, marketing, research and development and labour relations services or contributing to committees, such as those related to labour turnover and the environment. A Vancouver location also offers advantages to head offices in the hiring and keeping of employees and in terms of air access, within the province as well as externally, a point of some significance with respect to coordinating geographically dispersed activities. The importance of these considerations was recently exemplified by Scott Paper's relocation of its head offices from New Westminster to downtown Vancouver, a decision which was strongly influenced by a desire to reduce executive travelling times.

A number of other centres in the province have also attracted head office activities of large integrated firms, in particular Prince George, Kamloops, Kitimat and Cranbrook. Even so, all these firms also have or once had offices in downtown Vancouver, and consideration of the factors influencing recent changes in their function and status is instructive as regards the role of Vancouver as a decision-making centre. Crestbrook Forest Products has apparently decided to re-locate its head offices from Cranbrook to Vancouver and as a first step has established executives offices on Granville Street. The advantages of this move are seen, firstly, as freeing decision-makers from the details of day to day manufacturing operations, the profitability of which had been until recently the main concern of the firm;

and, secondly, as providing access to industry and government information pools at a time when the firm is considering more expansion-oriented strategies. For similar information-access reasons, Weyerhaeuser Canada also maintains in the Pacific Centre its president and a few senior executives responsible for forestry policies and off-shore transportation. In fact, most executive personnel and support staffs have recently returned from Vancouver to their head office in Kamloops, the main centre of the firm's manufacturing operations. Vancouver would have become the location of the firm's head office had a planned major expansion in Ontario been implemented. Similarly, Eurocan has recently decided to re-locate its head office from Vancouver to Kitimat where the profitability of its manufacturing complex continues to be a major executive problem but, at the same time, has left almost half its head office personnel in its Thurlow Street office. Three joint enterprise companies have also decided to maintain head offices adjacent to their principal manufacturing facilities at Prince George. Two of these firms, which share the same president and executive staff, maintain close relationships with Vancouver through ownership and functional ties, while Northwood Pulp's only link with Vancouver is a small public relations function.

With few exceptions then, Vancouver dominates the head office activities of the forest industries of the province and exercises control over the provincial hinterland through the supply of coordinating services and information and the calculation, evaluation and ratification of long-range plans and investment strategies.

Organization and decision-making structures

In order to maintain control of operations of increasing size and complexity, the vertically diversified forest product corporations of British Columbia have developed organizational structures comprising specialized groups, divisions and sections which are responsible for particular corporate functions and products and which are based upon hierarchical lines of authority. Characteristically, most of the larger firms are organized along product lines with functional and geographical groups occasionally supplementing the basic structure.

Such organizational decentralization and specialization of roles introduces the possibility of spatial decentralization and an hierarchy of services. With few exceptions, however, coastal firms have traditionally concentrated virtually all planning and administrative functions in downtown Vancouver head offices. Only the day to day operating responsibility for mill and logging performance and the hiring of employees has been decentralized to hinterland communities. Even decisions related to number of shifts, operating levels, market destinations and source of logs are usually made in Vancouver rather than at plant sites. This spatial concentration of authority has required, for coordination, a high degree of personal interaction between head office functions and dispersed manufacturing activities and the larger firms have thus been able to justify owning executive jets, helicopters and amphibious airplanes.

Conclusions

The pattern of forestry exploitation in British Columbia has led to close ties between Vancouver and the provincial hinterland and has contributed significantly to Vancouver's sphere of influence as a decision-making centre of provincial, national and even international importance. Within the province, Vancouver's decision-makers dominate the coastal hinterland and exert considerable influence over interior operations where, however, several forest product corporations without traditional ties with the coastal industry, and oriented to the head offices of other metropolitan centres, have also established facilities in recent years. Further, Vancouver's forestry technostructure is itself subject to the higher level of authority of parent companies, especially with regards to capital investment decision-making and the geographical scope of planning. So far the impact of 'subsidiary' status has been most clearly seen in the low level of (corporate) research and development activity in the province.

In future, however, as forest product potentials within the province become less attractive, there is likely to be more explicit concern for such external influence over development, especially as metropolitan and provincial policy-makers become increasingly interested in diversification strategies. In this regard, the relationships between industrial organization and industrial structure would seem to be a topic worthy of further study.

References

Careless J M S 1954 Frontierism, metropolitanism, and Canadian history *Canadian Historical Review* **35** pp1–21

Denike K G and Leigh R 1972 Regional economic development in British Columbia, in *British Columbia* ed J L Robinson (Toronto: University of Toronto Press) pp87–118

Hardwick W G 1961 Changing logging and sawmilling sites in coastal British Columbia (Vancouver: Tantalus) *Occasional Papers in Geography No. 2*, pp1–17

—— 1963 Geography of the forest industry of coastal British Columbia (Vancouver: Tantalus) *Occasional Papers in Geography No. 5*, pp57–9

Hayter R 1976 Corporate strategies and industrial change in the Canadian forest product industries *Geographical Review* **66**(2) pp209–28

Kerr D P 1968 Metropolitan dominance in Canada, in *Canada: A Geographical Interpretation* ed J Warkentin (Toronto: Methuen) pp531–55

Pred A R 1974 Major job-providing organizations and systems of cities, *Commission on College Geography, Resource Paper No. 27* (Washington: Association of American Geographers) p9

Robinson J L and Hardwick W G 1968 The Canadian Cordillera, in *Canada: A Geographical Interpretation* ed J Warkentin (Toronto: Methuen) pp438–72

Note

Acknowledgement: I am extremely grateful for the kind cooperation of many executives of Vancouver-based forest product corporations, especially with regard to interviews granted during August and September 1976.

9 Structure and Development Trends of the Cracow Agglomeration

by B Kortus

The Cracow urban–industrial agglomeration includes the city of Cracow (586 000; 120 000 industrial employees in 1970) and a few other industrial towns: e.g. Skawina (population 15 900), Wieliczka (13 600), Niepołomice (5200) and others, with a total employment in industry of over 10 000 (figure 9.1).

The Cracow agglomeration in 1966 ranked fifth in Poland in terms of population size and fourth with regard to the number employed in industry (table 9.1). It is a relatively young city in comparison with Warsaw or Łódź, and developed mainly after World War II as a result of industrial development in the city proper and its satellites such as Skawina (table 9.2).

At this point we should discuss the most significant

Table 9.1. Poland's largest urban–industrial agglomerations, 1966.

Urban-industrial agglomerations	Population (in thousands)	Employment in industry (in thousands)
Upper Silesia	2718	725
Warsaw	1623	295
Łódź	905	263
Gdańsk	600	100
Cracow	560	115
Wrocław	492	97
Poznań	480	103

Source: S Leszczycki, P Eberhardt, S Herman, 1971 *Aglomeracje miejsko-przemyslowe w Polsce 1966–2000* (Urban–industrial agglomerations in Poland 1966–2000) (Warsaw: PAN)
Data for Cracow agglomeration calculated by the author.

Source: *Geographia Polonica* 1975 **30** pp113–23. By permission of Państwowe Wydanictwo Naukowe, Polish Scientific Publishers, Warsaw.

Table 9.2. The development of industry in the Cracow agglomeration, 1938–1970 (according to the number of employed in industry).

Year	The city of Cracow (in thousands)	Cracow's satellites (in thousands)	Cracow agglomeration (in thousands)
1938	20.7	3.4	24.1
1946	28.7	3.4	32.1
1956	78.2	6.8	85.0
1960	89.5	8.5	98.0
1965	104.5	9.6	114.1
1970	120.0	10.5	130.5

elements in the development of Cracow's economic structure. Up to World War II Cracow was the main centre of education, science, art and place of historical monuments. Its industrial functions lagged far behind service, trade, educational, cultural and tourist functions. Historical tradition was the dominant force. During the post-war period, however, significant changes in Cracow's economic structure took place. In 1931 the number of people employed in industry and construction was equal to 32.6% of the total number employed; by 1950 it had risen to 44.2%, by 1960 it was 53.4% and in 1970, 57%. Cracow became a large industrial growth centre; the numbers employed in industry and handicrafts increased fourfold from 30 000 in 1938 to 120 000 in 1970. The population of the city doubled during that period from 260 000 to 586 000, and in 1970 Cracow was the third largest Polish city. These facts and figures illustrate the dynamic development of Cracow during the post-war period. No other city in Poland, with the exception of Warsaw, underwent such enormous change. Industry was the driving force of Cracow's growth, and today it is one of the most impor-

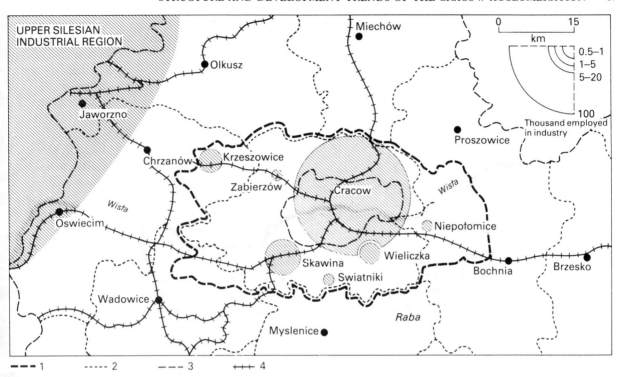

Figure 9.1 The Cracow urban–industrial agglomeration. 1, agglomeration boundary; 2, voivodship boundaries; 3, *powiats* boundaries; 4, main rail routes.

tant functions of the city. This, however, does not mean that Cracow lost its traditional functions. It is the country's second cultural and scientific centre, as well as one of Europe's major tourist centres.

The growth of Cracow after World War II was a product of its industrial development. If we take the percentage of people employed in manufacturing as an index of industrialization, Cracow went from 10% to over 21% during 1938–70 (figure 9.2). Rapid industrialization has been a characteristic feature of post-war Poland. While the index of industrial growth (measured according to production) in 1950–70 was 760 for the country as a whole, it amounted to 2100 in the case of Warsaw, 1300 for Cracow, 795 for Wrocław, 733 for Poznań and 440 for Łódź. The post-war industrialization of Cracow has been much more rapid than that of other Polish cities (except Warsaw), at about twice the national average. The main component in industrialization has been the Lenin steelworks, the biggest industrial investment in Poland.

In the period 1946–60 some 100 000 persons migrated to Cracow, 60% of whom came from rural areas. In 1973 the Lenin steelworks produced 6.5 million tons of steel (50% of the national total) and over 30 000 people are employed in the still expanding works. Thus the Lenin steelworks became Cracow's dominant industry employing 26% of the labour force, and achieving 46% of industrial production. About 20 large and 50 other, smaller industrial plants have been constructed in Cracow since 1945 and a number of already existing factories expanded. Cracow has become one of the biggest industrial centres in Poland, ranking after Upper Silesia, Warsaw and Łódź. Its industrial structure has also been subject to major changes (table 9.3). Before World War II machinery (31.2% employed), food processing (28%) and the chemical industry (10%) were dominant, whereas metallurgy, which was added to the three traditional branches, is now the most important. Cracow has become a significant metallurgical and printing centre, and also specializes in chemical, electrical engineering and leather industries. However, the role of machinery, paper, textile and food processing industries has diminished since 1938, caused by the fact that priority was given to steel production, while other industries were relatively neglected.

In comparison with Wrocław and Poznań, cities similar in size and function, Cracow's machinery and electrical engineering industry accounts for only 19.2% of its industry; whereas in Poznań, Wrocław and War-

Table 9.3. Branch structure changes in Cracow's industry, 1938–1970

Industrial branches	Employment (%)		Location index †	
	1938	1970	1938	1970
Energy	3.3	5.0	0.3	0.4
Metallurgy	—	22.8	—	5.4
Metal and machinery	23.5	20.3	1.4	0.8
Electrical engineering	7.7	6.9	3.5	1.3
Chemicals	10.0	9.0	1.4	1.4
Minerals	5.5	6.0	0.5	0.9
Wood	2.6	1.7	0.3	0.3
Paper	4.5	1.3	2.0	1.0
Printing	6.3	3.6	3.5	3.0
Textiles	1.9	1.2	0.1	0.1
Clothing	6.1	4.3	3.0	1.1
Leather	4.3	4.6	2.7	1.4
Food	23.6	11.1	2.2	1.0
Other branches	0.7	1.8	0.9	1.3
Total	100.0	100.0	×	×

Source: Statistical Yearbooks of the Central Statistical Office and calculations made by the author.

†Location index (Wlok) was calculated according to the following formula:

$$W_{lok} = \frac{Kx/K}{Px/P}$$

where Kx/K = per cent of employment within a given industrial branch to total employment in Cracow's industry, Px/P = the respective quotient for the country as a whole.

saw the percentage is 51.5%, 54.8% and 55.3% respectively. The situation in Łódź is similar to that in Cracow (19.8%), which is why the contribution of the so-called 'new branches' (electrical engineering, chemicals) to industry as a whole is 66% and 64% in Poznań and Wrocław, but only 28.1% in Cracow. Cracow, on the other hand, has a bigger university and industrial research centre: in 1970 the numbers employed in specialized research institutions was 16 000, in Poznań 11 000 and in Wrocław 13 000. In this respect Cracow ranks third in the country, after Warsaw and the voivodship[1] (region) of Katowice. Accordingly, various processing (rather than primary) industries should be developed in Cracow, especially those requiring close links with the scientific and research institutions. However, Cracow's scientific potential is to a higher degree connected with non-local, rather than local industry.

The one-sided development of Cracow's industry, where metallurgy accounts for 42% of total production

and 23% of the numbers employed, has had some negative effects. Cracow is becoming a mono-industrial centre, which reduces the city's localization advantages. This means that Cracow's industrial structure is becoming more like that of the whole country. This in turn points to the dominance of heavy industry, mainly metallurgy.

The industrial structure of Cracow's hinterland is also dominated by heavy industries: building materials (23% of the total number employed), metal and machinery (22%), aluminium and power (18%) and the chemical industry (10%). The common feature of industrial growth in Cracow and its hinterland has been the emphasis on primary metals such as steel and aluminium (see table 9.4).

In 1970 the Lenin steelworks (together with its cement plant) and the aluminium mill at Skawina accounted for 30% of the total number of industrial employees and 50% of production within the agglomeration, and in 1972 produced 45% of the country's steel and 51% of its aluminium.

An important locational advantage of Łódź and Warsaw is their situation in the centre of the country; in the case of Cracow an additional factor is its proximity to the Upper Silesia industrial district, which has determined the industrial structure and the rate of growth of

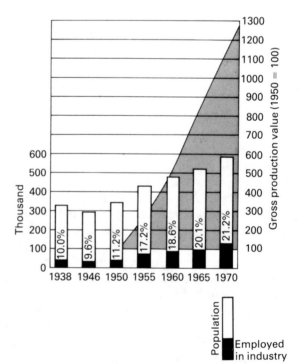

Figure 9.2 The growth of industry in Cracow, 1938–70.

Note:
[1] Voivodship – similar to county, or regional authority.

Table 9.4. Cracow — structure of employment, 1970.

Branches of economy	Employment (in thousands)	%
National economy (total)	330.6	×
Non-private sector (total)	307.6	100.0
industry	114.3	37.1
construction	60.5	19.6
agriculture and forestry	1.9	0.3
transportation	24.0	7.8
trade	26.3	8.5
education, science, culture	33.3	10.8
others (health services, administration, etc)	39.9	15.9

Source: Statistical Yearbook of Cracow 1971 (Cracow: MUS).

the agglomeration. This area specializes in resource-oriented heavy industry (metal and machines, metallurgy, building materials, soda and artificial fertilizer production), the growth of which has been based on the local coal and metallurgical resources.

During the intensive period of the country's industrialization after World War II, Cracow as a peripheral industrial centre of that type, acquired a number of industrial investments which the Upper Silesia industrial district was unable to accommodate. The localization of steel and aluminium works in Cracow and its satellite centre, Skawina, is an example of a policy of passive deglomeration with regard to Upper Silesia.

The scientific and cultural functions are second to those of industry as far as the number employed is concerned, while taking first place among the non-productive (service) functions. At the same time they constitute the oldest functions introduced by the foundation in 1364 of the Jagellonian University, and they play a prominent role both in the city's functional structure and on a national scale, with Cracow taking the second position only after Warsaw. The development of higher education (11 colleges at university level with over 50 000 students) has stimulated the growth of scientific institutions affiliated to the Polish Academy of Sciences, as well as numerous industrial research centres. In terms of the number of persons employed in these institutions Cracow is the country's third largest centre, after Warsaw and the Katowice voivodship. With the post-war development of industry and construction Cracow became an important scientific and research centre meeting the needs of southern Poland's coal-mining and other industries. The territorial range of Cracow's influence as a centre of university education, science and cultural functions encompasses most of southern Poland.

Another function of Cracow on a supra-regional, national and to a large extent international scale, is its function as a tourist centre. The tourist movement to Cracow which in the inter-war period stood at about 80 000 persons per year, now exceeds 2 million per year. Foreign visitors constitute about 10% of the total.

The following elements make Cracow a major tourist attraction: numerous and well preserved historical and art monuments; widely known cultural institutions, especially museums containing valuable and varied collections; the proximity to such tourist centres as the National Park of Ojców, the Wieliczka salt mine and the Oświecim (Auschwitz) Museum of Martyrdom; and a convenient location with regard to transport.

There are 713 historical monuments in Cracow, both secular and sacred, a record number in comparison to other Polish cities. Out of Poland's 52 monuments graded in the '0' group, that is monuments of the highest artistic and historical value on an international scale, Cracow has 11, outnumbering by far Poland's remaining regions and cities.

Finally, Cracow's transportation function is also one of supra-regional importance. Its railroad junction, the airport and partly its highway junctions are of national importance. The expansion of the city's economy and population has caused a substantial increase in transportation demand. About half of Cracow's rail and bus passenger trips are journeys to work by commuters. The large labour deficit due to the constant development of industry and construction makes commuting necessary with 50 000 (in 1970) persons travelling daily. After Warsaw, Cracow has the highest number of commuters.

The ranges of this commuting in the western (up to Krzeszowice) and eastern (up to Bochnia) directions clearly demarcate the Cracow agglomeration's sphere of influence from that of Upper Silesia and Tarnów. In the southern and northern directions Cracow's commuting ranges are fairly small, and in the south most of the journeys are in the direction of Skawina and Wieliczka.

In the vicinity of Cracow are several small industrial centres which might be called 'industrial satellites' (Wieliczka, Skawina, Niepołomice, Zabierzów, and others). Like Cracow, the industrial growth of these towns is mainly a post-war phenomenon. Skawina, where in 1954 Poland's first aluminium mill was erected and later a power station (570 MW), has developed the most. Wieliczka, on the other hand, is gradually ceasing to be Cracow's industrial satellite. Its salt mine is nearly exhausted, so that Cracow's soda plant takes its brine from the more distant Bochnia. Wieliczka's historic mine is presently mainly a tourist attraction as well as a health resort (an anti-asthma sanatorium). However, Wieliczka is still Cracow's satellite since over 6000 persons (40% of the population) commute daily from there to Cracow.

It is likely that in the future Cracow's strong and vigorous industry will cause development of further industrial centres in the vicinity. For several years in Cracow — as in other large industrial industrial centres — there have been difficulties in the expansion of industry due to labour shortages, water shortages and so on. One of the ways of overcoming these difficulties has been the establishment of branches of larger industrial plants in the voivodship area where labour is still available, that is, mainly in the east and south. For example, in 1968 a branch of the Lenin steelworks was set up in Bochnia. In the years 1969–70 branches of other factories producing transport equipment, measuring apparatus, etc, were established in Sucha, Limanowa and elsewhere. The development of the tin plate packing factory in Brzesko was based on plate produced in the Lenin steelworks. The voivodship authorities encourage other large industrial plants which meet growth thresholds to establish branches in smaller towns of the voivodship. This is undoubtedly the right kind of policy since it is in accordance with the deglomeration policy of Cracow as well as with the policy of stimulating economic expansion in less developed areas. In the plants that have been established as a result of the deglomeration policy, by 1972 about 3000 persons had been employed.

The spatial growth of the agglomeration of Cracow is headed in the western and eastern directions along the most important transport lines: the Upper Silesia–Cracow–Rzeszów–Przemyśl electric railway, highway and natural gas pipeline. The eastward expansion must be regarded as logical, and was stimulated by appropriate location decisions in places like Bochnia, Brzesko and others. The same cannot be said about the westward expansion, where growth should be stopped. The area between Cracow and the Upper Silesia industrial district is especially attractive to industry due to the existing technical infrastructure (transport, energy, etc), as well as the possibility of cooperation with established industries. But integration of the Cracow agglomeration of over 700 000 inhabitants with that of Upper Silesia with its 2 million population should not be allowed because this would worsen the bioclimatic, health and sanitary conditions in that area. The Cracow voivodship aims at preserving the biological protective zone between Cracow and Upper Silesia, that is, agricultural and forest areas which are industrialized only to a very small degree. The future joining of the Upper Silesia and Cracow agglomerations is unavoidable but the connecting area should be as narrow as possible, in other words, only along the transport routes.

The spatial development of the agglomeration core, Cracow, will head beyond the city's present administrative boundaries. All the vacant land between Nowa Huta and old Cracow, as well as on the outskirts of the city's present territory will soon be used up. The city's future eastward expansion will be prevented by the Lenin steelworks, while to the north it is not advisable because of valuable agricultural land. In the west the terrain is partly unsuitable for construction, and forms attractive recreational areas which should be protected. Thus there remains only the southern direction which is designated for the city's urban development. The present satellite towns of Skawina and Wieliczka will probably be incorporated into the city. Lately, more and more attention is being paid, within the agglomeration and its surroundings, to the protection of the environment.

Due to the location of a large part of the city in the valley of the Vistula River, Cracow has very unfavourable micro-climatic conditions; because of the lack of wind, smog is often observed over the city. The aim should be, of course, to limit or eliminate the sources of pollution, and the Lenin works have made some marked achievements in this field. It has limited air pollution and the pollution of the Vistula River by sewage. Nevertheless, the mill still constitutes a threat to the Niepołomice Forest to the east. Industry as well as communal heating systems should gradually switch from coal to natural gas to be supplied by pipeline from the Rzeszów voivodship (natural gas has recently been discovered in the Bochnia area).

The Upper Silesia industrial district, especially its eastern part, still contributes to air and water pollution in the Cracow agglomeration. Due to the prevailing west and north-west winds in this area, smoke and dust reach Cracow. Also the Vistula River is polluted by the industry of the Katowice voivodship (mainly through the Przemsza River) and by the industry of the western part of the Cracow voivodship.

10 Changes in the Character of Migration Movements from Rural to Urban Areas in Poland

by E Iwanicka-Lyra

The intensity of the influx of the rural population to urban centres has always been influenced by general migration movements in Poland, and migration on a mass scale occurred during and after the two World Wars.

Between 1914 and 1917 migration movements were connected with the evacuation of civilians by the Russian authorities and with the mobilization of the male population. After the war there was considerable repatriation of both Polish and German population groups as a result of boundary shifts. During World War II the intensity of migration movements was much higher; together with the migration resulting directly from the war they involved about 22 million people. These migration movements comprised the deportation of a part of the Polish population to Germany, resettlement of the population of whole villages within the boundaries of what the Germans called *general-gouvernement*, deportation to concentration camps or to compulsory work in Germany, the evacuation of the population of Warsaw after the 1944 Warsaw Uprising and from certain areas after bombardment, and the immigration of rural populations to the voivodships of Lublin, Cracow and Rzeszów from the south-eastern areas, harassed by nationalist bands of Ukrainians. As a result of the war there were also compensatory movements of populations, i.e. the repatriation of Poles who had been deported from their original place of residence by the Germans and resettlement of Poles due to the shift of Poland's borders.

The migration of the rural population to the cities constitutes an integral part of these general move-ments. The direct motivations behind these movements are to be seen in the ease of settling in urban centres and of repopulating the cities left by the Germans. These two motivations were much stronger after World War II than they were after the First war because of the higher losses in urban population and also the government's action of repopulating the old Polish territories regained from Germany. More recently, as a result of Poland's industrialization, migration has been caused by economic incentives, i.e. by the possibility of better-paid jobs in the rapidly developing industrial districts.

The extent of emigration from rural to urban areas up to 1960 is presented in table 10.1. Both the absolute (column 4) and relative (column 6) figures show that migration from rural to urban areas during the 14 years after World War II was more intense than during the 16-year period between the wars. Moreover, such measures as the mean annual emigration from villages to cities (column 5) or the intensity of annual emigration (defined as the ratio of net emigration to natural increase) in the years following World War II were

Table 10.1. Emigration of rural populations to urban areas.

Years	Mean number	Natural increase	Net rural–urban migration		Net emigration (%)	
	of rural population	total	total	mean annual	total rural pop. (5:2)	natural increase (4:3)
			million persons			
1	2	3	4	5	6	7
1922–31	21.8	4.0	1.1	0.11	0.5	27
1932–38	24.1	2.4	0.5	0.07	0.3	21
1946–50	16.1	1.3	1.2	0.24	1.5	95
1951–60	15.7	2.9	1.3	0.13	0.8	46

Source: *Geographia Polonica* 1972 vol. **24**. By permission of Państwowe Wydanictwo Naukowe, Polish Scientific Publishers, Warsaw.

twice as great as those for the period 1922–38.

As to the value of the net rural–urban migration (column 6), it is seen that after a period of intense migration movements of the rural population after World War I there was an abrupt slowing down of the efflux: this was caused by the economic depression of the 1930s.

In spite of the heavy damage to cities during World War II, there was an increase in the number of emigrants from rural areas to cities, but the numbers decreased during the statistical period 1950–60, due to the completion of the settlement of the western and northern territories. Since 1960 rural–urban migration has been steadily diminishing both in absolute figures and rate per 1000 of population.

An analysis of the migration of the rural population to urban centres discloses the significance of the movement in the process of urbanization. During the years 1922–38 the immigration from rural areas amounted to about 130% of the urban natural increase, the percentage of urban population being relatively low. In 1946–50, this index increased to 170%. During these periods, migration from rural areas to urban centres constituted the decisive factor in the increase of the urban population. An analogous index calculated for the years 1950–60 implies a smaller share of the rural migrants in the process of urbanization: migrants to cities constituted only 60% of urban growth. This index is, however, hardly comparable to the indices calculated for the earlier periods, for between 1950 and 1960 certain events contributed to a considerable increase of the urban population. This phenomenon was connected with the inclusion of parts of adjacent rural areas in the administrative boundaries of towns, as well as with the raising of a number of urban settlements to the status of towns. At the same time, there was a growth in the natural increase in the urban population whereas in 1931–32 it was 8⁰/₀₀, in 1960 it was 1.3⁰/₀₀. This was partly a result of rural immigration to urban areas.

Thus, rural–urban migration was one of the main factors of urbanization, and in 1950–60 migration produced an increase in the urban population of about 19%. In view of the significance of migration, it seems desirable to study its characteristic features and mechanisms.

Apart from the common features of all migration movements, observable also in other countries, rural–urban migration movements in Poland show two specific features:

(1) a higher intensity of migration when compared with other countries at a similar stage of socioeconomic development;

(2) the dependence of migration not only on the labour market but also on planned centres of growth.

Because of the lack of accurate statistical data on rural–urban migration during the inter-war period, the ensuing considerations are limited to the analysis of the phenomena after World War II. Following the main source of information, i.e. the population censuses, this period is divided into three phases:

(i) the first period, 1945–50, was one of intense population migration coinciding with a period of reconstruction of the country and the formation of a centrally planned economy;

(ii) the second phase covers the years 1950–60 and was marked by a natural increase, a higher stability of the population as regards place of residence, and regional, multi-phase migration from rural to urban areas;

(iii) the third phase extending from 1960 up to the present has been characterized by further processes of industrialization and urbanization, accompanied by a declining natural increase. Rural–urban migration has mostly taken the form of multi-stage moves within particular regions.

Changes after World War II

Migration in the period examined underwent changes not only with respect to the intensity of the migration movements of the rural population, but also as regards *the direction of migration*. Thus, in the first phase of migration, the predominant trend of movement was to the northern and western territories. In consequence of war hostilities, the towns of these areas were, on average, destroyed to the extent of 54%, and the losses in the housing resources in the cities of Wrocław, Szczecin, Gdańsk, and Opole, and especially in small towns, sometimes exceeded 90%. Characteristically, although the first wave of settlers went to towns that were relatively less devastated, the destroyed towns were ultimately repopulated and redeveloped, for they already had basic functions. Migration was connected with the possibilities of finding employment, at first in the reconstruction of factories and afterwards in manufacturing itself. This circumstance later had an adverse effect on the development of the smaller towns, which were slower to recover from war damage and unable to regain their functions as centres of commerce and handicrafts, now superseded by cheaper industrial products. This 'crisis of the small towns' affected the settlement movements in the western territories as well as in the rest of the country.

In consequence of the repatriation from the Soviet Union between 1944 and 1949, about 1.5 million people came to the present territory of Poland. Of these, 1.24 million settled in the western and northern territories, mainly in the towns, because of better possibilities of finding jobs and also in expectation of improving their living conditions.

The most numerous group among the settlers in the towns of the northern and western territories were immigrants from those parts of pre-war Poland that still remained within the revised national boundaries. The resettlement movement from central Poland comprised altogether 2.2 million people, i.e. 12% of the total population of pre-war Poland. The migration movement affected mainly the neighbouring voivodships; for instance, people from the voivodship of Poznań went chiefly to that of Zielona Góra, while inhabitants of the voivodship of Kielce settled in Lower Silesia. Simultaneously, apart from these short-distance movements, there was also migration from more distant areas, such as the voivodships of Białystok, Lublin, Rzeszów or the overpopulated voivodship of Cracow. The migrants from these districts moved to the big cities, especially the urban centres of Upper Silesia and Wrocław.

Organized mass migration to the western and northern territories ceased in 1947, after the existing housing resources had been exhausted, and thereafter further settlement could be achieved only by building new residential units or by major repairs to existing buildings. One consequence of these migration movements was that in 1947, for instance, 41% of the inhabitants of Wrocław were immigrants who had come directly from rural areas. In the case of smaller urban settlements, e.g. Kędzierzyn, about 90% of the population was of rural origin.

The first phase of the migration movements in the areas that had formed part of pre-war Poland was also marked by migration from rural to urban areas. This influx contributed to the growth of large cities, which offered opportunities in construction jobs, even for unqualified manpower. In this period there were several centres of migration from rural to urban areas, especially Warsaw, and the cities of Poznań, Cracow, and Łódź. Whereas Warsaw and Cracow (after construction of Nowa Huta had begun) were destinations of rural migrants from the whole country, the other cities attracted migrants mainly from the neighbouring voivodships. During that period migration took place mainly to large and medium-sized urban centres; migration to small towns was rather limited because the reconstruction of the larger urban settlements promised a substantial improvement in living standards, owing both to the provision of modern facilities and a broad network of services, and to the fact that such movements were organized by industrial establishments themselves.

A characteristic feature of the second phase of migration (1950–60) was the appearance of regional centres of migration. This was connected with short-distance migration and with a tendency for migrants to settle in the capital cities of their native voivodships.

A supra-regional significance is to be ascribed to the cities of the Cracow voivodship (Cracow, Nowa Huta) and to a number of industrial urban centres in the regained territories; these latter attracted immigrants mostly from the neighbouring voivodships, but not infrequently they were also the destination of migrants from distant voivodships as in the case of migration from the voivodship of Lublin to that of Wrocław.

In the period under examination, 40–70% of migrants lived outside the boundaries of their 'voivodship of origin'. An analysis of the directions of migration of this group shows that there were centres of absorption on a national scale. These consisted chiefly of towns in the voivodship of Wrocław (immigrants from Poznań and Lublin), and the voivodships of Warsaw (from the whole country), Katowice (from southern Poland) and Gdańsk (from the northern and central voivodships).

Studies of micro-regions have revealed another feature typical of the second wave of migration movements, namely the 'multi-stage' character of the migration process. Settlers from rural areas used to go first to small towns performing mixed functions, where they could more easily find employment as unskilled workers. After having obtained rudimentary training for their jobs or having completed vocational evening courses, they went to the bigger, more industrialized towns or cities which had a higher demand for skilled manpower. This 'multi-stage' character of migration did not completely eliminate rural–urban migration directly, but the latter did not significantly affect the proportions of the respective absolute figures at that time.

The third phase of the migration movements in Poland, which started in 1960, began during the second phase. Short-distance migration continued to predominate and this conditioned multi-stage migration. Also, the earlier-established division into national, regional and local centres of absorption exists to this day.

The changes in the dynamics and directions of migration have been accompanied by changes in the demographic characteristics of the migrants. In the first phase, the *age structure of the migrants* exhibited a predominance of persons in the productive age group. In the 1950s this structure shifted towards the younger age groups, and most emigrants left their villages before the age of 22–24. This tendency survives in the third phase, which is connected with the entry into the productive age group of the young people belonging to the post-war population explosion.

The selection of migrants according to age is a common fact also observed in other countries due to the easier adjustment of young people to new conditions of urban life, as well as to weak family ties and emotional bonds and lower financial status. In Poland the selection of migrants by age has also resulted from the higher natural increase of the rural population, from the mechanization of agriculture and from the resulting decrease in the demand for manpower in rural areas (and limited opportunities of employment in non-agricultural occupations in villages). In addition, the availability of a broad network of educational institutions of secondary and higher levels in the towns has undoubtedly stimulated the emigration of young people. The possibility of obtaining vocational training or higher education was traditionally identified by the rural population with social advance. In later years the motivations for migrating were reinforced by the financial aspect: on 5 July 1963, a bill was passed preventing the partition of farms. This bill, based on the recommendations of the Polish United Workers' Party, was intended to prevent the partition of farms through inheritance. It imposed the rule of passing the whole farm on to one of the children, with the obligation of that child to pay off those of his brothers or sisters who earned their living by working on the farm. Apart from preserving existing farm sizes, the bill also aimed to prevent the outflow of capital from the rural areas and to encourage superfluous manpower to move to urban centres.

On the basis of the age structure of migrants in recent years we may draw the conclusion that the new law has achieved its aims with regard to the gaining of additional manpower for industry. But sociologists still discuss the question whether the outflow of the most valuable manpower to the cities will not result in the maintenance of the traditional model of agriculture and thus retard the intensification of agricultural production. This is a statement based on intuition not yet justified by empirical results.

In recent years, there has occurred an imbalance in the age structure of the rural population, resulting from an increase of population in the pre- and post-productive age groups and a decrease of the wage-earning population. This causes financial strain on the working population of the villages, mitigated, however, by relatively low costs of living in rural areas and by the support of the state regarding the education of children.

The *sex structure of the migrants* in the period examined was marked by a higher proportion of women, because the possibilities of employing women in villages are smaller than for men. Exceptions to this rule occurred in some years during the industrialization of the country, in the second phase of the migration movements. The manufacturing plants opened in that period created a high demand for male workers.

A different picture of selection of migrants by sex results from an analysis of the outflow of manpower from agriculture. Here the share of men in the total number of migrants is twice as large as that of women. This results partly from the large share of what are called 'peasant-workers'. They are, in fact, engaged in both non-agricultural and agricultural activities and thus are only potential migrants, in view of their permanent residence in the village.

Although there is a relatively higher rate of migration of women to towns, the index of their employment activity is decidedly lower than that of men. Out of 100 female migrants, only 50 are employed, whereas the corresponding figure for males amounts to 90.

The structure of employment of the migrants shows that most of them work in the various sectors of industrial production (70%), and a smaller number (mainly women) are employed in state institutions concerned with administrative and service activities (22%).

Final remarks

In recent years the problem of migration from rural to urban areas has been frequently studied by specialists in different disciplines. In spite of this active interest, many questions remain to be answered. The Polish state is greatly interested in the problem of migration, and has taken over the initiative in directing population movements by exerting control over the labour market, wages, investment, housing and the training of manpower. At the same time, the state finances the development of the study of migration.

11   Rural Social Change in Poland

by B Galeski

Migration from village to town, the settlement of the western territories, and the growth of earnings outside the village have had a particularly strong influence in Poland. One can no longer say that the village constitutes a single social estate. Formerly, landless peasants who lived in the villages did not constitute a separate group. Today not only have their numbers increased but the majority work outside the village and agriculture, and belong to other social strata and classes. The same can be said of the majority of the peasants working smallholdings, except that they form a marginal category, in between two social strata and milieux.

The village has thus become a place of residence for people following various occupations and belonging to different social strata. This differentiation is only partly (in Poland only very slightly) a function of the internal needs of the rural community. It is much more due to urban influences, even the direct penetration of the town into the village. This makes it difficult today to demarcate the boundaries between village and town precisely: in the case of those areas which have been most strongly subject to the influences of urbanization and industrialization one can even speak of the emergence of local aggregations of an 'urban–rural' character. Certain features peculiar to Poland are intensifying this process. Mass migration from village to town, which strengthens mutual contacts, urbanizes the village but also 'ruralizes' the town. Improved communications facilitate the use of large urban centres as sources of supply and as places of amusement for villagers within the ever-extending orbit of the towns. The trend towards the depopulation of the small towns, which in many respects worsens the economic, cultural and even administrative services available to

the village as compared with the larger urban centre, is a further factor peculiar to Poland which tends to make the village increasingly a 'suburban' place. The small towns also change their functions or go into decline, and their suburbs grow larger. The village changes its character in terms of land use: it is no longer exclusively an agricultural area, but becomes a residential and recreational area for the urban population.

One could go on multiplying these observations; they are all evidence of the unidirectionality of change, of the weakening of the traditional local village community and the blurring of fundamental social differences between town and country. To a large extent, then, theories based on such assumptions are becoming useless.

Although class divisions are not a myth and although one can point to actual rural capitalists and proletarians, those who conceive of the future of the village in terms of a class struggle 'between the poor and the kulaks', and who believe that this struggle will lead to collectivization, draw no support for their views from our knowledge of actual conditions today. The most numerous social categories in the Polish village today are (1) peasant-owners of family farms, and (2) the highly diversified category of 'peasant-workers', i.e. families living in the village and in varying degrees combining work on a farm with regular employment outside the village and outside agriculture. Thus differentiation along the village–town axis has become the dominant division in the peasant stratum, and in Poland this differentiation is *not* associated with the class divisions to which Lenin pointed in his works on the pre-revolutionary Russian village with regard to changes in the urban class structure or with regard to rural change.

Because of marked differentiation among 'peasant-workers' it is difficult to analyse this category as a social force. However, it cannot be left out when considering the future of the village. It would seem that, apart from

Source: B Galeski 1972 *Basic Concepts of Rural Sociology* (2nd edn 1976) (Manchester: Manchester University Press). Originally published in Polish by Państwowe Wydanictwo Naukowe, Warsaw (Socjologia wsi pojecia podstawowe).

problems arising from their new vocations, peasant-workers are also concerned about being near their place of work, about freeing themselves from the burdens imposed by farming (by renting or selling their land, etc), and about the development of the village as a residential settlement. This can be interpreted as an interest in the urbanization of the village; in its transformation into a rural–urban community. This is the attitude towards the village on the part of what today is one of the most numerous categories of the rural population and one which is fast becoming a social force, though in Poland we still cannot definitely say what part the peasant-workers will ultimately play in social change.

Demographic and Social Change in the West Midlands

by A J Rugman and M D Green

Fundamental changes in the size, distribution and structure of the population of the West Midlands conurbation and region have occurred since 1950. Population growth, faster than in any other conurbation or region in Great Britain during the 1950s, has slowed, stabilized and recently changed to decline. Most of the growth was accommodated in Birmingham and Coventry and their hinterlands, but there has been an increasing tendency for the population of this central area to move outwards towards its periphery. The area surrounding the West Midlands metropolitan county, rather than the county itself, is now the dominant population growth area of the region. At the same time, there have been important changes in age and social structure. These developments reflect social evolution in the country as a whole as well as locally, the changing economic fortunes of the West Midlands and the trend experienced in all major British conurbations in recent years for population to move away from older urban centres. Demographic change is inextricably linked with social and economic change. Its spatial expression is in terms of the pattern of urban development and it is, therefore, a critical element in planning policy formulation. This has been particularly true of the West Midlands where demographic projections and their variability have been closely connected with the debates about containment and overspill.

The definition of geographical boundaries, which are particularly important for demographic analysis, is complicated by successive local government changes during the post-war period. The West Midland 'conurbation' — a statistical rather than a local government unit — has remained largely undisturbed since 1950,

although in 1974 it was superseded even for statistical purposes by the West Midlands metropolitan county (WMMC), which since that date has also included Coventry and the Birmingham–Coventry corridor.

Although the WMMC includes the major urban core of the West Midlands region, it is surrounded beyond the green belt by a ring of towns which have experienced rapid population growth during the past 25 years. The area including these towns and the green belt itself has been identified as an 'outer metropolitan area' (OMA) reaching from Stratford-upon-Avon to Cannock and Kidderminster to Rugby.[1] Whilst the population of the OMA has grown rapidly by outward migration from the older urban core, inner areas have generally experienced an extensive population loss.

Total population

From 1911 until 1951 the West Midlands conurbation was growing faster than any other as the dominant urban area of a booming and prosperous region. Most of the growth occurred in the WMMC area, which by 1951 contained 58% of the region's population. Over this 40 year period, the conurbation's population grew from 1 630 000 to 2 260 000 and Coventry's from 150 000 in 1921 to some 270 000 in 1951.

The 1951–61 period saw some continuation of earlier trends (table 12.1). The population of the region and the WMMC area continued to grow faster than that of England and Wales, but there were marked variations within the county area and signs of a new pattern. The dominant growth areas within it were around the periphery where land was available for new development, thus continuing the process of suburbanization which had commenced before the war (Eversley *et al* 1965). Solihull CB, effectively a Birmingham suburb,

Source: F Joyce (ed) 1977 *Metropolitan Development and Change: The West Midlands — A Policy Review* (London: Saxon House) pp50–74.

Table 12.1. Population change by area, 1951–76 (in thousands).

Area	1951	Change 1951–61		1961	Change 1961–71		1971	Change 1971–76		1976	Change 1951–76	
		No.	%		No.	%		No.	%		No.	%
Birmingham MD	1161.6	21.7	1.9	1183.2	−85.3	−7.2	1098.0	−39.2	−3.6	1058.8	−102.8	−8.8
Coventry MD	270.4	48.0	17.7	318.4	18.4	5.8	336.7	0.1	0.0	336.8	66.4	24.6
Dudley MD	231.6	22.6	9.8	254.2	39.7	15.6	293.9	6.3	2.1	300.2	68.6	29.6
Sandwell MD	342.8	−3.3	−1.0	339.5	−9.4	−2.8	330.2	−17.3	−5.2	312.9	−29.9	−8.7
Solihull MD	81.1	47.1	58.0	128.2	63.9	49.8	192.1	7.5	3.9	199.6	118.5	146.1
Walsall MD	216.4	48.4	14.1	264.8	8.5	10.7	273.3	4.7	−1.7	268.6	52.2	24.1
Wolverhampton MD	242.6	18.9	7.8	261.6	7.6	2.9	269.1	−2.7	−1.0	266.4	23.8	9.8
WMMC	2546.6	185.3	7.3	2731.9	61.4	2.2	2793.3	−50.0	−1.8	2743.3	196.7	7.7
W. Midlands conurbation	2259.8	118.2	5.2	2378.0	−6.4	−0.3	2371.6	†	†	†	†	†
Birmingham inner area	†	†	†	327.0	−84.3	−25.8	242.6	†	†	†	†	†
Outer metropolitan area (OMA)	654.4	101.3	15.5	755.7	185.5	24.6	941.2	69.1	7.3	1010.3	355.9	54.4
W. Midlands region	4422.9	334.8	7.6	4757.6	351.9	7.4	5109.6	55.5	1.1	5165.1	742.2	16.8
England and Wales	43757.9	2436.7	5.4	46104.5	2645.0	5.7	48749.6	434.8	0.9	49184.4	5426.5	12.4

Notes: †Not available.
       All data independently rounded.

Sources: 1 Census of Population 1951, 1961 and 1971;
         2 Office of Population Censuses and Surveys, provisional estimates of population at mid-1976 (these data are not
           precisely compatible with 1951–71 Census results because of a slightly different definition of population).

grew in population by some 28 000. This was much less than the 51 000 growth in Coventry CB but at 43.2% and 19.1% respectively, was much higher in relative terms. In the enlarged Solihull Metropolitan District (MD), population grew by about 47 000 (58%). Sutton Coldfield MB (now in Birmingham MD) gained 51.7% in population and Aldridge–Brownhills UD (now in Walsall MD) 56.3%. At the same time, the population of the former Birmingham CB was roughly stable, which in the light of trends towards suburbanization suggests that the Birmingham inner area was already losing population. Altogether, the WMMC area grew by 185 000 people or 7.3%. Nevertheless, population growth in the OMA was already pronounced; the total rose by 101 000 representing 30% of the regional gain, and the relative growth of 15.5% was over twice that of the WMMC.

The following decade marked a significant change from previous patterns and an acceleration of the trend toward dispersal beyond the metropolitan county boundary. Whilst the population of the West Midlands region continued to grow faster than that of England and Wales, growth in the WMMC area was lower, at only 2.2%. Migration to the suburbs continued

although these areas were growing less rapidly. For example, growth rates in Solihull CB, Sutton Coldfield MB and Aldridge–Brownhills UD declined to 15.6, 14.8 and 25.5% respectively. Solihull MD gained nearly 50% in population due mainly to Birmingham city council's peripheral housing development at Chelmsley Wood.

Significant new trends were at the same time becoming apparent in the older urban areas. The former Birmingham CB lost 96 000 people or 8.6% and the inner area lost 84 000, over 25% of its population, in only ten years. Population decline in these areas tended to coincide with lack of land for new housing, coupled with the effects of redevelopment and a decrease in the average size of households. In contrast, the OMA gained in population by nearly 186 000, 83% more than its gain of 101 000 in the previous decade, and equal to nearly 25% of its 1961 total. Its absolute growth was about three times that of the metropolitan county and accounted for 53% of the regional gain. Thus the main areas of fast population growth were increasingly the free-standing towns and villages within and beyond the green belt.

Since 1971, the Registrar General's population estimates show that the centrifugal trend in population redistribution has continued but has been affected by a very marked reduction in national and regional population growth due primarily to a much lower rate of natural increase. Between 1974 and 1976, the region experienced a population decline, the first recorded since the first census in 1801. The WMMC itself lost some 50 000 people (1.8%) between 1971 and 1976, predominantly from the older areas of Birmingham and Sandwell. Significantly, population growth in the OMA for the first time exceeded that of the region as a whole, although at 69 000 it was relatively lower than in 1961–71. Thus the OMA had emerged by 1976 as the main large area of outstanding population growth in the whole region.

The picture for the whole period from 1951 is one of accelerating decentralization. In the 1950s, this tended to take the form of classical suburban growth and a relatively stable older urban core. After 1961, the focus of population growth shifted beyond the green belt to the growing towns in the OMA. Whereas in 1951 the OMA's population equalled about a quarter of that of the metropolitan county, by 1976 it had risen to over a third. This trend was in contrast to the marked population decline in inner areas.

These trends are closely linked with changes in the scale and distribution of employment. The WMMC area experienced high absolute and relative employment growth until the mid 1960s, when the situation began to change dramatically. Part of the employment loss in the older urban areas was offset by expansion in peripheral locations and the growing towns of the OMA but population was decentralizing at a faster rate than employment (Department of the Environment 1976a). This suggests that much of the population decentralization was housing — rather than employment — motivated; it was certainly associated with a rapid growth in commuting by people living outside the conurbation but working within it (Office of Population Censuses and Surveys 1976a).

Components of population change

Changes in the total population of an area and its age structure are the result of changes in birth and death rates and the balance of inward and outward migration (table 12.2). The period under review covers two extremely significant changes in the rate of natural population increase: a sudden and unexpected growth in births throughout the country followed by an even

Table 12.2 Components of population change West Midlands metropolitan county, conurbation and region, 1951–76 (in thousands).

Area	1951–56	56–61	61–66	66–71	71–76
WMMC					
Natural increase	†	†	125	108	47
Net migration	†	†	−96	−69	−96
Total change	†	†	29	39	−49
WM conurbation					
Natural increase	64	78	106	88	†
Net migration	−28	−1	−97	−96	†
Total change	36	77	9	−8	†
WM region					
Natural increase	121	155	206	192	86
Net migration	1	59	−22	−17	−42
Total change	122	214	184	175	44

Notes: 1. 1951–61 data for the conurbation excludes Brownhills UD.
2. Net migration is the balance including net civilian migration.
3. 1971–76 data are provisional.
† Data not available.

Source: Annual population estimates and other data included by courtesy of the Office of Population Censuses and Surveys. Crown Copyright Reserved.

greater decline. During the 1950s, the region gained population through migration in reflection of its relative economic prosperity. In the 1960s and the first half of the 1970s, there was a net loss. The interrelationship between natural increase and net migration trends has been particularly significant, especially from 1961 onwards. Since then, the net migration loss from the region has tended to rise, although it has been outweighed by very high rates of natural increase. The recent decline in the latter, however, has been relatively greater than the growth in net migration loss and by 1974, the two factors combined to produce a small drop in total population. The greater relative effect of lower natural increase has been even more marked in the WMMC where the average net migration loss remained broadly constant from 1961 to 1976.

Migration

The 1966 and 1971 censuses show gross migration flows, origins and destinations, and the age, occupation and social structure of migrants. The net migration balances shown in table 12.3 are not directly comparable with those in table 12.2 because of differing

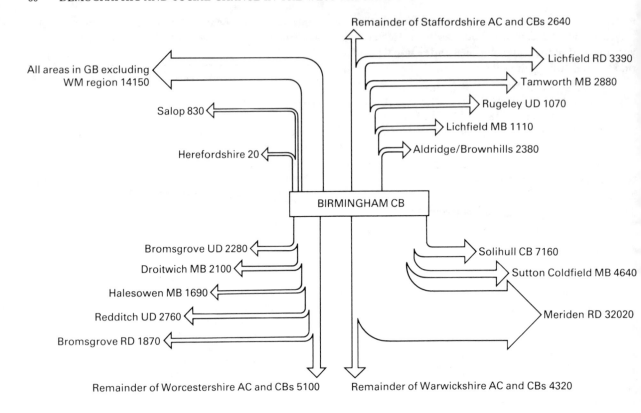

Figure 12.1 Volume and direction of net immigration, Birmingham CB, 1966–71.

sources and the exclusion of overseas emigrants. Nevertheless, the data do show the large volume of gross migration in relation to the net balance, particularly in the case of the region. It has been estimated that about one in ten of the region's population moved during 1970–71. Both inward and outward migration to and from the region and conurbation increased between 1961–66 and 1966–71, but in both cases outward migration by a larger absolute amount, thus raising the net migration loss. Net movement from the conurbation to the rest of Great Britain increased by 30.6% between these periods and the net balance in 1966–71 was −118 110 people. Most of this increase was attributable to a rising net loss to the rest of the West Midlands region. Inward migration from the New Commonwealth was falling and that from the British Isles outside Great Britain (mainly Northern Ireland and the Irish Republic) declined even more.

Most of the outward migration from the conurbation to the rest of the region was across the green belt to the smaller towns in the OMA. Birmingham CB was the principal source of this migration, although movement to the suburbs of Sutton Coldfield, Solihull and

Aldridge–Brownhills was still significant (figure 12.1). Of the 124 000 persons moving from the conurbation to the rest of the region in 1966–71, only 15 000 (12%) moved to the four new and expanded towns in the region: Redditch, Telford, Droitwich and Tamworth. At that time, however, some of these schemes were still in their early build-up period. An additional 37 000 people moved from Birmingham CB to Meriden RD, mainly resulting from the public sector housing development at Chelmsley Wood. Most of the movement was therefore 'voluntary', mainly in the private sector of the housing market. Of the 92 000 people (net) who left the WMMC area in 1966–71, 34.3% moved outside the West Midlands region and the largest flows to the new West Midlands counties were to Staffordshire and Hereford and Worcester (table 12.3).

Between 1966 and 1971, 56% of the net migration loss from the conurbation comprised people aged 15–44, although that group accounted for only 43% of the total equivalent population in 1971. In the 15–29 age group, the figures were 38% and 23% respectively. These are the age groups who are always most likely to

Table 12.3. Net migration, West Midlands metropolitan county, 1966–71.

Net migration from/to	Number	%
Rest of West Midlands region	−60 520	65.7
Hereford and Worcester	−18 730	20.3
Salop	−5790	6.3
Staffordshire	−22 450	24.4
Warwickshire	−13 550	14.7
Rest of Great Britain outside West Midlands region	−31 560	34.3
Rest of Great Britain outside West Midlands metropolitan county	−92 080	100

Note: Figures exclude students, armed forces and institutional population.

Source: Department of the Environment (South West Regional Office) migration research project, using Census of Population 1971. The help of the SWRO migration research project team is gratefully acknowledged.

move, both for employment and housing purposes, and the loss of younger people is significant when, as in the conurbation and WMMC area, there is a large negative migration balance. The social structure of migrants showed similar deviations from that of the whole population. Of the net balance of economically active and retired males who migrated from the conurbation in 1966–71 some 26% were professionals, employers and managers compared with 14% of the equivalent resident population in 1971. On the other hand, less than 2% of net male migrants were unskilled workers, compared with 8% of 1971 residents. The long-term consequences of these differentials are disturbing, and it will be seen below that there have consequently been divergent trends since 1951 between the social structure of the WMMC area, particularly the inner Birmingham area, and that of the OMA.

Population, households and housing need

One of the most important effects of population change is on housing need, in terms of both numbers and type of dwellings. It is self-evident that population growth due to migration, as has occurred around the periphery of the WMMC area and beyond, must presuppose additional new housing. What is less clear is that a stable or even declining population can still generate a rising housing need because of its grouping into smaller households. This trend, together with the need for substantial clearance of obsolete housing in the 1950s and 1960s, has been responsible for much of the housing pressure in the WMMC area.

This reduction in average household size (from 3.41 persons per household in the WMMC area in 1951 to 3.0 in 1971) has resulted from the reduction in the backlog of overcrowding and the tendency for younger and older people to live independently, together with the lower birth rate since 1964. The number of one- and two-person households in the region rose by 37% between 1961 and 1971 (one-person households by 67%) and 78% of this increase included people of pensionable age (JMSG 1976a). These trends have had far reaching consequences for urban and regional planning. Firstly, they have served to counteract any reduction in housing pressures which might have resulted from lower population growth and have meant that a given housing stock has tended to contain fewer people. The overall need for new housing land has therefore grown while the total population has declined in older urban areas where little land is available. Secondly, the type and size of existing (and many recently built) dwellings are often ill-suited to the needs of small households. Current projections suggest that the trends will continue, thus adding to the housing need in the 1980s arising from the higher birth rates of the 1960s and often reducing the population capacity of areas already developed. In consequence, and coupled with the redevelopment of obsolete housing, the structure plans prepared for the WMMC area suggest a continuing excess between 1971 and 1986 in the need for housing in the county over probable supply (WMMC 1975, DOE 1976b).

Future population

The 1974-based population projections by the OPCS showed future population and its age structure after assuming that the net migration loss from the region will be at a rate of some 10 000 persons per annum (OPCS 1976b). These projections were based on existing trends and proposals and may well be affected by future planning policies, including those of individual local authorities. They showed a slowly growing regional (and national) population, in sharp contrast to the projections made only a few years ago. For example, the 1969-based projections showed a regional population of 5 671 000 by 1986; in the 1974-based projection the equivalent figure was 5 256 000, a reduction of 415 000 people, greater than the population of Coventry. This transition from rapid to relatively low population growth has many social and planning implications but the projections suggest that the process of outward population redistribution from the WMMC area will continue, with marked reductions in population in Birmingham, Sandwell, and Wolverhampton MDs. These are areas where the effect of lower household sizes is not being offset by the availability on the periphery of large areas of land for new housing. Dudley and Solihull MDs, however, should see population growth stemming from new housing development.

Socio-economic structure

Marked changes have occurred not only in numbers of people and their distribution, but also in social structure. This has resulted from two broad factors: changes in the whole population reflecting education, employment and social mobility, together with the more local effects of migration. Both factors have influenced distribution between social classes or socio-economic groups, as well as changes in the size of individual groups (table 12.4, figure 12.2). Between 1951 and 1971, there was a national growth in the proportion of non-manual 'white-collar' workers (social classes I and II)[2] but a decline in manual (particularly unskilled) workers (social classes III–V), reflecting the expansion of service employment in relation to manufacturing. These trends were also apparent in the West Midlands region but the migration factor has been especially influential in the relative change between the WMMC area, the OMA and inner urban areas.

In 1951, the WMMC area had a lower proportion of non-manual workers than England and Wales and a larger proportion of skilled manual workers (social class III), demonstrating its dependence on manufacturing and its low levels of service employment. By 1971 the growth in the proportion of non-manual workers had been less than the national average, as had the decline in the proportion of semi-skilled and unskilled workers (social classes IV and V) combined. The result was a greater proportion in the latter category in the WMMC area in 1971 than in 1951.

Table 12.4.   Socio-economic structure of economically active males by area, 1961 and 1971.

Area	Year	Socio-economic groups											
		1,2,3,4,13		5,6		8,9,12,14		7,10,15		11		Total	
		'000	%	'000	%	'000	%	'000	%	'000	%	'000	%
West Midlands met. county	1961	106.3	11.6	128.2	14.0	429.6	47.0	162.2	17.7	68.3	7.5	914.2	100
	1971	122.6	14.0	128.8	14.7	386.1	44.2	155.0	17.7	62.8	7.2	874.3	100
Birmingham inner area	1961	6.0	5.6	10.8	10.0	51.7	48.0	22.4	20.7	16.9	15.6	107.8	100
	1971	3.9	5.2	8.5	11.3	31.5	41.7	19.0	25.2	12.4	16.4	75.6	100
Outer met. area	1961	37.3	15.1	33.0	13.3	102.3	41.3	51.5	20.8	14.9	6.0	247.3	100
	1971	55.2	19.5	44.4	15.7	117.9	41.6	46.2	16.3	14.8	5.2	283.6	100
West Midlands region	1961	200.5	12.7	214.5	13.6	703.6	44.7	293.6	18.6	117.8	7.4	1574.4	100
	1971	244.6	15.5	233.4	14.8	680.5	43.2	268.6	17.1	109.4	6.9	1574.4	100
England and Wales	1961	2088.4	14.3	2415.8	16.5	5757.6	39.3	2624.2	17.9	1222.6	8.3	14649.1	100
	1971	2525.8	17.5	2548.0	17.7	5597.3	38.8	2190.8	15.2	1074.1	7.5	14408.0	100

Notes: 1. Armed forces and inadequately described excluded from groups (except for Birmingham inner area in 1961 where included in SEG 11) but included in totals.
2. Data for the whole of Meriden RD (a small part of which lies within the OMA) have been included in WMMC for both 1961 and 1971.
3. Socio-economic groups have been classified as follows:
1,2,3,4,13   Professional employers and managers
5,6   Intermediate and junior non-manual workers
8,9,12,14   Foremen and skilled manual workers
7,10,15   Semi-skilled manual workers
11   Unskilled manual workers

Sources: 1. Censuses of Population, 1961 and 1971.
2. City of Birmingham Abstract of Statistics 1964 and 1972–73.

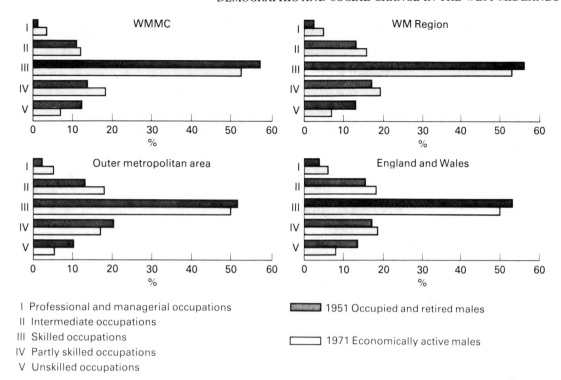

Figure 12.2 Social class structure in WMMC, outer metropolitan area, West Midlands region and England and Wales, 1951 and 1971. (Source: Census of Population 1951 and 1971).

The trends mentioned above are borne out by comparison of relative changes in socio-economic groups (table 12.4), which have slightly different definitions from social class. In the OMA, however, the proportion of professionals, employers and managers grew more than in either the metropolitan county or England and Wales, and there was a greater decline in that of semi-skilled and unskilled workers. In the inner Birmingham area, on the other hand, there was a pronounced drop between 1961 and 1971 in the proportion of professionals etc, and skilled manual workers and a rise in that of semi-skilled and unskilled workers.

There were also marked contrasts between the former local authorities in the WMMC area, both in the proportions in each group and the changes between 1966 and 1971. Birmingham, Warley and West Bromwich, forming the conurbation core, had a distinctly lower proportion of workers in the non-manual groups in comparison with the whole conurbation, and a higher proportion in the partly skilled and unskilled groups. A reverse situation existed in the peripheral areas of Solihull CB and Halesowen, Stourbridge and Sutton Coldfield MBs, where the growth in non-manual groups in both absolute and relative terms was marked (JMSG 1976b).

Changes in the size of groups over time, as distinct from proportions of the total, are revealing. Each socio-economic group in the Birmingham inner area declined in numbers between 1961 and 1971 because of an overall population loss but the greatest percentage decline was in skilled manual workers, the largest group in absolute numbers. In contrast, the number of professionals, employers and managers living in the OMA increased by 48% and skilled manual workers by 15%. In the metropolitan county itself, non-manual groups grew much more slowly than in the OMA, the region or England and Wales. Skilled manual workers decreased relatively more than in the two latter areas whilst the partly skilled fell relatively less than in any other area analysed. It is clearly apparent that between 1951 and 1976 there was not only a widening difference between social trends in the WMMC area and the rest of the country but that there was an even more marked gap between trends in the inner Birmingham area and the OMA. It is reasonable to assume that the gap applies to most of the inner areas of the metropolitan county.

Table 12.5. New Commonwealth immigrants (and dependants in 1971) by area, 1961, 1966 and 1971.

Area	Residents born in New Commonwealth (NC)						Both parents born in NC	
	1961		1966		1971		1971	
	Number	% Total Population	Number	% Total Population	Number	% Total Population	Number	% Total Population
Birmingham MD	—	—	50 670	4.4	69 140	6.3	93 175	8.5
Coventry MD	—	—	10 770	3.3	15 190	4.5	19 971	5.9
Dudley MD	—	—	3140	1.1	4835	1.6	5977	2.0
Sandwell MD	—	—	11 040	3.3	15 630	4.7	22 155	6.7
Solihull MD	—	—	560	0.4	1610	0.8	1665	0.9
Walsall MD	—	—	6190	2.4	9320	3.4	12 169	4.5
Wolverh'ton MD	—	—	13 310	5.1	20 065	7.5	28 853	10.7
WMMC	35 800†	1.4	95 680	3.5	135 790	4.9	183 965	6.6
Birmingham inner area	19 155‡	5.9	32 930	10.9	42 535	17.5	60 075	24.8

†Conurbation plus Coventry CB.
‡This figure includes all Commonwealth countries.

Definitions: 1961, Jamaica, other Commonwealth Caribbean territories, India, Pakistan, Commonwealth countries in Africa (excluding South Africa), Cyprus and Malta.
1966, Commonwealth and colonies other than Australia, Canada and New Zealand.
1971, Commonwealth countries in Africa, Caribbean, Asia, Cyprus, Gibraltar, Malta and Gozo.
Sources: Censuses of Population 1961, 1966 and 1971. City of Birmingham Abstract of Statistics, 1964, 1966–67 and 1972–73.

This leads to questions about social polarization and the increasing spatial segregation of different socio-economic groups (extensively discussed by Hall *et al* 1973). The changing spatial distribution of skills in the labour force is certainly likely to have implications for the location of future employment growth as well as for social policy.

These trends were due in part to the tendency for outward migration to contain a disproportionately large number of people in white collar occupations and a smaller proportion of unskilled and semi-skilled groups. This undoubtedly had many causes but an immensely important factor has been the growth of car ownership since the 1950s, allowing easy commuting across the green belt. As might be expected, therefore, a far higher proportion of households in 1971 in the OMA (64%) owned a car than in the WMMC area (49%), whilst the level in the Birmingham inner area (27%) was only half the regional average (54%).

Immigration from overseas
Western Europe has experienced high levels of international migration for the last 20 years. Most of the immigrants to Britain came from the New Commonwealth and settled primarily in the inner areas of the conurbations. In the WMMC area immigration from Ireland has also been important since before 1950, and in 1971 over 73 000 of the county's population (2.6%) were born in the Irish Republic, compared with nearly 136 000 (4.9%) born in the New Commonwealth.

Immigration from the New Commonwealth became significant during the 1950s (Rose *et al* 1969) when a labour shortage in Britain provided plentiful employment opportunities, particularly in less attractive jobs. Jamaica and the Caribbean generally, were the principal origins at first, but Indians and Pakistanis were dominant during the 1960s. With its economic prosperity, the West Midlands conurbation was an important area of settlement from the outset and by 1966 had emerged as the main focus of coloured immigration outside Greater London (Jones 1970), a situation which still prevailed in 1971 (Jones 1976). In 1961 there were some 36 000 immigrants born in the New Commonwealth living in the metropolitan county area. Five years later there were nearly 96 000 and by 1971 the number had risen to nearly 136 000 (table 12.5). Persons with both parents born in the New Commonwealth (thus including children born in the UK to earlier immigrants) numbered nearly 184 000 in 1971, 6.6% of the total population.

The main concentration within the WMMC area is in Birmingham MD, which accommodated over half the total persons born in the New Commonwealth in 1971. The areas of settlement within Birmingham, however, were highly concentrated into the central part of the city, with nearly two-thirds of the total living within the Birmingham inner area wards selected for analysis. Nearly 25% of the total 1971 population of the latter area had both parents born in the New Commonwealth. During the 1960s, these concentrations in the inner areas intensified, with little evidence of dispersal and suburbanization (Jones 1970, 1976). Growth of coloured minorities in the inner areas was generally paralleled by an outward movement of the original population; whilst the inner wards of Birmingham lost 25% of their total population between 1961 and 1971, residents born in the New Commonwealth grew in number by over 120% (tables 12.1 and 12.5). The migration of coloured people into Birmingham and other inner areas was therefore part of a population replacement process (Jones 1976). Indeed, on a regional scale, the net migration loss which became apparent during the 1960s might have been larger still had it not been for Commonwealth immigration.

The distribution of immigrants from the various countries of origin is uneven. In 1971, some 58% of the total New Commonwealth immigrants in the WMMC area were born in the Indian sub-continent and about 31% in the Caribbean. Indians and Pakistanis, however, were more concentrated in Coventry, Sandwell and Walsall, with West Indians more so in Birmingham.

In 1971, persons in the WMMC area with both parents born in the New Commonwealth had a distinctly 'young' age profile. 42% were aged 0–14 (compared with 25% of the whole population); 47% were 15–44 (39%) and only 0.8% were over 65 (14%). In the same year, nearly 58% of this group age 15–44 were males, and of the single people aged 15 and over, nearly 63% were males. Partly in reflection of the relatively high proportion of young people and despite the male predominance in the child-bearing age groups, 17.5% of total births in the West Midlands conurbation in 1973 were to mothers born in the New Commonwealth and Pakistan, a considerably higher proportion than that of such persons in the total population.

Conclusions

The Abercrombie–Jackson Plan (1948) and the later green belt provided for the solution of urban problems by a strategy for the dispersal and containment of a population that was expected to remain broadly stable (e.g. West Midlands Group 1948). In the event, the region and metropolitan county experienced a considerable population growth, particularly through natural increase. When added to physical housing problems and the trend towards smaller households, the result was a level of housing pressure for which regional policy did not adequately provide. The nature of the dispersal which did occur, when combined with other demographic, social and economic forces, produced a widening diversity between growing towns beyond the green belt and inner urban areas of the metropolitan county. More recently, urban population growth has changed to localized population decline.

Between 1951 and 1976 the population of the WMMC area grew by 7.7%, mostly during the 1950s; since 1971 its population has declined. The Birmingham inner area lost 25.8% of its population between 1961 and 1971 alone. On the other hand, the population of the OMA grew by 54.6% between 1951 and 1976, far in excess of that in either the region or England and Wales. Moreover, the growth was considerably higher during the 1960s than the 1950s, and although the growth rate since 1971 has been lower, it has remained substantially higher than in the region or the rest of the country. Whilst peripheral growth was expanding the WMMC area's population during the 1950s, and high-density development maintaining it during the 1960s, the focus of growth shifted beyond the green belt to the growing towns around its perimeter. Job mobility, however, has been less than that of population and employment has not decentralized to the same extent. Separation of home and workplace has been facilitated by the expansion of mass car ownership since the 1950s, particularly amongst middle- and higher-income groups, making possible easy commuting into the metropolitan county area across the green belt. It has also coincided with growing housing expectations, a shift towards owner-occupation and, until recently, cheap energy. Thus travelling costs could be set against cheaper housing in areas where land was in plentiful supply.

The people most willing and able to make this move have predictably been those in the younger and white-collar groups. Although there have not been dramatic changes in age profiles, there has been a tendency for the OMA to become 'younger' than the WMMC area and to show widely differing trends in social structure. The WMMC area had in 1951 a lower proportion of white-collar workers and a higher proportion of semi-skilled and unskilled workers than England and Wales but by 1971 the growth in proportion of the white-collar groups and the decline in the semi- and unskilled had both been less than the national average. This situation was even more marked in the inner Birmingham area, where the proportion of semi-skilled and unskilled workers actually rose between 1961 and 1971 against the national trend. In the OMA, however, a rapid growth in white-collar and skilled manual groups has resulted in a socio-economic structure diverging from that of the WMMC area and contrasting sharply with that of inner areas generally.

What general conclusions can be drawn about the relationship between the course of events and planning policy? Many of the changes were country-wide and the result of economic and social forces on which policy could have little or no effect. These changes included the high population growth of the late 1950s and early 1960s, smaller household sizes and the growth of car ownership. Regional policies must respond to such events rather than vice versa, although time lags have been clearly apparent. Planning does, however, have a leading role in accommodating the spatial dimension of overall economic and social changes and in resolving the conflicting demands on land use. It is in this field that controversy has arisen in recent years, particularly in the efficiency and effects of the policies of urban containment, dispersal and green belt (e.g. Hall *et al* 1973). The judgment must lie elsewhere, but there is too little evidence as yet on which to draw any general conclusions about direct causal relationships between the dispersal of population and the problems of inner areas. Employment decline, low incomes, physical obsolescence and reservoirs of cheap rented housing have each been important in the 'inner city'. In any event, a reduction in inner-area population densities was both necessary and desirable.

What can be firmly concluded is that we should always be cautious about our ability to predict anything with certainty and that uncertainty about the future has never been greater. Nowhere is this more true than of the basic questions in social policy: how many people, where, and of what characteristics?

Notes

[1] The outer metropolitan area (OMA) includes the new districts of Redditch, Bromsgrove, Wyre Forest, South Staffordshire, Cannock Chase, Lichfield, Tamworth, North Warwickshire, Nuneaton, Rugby, Warwick and Stratford-upon-Avon.

[2] Since 1911, the Office of Population Censuses and Surveys has used the term 'social class' in its enumeration of the British population. There are five social classes, based broadly on the nature of the enumerated person's employment. A more recent classification — socio-economic grouping — is based on a finer breakdown of occupational types although these can be aggregated to correspond roughly to the five social classes described above as, for example, in table 12.4.

References

Abercrombie P and Jackson H 1948 *The West Midlands Plan*, Ministry of Town and Country Planning, London

Department of the Environment 1976a *British Cities: Urban Population and Employment Trends 1951–1971*, Research Report 10

—— 1976b Examination in Public of the Structure plans for Birmingham, Dudley, Walsall, Warley, West Bromwich and Wolverhampton. Report of the Panel

Eversley D E C, Jackson V J and Lomas G M 1965 *Population Growth and Planning Policy* (London: Cass)

Hall P *et al* 1973 *The Containment of Urban England* (London: Allen and Unwin)

Joint Monitoring Steering Group 1976a *A Developing Strategy for the West Midlands, General Housing Analysis 1961–1974*, Department of the Environment and West Midlands Planning Authorities Conference

—— 1976b *A Developing Strategy for the West Midlands, Analysis of Socio-Economic Groups*, Department of the Environment and West Midlands Planning Authorities Conference

Jones P N 1970 Coloured immigrants in Birmingham, 1961–66 *Transactions, Institute of British Geographers* No. 50 pp199–219

—— 1976 Coloured Minorities in Birmingham, England *Annals of the Association of American Geographers* **66** pp 80–103

Office of Population Censuses and Surveys 1976a Travelling to Work: the 1971 Census Picture *Population Trends* **4** pp 12–20

—— 1976b Local Population Projections *Population Trends* **5** pp9–12

Rose E J B *et al* (1969) *Colour and Citizenship: A Report on British Race Relations*, Institute of Race Relations (London: Oxford University Press)

West Midlands County Council 1975 *Coventry Structure Plan*

West Midlands Group 1948 *Conurbation*, Table VIII (London: Architectural Press)

Section III
City Centre Development and Change

Introduction

The internal structure and pattern of cities are rarely if ever static. They are instead in a state of constant flux. As the economic fortunes and population of cities change, so do the type and pattern of land-use. From the mixed pattern of land uses characteristic of the pre-industrial, feudal or pre-capitalist city where residential and industrial uses were frequently jumbled together, to the beginnings of land use and spatial segregation of different social groups at the start of the industrial revolution, through to the more developed pattern of functional and social segregation found in the contemporary Western city, there has been a more or less constant process of change. The capitalist city in the nineteenth and twentieth centuries has seen the steady development of a central commercial area, typically surrounded by a 19th century and early 20th century industrial zone, and a sequence of housing types differentiated both by age, condition and social status.

Over time, city growth combined with a relatively free market in land and property, have resulted in the expansion of a commercial office and retailing core which has gradually displaced outwards residential and industrial uses as it has grown. In the great majority of cases the causes of this process have been the greater accessibility of the central area as a focus of transport routes, the premium placed on centrality and accessibility by commercial users and, crucially, their ability to outbid other potential users or pay more for scarce central sites on the basis of the greater turnover, sales or rents such users can command. Similarly, with the growth of public and, subsequently, private transport, the process of suburbanization of both population and, later, industry and retailing, have proceeded apace. Competition for land, and land-use and residential seg-

regation, have been equally marked in the suburbs but the most intense competition is commonly found in the central areas of cities. It is for this reason that we have concentrated our attention on land-use change in the central areas as they exhibit most clearly the competition for scarce sites and the associated process of displacement.

Lest it be thought that these changes occur of their own volition, the central area expanding and developing as a result of its own logic of growth, it should be clearly stated that this is not the case. The motor of land-use development and redevelopment in the West is, at root, that of private ownership and the drive to maximize profitability. Working through the instrument of the development industry, the process of land-use intensification and the greater profits such intensification brings, have brought about the changes we are so familiar with. An understanding of these processes is central to an understanding of city centre change. To imagine that they somehow occur of their own volition is to fall into the trap of reifying the pattern of land-use change as something which occurs in its own right. That it does not is clearly indicated by the relative absence of Western-style commercial development and land-use intensification in East European cities. There is no free market in land or property in such societies and no Western-style development industry geared up to profit maximization. The problem in the West is that whereas the land use outcomes are highly visible to the general public, the underlying development processes are not. There is therefore a tendency to remain, as it were, at the level of surface appearances, rather than trying to penetrate deeper.

The value of looking deeper into the development process is shown by the extract from chapter 14 of

Oliver Marriott's book *The Property Boom*, where he sets out much of the story behind the development of the Bull Ring shopping centre in Birmingham. A down-at-heel area only a few hundred yards from the hub of Birmingham's retail core, the redevelopment of the Bull Ring arose out of Birmingham's famous Inner Ring Scheme which though conceived pre-War was not started until 1957, largely as a result of a growth-oriented, prodevelopment council wishing to revamp the image of Birmingham. Initially, those parts of the land owned by the council or compulsorarily purchased by them and not needed for the road itself, were leased off to the developers. As Marriott shows, the role of city architects in promoting the Bull Ring scheme was crucial, the details being worked out in tandem between public and private enterprise. Eventually, at the end of 1959, when the site was offered to developers by public tender, Birmingham merely set out in general terms what they needed, leaving the developers to decide on the number of shops. As with the current scheme for the redevelopment of Snow Hill station (which is treated in the TV programme on city centre change associated with the course) the council were concerned to try to maximize the return offered by the developers in the form of annual ground rents.

Finished in late 1963, the Bull Ring faced considerable letting problems and the eventual commercial success of the scheme was dependent on a high-power marketing campaign combined with a reduction in initial rents as Marriott indicates. He also points to the not inconsiderable design defects of the scheme which is inconvenient for shoppers and visitors alike. This raises the question posed by Donald Gutstein in his polemical book *Vancouver Ltd*, of 'who is downtown for?'

As Gutstein indicates, the level of new development in Vancouver is adding a growing number of central office workers with the result of more congestion and pollution and a reduction of the spectacular views of mountain and sea. He asks whether downtown Vancouver is for the banks and national and multinational corporations who want a concentrated node of prestigious high-rise office towers to 'oversee the exploitation of British Columbia's natural resources' or whether it is for Vancouver's citizens who want 'an open, pleasant, liveable downtown full of activity and public amenities'. The answer according to Gutstein, is all too evident, in that the multinational corporations have designated Vancouver as an administrative centre for the Pacific Basin trading block. In consequence, there

will be 'a growing demand for prestige office space'. This is undoubtedly correct, and whilst it is possible to disagree with Gutstein's view that there is no congruence of interest whatsoever between Vancouver's residents and the developers and corporate interests, he is also correct that 'Developers will build wherever the potential profit is greatest'. In consequence whilst there is a periodic over-production and surplus of office space, there is an enormous demand for scarce low- and moderate-income housing, the income–housing cost relationship being such as to render its production unprofitable.

Gutstein's article provides an insight into the commercial development process itself, its financial basis and returns, the limited power of planning to do anything but work with and seek to guide or channel the development pressures, and the limited ability of the general public to influence the process.

A number of these issues are hinted at or mentioned in passing in Hardwick's more comprehensive paper *Downtown Vancouver: One Hundred Years of Change*. As well as outlining the role of downtown, its development and structure, Hardwick mentions the role of the Canadian Pacific Railway in the early promotion of the downtown area which it owned, and the subsequent plans of Marathon Realty for the old goods yards adjacent to the downtown area. In touching on the renaissance of the historic Gas Town area, the core of the initial settlement, Hardwick hints at the role of functional change and the profits to be derived from this process and the subsequent land-use intensification. The same point emerges from the discussion of the projected Project 200 waterfront development. Hardwick also discusses the use of TEAM (The Electors' Action Movement) as a response to the 'big is beautiful' development policy. Opinions vary as to the success of TEAM and the extent to which the changes they effected were merely cosmetic. What is clear is that in a market economy it is remarkably difficult without considerable determination and strong legal powers to fundamentally change the pattern of land-use development and change. Even then, the lack of positive control over the pattern of investment renders planning problematic.

As Z Gorka's brief descriptive article indicates, the structure of the old medieval centre of Cracow is very different. The land-use structure is atypical, even for East European countries, in that the city centre has remained basically unchanged for several hundred years. A new city centre was planned in the area between the existing centre and the railway station but it is now uncertain whether this will proceed. Meanwhile the process of state initiated and funded rehabilitation of old buildings proceeds apace (as the TV programme associated with the course shows) with the linked aim of expanding the service component on the first and higher floors of buildings, reducing the residential component and the overall residential population. Whether this has resulted from high land values, as Gorka suggests, is questionable though it is certain that the centrality and accessibility of the old city have played a contributory role as has its important tourist function.

The old medieval core of Cracow is, of course, merely the oldest and most central of several zones within Cracow. This is a common pattern as F E Ian Hamilton shows in the extract from *The Socialist City*. The old core is commonly surrounded by a 19th century zone and post-World War II socialist housing developments which differ significantly from the pre-socialist areas. Though subject to socialization, these areas still pose a pre-socialist legacy which is difficult to change radically. The growth of post-War areas has however greatly altered the nature of the physical pattern of settlement facility provision and social differentiation. As Hamilton points out, the displacement of routine functions from the old city centre in Cracow and elsewhere, in favour of more specialist tourist functions, is the result of deliberate planning policy. So the densely populated 19th century inner zones, which Hamilton terms the relict capitalist city, have been subjected to considerable change, even though some are still awaiting the realization of comprehensive long-term plans. Hamilton states that the 1970s saw the resurgence of a desire to create new socialist city centres, as urbanization, population growth, and rising living standards 'stretched the capacities' of the inherited physical fabric to supply even existing needs. 'Sustained economic growth in all socialist countries is generating more resources for urban renewal,' says Hamilton, but although Cracow fits this ideal type model he outlines, recent events in Poland must cast grave doubts on the availability of new resources for such purposes.

Taking an overview, all the articles referred to serve to highlight the constant process of urban land-use change and the tendency towards land-use intensification. Obviously, this process is far more marked in Western societies where a free market in land and property obtains, but it would seem that even in socialist economies the attractions of centrality and accessibility are still such as to encourage planners to seek to introduce more 'central area' type land-uses. Unlike in the West however, these are not usually major office and retail developments but, instead, cultural and tourist-oriented service facilities. It would thus appear that whilst there is a common tendency toward land-use intensification, these tendencies result from different bases and produce very different outcomes.

Chris Hamnett

13 Troubles at the Bull Ring and the Elephant and Castle

by O Marriott

Two major and uncomfortably visible blunders, born of over-confidence, helped to cool the optimism generated by the property world as the boom faded away in the 1960s. As the plans were unveiled to the public in 1960, the shopping centres to be built at the Elephant and Castle in south London and at the Bull Ring in Birmingham were seen as the first two examples of a revolutionary concept: a large number of shops — 140 at the Bull Ring and 120 at the Elephant — all under one roof and on different levels. Here was a chance for property developers to show their sophistication.

As they grew 113 miles apart — publicists on each side preparing to claim that theirs was the biggest self-contained shopping centre in Europe — both projects had a remarkable amount in common. Each was essentially a by-product of a road traffic plan, each was leased after a competition by the local authority to a developer, and each was initiated, quite by coincidence, in the same month, September 1959. In both cases, partly in order to cram a sufficient number of shops on the site to justify the ground rent offered by their clients, the architects designed the hybrid buildings on several levels, with a curtain-walled, rectangular office block perched on top. But the Bull Ring, which cost £5½ million to build compared with the £2¼ million for the Elephant, was a much more complicated affair, housing Birmingham's central bus station, a car park for 550 cars, a ballroom and a large retail market of stalls operated by the Corporation.

As their births fade into the distance, these two shopping centres provide some object lessons in how not to plan.

With something of the same character as the Elephant, the Bull Ring before reconstruction was a traditional cheap and vigorous mixture of barrow boys and shops, the most celebrated of old Birmingham's street markets. But it was less of a self-contained concentration than the pre-war Elephant, for it was adjacent to the glamorous national retailers and department stores of High Street, New Street, and Corporation Street, the equivalent of London's Oxford and Regent Streets. Separated by a few hundred yards from those increasingly prosperous streets, the Bull Ring varied the conformity of the multiples' neon with a welcome down-at-heel hubbub.

The redevelopment of this area sprang as a side-issue from the Birmingham Corporation's £27 million Inner Ring Road, encircling the heart of Birmingham. This plan was conceived between the wars by Sir Herbert Manzoni, city engineer of Birmingham from 1935 to 1963. Although it had several features which ran directly counter to the modern theory of planning, the ring road was pushed ahead by the buccaneering, hard-headed officials and councillors of Birmingham and was begun in 1957. One business-like aspect of the plan was to lease off to developers all spare slivers of land which had been compulsorily acquired for the road.

Frank Price, then chairman of the Public Works Committee, later Lord Mayor of Birmingham as well as a director of Walter Flack's Murrayfield Real Estate, has recalled in an article the beginning of this policy: 'Once we had started on the physical work of the road I saw quite clearly that if our vision of the New Birmingham was to take shape it was essential to make it as commercially successful as possible.'

The first section of the road to be built, Smallbrook Ringway, was lined with offices and shops on one side, and on the other with offices, shops and the most luxurious hotel to be built at the time outside London,

Source: Oliver Marriott 1969 *The Property Boom* (London: Pan Books) Ch. 14. Reprinted by permission of A D Peters & Co. Ltd.

the Albany run by Lyons, the tea-shop people. But one comfort which the Albany lacked was quiet. The roar of traffic from its location beside a three-lane dual carriageway was overpowering and soon after the hotel was first occupied the builders had to move back in to fit the windows with double glazing.

For Birmingham Corporation, though, the policy of reducing the cost of the road by selling off leases on the roadside land was amply justified in financial terms. After initial hesitation, since this was not an established place for either shops or offices, a combination of the Birmingham architect Jim Roberts, a property developer, Jo Godfrey of Property & General Developments, and a firm of contractors-cum-developers, John Laing, tackled the first site on the south of the Ringway. Frank Price said that 'after the publicity given to this scheme investors came pouring in'.

Jo Godfrey continued the good work for Birmingham's coffers and his own company's finances alongside the ring road with more office buildings designed by Jim Roberts. Their last and most revolutionary building for Birmingham was the slick, 21-storey circular tower of offices, the Rotunda, which was slow to let as the famine of offices turned to glut but was a proud landmark for Birmingham and for Roberts, who set up his thriving practice on the highest two floors.

Meanwhile, at much the same time in 1958–59 as Godfrey and Roberts were planning the Rotunda, they were also negotiating with Birmingham for an even more ambitious project across the ring road from the Rotunda on the Bull Ring site. The ideas of Roberts fitted in well with those of the city's architect, the scheme for a vast centre of shops and market stalls was publicly discussed and published in the architectural magazines, and the details worked out in tandem between public and private enterprise. But then a great wrangle began over what price Godfrey should pay for the site. After months of haggling there was an impasse. Godfrey was prepared to offer only £50 000 a year in ground rent. Birmingham wanted £75 000 a year.

Eventually Birmingham decided to offer the site to developers by public tender and the brief to competitors was published on 11 September 1959. Unlike the LCC, Birmingham's officials did not lay down in their brief the details of the volume of shops to be built. They just set out in general terms what was needed: car park, bus station, market stalls, shops, and so on. The vital decision on the number of shops was left for the developers to decide. Since Birmingham, like the LCC,

had not done any serious research on the potential of the Bull Ring site as a shopping centre, it was wise to leave the decision to somebody else.

Developers were given three months in which to submit their plans; by American standards this was about half the normal time needed to make a trustworthy analysis for such a major project. One important feature of the winning scheme — to have it entirely covered over — was thought up only ten days before the closing date for entries. Laing, partner with the frustrated Mr Godfrey just down the road, won with a ground rent of £109 000 a year. Godfrey, for all his earlier deadlock with the Corporation, did compete and offered £80 000 a year for a somewhat enlarged version of his original plan. There were eleven competitors in all, less than a third of the number at the Elephant, although the Bull Ring's site had greater natural advantages, but developers were strongly oriented towards London. Both the LCC and Birmingham's officials, when they announced the result of the competition, were insistent that they had chosen the winner for its architectural and planning qualities combined with the financial offer, and that they had not just taken the highest bid, though they did not disclose what the higher offers were.

The Bull Ring was finished in late 1963, a year and a half earlier than the Elephant. It was a pioneer of its species. Any pioneer in business, be it in nylon or commercial television, faces a tough struggle to make a new product acceptable. But Maurice Robson, a manager as opposed to an entrepreneur, who headed Laing's property development side, was lumbered with an extra difficulty in trying to sell the Bull Ring to his customers, the retailers. It was an exceedingly complicated product. Moreover, Laing had jumped into this heavy £5½ million commitment largely on the strength of the developer's intuition, the acknowledged formula at that heady stage in the property boom and with insufficient research into the possible needs of the site or the possible reaction of the population to the new building.

From the outside the Bull Ring is an untidy jumble of a building. Apart from a magnificent, virile bronze bull, designed by Trewin Copplestone, and hoisted high on the end walls, it is hard to decipher the purpose of the sprawling structure. It says almost nothing to the passer-by. Undoubtedly the architects, Sydney Greenwood and Laing's staff architect, T J Hirst, within the limitations of Birmingham Corporation's brief, were faced with a great difficulty in relating so many uses on a small site and attempting to produce a cohesive whole. Car park, office block, one of the biggest Woolworths in the country, market stalls, rows of shops and a bus station, all have been thrown together into one heavy lump. Inside, this multiplicity of uses is also a great problem and again has been unsatisfactorily solved. The shopper is faced with the choice of no less than five different layers of shops.

To walk around the Bull Ring gives the impression that a highly sophisticated designer with a Meccano set, tied down to a restrictive brief, was the originator of the structure. There was a more natural reason for the five levels at the Bull Ring than the three at the Elephant: the ground fell by 50 feet from one side of the site to the other, whereas it was flat at the Elephant. But the Bull Ring's complexity gave the developers a severe headache.

Maurice Robson and his manager at the Bull Ring, Adam Hepburn, gave an unusually frank talk about the problems to the Chartered Surveyors in February 1965. Maurice Robson told the surveyors: 'At the very outset, our early publicity attracted a large number of tenants ready and willing to take accommodation. But after eighteen months or so had elapsed and construction work was under way they found it more and more difficult to understand how they could possibly carry on their business in such an apparently complicated maze of different levels. One or two began to fall out and, as so often happens in these cases, the rot began to set in, until we found ourselves, early in 1963, with a huge shopping centre which we knew would soon be involving us in outgoings approaching £500 000 a year, and pretty well devoid of tenants.

'Even worse than this, the drums were beating and the jungle telegraph had it that the scheme was doomed to failure . . .' Mr Robson had begun by saying that 'the RICS originally asked me to give this talk to you last winter, and I had to decline the invitation because at that time there was every prospect that the centre would be empty when the Duke of Edinburgh opened it in May of last year, and I had not the slightest desire to stand up here and talk to you about empty shops . . .'

It was at the point when the drums of the estate agents and retailers began to beat out the message of doom that Laing's experience and professionalism, greater than that of Willett at the Elephant, came into play. Robson saw that if the centre was open as planned in November 1963 with most of the shops unlet, the vicious circle of unlet shops, not enough shoppers and thus nobody willing to take the shops might turn his

£5½ million investment into a chronic white elephant. If the shops could be let before opening day, even at lower rents than would give Laing a profit in the early years, it would at least give the centre a chance.

So in the spring of 1963 Robson decided to put off the opening from November until the following May of 1964. This was not good for the morale of those who had already leased shops. Laing also added to the two firms originally hired as letting agents, John D Wood in London and Cheshire Gibson in Birmingham, both rather inexperienced at letting shops on a national scale, a third, with much more specialized skill, Edward Erdman. At the same time the campaign to let the shops was stopped. It was to be started up again with a high-powered thrust when building was finished in the autumn and 'the maze of internal scaffolding and paraphernalia' was out of the way so that prospective tenants could see their way around. But before the campaign was re-opened Robson personally asked some of the biggest retailers in the country to take space on concessionary terms in one or two key spots in the project in order to act as a magnet to pull in other traders. His great coup here was to persuade John Collier, the self-made millionaire head of the £120 million United Drapery Stores, to take a large slice of the shops at the pivot of the Grand Parade.

Robson's gamble on delay was a winner. It saved Laing from what could have been an outright disaster. By May 1964, after some tense months of hard work, around 85% of the shops were let. But the rents had had to be lowered sharply. Barratts the shoe people ('Walk the Barratt Way') took a shop, 38 feet wide by 67 feet deep, in the first letting campaign at £9 500 a year, rising to £10 500 at the seventh year and £11 250 from the fourteenth to the twenty-first year. Stylo Shoes leased a shop in a similar position almost exactly opposite Barratts which was the same width but only 37 feet deep. This difference in depth might normally give a 50% lower rent. But Stylo arranged its lease in the hard push of the second campaign and its lease was at £4 000 for the first seven years and £4 500 for the remaining fourteen. Instead of 50%, Barratt was paying between 137 and 150% more.

All the leases varied much more than is normal with a clutch of new shops, depending on how hard a bargain the particular retailer or his agent could strike. Most of them knew that Laing was desperate to have the centre let by opening day. A handful of traders leased their shops on percentage rents. The percentage rent is common in North America, but virtually unknown in

Britain. The retailer pays a low basic rent, and a determined proportion of his turnover after it tops a certain level. It has not caught on largely because it is more difficult for a developer to finance a project neatly under British methods, and because retailers who have operated through almost incessant inflation have preferred to have fixed rents as far as possible. But in their time of trouble Laing tempted a few traders in this way by offering extremely low basic rents to compensate for the uncertain prospects at the Bull Ring. John Collier the tailors and Richard (dress) Shops, both in the United Drapery group, took percentage rents. This type of lease has subsequently proved popular at the Bull Ring and all new lettings are on this principle.

The shopping public of Birmingham did not flock to the Bull Ring. It responded slowly. To start with there were private cries of woe among the traders at the relative dearth of shoppers, though there was a fair turnout on Saturdays. But in the second year trade was 30 to 40% up, that is, '30 or 40% up from damn all', as one trader put it. And on Saturdays there was a huge, swirling crowd before very long. This, however, showed one of the deficiencies in design. On a Saturday afternoon when the crowd was at its thickest, the escalators carrying shoppers between levels could not cope with the numbers, even though the capacity to serve customers in the shops was not yet stretched as it should be at the peak of the week. Laing has been altering the escalators. In any event shops cannot do well on little more than one reasonably good trading day a week.

What were the snags at the Bull Ring? Laing had one big excuse, which was that the link into New Street Station could not be joined through the long delays by British Rail in its complete rebuilding as Birmingham's one passenger station by a consortium of three developers. Once this was built, Laing claimed, the flow of pedestrians would be much increased and properly balanced.

The two main faults at the Bull Ring seem to me that it was too big for its location and that it was poorly designed. Both these drawbacks could have been lessened if not avoided by greater care and research at the planning stage. One of the more ominous patterns to emerge in the early days of the Bull Ring was the flow of pedestrians out of the bus stations, into the Corporation's bustling retail market on the same ground floor level, out past the open-air stalls and sweeping round under the subway into the traditional centre of Birmingham. This suggested two things. First, that the selection of shops in the Bull Ring did not satisfy any needs which the existing main streets did not already meet. Secondly, that the environment in the centre, for all its absence of traffic, its air-conditioning and canned music, did not have any particular appeal to shoppers.

The Bull Ring was more ingenious than the Elephant, it was more professionally handled, but the disfiguring birthmark with which each started life was that they were in the wrong place. These decisions of location were taken by the local authorities and accepted by over-enthusiastic developers. The Bull Ring was either too near the centre of Birmingham or too far from it: if, instead of being 200 yards or so away, it had been sited cheek by jowl with established central pitches of the department stores and other big-time shops or perhaps in the middle of a city block surrounded by such shops, then it might have reaped more of the overspill quite naturally from the shoppers who converged on the centre from all over the vast sprawl of Birmingham, not just from the direction of the Bull Ring. If on the other hand, it had been 2 to 3 miles out from the centre in some prosperous but poorly served suburb, it might possibly have attracted all the normal variety of the High Street and acted as a counter-pull for those who were unwilling to brave the traffic of the city's centre. This would have been a great risk.

The whole concept of the Bull Ring, far from everyday experience, was difficult for the shopper to accept. Its atmosphere was unnatural. Whereas the Elephant has a sliding roof which can let in some daylight on fine days, the Bull Ring is totally enclosed. With its simple paved stone flooring the Elephant's arcades echoed the normal clatter of heels; at the Bull Ring the floors were of black rubber tiling, which absorbed the noise and could give an eerie feeling of unreality. With the several levels of shops, the atmosphere tended to be that of a giant, claustrophobic palace of multiple retailers, a far cry from the regularity of the High Street or the intimacy of the department store. A disenchanted local politician, Councillor Beaumont Dark, spoke in angry exaggeration in 1965: 'The Bull Ring is perfectly all right if one wants an army fortification within the city centre. As a trading area it is at present a flop.' He called it the biggest white elephant in the history of Birmingham.

But the general consensus in Birmingham of that level of opinion which interests itself in civic prides was to brandish the Bull Ring as an example of the Second City's progress. Phrases such as 'Europe's most advanced shopping centre' and 'internationally famous' fitted neatly into dignified speeches. For the daring promoter of the novelty the pleasure of pioneering was two-edged. Winning the competition put Laing firmly on the map alongside the big-time shop developers, next to Ravenseft and Hammersons, Sam Chippindale and Barry East and Walter Flack. But as the flaws in the project became clear to the property world Laing's reputation was somewhat tarnished. It was also an extremely expensive affair for Laing. Just how expensive is obscure. At the Bull Ring the money was put up on sale and leaseback by Pension Fund Securities, the alias for Imperial Chemical Industries' pension fund. This method of financing makes it impossible for the researcher to build up a rough financial picture of the project, in the way that it is possible, for instance, with the empire of Harry Hyams. However, Laing was clearly in the red at the Bull Ring, probably deeper in the red than Willett at the Elephant. My estimate suggests that the loss was between £50 000 and £100 000 a year for at least the first five years.

14   **Who is Downtown for?**

by D Gutstein

You cannot go downtown in Vancouver these days without seeing at least five high-rise office buildings under construction. When completed, each one will add another 3000 to 4000 office workers to the downtown daytime population; it will add to the growing congestion and pollution in the downtown peninsula; it will further destroy the natural amenities of view and sunlight; it will further contribute to the monotony and anonymity of the architecture; it will produce another barren windswept plaza; it will point out clearly the lack of public open space, the lack of civic focus, the concentration on private high-cost luxury development at the expense of the ordinary citizen.

Just who is downtown for anyway?

Is it for the banks and the national and multinational corporations who want a concentrated node of prestigious high-rise office towers to oversee the exploitation of British Columbia's natural resources? Or is it for Vancouver's citizens who want an open, pleasant, livable downtown full of activity and public amenities?

The answer is all too evident. The multinational corporations have designated Vancouver as an administrative centre for the Pacific Basin trading-block — Japan, the USA, south-east Asia, Latin America and Canada. Trade among these countries is destined to grow enormously; consequently there will be a growing demand for prestige office space to house the headquarters of the companies engaged in Pacific Basin trade, along with the bankers, trust and insurance companies, investment dealers, law firms, chartered accountants, engineering and architectural firms — all of those organizations that serve the large corporations.

The corporate planners are well prepared for the coming boom. Most of the major banks have already established regional and international headquarters in the downtown core of Vancouver. Many of the larger national and international real estate companies have descended on Vancouver in anticipation of the coming building boom.

This flood of office buildings is shocking compared to the meagre amount of moderate-income housing being provided by those same developers, even though there is an enormous demand for such accommodation. But office buildings are much more profitable, even if half-empty, so that developers will continue to build those and ignore our housing needs.

Developers will build wherever the profit potential is greatest. In large downtown commerical developments there are no ungrateful tenants organizing rent strikes, there are no militant citizens' groups opposing the assembly of land and the destruction of the existing buildings, there are no rent freezes being imposed by a hostile provincial government. There are only stable, predictable corporate tenants who like to cluster together in prestigious surroundings and who don't mind high rents because they can pass on the cost to the clients or customers.

Developers cannot build what the money men — the banks, trust and insurance companies — will not fund. Large commercial developments such as the $50 million Royal Centre, and large developers such as the $600 million Trizec Corporation, are much more attractive to the financial sources than small home-builders and single-family homes. For one thing large commercial mortgages are a more secure investment than a small mortgage on a single-family house. For another, one large $50 million mortgage is much cheaper to service for the bank than 1000 mortgages for $50 000 each. Finally, the financiers can take an ownership position in the development, and hence share in the profits and appreciation of the land, as well as receive the interest payments on the mortgage. One example was the Great West Life Assurance Company's involvement in the Bentall Centre. Consequently, a company like Trizec has a much easier time

Source: Donald Gutstein 1975 *Vancouver Ltd* (Toronto: James Lorimer) pp20–4.

getting $50 million for a downtown high-rise than you or I have in getting $50 000 for a house.

Each new downtown high-rise development increases the land values in the surrounding blocks, and since property owners like to see their property increase in value, they are all for more high-rises. Over the past eight years land values in the downtown core have increased at a compound rate of 20% per year. Therefore, owners of downtown property can only applaud whenever a new high-rise building is announced.

Even the utility companies — B C Hydro and Power Authority (a publicly owned company) and BC Telephone Co. (a privately owned company) — like to see high-density, high-rise buildings, because their operating expenses are reduced substantially compared to the servicing of more spread out residential property; consequently, their profits are increased.

Once a developer has assembled property for a development, he has to line up a major tenant before he can finalize the financing. In many cases, the financing institution itself can become the major tenant; in others, companies associated with the developer take space in the building. In still others, the federal and provincial governments, using public funds, lease space in private developments; this enhances the value of private property, increases the pressure for more downtown high-rise blocks and plays its part in the increasing downtown congestion and the deterioration of the urban environment.

If the past actions of city council are any indication, the developers and multinational corporations will continue to set our building priorities. It seems that developers make their plans to suit their own corporate needs. The city council then comes out with policies that turn out to be remarkably similar to what the developers wanted in the first place.

Schemes such as The Electors' Action Movement (TEAM)-inspired Granville Mall seem like attempts to divert public attention from the harsh reality of downtown — that the developers own it. In spite of such efforts, developers carry on much the same as before TEAM. The only difference between the TEAM-dominated city council and the Non-Partisan Association (NPA) city council that preceded it, is that NPA gave the developers *even more than* they wanted, whereas TEAM gives them *slightly less than* they ask for.

Over the years, the city planning department has made a great show of planning for downtown. Numerous reports have been produced. But the assumption of continued and increasing growth was never questioned seriously. The city planning department busied itself with the details — a few more buildings here, a few less there, a little taller, a little shorter, but the basic question was never asked: what do the people of Vancouver want from their downtown?

At least it was never asked of the vast majority of the public. The only groups involved in the process of determining what downtown should be were the usual business and professional groups and a few ratepayer groups from the more affluent parts of the city.

Few people actually live in the downtown core, so it is a relatively easy matter for developers to assemble property, to get the development permits, to get relaxations of the zoning by-law to permit denser developments, to tear down the buildings that were there before without a big public outcry, and to get the building up with a minimum of delay.

By the time the public does find out about the development, it is far too late to do anything about it. The decisions have been made, probably years before, in the corporate boardrooms of Tokyo or New York, that have led to the destruction of fine old downtown buildings and their replacement by the sleek, shiny towers that continue to dominate the downtown core.

Business interests and city politicians keep telling us how necessary all this development is for our own good, but there is one question that we should keep in mind at all times: *what does downtown development cost us?* Will all the proposed developments generate enough tax revenues to pay for the required public services and amenities that have become necessary because of the new developments? The roads, rapid transit and buses, the sewers, sidewalks, and fire protection, the parks and open spaces? Or will the home owner through his taxes and the tenant through his rent have to foot the bill and subsidize the big out-of-town developers?

In spite of what city council tells us — that the big downtown developments are paying their own way — the answer is not all that clear. A study done in San Francisco showed that it cost more to run the downtown than the downtown brought in revenues: downtown contributed $62.9 million in local revenues, but cost $67.7 million to run. Does the same hold true for Vancouver? Are the ordinary taxpayers and tenants bailing out the developers? Vancouver has never conducted the comprehensive research which would provide the answer to this question. If taxpayers are subsidizing this redevelopment, the situation is indeed appalling. Not only do the large multinational corporations have almost *carte blanche* to come in and develop downtown as they wish while continuing to destroy Vancouver's natural amenities, but the people of Vancouver are subsidizing them to do it.

There is a hierarchy of decision-making affecting downtown development. At the top level, the large multinational corporations are making broad overall policy decisions about the growth of the Pacific Basin and national trade and commerce. The consequences of these decisions are felt in Canada through the chartered banks who provide the necessary funds and who are the centres of power in the country.

Control flows through the banks, via the local directors of the banks, into the local business establishment. From the local business establishment the decision-making chain leads into the local political structure — the federal Liberals, the provincial Liberals and Social Credit, and the municipal parties, the Non-Partisan Association and The Electors' Action Movement.

Table 14.1   Downtown Vancouver's decision-making hierarchy.

Multinational
corporations
↓
Canadian
chartered banks
↓
Local bank
directors
↓
Local business
establishment
(corporations — law firms — old families — clubs)
↓
Local political
parties
(Liberals — Socreds — TEAM – NPA)
↓
Developers — planners — architects

15 Downtown Vancouver: One Hundred Years of Change

by W Hardwick

The role and form of downtown Vancouver is currently a central topic for public debate and discussion. Office towers are mushrooming and now represent the largest percentage of floor area and employment, whereas industry and retailing are in actual or relative decline. This is in direct contrast to conditions as recent as a decade ago when retailing, wholesaling, and industry were of relatively equal importance as propellants of the core.

For over 80 years, the downtown core had the largest proportion of retailing, business, entertainment, hotels and services in the metropolitan area, and the point of greatest pedestrian and vehicular traffic. Traditionally, the core had also had the highest land values in the city and had contributed handsomely to the city's tax revenue. For many, the core had been the place that contained the essence of urban life. Downtown expressed the prosperity and character of the city and its citizens.

In the past 20 years, this picture of the dominant downtown has been undergoing radical change and, in the process, confidence in the future of the city has been undermined. This is part of a fundamental re-arrangement of activities going on within most North American cities reflecting new technological, social, and economic situations. It is, however, a *selected* change. Some activities are decentralizing while others remain centralized and prosper.

Like many western cities in North America, Vancouver was originally part of the westward extension to the eastern manufacturing systems. The city and its region were seen as a market for processed goods and as a source of raw materials. Thus it is not surprising that the incipient city was blessed with a few hundred thousand square feet of warehouses for storing and distributing goods imported from the industrial heartlands. The merchant wholesalers served the logging and fishing camps, placed stores on ships, and supplied the retailers on main shopping streets. In these capacities, Vancouver was like hundreds of towns west of the Great Lakes and Mississippi Valley. The sawmills and timber-processing facilities differed in product and form from the grain elevators of the plains, but in function (supply of raw materials), *vis à vis* the east, they were similar. Nineteenth-century Vancouver was a city within which decisions were made more often on the affairs of Main Street than on the regional or national levels. The city was not a seat of power.

This description contrasts with the emerging regional capital of the 1970s, where office buildings housing thousands of servants of decision-makers made up the largest number of workers downtown. In a sense the city and its core has shifted from colonial status to regional dominance. In the process the city of the marketplace is being replaced by the city of 'power', a historic *raison d'être* of cities. But rather than the palace and cathedral being the symbol of 'power', the corporate high-rise is the new icon.

The transformation of the city from a mill and warehouse to a financial and management centre has not been without stress. Much of the conflict about the role and direction for Vancouver in the 1960s was between spokesmen for the old order and the new — those cultivating an industrial and merchant city and those cultivating 'the executive city'. Here the contrasting models of various groups interact in a very concrete way. As in so many cases, though, just at a time when one view — 'the industrial city' — is giving way to another — 'the executive city' — still another becomes identified — 'the post-industrial city'.

Source: W Hardwick 1974 *Vancouver* (Vancouver: Collier-Macmillan) Ch. 3, pp 43–62.

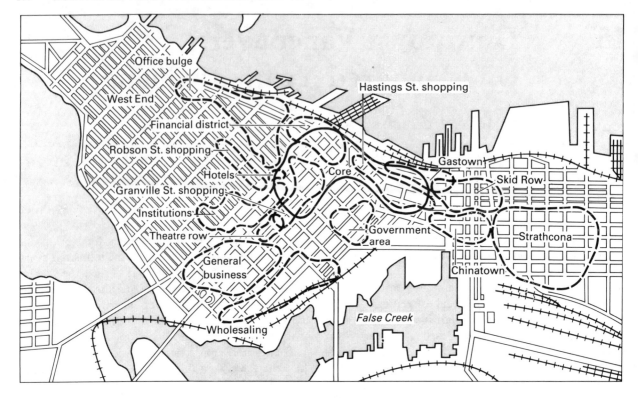

Figure 15.1   Downtown Vancouver: functional areas, 1972.

The persistence of the core, 1920–50

Much of the apprehension about the future of Vancouver's downtown in the 1960s stemmed from experiences of cities in the United States and the preoccupation of planners and consultants with conditions in those cities.

But in Vancouver, citizens were not dealing with an old city of the industrial belt of the eastern United States — with congestion, depressed industries, and large minorities. Although concentrations of various ethnic groups in the older residential areas adjacent to parts of downtown do exist in Vancouver, minority groups have not become the majority of the inner-city population nor in recent decades have they become a focus of conflict.

Despite the points of similarity between Vancouver and the various cities that have been studied in the United States, the trends of deterioration, giving so much concern there, are by no means as pronounced or advanced in Vancouver. Opportunities for the creation of a healthy urban core environment still exist in Vancouver, given proper recognition by public, government, and business interests of the nature of change

and a restatement of the goals of many people within the city.

The major elements of downtown landscape were in place by the end of the 1920s. During this decade office buildings had been constructed along Hastings and Howe Streets. The Granville Street area became fleshed out with the opening of the 'photoplay' theatres, new hotels and shops. The downtown area expanded, but its central focus in the region remained.

The severity of the depression in Canada, the longer war period as compared with the United States, and an extended sellers' market in Canada after World War II each contributed to holding down investment in suburban facilities until a decade or more after they had become the dominant characteristic of urban change in the United States. All of this, needless to say, served to preserve core dominance well into the post-war years.

Some signs, however, of the weakening attractiveness of the core had been evident in the 1930s, indicating that the advantages assumed to depend primarily on centrality were beginning to be shared by places other than downtown. The opportunities for individual mobility conferred by the private automobile was one such sign, but other indicators, such as the advent of the supermarket, were slow to have an impact on Vancouver.

Vancouver became the site of a vast new urban expansion after World War II. By that date, disposable income within the city had grown and demand for land for residential accommodation was rising. In addition, thousands of people who had involuntarily postponed settling into long-term occupations returned from the war and moved into Vancouver, which in the post-war years played, in Canada, the role played by Los Angeles in the United States, so far as the westward population shift was concerned.

It was during and following this post-war transition that the real impact of auto-mobility and suburban servicing of residents began to be felt in Vancouver, more than a decade after these catalysts of change had been demonstrated in the United States and their influences, real and inferred, had been built into the urban model that dominated academic and planning thought throughout the post-war years.

Manufacturing and wholesaling responded to those changed conditions, and a pronounced decentralization of these activities took place in the 1950s and 1960s. However, the total impact of this decentralization on the core was only nominal because of expansion in the managerial–administrative sectors located downtown.

The inner belt of older residential districts, on the margin of the downtown core, received much of the development thrust that was a corollary of provincial economic growth. There, homes of frame construction had by and large outlived their usefulness as residential accommodation, and, row after row, they were razed to provide open parking areas for the increasing number of commuters working in the new office buildings downtown.

Between 1945 and 1958, office accommodation had expanded westward from the old core, impinging on one of the older inner residential districts. The parking lots provided easy access to core areas and new residences added to an inner-city retail trade area.

The challenge to the core: the 1950s

By the mid-1950s, however, there was a retardation of the rate of national economic growth. In those years few new office buildings were built, and erosion of wholesaling and manufacturing employment followed as marginal sawmills were forced to close. In addition,

the kind of industrial, warehousing and storage facilities characteristic of Vancouver — that is, the six-storey building — became less competitive as modern facilities were built in suburban Burnaby and Richmond.

Over the same period of time that these changes were making themselves felt, an expansion of suburban retail facilities took place, most noticeably with development of major regional shopping centres — Park Royal, Oakridge and Brentwood, two of which were within three miles of the core itself. These developments were the final signal, as it were, of the change from sellers' to buyers' market in foodstuffs and general merchandise, and were in part evidence of recognition of the coming of age of Vancouver's suburban structure.

The result of these and associated changes were the most serious readjustment to be felt in Vancouver in the 80 years of its existence. And it is fair to say that by 1960, Vancouver no longer had the advantages of traditional attributes of a downtown core as enshrined in the classical literature on cities. Ideas of centrality were no longer of prime importance to the retailer, at least no longer in a simple, general sense. Concepts of minimum aggregate travel, which had been invoked to explain high-priced land within the core, had begun to dissolve from the general to specific cases. Also, the idea of a single focus of high real estate value for an entire metropolitan region was no longer appropriate.

Nevertheless, downtown Vancouver maintained advantages of maximizing face-to-face contact, principally among businessmen, especially in those years when expansion of business was slow and demand for new facilities was minimal.

Public policy reaction

This period of adjustment in the mid-1950s brought about a rise in political interest in the downtown and generated a number of proposals calling for major public intervention to stimulate its growth. Among the proposals put forward were: a major radial freeway system in order to capture the mobile populations of the suburbs; a large-scale, publicly subsidized Downtown Parking Corporation and the upgrading of existing street capacity to accommodate the captives; and the intervention of the city in land assembly for public and private urban renewal, to make more attractive and viable the focus of all this effort.

In brief, these interventions and proposals were

made by and through a civic government which believed that its most important goal was to rejuvenate the core along the development lines essentially reflecting concepts appropriate to the 1920s. Little of this, however, was to happen because the political and business leaders did not understand the nature of changes taking place in the core, which leads us to consider the nature of these changes which occurred between 1960 and 1970.

The role of the core: post-industrialism

Many students of urbanism have taken up the theme of the post-industrial city. Implicit in widespread acceptance of this theme is the idea that city growth for the next few decades will be more dependent upon the expansion of activities within service and management sectors than on growth in the industrial sectors. The idea has its roots and draws support from demonstrable changes recorded through recent decades in the employment structure of the economy. An associated assumption is that as the general education level rises and as free time expands, the population will increasingly purchase experiences and services such as entertainment and travel rather than demand more and more industrial goods.

It is clear that an increasing proportion of our national wealth is being created outside of the production, distribution, and consumption of material goods. These include the 'extra-economic' activities that act as catalysts to the producer economy, plus those activities which provide experiences to a rapidly expanding number of people. Much of the recent growth of the labour force in cities has been outside of the primary–secondary sectors, as is illustrated in table 15.1 from a study of the Canadian economy.

Growth is in the quaternary service sector, especially in activities dealing with non-tangible matters such as

Table 15.1. Growth of labour force.

Labour force	Production (%)	Services (%)	Marketing sub-total (%)
1950 Canada	58	42	(26)
1964	45	55	(25)
1950 USA	46	55	(25)
1964	39	61	(24)

Source: Economic Council of Canada *Annual Report* 1970.

research and design, entertainment, and services. In other examples, experiences are being marketed — sports, restaurants and travel. Traditional notions of location do not fit much of this new activity; some rethinking is needed.

Athough quaternary industries have always been with us, their scale was comparatively small. In the contemporary city, they are now major land users. They are also pace-setters and they are contributing to new patterns of activity in urban areas.

The impact of the experience industries is not uniform across the country. Clearly, however, those places that are associated with travel and those with physical or man-made amenities are going to benefit. Vancouver is one place that cannot be denied advantages on both counts. The core is the focus for many of these activities; thus, the planning of the core must take these activities into account.

The change in mix of activities that employ people has a fundamental impact on the structure of cities, and Vancouver is no exception. The role of the downtown in the region is changing because it is no longer the location of the majority of jobs. Those jobs that stay downtown have special roles to play and take on a specialized character. The vision of downtown dominating a totally radial city, therefore, should be dead. The idea of downtown as a centre of power (economic and political) and the services to power it is real. It remains the primate centre in an increasingly dispersed urban region. Its continued viability depends upon an understanding of the processes of change in various activities.

The office-management function

The high-rise office building has replaced the factory and shop as the most frequent downtown workplace. The large buildings dominate the skyline in visual terms as well.

In the founding period around 1890, office activities were not a major propellant of downtown. Office and management functions related to industrial–commercial establishments tended to be located on the premises of the establishment itself. This is, of course, natural enough, in light of the comparatively small population of the founding decades. In 1891, 13 685 people were hardly enough to warrant or generate a large managerial establishment.

The city grew slowly in the 1890s. The depression of 1893–94 had a retarding influence which was not counteracted until the Klondike rush of 1897–98. Nonetheless, the major period of growth of the city did not begin until about 1905 when the city entered upon a spectacular period of growth, running through one of the largest real estate booms in the history of Canada, and coming to a rather painful close in the autumn of 1913.

All in all, growth in the city through much of the early decades was based more upon anticipation of a future, confidently awaited, than it was upon expansion in the industrial and resource sectors of the economy.

The booms

The decade of development, culminating in the 'bust' of 1913, had brought into Vancouver an established infrastructure for business which, however dormant it may have been throughout the early years, stood available as a foundation for later growth. Many administrative and business service-oriented operations had established themselves in the core. Also to be found downtown were various banking and financial services, some regional headquarter offices, shipping and insurance agencies, together with specialized locations for many of the major forest and mining interests.

Office construction responded to demand. The Holden Building, the Province Building and the Dominion Trust Building on Hastings Street were all constructed before 1911, with the latter building giving Vancouver (in 1908) the tallest building in the British Empire, a symbol to many of that day of the city's potential.

In the post-World War I years, several new office buildings were constructed and the financial district in the area of Hastings and Howe Streets became established. The opening of the Panama Canal brought markets in Europe and the north-eastern United States within the reach of the Vancouver industrial, commercial and shipping interests.

These events contributed to growth in industrial production and shipping. In these years, chartered banks from eastern Canada established regional branches in Vancouver, the stock exchange was established, and local capital was increasingly generated for the development of the city–provincial economy. As one 1927 report stated:

No other figures speak so conclusively of a city's business growth as the annual record of its bank clearings. As a matter of comparison, the bank clearings of 1882 were $8 414 923, while in 1926 the total had reached the sum of $888 704 118. [These figures are uncorrected – illustrative, but not comparable.]

The growth of office employment and employment in tertiary activities culminated with the construction of the Marine Building at Burrard and Hastings Streets, the home of the Merchants' Exchange. The construction of this building added its weight to Vancouver's significance as a major office and management centre.

When the crash came in 1929, Vancouver's downtown office facilities were found to be overbuilt, and financial problems from this source were added to the general environment of economic hardship. The situation in office capacity was similar to that existing in land at the time of the 1913 collapse of the real estate boom.

However, through the two boom periods of 1905–13 and 1921–29, Vancouver had established itself as western Canada's leading commercial–managerial centre, displacing Victoria's previous dominance and leaving the capital city little more than the title and the associated governmental activities.

In looking through the lists of companies that occupied Vancouver's major office centre in the 1920s, one is struck by the importance of shipping agents and the prevalence of forest industrial firms, together with the legal, financial and technical services supporting the forest and shipping industries. The picture is clearly one of a centre characterized by managerial functions pertinent to a port and a port city. In morphological terms, the commercial construction in the downtown gave Vancouver an impressive skyline, with many office buildings rising between 12 and 20 storeys in height. It is interesting to note in passing that, although several office buildings had been built on Granville Street in the vicinity of the Hudson's Bay department store and the Hotel Vancouver, that area did not really share in major managerial–financial activities. A review of the occupants of this area shows a high proportion of doctors, dentists and lawyers, servicing a general rather than a corporate market. There was then a distinct contrast between the functions of the office buildings located along Hastings Street and those of the Georgia–Granville area.

Between 1890 and 1920 the central business district's role critically shifted from being simply a merchant-dominated centre, emphasizing the retail and service functions, to being a regionally oriented centre of power, controlling a larger hinterland.

The culmination of the building boom of the 1920s coincided with the adoption of the Zoning By-law of 1931, the outcome of the Bartholomew Report; and the pattern of development up to that point in time had established very clearly in the minds of most people the principle that office building and management occupancy, together with retailing, were the dominant propellants of the city core.

During the ensuing years, spanning the depression of the 1930s and the war of the first half of the 1940s, no major office construction took place in the Vancouver core. In fact, during these years, several office complexes experienced financial hardships, and some changed hands with substantial losses to the sellers.

The post-war period

When additional office space was eventually needed in the post-war years, considerable surplus was available to meet the demand, and new construction was not given high priority. As a result, it was not until the early 1950s that new construction appeared at a scale sufficient to change the skyline of the city. The building entrepreneurs were actually several corporations who built partly in accordance with their general financial investment programmes, partly for reasons of status and prestige, and partly to provide sufficient space of appropriate design for their own operations. Examples include several oil companies that built along west Georgia Street, a number of forest companies such as the Pender Street offices of MacMillan-Bloedel and the Tahsis Company, and the two major utility companies, B C Electric Co. and B C Telephone Co., both of which were built outside of but adjacent to the major financial district. The only very large general commercial building built in this period was the Burrard Building, constructed by the Utah Construction Company interests, which were involved in the province's expanding mining activities in the 1950s.

This period of expansion in office construction followed a period of rapid increase in investment capital flowing into British Columbia, especially into the mining sector and into power development. It is symbolic that mining interests, oil interests, and the utility companies were so visible in the development of the new office construction in downtown Vancouver.

By the mid-1950s, a slowing of growth in business activity in the province led to the cessation of office construction, with the exception of the erection of the Bank of Canada's western head office building, built in response to a commitment of long standing. The Bank of Canada building, erected on Hastings Street, did much to secure the Hastings–Howe district as Vancouver's financial core. It also provoked protest from

office building owners who, suffering high vacancy levels, resented the entry of public money into this competitive field.

It was in this period that various public agencies and private interests became concerned with the role of downtown office buildings in protecting and favouring the city core, much as earlier concerns had been expressed regarding downtown commerce. It was in this period that initial plans were made for the redevelopment of some downtown areas in the hopes of promoting and stimulating economic growth. All of this followed well publicized suggestions of American urbanologists that growth in the 1960s was going to be rooted in the service industries, which was frequently interpreted to mean that the construction of office buildings would in some way have a generating effect on the economy.

Although the linkage multiplier between the regional economy and its urban structure is by no means understood even now, significant relationships must be sought between investment capital flowing into various regions of the province and central city development in Vancouver.

In the early 1960s, when the University of British Columbia Urban Core Project was in its initial stages, I made the following comment in a speech to the Downtown Businessmen's Association:

Who's staying downtown? Those functions which originally were the *raison d'être* of cities, institutions of power, wealth, and presige, financial headquarters, commerce, the stock exchange, and the auxiliary services to these. And further the rejuvenation of our downtown can only take place with the expansion of these major propellants of the urban core. This will require increases in the number and size of head and regional offices of financial concerns, trade organizations and related enterprises, which require and can afford the downtown location. These new firms will not be created by civic finance promotions of new office facilities on prime land.

The concluding reference in that speech was to the then proposed redevelopment, with considerable civic input, on two strategic blocks of land on the western side of the downtown core area, Block 42/52.

As in the past, when rapid expansion of capital investment takes place in British Columbia, it will be followed in a few months by new office construction in the core. The new buildings will follow demand in precisely the way most service-orientated investments are made.

At that time we had already noted a major upturn in capital investment in British Columbia, related largely to the various hydroelectric and water storage projects carried out by the British Columbia Hydro Authority and also to the expansions taking place in the forest and mining industries in the province.

I went on at that time to say that these prime movers of downtown attract a whole range of ancillary services, from accountancy firms all the way through a long list that includes janitorial firms and mobile coffee vendors. In short, downtown development in the office sector was tied to regional economic growth. These statements, made in 1963–64, have been proven correct by the continued expansion of office floor space in downtown Vancouver.

Growth in the 1970s

The latter years of the 1960s were boom years in terms of office construction, setting records for Vancouver in the numbers of building permits granted for downtown construction. The result has been a whole range of impressive buildings, including the Bentall Centre, the Guiness Tower, the Board of Trade Building, the Royal Centre, the Pacific Centre, as well as a number of less ambitiously conceived commercial buildings. The pace of growth in the late 1960s in office construction is outlined in table 15.2.

One of the questions raised by this rapid increase in office accommodation is: to what extent have businesses been located by the availability of accommodation, and influenced by the prestige quality inherent in much of the newly provided floor space, and so encouraged into mal-locations, possibly at rents higher than their true economic position would justify? Another question is: what is likely to be the result of an economic slowdown, if indeed an appreciable number of businesses have been induced away from sites better suited to their real needs, both in terms of location and rent?

There are a number of trends evident that may already be signalling some of the changes we might expect in the near future. First, for many head offices there has been a decentralization of those services which are not central in the management process. MacMillan-Bloedel is one such example. Research and development, for instance, can be separated from central management and located out of the core in a suburban location, where the rent is considerably lower. Divisions such as these are, of course, facilitated by the modern communications systems available to every corporation. Secondly, a number of office facilities, once centralized in the downtown area, are moving out to suburban locations along with their plants. This is especially noticeable in cases where the plants are large and new and, for reasons of production efficiency, desire to have the managerial function close to the production location. The Crown Zellerbach Canada Limited paperboard plant is an example. Thirdly, there has been a separation between what might be called the major western head/branch office function and the more local function within such enterprises as insurance companies and various other financial and business service companies. The more extensive service, in these cases, will be maintained in the downtown, while the locally oriented sales force, or service division, will be located outside the core, perhaps along West Broadway or in one of the suburban 'downtowns'. As in the private sector, public services are showing a trend to decentralization, for example, in civic health and welfare services. The forces of dispersion are beginning to influence the downtown area. The expansion of management functions has been a major centripetal force. However, the kind of public decisions on transportation and land use to be made in the 1970s will condition, if not control, the shape of long-term growth.

Table 15.2. Net rentable office space in downtown Vancouver, 1957–73.

Year	Total square feet	Square feet added
1957	5 700 000	
1958	5 980 000	270 000
1959	6 500 000	520 000
1960	6 550 000	47 000
1961	6 550 000	
1962[a]	6 550 000	
1963	6 625 000	71 000
1964	6 646 000	21 000
1965[b]	6 757 300	111 000
1966	6 873 500	116 200
1967	7 372 580	499 000
1968	7 475 980	103 400
1969	8 752 983	1 277 000
1970	8 922 983	170 000
1971	9 537 770	614 785
1972	9 711 600	173 840
1973[c]	11 224 050	1 326 550

[a]Period when William Rathie became Mayor.
[b]Initiation of the Urban Core Study at UBC with CCURR funding.
[c]In 1973–74, well over 500 000 square feet were under construction. Forecast for 1980 is some 15 000 000 square feet.

Source: City of Vancouver Department of Planning and Civic Development 1973 *Information and Statistics Report No. 9* (August) p21.

16 Spatial Structure in East European Cities

by F E I Hamilton

Towards a model East European city

The typical East European socialist city of today comprises several quite distinctive zones which may be portrayed in model form (figure 16.1). These zones are clearly evident in townscapes throughout the region, irrespective of city size or location. Nonetheless, in reality, the relative scale and importance of each zone does vary from city to city. When travelling out from the city centre one can observe the following zones: (1) the historic medieval or Renaissance core; (2) inner commercial, housing, and industrial areas from the capitalist period; (3) a zone of socialist transition or renewal, where modern construction is partially and progressively replacing inherited urban or relict-village features; (4) socialist housing of the 1950s; (5) integrated socialist neighbourhoods and residential districts of the 1960s and 1970s; (6) open or planted 'isolation belts'; (7) industrial or related zones; and (8) open countryside, forests or hills, including tourist complexes. Broadly speaking, outward expansion of city areas yields a concentric zonal pattern, successive stages of building being readily recognizable in architectural styles and skylines. This pattern tends to 'overlay' a more sectoral or 'wedge-like' distribution of functional zones associated with particular site qualities, historic traditions, and major transport arteries. Fundamentally distinct, however, are the pre-socialist inner and socialist outer urban areas.

The *inherited inner area* is a pre-socialist urban tract which has been subject to socialization, yet it retains some — even much — of its former spatial and functional structure, physical appearance, and marked inter-zonal differentiation. Within it patterns of social behaviour are predominantly centripetal as people

Source: R A French and F E I Hamilton (eds) 1979 *The Socialist City* (New York: Wiley) pp 227–44.

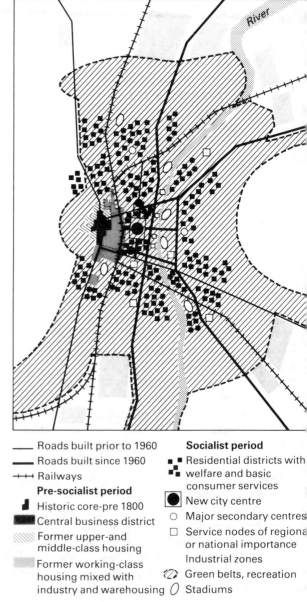

— Roads built prior to 1960
— Roads built since 1960
+++ Railways

Pre-socialist period

▮ Historic core-pre 1800
▮ Central business district
▨ Former upper-and middle-class housing
▨ Former working-class housing mixed with industry and warehousing

Socialist period

■ Residential districts with welfare and basic consumer services
● New city centre
○ Major secondary centres
□ Service nodes of regional or national importance
Industrial zones
〰 Green belts, recreation
〇 Stadiums

Figure 16.1 A model of the growth of an East European Socialist City.

gravitate to its highly localized central services. By contrast, the modern *socialist outer urban area* is far more uniform in appearance, layout and standard equipment. Within it, though, a much more 'polynuclear' spatial structure is evolving, generating comparatively more centrifugal patterns of social circulation in the outer city as people go about their daily lives in neighbourhoods and residential districts, with local welfare, consumer, recreation and entertainment facilities to hand, or as they make their journeys to work in the large industrial, transport or other employment zones that lie nearby 'in parallel' or beyond the city's built-up area. Figure 16.1 provides the barest skeleton model.

The historic core

This usually pre-dates the 1830s. Besides having as its focus a once-fortified medieval town, a castle, a church or mosque or a palace, the core usually comprises also a market square and a trading area with cooperatively or privately owned handicraft workshops, repair services, and some housing in courtyards, alleys and side streets. Although this zone contains the city's oldest buildings, many, if not most, have been restored or even reconstructed in their former style to preserve rich heritages of distinctive national culture, history and even religion. By virtue of their enhanced local socio-cultural value in smaller towns (e.g. Płock) and of their national or international touristic importance in larger towns (e.g. Gdańsk), city planners have cleared such cores of unaesthetic commercial or landscape features. In more extensive and medieval zones, as in Cracow or Prague, routine functions have often been relocated to the periphery of the old town. In their place have been substituted shops selling artistic goods and books, attractively decorated cafés and restaurants, and museums. This applies as much in bigger cities like Warsaw, Gdańsk, Gliwice, and Bratislava as in smaller ones like Eger, Sandomierz, Złotoryja and Suceava.

Yet there is also another type of core: some were so badly gutted during the last war that, in the face of the serious post-war shortages, they have been only partially rebuilt, or virtually abandoned. Szczecin is an example of the first, while Elblag, Gorzów, Głogów, Kołobrzeg, or Nysa are examples of the second where only selected buildings (often churches or bastions) have been restored, the remaining land having been planted as parkland or given over to new housing and modern central functions such as hotels or cultural facilities.

The relict capitalist city

Adjoining the historic core are the quite different, usually far more drab, inner zones of capitalist urban development. Built between the 1850s and the 1930s, such areas were invariably associated with industries, commerce and transport made possible or necessary by the advent of the railway. Elsewhere, as in Gdynia, Gottwaldov (then Zlin) and Stalowa Wola, whole new towns were built following national independence after World War I. The zones that pre-date 1940, however, are the most highly differentiated in East European cities. First, they are most extensive in Budapest, Łódź, Wrocław, Upper Silesia, Ploiesti, and in Czech and German towns, but are relatively restricted in their occurrence elsewhere. Secondly, in their intensity they exhibit very dense concentrations of population, services, and infrastructure (piped water, gas, electricity, cobbled roads and tramways) in the towns located in the areas of pre-1918 Prussian occupation. Their development is much sparser by all criteria in the eastern and south-eastern towns. Such a contrast is still observable, for instance, in Upper Silesia (which was politically divided until 1945) in the adjacent cities of Katowice and Sosnowiec. Thirdly, they display great internal differentiation. Congested commercial streets lined with continuous rows of shops and offices convey the image of the former capitalist central business district (CBD), especially in cities which experienced an industrial or commercial boom in the nineteenth century: Piotrkowska Street in Łódź, Rakoczi út in Budapest and Ilica in Zagreb are classic examples. Adjacent to the inherited CBD are well appointed, spacious apartments once belonging to the aristocracy, and middle and professional classes, as in eastern Donji Grad in Zagreb. Representative of the inter-war beginnings of the 'flight to the suburbs' among wealthier people are the villas or suburban-type housing in areas with gardens, as in Tuškanac in Zagreb, in Saska Kępa and Żoliborz in Warsaw, or in Buda. Near the railways and interspersed with smaller or larger industrial plants are the poorer, former working class residential areas. Sometimes built in 'planned' rows of urban workers' and miners' housing — as in Upper Silesian towns or in semi-rural 'wild settlements' as in Tresnjevka in Zagreb, Praga in Warsaw, or on the north side of Łódź — these areas were inherited in 1945 and invariably lacked piped water, proper sanitation or hard-surfaced roads.

Socialization has brought significant changes to these zones. During the late 1940s city authorities effected some population redistribution within the existing housing stock. Imposition of norms of living space per capita, often of around 7–9 m² per capita, resulted in expropriation of 'excess' rooms or floors in premises belonging to the 'bourgeoisie' and in its re-allocation to more needy families. This process was short-lived; indeed, for much of the 1950s it was pre-cisely those highly differentiated and still largely pri-vately owned housing areas from the capitalist period that bore the brunt of population growth. Rural–urban migration and indigenous city population growth led both to overcrowding and often raised in equal measure the inherited differences in housing densities between areas. Sometimes the environments of former working-class areas were further worsened in the 1950s by the planned expansion there, on grounds of short- or medium-term economic necessity, of existing indus-trial plants. Since the mid-1960s some have been closed and removed from inner-city areas: the copper-processing and chemical industries moved from the Kvaternikov Trg-Kanal areas of south-east Zagreb provide an example.

Such trends form part of long-term city plans to rationalize and to zone land uses more effectively and to improve residential and service or industrial site condi-tions. Indeed, these intentions of change partly explain why, in many cities, little has been done beyond basic repairs to modernize or to 'shore up' the urban fabric inherited from the capitalist period. Nevertheless, long term neglect of these areas has led to a continued increase in the differentiation of living conditions in cities by comparison with the new socialist residential areas, with some undesirable consequences. The need for modernization is recognized more and more, there-fore. When such processes begin to operate, however, the inherited zones enter the phase of transition towards a socialist urban spatial structure.

Zones of socialist transition: the question of urban renewal
These zones appeared first in rebuilding the war-damaged cities. Indeed, much of Warsaw on the west bank of the Vistula — the central area of the city today — has seen 30 years of the ebb and flow of such zones as rubble, remnant or ruined pre-socialist buildings were surrounded and then completely replaced by new socialist construction. First, streets were widened and straightened, and infrastructure networks were rationalized and modernized. Secondly, in the early 1950s, the 'Stalinesque' government office, hotel, and housing and shopping complexes were completed to the south, and the Palace of Culture to the west, of the historic core. Thirdly, some older industrial 'sub-urban' and 'village' relict features on the periphery of the pre-socialist city were partially or wholly replaced by large and expanding industrial zones. Fourthly, in the 1960s and 1970s, the new 'central city' took its final shape with the building, around the Palace of Culture, of the Centrum services complex and, on the site of the war-time ghetto to the north-west, of massive residen-tial neighbourhoods. Once completed, these develop-ments exhibited fully fledged socialist urban struc-tures: the zone of socialist transition 'moved' elsewhere in the city or disappeared from it altogether.

Clearly, these zones are temporary features of the city landscape. They may replace whole sections of the inherited inner city or the relict villages on the urban–rural fringe, usually the most sub-standard housing zones. However, some zones of socialist transi-tion are less temporary than others. The reasons for the persistence of villages on the city periphery have already been outlined. Yet, commonly, cities with a large capitalist 'inheritance' which survived World War II (as in Cracow, Prague or Zagreb) often still exhibit only small 'nests' of socialist building: the rather uneconomic urban *plomba* (fillings). The major-ity comprise housing projects which range from the individual block, which may increase congestion or make comprehensive renewal more difficult, to the 'mini-neighbourhood'. This kind of renewal also typifies the central areas of older cities like Łódź. There, new premises scattered between four- and five-storey buildings (from 1870 to the 1930s) increased total office and service floor space by almost 200 000 m² between 1964 and 1974. Offices in the *Neboder* (sky-scraper) building in Zagreb or the *Energoinvest* offices in Sarajevo are other examples. Of course, the ultimate aim is to remove all vestiges of urban capitalism, save for buildings deemed to have special architectural, functional or historical merit. Yet much of the capital-ist legacy has had to remain simply because of the scarcity of financial and material resources and time to replace it.

The need for new city centres
Despite this, the past decade has seen the necessity to create *new socialist city centres* in more and more East European cities (figure 16.1). This is now deemed to be a very urgent construction task, for several reasons. The lack of modern attractive town centres — symp-tomatic of restricted consumption generally — is a source of 'negative social phenomena'. Urbanization,

population growth and rising living standards have stretched the capacities of inherited commercial streets and market squares and of new neighbourhood service centres, often beyond belief, even to satisfy existing needs. Sustained economic growth in all socialist countries is generating more resources for urban renewal. Yet it has also created the thresholds to support 'take-off' in personal consumption: levels of consumption are planned to double or treble throughout Eastern Europe by 1985 and to increase five- to sevenfold by 2000. Greater private car ownership and the outward expansion of socialist cities is creating a demand for city centres of new design and layout, of bigger scale, and often on newer sites.

Two problems are currently under discussion concerning city centres. New approaches in socialist urban economies must be devised to replace the still widespread notion that simple repairs to existing buildings are good enough. Sophisticated criteria and techniques are required to assess the benefit costs of comprehensive urban modernization and renewal. Moreover, the architect-dominated city planning profession has still much to learn, through well organized and intensive training courses and project competitions, about the purposes of and the art and science of flexible city-centre design. No longer can such centres be based on the use of iterative and simple planning norms applied hitherto to residential districts and neighbourhood service centres of third or fourth order.

Despite this learning process, new first-order city service centres already exist in East European cities today and are of two types. First is the former capitalist (or imperial) CBD that has undergone substantial conversion and extension, demanding inner city renewal. Second is the completely new socialist city centre that is constructed on a near-virgin site and, lying on the periphery or rural–urban fringe of the pre-socialist city, will *become* (or already is) centrally located within a rapidly expanding planned city.

Not unnaturally, the first type is currently best developed in heavily war-damaged cities which could be rebuilt after 1946 on new planned lines, such as Warsaw and Berlin–Hauptstadt. Yet where the physical volume of clearance necessary to make way for a new centre has been quite limited, involving removal of 'low-density' and 'semi-rural' housing, many smaller, unscathed towns have also acquired impressive new city centres, often their first true centres e.g. Bîrlad and Vaslui in eastern Romania. That many other cities will acquire new city centres in the next decade cannot be doubted, though this will entail much bargaining between city councils and state organizations, cooperatives, or private persons owning the property that will have to be cleared. It has been estimated, for example, that more than 1000 plans for city-centre redevelopment have been submitted to city design competitions in Poland alone since 1965, but very few have yet proceeded beyond the drawing board. Crucial to many are much-improved road communications. At least this process has begun in Cracow and a plan for building a new city centre immediately to the north-east of Stare Miasto and the railway station has been accepted.

The residential neighbourhoods
In many cities the greatest extent of socialist building is vested in housing areas. Since the early 1950s these have been organized in all East European cities as residential neighbourhoods with their own welfare and consumer services. Today they house at least half (35–40 million) of the region's urban population. In concept, scale and quality of life that they offer, such neighbourhoods share very much in common, whether located in Grbavica (Sarajevo), Titan–Balta Alba (Bucharest), Uranvaros (Pecs), Dablice (Prague), Jelitkowo in Gdańsk or Rostock Lütten–Klein. Remarks here, therefore, are confined largely to three case studies, drawn from Halle-Neustadt, Novi Beograd and Warsaw.

Nevertheless, some important differences are observable between districts in the same and in different cities. In architecture and layout the uniform five-storeyed 'Stalinesque' of the early 1950s in Mokotów, Nowa Huta or Eisenhüttenstadt has given way everywhere to what in 1957 was described as 'weaknesses towards formal abstraction and revisionism'—then visible in some residential planning, notably in Poland for the Tatary district in Lublin and for Gołonóg in Upper Silesia. Districts built in the 1960s and 1970s are far more varied in layout, design, elevation and colour, but many newer developments suffer from significantly higher densities, higher 'wall' blocks which cast dark shadows, and very inadequate provision for the new fact of consumer life — the private car. Parking has recently become a very serious problem in larger Yugoslav cities. Even in the newest residential neighbourhoods like Travno in Novi Zagreb, where car-parking space greatly exceeds that in Polish or Soviet cooperative residential areas, double parking and use of pavements is common. Yet even elsewhere, as in Warsaw, many children's play areas in neighbourhood courtyards are effectively 'nullified' by the presence of cars. Generally the five-storey quadrangles of Stalinesque and the rigid rows of Khrushchevian residential blocks — so widespread in Soviet cities till 1965 and which often have more 'footpath only' access and extensive green areas — gave way much earlier in Eastern Europe to higher-density, high-rise blocks. A major cause was the relative growing scarcity of land in general and of state-owned land in particular in and around cities, whether in Poland, Czechoslovakia or in Yugoslavia.

This point is brought out clearly in examining the first residential case, *Halle–Neustadt*. Population densities in this, one of Eastern Europe's newest urban developments, *commenced* at higher levels than those existing in a typical 'Stalinesque' new town, Eisenhüttenstadt, and they have surpassed, at more than 11 000 people per km², densities in Berlin Mitte (7780 per km²). Indeed, this case serves to underline the specific characteristic of the socialist city that housing densities in neighbourhoods do not decline from city centre to periphery and in many cities actually increase as between the older 'lower' inner city and the 'high-rise' periphery. What may happen, of course, is that the *frequency* of neighbourhoods decreased with distance from the city centre so that *overall* population densities do appear to decline. Fundamentally, however, the socialist city contains no suburbs — only high-rise flats to the very edge of the urban area. In reality, vestiges of suburbs may remain as relict-village features, illegal 'wild settlements', or limited but legal 'new class' villa development. Typically, for socialist residential construction, the city has advanced in 'sectors' through time, mostly from the centre outwards, so as to achieve economies of scale in construction. On completion, each of the six housing districts will house 15 000–20 000 people. These comprise residential complexes in 'box-like' layouts surrounding courtyards within which are located welfare facilities (e.g. schools, kindergartens, clinics), while shops are located in small clusters between residential complexes. By 1974, 21 000 flats in the town were occupied by 53 000 people. The following list of services available to them says much about the priorities of German socialist planning and local population structure: 30 crèches, 29 kindergartens, 17 schools, three clinics, two pharmacies, two children's libraries, a children's hospital, two sports centres, eight gymnasia, five supermarkets, seven food stores, three household appliance shops, three warehouses, two car-service stations, one petrol station, a sports stadium, swimming pool, dormitory, canteen, industrial training school, university institute, laundry, post office, fire station, railway station, bakery and district central-heating unit.

Such provision clearly underlines the difficulties which may be experienced by living in such urban areas — at least in the short run. That few new facilities have been added to this list since 1974 reflects a failure to build the city centre. Inadequacies in shopping and entertainment services in particular mean extra journeys for residents by bus to old Halle. Thus while the young are well catered for, the adult are not. Not surprisingly, some workers are changing their jobs from the chemical plants to jobs in old Halle near shops and cinemas. Yet without population mobility, by the 1990s many of the crèches, kindergartens, and schools will be empty. *That* problem is widespread already in neighbourhoods in East European and Soviet cities built in the 1950s and early 1960s. There is evidence from Halle–Neustadt, however, that population mobility is already beginning. Some people are leaving to live in older properties in old Halle or nearby. They do so for two reasons: to avoid the arduous daily journeys to work or shopping trips on congested public transport (by bus and train); and to seek housing which offers more space and air. As many Poles can also testify, perceived health and comfort can suffer in the new prefabricated concrete residential blocks with district central heating because, unlike the stone or brick of pre-socialist and Stalinesque buildings, their walls cannot 'breathe'. Yet the majority of people live where new housing areas are built, not where they choose to live.

The second case study investigates the quality of life in a neighbourhood in Novi Beograd as assessed by its residents. Although drawn from Yugoslavia, it points to problems which may be as common in Brandenburg or Bratsk as in Belgrade. The results were obtained from a questionnaire survey of 8200 residents living in 2400 flats in one neighbourhood in central Novi Beograd in 1975 by members of the Yugoslav Institute for Town Planning and Housing. The neighbourhood was selected because it satisfied the following basic criteria: occupance for more than a decade, giving sufficient time for habits, objective opinions, and social relationships to form among residents; varied housing units of 5, 9, 11 and 17 storeys; and a fair cross-section of the Belgrade population. Replies were obtained from 924 families each with two children, 674 each with one child, 220 childless couples, and 85 families with three children each. In fact, the residents appeared to be above average since 32% had higher qualifications, 27% had completed high schools, while 71% of all families owned cars. The vast majority of residents worked within 25–30 minutes of their homes either in Novi Beograd or in the old city across the Sava.

The questionnaire revealed a very high level of satisfaction with the location of the neighbourhood since it lay within easy reach of work, the river, good public services, and enjoyed good transport links with Belgrade, although there was much dissatisfaction with the neighbourhood itself. On balance, however, residents considered that conditions in other neighbourhoods were worse; thus they did not wish to move.

They argued positively that their flats were comfortable, centrally heated, and functionally well planned, while the balcony offered excellent views. However, 'a whole series of defects were perceived concerning the arrangement and use of space in the neighbourhood and point to deficiencies in the details of urban planning'. This view certainly finds support from Poland, too; the defects concerned living both inside and outside the housing blocks. Most residents complained that the flats were too small, with too few rooms. Individual rooms frequently had to perform several functions. The interviewers observed that the living room in 61% of flats became a bedroom at night (a feature widespread in socialist cities where two-roomed flats are the norm). There was nowhere to dry clothes — *that* was the major use of balconies (37% of cases). Almost two-thirds of residents (61%) complained of noise. The majority considered neighbourhood services to be unsatisfactory or non-existent, whether these concerned children's facilities, shops, repair services, cultural amenities, or opportunities to cultivate fruit and vegetables. Only very basic daily needs could be fulfilled locally and 'weekly shopping required journeys to the Belgrade market or to Zemun, and monthly shopping to central Belgrade'. More than 57% of residents would have preferred to live in the five-storey building and not in their present blocks, because of the ease of exit it offered to ground level. Yet 84% perceived the neighbourhood to be overcrowded, offering nowhere for anyone to be alone, and having congested pathways and roads: these were all of a standard width, irrespective of the size of the building that they served. Thus residents preferred (56%) to spend their spare time in old Belgrade (especially in Kalemegdan), although children were quite happy to be in the neighbourhood since all their school friends lived in the same or in adjacent housing blocks.

17 The Centre of Cracow

by Zygmunt Gorka

The medieval quarter of Cracow, called *Śródmieście* (the town centre), constitutes a major part of the city centre; this small area of only 78.8 ha (0.34% of the area of Cracow) fulfils a number of important urban functions. It is the most important retail trade centre of Cracow, containing 15% of shops and achieving 20% of trade sales, and specializes in clothes, souvenirs and books. The two million tourists who visit this part of the city can find here 60% of Cracow's historical monuments, including 8 out of 11 of the most valuable ones. Branches of craft and industry are also represented, but their activity is of minor importance (employing 4% of the labour force and 1.8% of production value), with the exception of engraving. The old medieval buildings of the centre are unsuitable for industrial development, and so many of the quaternary sector services such as scientific institutes, colleges of the Jagellonian University, theatres and other cultural organizations are concentrated there. As a result of these numerous functions, motor and pedestrian traffic is very heavy due to the narrow streets and lack of adequate parking facilities. The population of the centre is 13 000, only 2.1% of the total population of Cracow. High land values have resulted in an expansion of services on the first and higher floors, a reduction in the amount of residential space, and a consequent depopulation.

The land use structure is quite distinctive because of the thousand-year period of settlement, a succession of urban functions, the historic nature and central location within the Cracow urban area (tables 17.1 and 17.2). This complicated structure of the centre led to the author's study of the various uses of building storeys; the higher the storey, the less diversified is the structure (see figure 17.1), and the percentage of downtown-type uses is smaller (commerce, banks,

Figure 17.1 The use of building floors in a block in the centre of Cracow, 1970. a, plot boundaries; b, plot usage (downtown type land use shaded). A, Administration (offices); B, banks; C, cultural institutions (theatres, clubs, etc); CI, industrial crafts; D, dwellings; E, education; G, garages; R, restaurants, bars, cafes; S, shops; X, warehouses, storage; Y, renovated or unused buildings; c, storeys; O, ground floor; 1–4, floors.

administration, cultural institutions, etc). Residential accommodation can be found on all storeys, and services are rarely found above the third floor. Thus the centre still has reserves of potential office space in the upper parts of buildings. The central quarter is surrounded by a green belt (*Planty*) which replaced the medieval town walls, and covers an area of about 20 ha.

Source: *Prace Geograficzne* 1976 **43** (Cracow: Jagellonian University).

Table 17.1 Land use structure in the central district of Cracow in 1970 (in percentages).

Uses	Ground area (ha)	Utilized floors					% Total area	% Ground area
		Ground floor	1st floor	2nd floor	3rd floor	4th floor		
Craft and industry	3.74	10.20	1.94	0.76	0.53	0.20	4.11	2.65
Residential	7.72	21.01	42.43	58.46	65.97	72.43	42.73	27.51
Monasteries	2.17	5.90	6.55	3.39	0.94	—	4.79	3.08
Hotels	0.40	1.08	2.38	2.98	5.33	3.04	2.41	1.55
Shops	6.05	16.49	0.78	0.57	—	—	5.66	3.65
Restaurants, cafés	2.02	5.50	0.29	—	—	—	1.85	1.19
Schools, scientific institutes	2.02	5.50	6.93	7.87	6.56	4.67	6.57	4.23
Cultural institutions	2.53	6.90	8.95	5.13	5.48	4.78	6.84	4.40
Churches, chapels	2.16	5.87	6.05	—	0.29	—	3.75	2.42
Administration, offices	2.44	6.70	14.67	13.34	9.42	8.30	11.12	7.14
Renovated, unused buildings	2.04	5.54	4.53	4.53	3.17	1.72	4.60	2.97
Other uses	3.42	9.31	4.50	2.97	2.41	4.86	5.57	3.59
Total built-up area	37.71	100	100	100	100	100	100	64.38
Share of downtown-type uses	x	37.32	26.17	20.56	15.96	17.94	27.20	x

Table 17.2. Land use structure in the central district of Cracow in 1980 (in percentages).

Uses	Ground area	Utilized floors								% Total area	% Ground area
		Ground floor	1st floor	2nd floor	3rd floor	4th floor	5th floor	6th floor	7th floor		
Craft and industry	2.5	6.9	1.6	0.5	0.8	—	—	—	—	2.9	1.9
Residential	5.6	15.4	35.3	49.5	57.3	64.3	65.1	71.5	—	35.4	22.6
Monasteries	2.1	5.7	6.4	4.4	0.8	—	—	—	—	4.8	3.1
Hotels	0.2	0.4	1.0	1.3	2.4	3.4	—	—	—	1.1	0.7
Shops	5.4	14.7	0.6	0.6	—	—	—	—	—	5.1	3.3
Restaurants, cafés	2.0	5.6	0.7	0.4	0.3	—	—	—	—	2.1	1.4
Schools, scientific institutes	2.7	7.5	9.7	10.5	7.5	5.0	8.1	—	—	8.7	5.7
Cultural institutions	3.1	8.6	10.0	6.1	6.7	8.5	—	—	—	8.1	5.2
Churches, chapels	2.2	5.9	6.1	0.0	—	—	—	—	—	3.8	2.4
Administration, offices	2.2	6.4	11.6	10.1	10.0	10.3	13.7	28.5	100	9.5	5.9
Renovated or unused buildings	4.7	12.8	11.3	12.3	11.9	5.2	—	—	—	11.8	7.6
Other uses	3.7	10.1	5.7	4.3	2.3	3.3	12.3	—	—	6.7	4.2
Total built-up area	36.4	100	100	100	100	100	100	100	100	100	64.0
Share of downtown-type uses	18.7	37.6	24.7	19.3	18.1	22.1	26.8	28.5	100	26.8	17.2

Inside the green belt the buildings have been built very close together with few open spaces.

Only the northern and central parts of the centre possess features characteristic of a city centre, and comprise mainly three-storey buildings. The rest of the area has a large number of tenements, gardens and monasteries, as well as the green belt. As the old historic buildings cannot accommodate all the various functions typical of a city centre, a large new service centre and some smaller ones will be built in the neighbourhood. When the buildings of this part of Cracow are renovated, these will form the centre of the tourist and cultural institutions — functions most suitable to its character (see table 17.2).

Section IV
Housing, Class and Space

Introduction

In this section of the Reader the focus of attention is turned from the spatial distribution of urban land uses — the theme of the previous section — to the question of the allocation of scarce urban goods and resources between the urban populations of the three cities. Hence, issues of social allocation take their place with the question of spatial allocation. The particular issue chosen for comparative analysis is housing. Its selection hardly needs justification. Shelter, after food and clothing, is perhaps the basic need of households. It is, however, much more than this, including the location of a high proportion of many people's leisure time, the workplace of many women, a source of pride, anxiety and an indication of the social status of the family. In addition, housing is the major land use in cities, as well as a major item of expense in the budget of most households. It provides access to a wide range of goods and facilities in the immediate vicinity, a feature of major importance to those household members whose daily lives are basically restricted to a very small local area. This includes most old people and children, many women, the unemployed and also a varying proportion of the workforce who find employment within relatively close access of their homes.

Many of the attempts by English-speaking scholars to describe the structure of urban housing markets in different countries of the world — comparing the spatial distribution of housing within cities and its allocation between households of varying social characteristics — are flawed by a seemingly inevitable ethnocentricity. It is hard to avoid the blinkers of one's own society, easy to rely on conventional methods of modelling city structure that may not have equal applicability to all societies or periods of time. For many years, studies of residential structure and processes were constrained by the perspective of the Chicago School and its North American disciples and descendants. Spatial patterns conforming to idealized models of zones, sectors or multiple nuclei were mapped in different parts of the world. A volume published in 1974 by Schwirian (ed), for example, included studies of the ecology of cities as diverse as Chicago, Bogota, Calgary, Edmonton and other Canadian cities, Helsinki, Alexandria and Poona. The common method was to demonstrate statistical associations between where households lived in the city and a range of their social characteristics, such as age of the head, social class, life cycle stage and ethnic origins. Increasingly, however, as the number of comparative studies of the social ecology of cities, of their residential patterning, grew, the limitations of the approach became apparent. Such descriptive statistical modelling failed to provide explanations of why people lived where they did in different cities in the world, of why variations in the regular patterns could be observed between cities. When attention was turned from the capitalist cities of the advanced and less developed economies to the cities of the Eastern bloc, it became clear that the assumptions of an unregulated land market and individual competition for housing, whether to rent or to buy, in an open market that lay behind explanations derived primarily from North American experience were inadequate to cope in state socialist societies, and indeed in other economies where the degree of state intervention had increased during the twentieth century.

In Eastern Europe, land use and housing allocation is controlled to a far greater extent by the state than in the free-enterprise or mixed economies of the capitalist world. Thus key questions about the resulting patterns of residential location and housing distribution in societies in which the mechanisms of the allocation of scarce urban resources are based on totally different ideological precepts are raised. Is housing space distributed more equally in socialist societies? Are there marked spatial variations between small areas within cities such as are common in Western cities?

To try and answer these questions, certain aspects of the allocation of housing and the resulting spatial patterns in Birmingham, Vancouver and Cracow are described in the three articles in this section of the Reader. Vancouver and Cracow provide examples of societies, and cities, where the rhetoric of distribution is in total contrast. In the Canadian city, individual preferences and free choice, the unquestioned desire to become a home owner, are the basic premises on which the housing system operates. In Cracow, the official ideology is egalitarian. A large proportion of the housing stock is state-owned and controlled and families are allocated to these dwellings to rent according to bureaucratic definitions of social need, rather than on the basis of their financial circumstances, although occupational criteria are also taken into account. In Birmingham, a mixed system is in operation. Although the major part of the housing stock is for sale or for rent in the private market, a substantial proportion of the stock (almost 40% in 1980) is owned by the local authority and, as in Cracow, is allocated according to criteria of social need, although the exact operation of the allocation systems in the two cities obviously differ.

To some extent, the differences between the three cities have been exaggerated to clarify the different ideological bases of allocation policies. The state does intervene in various ways in the owner-occupied market in Canada to subsidize both suppliers and consumers of residential property. Financial institutions act to mediate the market relationship and to provide mortgage finance for these households — in fact the vast majority — who cannot afford to purchase property outright. They operate systems to assess the credit worthiness and security of potential home purchasers as well as spreading the financial burden over several years and thus to some extent mediate the direct relationship between social class and income on the one hand, and quality of housing — whether measured by size, age, type or location — on the other. However, the overall importance of social class and income in determining access to housing is apparent. Substantial inequalities in the distribution of housing are common in Canada, and Vancouver proves no exception to this rule. There is a very small public housing sector in the city, where dwellings are allocated on non-market criteria, but it plays a residual welfare role for extremely disadvantaged groups rather than providing a real alternative to the market.

In Poland, the extent of state penetration of the housing market in general and in Cracow in particular, is not complete and Poland by no means conforms to a pure command economy. Housing is in fact available to rent and to buy in a range of different sub-markets. Owner-occupation, particularly in rural areas, is still a common feature and indeed there seems to be evidence of its growing contribution as efforts are made to attract private savings into housing to alleviate partially the increasingly severe financial constraints on the house-building programme. New individual construction is not uncommon on peripheral sites in small towns, as well as in the countryside. In addition to state housing to rent and owner-occupation, there is a cooperative sector in Poland of dwellings rented or owned by private shareholders. Rents in this sector are generally higher than in the state-owned buildings, and, according to one East European commentator, 'consumer preferences can and do find economic expression' (Andrzejewski, in Nevitt, AA (ed) 1967, p157). There is also a small private rental sector of dwellings that were built before 1945 and were not nationalized.

The British system stands somewhere between the Canadian and Polish systems. Despite the growing reliance on market mechanisms, there is still official support, especially by the Labour Party, for the public provision of housing to cater for a relatively wide sector of the population. However, the majority of houses and flats are sold or rented on the open market, which, as in Canada, is influenced by a system of legislation and financial institutions to mediate the direct relationships between supplier and purchaser. Various degrees of security and tenure and rent control have been in operation in the private rented sector since 1915 and owner-occupiers are assisted by a range of preferential tax incentives available to them individually and as members of the building society movement. The public sector at present houses a third of all households, greatly exceeding Canada's 10% but probably not reaching the figure for Poland where over 50% of urban housing is directly state-owned or owned by industrial enterprises, which are themselves state-owned (Ball and Harloe 1974). As in Britain, however, the percentage of new building being undertaken by the state in Poland has fallen in the last decade and the relative share of the state sector is in decline. Emphasis has swung towards cooperative housing which now accounts for over half of all new construction, compared with less than a quarter for direct state provision. In Britain the decline of public housing will be exacerbated by legislation introduced in the 1980 Housing Act to sell public housing to sitting tenants. The existence of a substantial public housing sector in Britain has to some extent altered the pattern of associations between class, income and housing conditions by enabling less affluent households to gain access to relatively high-standard accommodation, but the clear associations between housing type, standards and location, and professional, managerial and white-collar employment that are found in Canada are also evident in Great Britain, particularly in the owner-occupied sub-market.

One of the key questions to attempt to analyse in a comparative study of industrial capitalist and socialist cities is the extent to which their differing official ideologies and systems of allocation result in different or similar inequalities in the distribution of housing between social groups. Additional, related questions are how far similar spatial patterns develop and whether there are similar consequences for access to locally distributed urban goods and resources in each society. All housing has the characteristic of influencing access to the goods and services in its vicinity. Consequently, where a household lives has a material significance if the quality of local environments and the quantity and quality of urban services vary spatially. All economic systems have to make decisions about how to distribute scarce goods and resources in space, of whom to include and whom to exclude from proximity to employment, to shopping and schools and crèches, to noxious or noisy land uses as well as to the more desirable attributes of open space, parks and other leisure facilities. There is also a further factor that will affect the extent to which societies and cities exhibit similar or different patterns in their housing markets and this is their historical development. The inheritance of housing built under earlier social and political conditions, under a different mode of production, will limit the extent to which present-day objectives, whether egalitarian or inequitable, may be implemented. Housing has a relatively long life (60 years or more is common in industrial societies), and so previous standards influence present distributions and locations.

An ideal comparative analysis of the residential structure of Birmingham, Cracow and Vancouver would require that we tackle all these questions and attempt to untangle the influence of the historical development of the three cities from the economic and political systems in operation at particular periods of time. An analysis of the changing employment structures and hence of levels of demand, of the organization of the building industry, of the strength of local political parties and action groups, and of the influence of regulatory legislation would all need to be included and their relative importance assessed. In addition careful and detailed collection of data relating to household and dwelling characteristics on a fine spatial scale would be needed to compare the spatial distribution of households in each city, always presuming, of course, that the concepts we are using and the characteristics we are measuring mean the same thing across each society, if — and it often is a big if in comparative research — comparable data are ever available. Are status, location and housing type related in the same way in different societies, in Poland as well as in Canada, for example? This and similar questions need to be continually posed as the three articles are read. In reality, of course, the ideal requirements are easier to specify than to meet. The investigation of East European cities by Western researchers is comparatively recent and is frequently hindered by the lack of data for small urban areas, by the absence of large-scale maps and, more seriously, by the financial and political difficulties that prevent long periods of fieldwork being undertaken. In addition, for many erstwhile comparative investigators, language difficulties pose another substantial barrier.

The articles which follow were not commissioned specially for this volume nor for the Open University course *Urban Change and Conflict* with which it is associated. Rather they are representative of what has been written in English about each of the three cities, and so they address a rather different range of concerns. This is immediately apparent on even the most superficial comparison of the three pieces: each of the authors picks out a different range of factors to concentrate on. The emphasis on the importance of individual and social beliefs in Hardwick's description of Vancouver's suburban development reflects both the lack of state intervention in Vancouver's housing market as a whole and his emphasis on the growth of the suburbs where, for more affluent households, the overall quality of the environment and desires for a particular lifestyle are important factors in deciding where to live. In the article on Birmingham, the emphasis shifts from social class and income level to a consideration of the significance of ethnic group membership for residential location. Racial origins appear to have a crucial influence on access to housing in this city. In the extract, Rex and Tomlinson modify the original model of housing classes put forward by Rex and Moore (1967) in an earlier study of Birmingham but they continue to emphasize the hierarchical nature of the housing system in Britain. Their survey of the housing opportunities open to black immigrants in the city demonstrates that access to the categories of housing at each level in the hierarchy is uneven and that certain groups of people consistently lose out. Members of ethnic minorities are found in greater numbers than their overall presence in the city would lead one to expect in particularly run-down parts of the inner city. The extent to which this is a reflection of a desire to live in close proximity to their own kin is difficult to measure. However, Rex and Tomlinson's study adds to the evidence of the operation of exclusionary practices in both the public and private sectors of the housing market in Great Britain.

The characteristics that exclude immigrant families from certain areas and types of property in Birmingham are not limited to these families alone. Low incomes, job insecurity and frequent movement within the city also exclude many native-born households from decent housing in salubrious areas, and particularly from owner-occupation in the suburbs. However, many immigrants suffer the additional disadvantages of conspicuousness because of their skin colour, a lack of familiarity with the operation of the housing system and, for some groups, language problems. These problems are also experienced by immigrant minorities in Vancouver, difficulties which Hardwick, because of his focus on the suburbs, does not discuss. But Vancouver too has its ethnic areas, although here the main minority groups are Chinese and South-East Asians and native Indians rather than West Indian, Indian and Pakistani as in Birmingham.

It is when our comparative focus shifts to Cracow that the difficulties inherent in any comparative analysis become acute. Information about the mechanisms of allocation of housing is less easily obtainable in socialist states, whether to scholars working within a particular country or to external researchers. The number of articles on the allocation of Polish housing, particularly when the scope is restricted to those published in the English language, is still very limited. French and Hamilton's book *The Socialist City* (1979) represents a large step forward in British awareness of the social and spatial structure of cities in a number of countries in Eastern Europe. The piece included in this

Reader is from their chapter on 'Social Processes and Residential Structure' and has a less exclusive emphasis on the particular city than either of the other two pieces. Migration has also been a significant influence on the social structure of Eastern European cities, although the flow has more usually been from surrounding rural areas than other countries. In many of the newly planned settlements and in cities experiencing a rapid and large increase in their population, particularly of people with little or no previous knowledge of urban life, problems of adjustment have been noticeable. Perhaps surprisingly, given that many households are allocated to whatever accommodation is available rather than to areas of their choice, the patterns of pre-war spatial segregation between social classes have been perpetuated in a number of cities, although elsewhere 'decomposition and fragmentation of the socio-spatial structure has proceeded', in other words class segregation is decreasing.

French and Hamilton also provide some evidence on allocation policies and the relationship between rents, housing quality and occupational status. There appear to be systematic trends that lead to associations between the more expensive and better quality housing and certain groups of workers; trends that are also made visually evident by the apparent higher status of the older, pre-socialist housing stock.

Thus it seems that considerable social differentiation in access to housing is not limited to capitalist cities, but is also found in socialist societies. From reading the three pieces, it is clear that housing is unequally distributed in all three case-study cities. However, the reasons for and the methods by which this unequal distribution is reached differ. The extent of state intervention in the housing market varies between the three cities and has a crucial influence in determining the degree of separation of each city's housing system into a number of different categories which are based on different systems of allocation. To the extent that each city, and society, has developed a 'mixed' system, however, based on a combination of renting and owning, on market and controlled prices, and has to grapple with the consequences of the uneven spatial distribution of housing and other resources, some of the arguments of convergence theorists outlined in the introduction to the Reader, may deserve a second, and serious, look.

Linda McDowell

References

Andrzejewski A 1967 Housing policy and housing-system models in some socialist countries, in *Economic Problems of Housing* ed A A Nevitt (London: Macmillan)

Ball M and Harloe M 1974 Housing policy in a socialist country: the case of Poland *Research Paper No. 8* (London: Centre for Environmental Studies)

Rex J and Moore R 1967 *Race, Community and Conflict* (London: Oxford University Press)

Schwirian K P (ed) 1974 *Comparative Urban Structure: Studies in the Ecology of Cities* (Lexington: D C Heath)

Black Immigrants and the Housing System in Birmingham

by J Rex and S Tomlinson

The concept of housing classes

In an earlier study in Sparkbrook, Birmingham, Rex and Moore (1967) isolated the study of 'housing-classes' from the conflicts between other interest groups in the various systems of resource allocation in Birmingham. They saw the conflicts between groups differentially placed in relation to the control of housing as the crucial factor exacerbating if not determining racial conflict. The present study seeks to correct this over-emphasis and to see housing conflict as one amongst a number of possibly interconnected forms of class conflict. None the less, it would be misleading even in this context not to recognize that men's relation to their houses and homes is one of their most important life-interests and one around which they are likely to organize in the course of ethnic and class conflict.

A great deal has been written about the concept of housing-class since the publication of *Race, Community and Conflict*, ranging from some writings which see the concept as a crucial and path-breaking one in urban sociology, through others which draw attention to its internal ambiguities, to still others which see it as essentially diversionary, drawing attention away from the central social process of industrial class struggle.[1] Some of the literature which this debate has generated is referred to below. Here we need only briefly recapitulate the main points about the concept's use which are relevant to the analysis of Birmingham's housing system as it has changed between 1965 and 1978.

The central notion indicated by the housing-class concept was that in any city there was a stock of housing of varying degrees of desirability to which different groups of people having different characteristics had differing degrees of access. The crucial point was not that of having different possessions or even a different lifestyle at the moment of observation, but of being able to command a certain type of tenure in relation to 'desirable' housing in the overall system of allocation. It would, however, have been nonsensical not to recognize that the actual kind of house and tenure which a man actually possessed when observed was one indicator of his power in the housing market or allocative system. Again, it is true enough that in the model of housing-class relations which was posited, the over-simplifying assumption was made that there was an agreed scale of what was desirable in terms of housing style and tenure, and that, in any actual model, particularly in a multi-ethnic society, such an assumption was unrealistic. It was important, none the less, not to allow the formulation of this more complex model to build in a justification of discrimination against minority groups, because they were held not to want what the majority wanted. Finally, because this was a variable concept only and not a description, it was never claimed that the housing-classes which seemed more relevant to explaining ethnic political conflict in Sparkbrook in the mid-1960s could be taken as a kind of inductive generalization covering all cases at all times.

What was new about the Sparkbrook study was precisely its recognition that, while established members of the locally born working class had the security which came from actual or potential access to publicly provided rented housing, there were others who had of necessity to own, and that their ownership indicated a weaker position in the total allocative system than that of the established council renters. Socialist prejudice, however, dies hard, and this argument was difficult for many of our radical and reformist readers to accept.

Source: J Rex and S Tomlinson 1979 *Colonial Immigrants in a British City* (London: Routledge and Kegan Paul Ltd.) Ch. 5, pp127–45; 156–7.

One way of reformulating what Rex and Moore were trying to say is to emphasize that there are some who 'must buy' while amongst those who 'must rent' there are some who have to rent on worse terms than others.

Valerie Karn, in reviewing *Race, Community and Conflict*, accused Rex and Moore of concentrating attention upon a particular type of owner-occupation, that of the lodging-house proprietor, while ignoring the widespread phenomenon of non-pathological forms of owner-occupation, which not only seemed to be a preferred form of tenure amongst immigrants, but was actually furthered by the local council, who, by giving mortgages of its own generously and even disproportionately to immigrants, actually strengthened their housing-class position.

Karn may have been correct in suggesting that the multi-occupied lodging-house in Sparkbrook was not typical of owner-occupation. Indeed, we would reinforce the point by pointing out that the pathology of Sparkbrook in particular had much to do with the disturbed sex-ratio attendant on the panic 'beat-the-ban' migration of Asians in 1960–62. Nonetheless, we would emphasize that the multi-occupied lodging-house is still a reluctantly acknowledged part of Birmingham's housing system, and, even more important, that many of the other forms of owner-occupation to which Karn refers are underprivileged housing situations of those who are forced to buy.

The crux of this matter is that many West Indians and Asians, who may indeed have had a cultural preference for owner-occupation, were trapped into a form of owner-occupation, which was to represent a new bottom of the housing system, and which not merely left them with inferior houses, but actually denied them the chance of moving to the privileged rented sector. The fact was that, however hard it might be to get a council tenancy or a mortgage on suburban property, it was possible by unorthodox forms of finance (e.g. council mortgages and bank loans) to obtain inferior inner-city property for purchase. Anyone who did this thereby made himself ineligible for rehousing through slum clearance and redevelopment and probably also through the waiting list. It is also the case that there was an unorthodox way into the privately rented sector, through gaining the tenancy of a housing association converted flat or house, but this sort of charitable, and sometimes anti-racist, activity placed its tenants primarily amongst the run-down inner-ring properties referred to above.

In a word, what Karn has done is to identify housing-classes of owner-occupiers and private renters, who, while they are clearly better off than the lodging-house proprietors and their tenants, are none the less distinctly underprivileged classes. Denied normal access to the legitimate and desired sectors of the housing market, they have been channelled into that complex entity which comes gradually to be known as the pathological inner city.

Turning now to those who were 'forced to rent' and, indeed, to those who chose to do so, it is important to realize that amongst these, some had certain avenues closed to them which were open to their competitors. In the first place those who lacked local connections would either be denied access to private lettings altogether, or would have to pay a substantial premium to outbid the natives. But much more important was access to the public sector, and here the Sparkbrook study identified exclusion of larger houses from redevelopment schemes, residential qualifications for access to and acquiring points on the list, and discriminating actions by housing officers faced with matching qualified applicants with actual houses, particularly through offering the less fortunate applicants slum property awaiting demolition rather than council-built property.

Matters, however, have moved on since 1965 when the survey in Sparkbrook was undertaken and housing policies as well as the available housing stock have changed. This has led some researchers, notably Lambert et al (1965) to conclude that the whole question of the housing queue or queues is now so complicated that it can be construed as a device to mystify the applicant by the bureaucratic authorities.

Taking into account all of these arguments and looking at Handsworth between 1974 and 1978, we suggest that analysis of the situation there and more widely in Birmingham can still fruitfully be looked at in terms of housing-classes of which the following are the most important:

1a   Outright owner of house } in suburban or
1b   Owner of mortgaged house } desirable area.
2a   Tenant of good post-war or inter-war council housing.
2b   Tenant of inner-city council housing or housing on undesirable estates.
3   Tenant in redevelopment area with possibility of rehousing.
4   Homeless person eligible to be rehoused.

5a   Outright owner of house ⎫ in general
    (i) freehold (ii) leasehold ⎪ improvement,
5b   Owner of mortgaged ⎬ housing action or
    house ⎪ other undesirable
    (i) freehold (ii) leasehold ⎭ area.
6   Tenant of charitable housing association.
7a   Owner-occupier of multi-occupied lodging-house.
7b   Tenant of multi-occupied lodging-house.

Of course some reservations may be held here about the evaluations of what is and what is not desirable built into this set of categories. That they are not the values of the present authors should be made clear at once. What is perhaps more important, however, is that they are disputed amongst the observed population themselves. We believe that there are three separate factors involved here. The first is a continuing widespread belief in the value of suburban semi-detached migration, which is shared by better-off West Indians and even Asians. The second is that the very attempt to improve the houses beyond the original redevelopment areas stigmatizes them. But the third is forced dispersal, whether of the old and retired who are attached to the inner areas for traditional reasons, or of the immigrants who may resent or be afraid of the consequences of the forced dispersal policy and influenced by a counter-tendency to stay in their own safe, enclosed and protected communities. This third factor should be taken into account, but it really does not alter the fact of the existence of housing-classes (at least in themselves) since access is in effect denied to those who do wish to move.

Housing policy in Birmingham

It is now necessary to look at the way in which the new situation in Birmingham, indicated by the new account of the housing-classes mentioned above, has come about through developments in housing policy. This includes looking at two separate aspects of the problem. One is the general housing policy enshrined in the 1969 Housing Act, which succeeded the phase of slum clearance and redevelopment. The other was the new set of policies worked out for council housing, including the place of immigrants within this system.

By 1975 it was clear that the slum clearance programme which Birmingham had begun in the immediate post-war period was coming to an end. Two new problems were emerging. One was that of how to deal

with the sites vacated by slum clearance, the other that of what to do about the next oldest houses. The redevelopment of clearance sites would appear to be a simple problem, namely that of knocking down old houses and replacing them with new ones. But this could not be done according to the same style or formula as that which applied in the case of council rehousing in the suburbs. Here, on these formerly overcrowded sites, there had to be a net housing gain in terms of the numbers of people per acre. This was one reason given in 1965 for not rehousing immigrants from the lodging-house areas in Sparkbrook. That sort of move would have meant that when the lodging-houses, with their intensive over-occupation, were knocked down, there would have been an actual surplus of people for whom there was no room in the new houses.

Obviously what had to be done was, on the one hand, to find more land on the outskirts which could be incorporated into the city and, on the other, to build tower-blocks or high-rise apartments. Moreover, if this was done, with the highest 'housing gain' and, one might add, the greatest gain in popularity by the council, it had to be done by demolishing first the old red-brick, two-storey, single-family houses. In so far as this was done, the 'net housing gain' would be achieved, and there would be a surplus of space for the population of the more overcrowded larger houses.

The two positive symbols of this housing policy, taken by itself and leaving aside the question of those who would not be rehoused, were the Chelmsley Wood estate to the east of the city, and the tower blocks which began to spring up on the cleared inner-city sites and on the periphery.

Chelmsley Wood was built on a stretch of land won back from what had originally been thought of as a green belt, as the result of negotiations with the neighbouring authority. It was thought to be such a significant development that the Queen was brought up to open it. Unfortunately it quickly became evident that it was to be one of the least desired estates in the city. Its small shopping precinct became a kind of wind-trap, humanly deserted and littered with paper at weekends; and down some steps near the car park, special works' buses seemed to indicate that this place was not on normal transport routes. 'Even' immigrants, as they qualified for housing, refused to go there (though since many of them worked across Birmingham's western border in the Black Country this was not surprising). In the town hall there was still hope for the place, and when under local government reorganization the estate passed from the Birmingham to the Solihull district council, Birmingham District saw it as essential that it should control the re-lets. Moreover, the leader of the Labour group on the council looked forward to a future railway line which would make the estate desirable. Up until 1977, however, this net housing gain looked like a human loss.

The tower blocks gave as little satisfaction. Like so many housing and planning developments which went to the drawing-board in 1945, they represent a cheap and vulgarized version of what had been described in the little Penguin books on planning, housing and reconstruction at that time. But whereas the Penguin reconstruction architecture presupposed green spaces and playgrounds between the blocks as well as communal facilities within them, the actual new tower blocks seemed to rise directly from ungrassed rubble, while, inside, circulation space was confined to not always effective small lifts and badly lit corridors.

When the Rex–Moore study of Sparkbrook was conceived, it was thought of as the first of a series of studies in urban sociology, a study of Birmingham's zone of transition to be followed by a study of the first tower blocks. It was suggested then that, given the dominant ideology surrounding the rehousing business, namely that social status improvement lay in semi-detached suburbia, rehousing in tower blocks in the inner city was at best an poorly-understood alternative unlikely to be acceptable to those to whom it was offered. Very quickly, in the first stage of redevelopment, the policy was modified by easing out the gaunt appearance of the tower blocks with exaggerated cottagey types of development, but, as rehousing moved into its second stage, and the British economy deeper into crisis, even this easing out ceased. The tower blocks now rose directly from the demolition sites and from the new network of urban motorways which made them even more terrifying islands for isolated pedestrians.

Rehousing, then, presented unexpected problems and the newly housed did not necessarily feel that they had been translated to Utopia. But their lot was significantly different from and superior to the un-redeveloped areas which now came to form the oldest portion of the city's housing stock. If, at the time of the Sparkbrook study, the city's biggest shame and anxiety had been called 'the twilight zones' now it was called the 'inner city'. According to the new mythology the inner city was the focus of all pathology, including pathological race relations. Cure the apparently

intractable problems of the inner city and you would cure the problem of race relations. This was of especial interest to us because it was a brief study of Handsworth, Augustine John's *Race in the Inner City* (1972), which became the very symbol of the inner-city problem in Great Britain.

In one part of the inner ring are demolition sites which have not yet been replaced by new housing or other buildings. Some of this land, of course, was scheduled for industrial use, but has not been taken up, partly, no doubt, because of the high cost of land, partly because of the absence of entrepreneurship and investment funds, and partly because it was the policy of the national, if not the local authorities that industry should migrate to new satellite towns. Other parts of the area, however, are scheduled for housing developments and these too are long delayed, because demolition itself may not yet be quite complete, and because there are uncertainties about the desirability of inner-city housing redevelopment anyway. The result is that the typical redevelopment area is a waste-land of rubble-strewn ash, pock-marked here and there by a house or two which, although boarded up, has escaped the bulldozer. No one looking at such sites, except perhaps an elite amongst the planners, knows for sure what the destiny of these sites will be, and to be told that one might be rehoused there one day would seem quite literally to be offered a fate worse than death. They are an eyesore and for many people they *are* the inner city.

What is commonly called the inner city, however, really refers to a secondary ring neighbourhood. It is essentially the archaeological residue of an Edwardian or late-Victorian industrial working-class culture and society. It includes usually a declining number of factories; a park of some grandeur, but somehow now under-used and gone tatty; a football ground which still brings noisy and turbulent crowds onto the street, but which is essentially divorced from ordinary domestic living; demolition sites, whose future has been pencilled in by planners, but which is uncertain and unknown to the local populace; some odd pockets of boarded-up houses not yet demolished; old working-class shops, some with new garish fronts as they are taken over by the supermarket chains; and, finally, the huddled, though often tree-lined terraces which actually constitute lodging-house zones, general improvement areas and housing action areas. This is the stage set on which many native old people, hard-working immigrant adults and black-minority children work out the pattern of their lives.

Meanwhile, despite all the arguing which attached to the inner-city policies and to the concept of improvement, private and public estates continued to be built, and those who succeeded in their occupations tended to move away from the improvement areas and housing action areas altogether. Those who remained were, as we have suggested in our regrouping of the housing-classes mentioned above, near the bottom of the heap, above only the tenants and owners of the lodging-houses. (It should be noted that there were still many of these, for between 1965 and 1975, according to the management team of the Policy and Resources Committee, some 4000 houses in multiple occupation were registered, estimated to be occupied by some 25 000 people in 11 000 households, with a further 100 properties a year being referred to the planning officer for enforcement action.)

But what of those who moved? The richer amongst them made not merely a suburban move, but a move outside the city altogether. Solihull became the smart district in the West Midlands conurbation, and Sutton Coldfield, while actually being included in the Birmingham district, retained its own identity as a centre for upper-class communities. Those who could went even further afield to Warwickshire and Worcestershire villages, to Herefordshire or to the Cotswolds. There was *not*, it must be emphasized, anything parallel to the subsequent inward migration of the rich and the white-collar people leading to a gentrification of the inner areas which occurred in London. At most there was an area of middle-class apartments in Edgbaston, but even that threatened to be engulfed by Balsall Heath on the one hand, and Ladywood on the other. Generally speaking, if one wanted to keep away from immigrants and council tenants, Sutton Coldfield and Solihull were safer. It should be noted that immigrants participated in these moves hardly at all. Those who did well made a more modest move such as from Handsworth to neighbouring Erdington.

The council housing stock of new houses continued to increase and the stock of new houses continued to increase and the stock of slums awaiting demolition in council ownership declined in significance both as an embarrassment and a resource. The most astonishing development, however, came in 1976 and early 1977. On 23 January 1976 the chairman of the housing committee called for a review of the housing waiting-list. Only fourteen months before, the *Post* had reported a Birmingham MP as saying that '30 000 families were on the council list and new applicants were coming on at the rate of 200 per week'. Yet on 27 January 1977 the *Evening Mail* was able to report that there were only 10 000 'live' applicants and that, of these, not all wanted housing immediately. Little wonder that in September 1977 the council finally responded to the pressure of the Cullingworth committee and reduced the waiting period before applicants could go on the active housing list from five years to two, and also lowered the age limit for the rehousing of single people. We believe that, in the late 1960s, Birmingham systematically exaggerated the numbers of those of its native population requiring council houses as an argument for not rehousing immigrants, and that by 1976 the figures had simply become incredible. In the mid-1970s, immigrants, who would by now have got by on the five-year rule anyway, stood as good a chance of getting an offer of a council house as whites, except that owner-occupiers in the improvement areas would not qualify anyway, and that it was possible that different kinds of offers might be made.

Discrimination in the public sector

We must recapitulate here the stages through which discrimination against immigrants in the public housing sector has gone, because there are some aspects of this discrimination which have had irreversible consequences in segregating the coloured population, short of some new act of positive discrimination of a kind unprecedented in Britain.

Obviously the principal barrier to the public rehousing of immigrants in the early 1960s was the period of residential qualification, and a great many of those whom we describe in this survey living in poor houses as owner-occupiers might well have been forced to buy at this time. But, even amongst those who qualified, there was a further hurdle to overcome. They had to be assigned to houses by housing visitors whose attitudes are well summed up in the following quotations from our own interviews:

We can't hide the fact that people have different standards of housekeeping. We don't want to offend people. We try to put people in neighbourhoods where they won't conflict. After all, some of the Asians may just be getting out of the stage where they made curry patties on the floor. It's like the English working class — they kept coal in the hall and donkeys in the kitchen when some of them were put in council houses in the twenties. It takes education to raise standards.

The standards haven't changed since 1969. People haven't learned a thing. It's what we call central area standard, and of course we are down to the dregs now. People with anything about them have moved out and it's the Irish, the immigrants and poor Birmingham people left — people we've moved around into the clearance houses. Now we are having to move them to the inter-war estates and they are turning these into slums.

Finally, one visitor, referring to Handsworth in particular, said:

It's a very mixed place. After the first war it was a lovely place — Holly Road, Antrobus Road, Chantry Road — they were all big houses with servants and huge rooms. Then after the second world war it began to go down. A lot of Irish came and then the West Indian people. There are still some very respectable white people living there. Mind you, I'm not saying West Indians aren't respectable . . .

It was on the basis of opinions such as these that, as our second quotation suggests, immigrants, instead of being rehoused in council-built houses, were 'moved around into the clearance houses'. Thus, before about 1966 there were only a few immigrants in council-built houses.

Some change in policy was inevitable, however, once the slum clearance programme neared completion. Those immigrants who were qualified in terms of residence for rehousing, and had enough points in total, could no longer be shunted around the clearance houses and it was necessary to move them to council estates.

What exactly the council's policy was with regard to which estates it assigned the immigrants to between 1965 and 1970 is not clear. The Conservative chairman of the housing committee in 1968 was forced to justify the allocation of council-built houses in the inner-city area of Ladywood, and refused to change his policy, even in the face of a rent strike by white tenants there. We do not know, however, whether there was at this time any further policy of discrimination so far as suburban estates were concerned. Possibly, as the second quotation above suggests, those who were sent to the suburbs were assigned to inter-war (i.e. older) estates and poorer houses. But matters might have been further complicated by an immigrant preference for the inner-city estates where they could maintain communal ties.

A wholly new situation faced the council by 1970, however. The question was no longer one of whether immigrants should be put in council houses at all, but of how they should be concentrated or dispersed on council estates. This was a difficult policy question and one which produced cross-voting. There were 'liberals' on the race issue who feared segregation on particular estates, but others who for equally liberal reasons opposed forced dispersal. On the other hand, there were 'racialists' who wanted to prevent estates 'going down' through having too many blacks, and others who thought that it was best to concentrate immigrants in a few areas and avoid putting them on other white estates at all.

Subject to this sort of cross-cutting pressure, the Conservative-controlled council in the early 1970s adopted the policy of 'dispersal'. The policy was that when a black family was offered a property, six properties on either side were marked 'NC' (not coloured) on the index of property. There was some confusion within the housing department as to whether the ratio was in fact one in thirteen rather than one in seven.

The new policy resulted in a reduction in the housing stock available to black families and to the stockpiling of coloured families who had asked for areas where the quota of houses available for coloured families had been reached. On the other hand, the policy could not in fact be fully applied, because, even though the housing department might have wished it, actual records of the ethnic origin of applicants were imperfect.

In effect, dispersal was very far from effective. A social development department was set up in the housing department in the late 1960s with the task of monitoring allocation procedures, policies and housing preferences. In 1975 this department undertook some research on the distribution of immigrants within the council housing stock. This showed that New Commonwealth immigrants were seriously under-represented in council tenancies based on the proportion of immigrants in the total population. Immigrants formed 10% of the population of Birmingham, but only 3.3% of those renting council housing.

In the inner wards of Highgate, Newtown, Nechells and Ladywood, the ratio of immigrant to non-immigrant tenants was well above the average for all council estates, while in Highgate and Nechells as a whole, as well as in small areas (enumeration districts) in all four wards, it was above the proportion of immigrants in the total population. The ratio of immigrant to white tenants in Highgate was 1 to 5.8 and in Nechells 1 to 9. In the most concentrated enumeration districts in the four wards the ratios were, Highgate 1 to 3, Newtown 1 to 4, Nechells 1 to 6 and Ladywood 1 to 4.

It will at once be apparent that, so far as certain parts of these estates of flats and houses are concerned, immigrants, far from being kept out, are actually over-represented. This by itself suggests that the problem of discrimination in the public sector has changed since

Rex and Moore's Sparkbrook study. Immigrants do now get council houses, but in the inner city there has arisen a *de facto* type of segregation and even a tendency towards making ghettos of certain small areas.

On the other hand, a look at the figures for some of the outer estates suggests an entirely contrary pattern. In Primrose Hill and Walkers Heath only 19 out of 400 tenants were immigrants, in Shenley only 25 out of 610, and in Woodgate Valley 30 out of 2754.

These figures suggest that the dispersal policy has not worked as yet. Immigrants are heavily concentrated in inner-city estates and badly under-represented on the newest suburban estates. How far is this a matter of immigrant choice and how far a matter of discriminatory application of the dispersal policy to certain areas only?

To our surprise we found that immigrants did not even mount a campaign for equality of access to suburban housing on the new estates. The social development department found that 90% of immigrants interviewed preferred central areas and there was a marked unwillingness to move to estates like Chelmsley Wood. What immigrants did oppose as discriminatory was the dispersal policy itself, partly because it effectively reduced the number of offers they were likely to receive, but also because it involved the forced break-up of black neighbourhoods.

So far as the council was concerned, it was committed in principle to the policy of overall dispersal or 'thinning out'. This could be justified on liberal assimilationist grounds and would also satisfy those more 'racialist' councillors and voters who wanted to limit the effect of the black presence. But this double and contradictory justification had important consequences. It produced three kinds of situations:

1 Fewer offers of houses in central areas than immigrants wanted.

2 More offers of houses in some undesirable suburban estates than immigrants were willing to accept.

3 Few offers of houses in some desirable suburban estates which, however, might have been turned down, had they been made.

The dispersal policy was eventually challenged by the Race Relations Board and, after some confused reporting in which the Board was represented in the press as having cleared the Birmingham Council of discrimination, a committee was set up to ensure that a discriminatory policy of forced dispersal was not pursued. Since this so-called 'watch-dog' committee, including representatives of the Community Relations Council, has only recently begun its work it is too early to say whether it will effectively prevent discrimination.

The adjustment which Birmingham has made to the rehousing of immigrants in the public sector thus turns out to be somewhat different from either of the two possibilities which appeared open in 1965. At that time it appeared that either Birmingham would keep immigrants out of council houses altogether or that immigrants would make the suburban migration through the public sector. What has happened is that many of the earliest New Commonwealth immigrants have bought inner-ring property and thus withdrawn themselves from the public sector, while those who have been lucky or unlucky enough to have stuck it out, without resort to house purchase, have more frequently finished up in inner-city estates where they could maintain communal links with their property-owning kinsmen. Very few have made the suburban migration.

The problem which actually confronts us now is a different one from that which Rex and Moore may have led us to expect. There are not two groups of immigrants, one discriminated against and united by strong ethnic bonds, and another assimilated through having acquired equal rights to suburban housing. Private property-owners and renters on the one hand, and immigrant council tenants on the other, have tended to be much the same sort of individual, and, to all intents and purposes, we found very little differences in the observed attributes of those housed in the public and private sectors.

The immigrant community in Handsworth now consists of a number of groups in different housing situations. There is a core of private owners, either outright or with a mortgage; there are private renters either from private landlords or from housing associations; there are still some tenants of council property awaiting improvement or demolition, and there are council tenants. The proximity of the houses of all our council tenants to the improvement areas and housing action areas, however, means that they form part of one community with the inhabitants of those areas, and have shared communal institutions.

But, while we are seeking to emphasize here that being a council tenant is a less privileged status than Rex and Moore imagined, we would not wish to suggest that being an owner-occupier, or living in the private sector, represents a position of privilege for those who live in improvement or action areas. For, in spite of all that has been done to develop special policies for these areas, beyond the original renewal areas, the fact is that they contain some of the worst housing and some of the most depressed conditions for their inhabitants of all areas of the city today. We may not be talking of groups quite as disadvantaged as the Pakistanis and their tenants in Sparkbrook in 1965, but we are talking about some of the most disadvantaged housing classes and sub-classes.

Conclusions

It is important that we should conclude by saying what we think would be necessary to eliminate the effect of housing-class conflict on race relations.

Crucially, we believe that a situation would have to be created in which West Indians and Asians could choose their housing freely without being subject either to discrimination or to the need to use their housing situation as a resource for strengthening ethnic ties.

The ending of discrimination will not be achieved simply by allowing the West Indian applicant who perseveres with his application despite all discouragements to obtain rehousing in inner-city council housing. Nor will it be achieved through a punitive policy of dispersal. What is necessary is that the council should actively pursue a policy, as it does with its white electorate, of making known the kinds of housing which are available, and of allowing all applicants the opportunity to make a fully informed choice. Such an information programme would include discussion with ethnic organizations as well as individuals about their attitudes to housing. We would be misleading our readers if we suggested that the move from deliberate discrimination and segregation to dispersal and then to the abandonment of dispersal is a policy which in any way meets this need.

Paradoxically, however, even though discrimination in housing is something which immigrant leaders would oppose, it has helped to provide them with a communal resource. Just as exploitation in industry gave rise to the trade union movement and more widely to the Labour movement amongst native British workers, so the fact of discrimination in housing has given rise to partially segregated areas, and to locally based and relatively effective communal and ethnic organizations, which are useful as a means of protecting the rights of minority groups. Thus to propose dispersal in terms of housing alone, before minority group rights have been assured right across the board, seems to minority group leaders, not so much a sound reform,

but rather an attempt to weaken them politically. Thus the 'high-profile minority rights programme' would have to be one which dealt with all those areas in which, at present, ethnic organizations are necessary to defend rights and not merely housing by itself.

We believe that it would be unrealistic in the present political situation to expect the adoption of this total package. Clearly the new Commission for Racial Equality set up in 1977 might see its task as lying in the carrying through of just such a programme. But the Commission has to operate in a hostile political situation in which the dominant trend is that of the anti-immigrant lobby. In such circumstances we can well understand the importance of political militancy amongst the immigrants. Such militancy is not an obstacle in the way of the Commission achieving its task. It is the essential condition of its success. Equal rights in housing are in fact dependent, above all, on effective political representation.

Our task in this paper, however, has not been primarily to advocate change of this kind. It has been to ask what changes have occurred in the housing situation since black immigration began. Clearly there have been changes and the situation in Handsworth or in Sparkbrook in 1978 is not the same as it was in Sparkbrook in 1965. None the less, we have not been describing a smooth process of assimilation. What we have seen is the emergence of a set of housing policies, which have produced the new social phenomenon of the 'inner city'. What its destiny will be, particularly as it is affected by new and deliberate inner-city policies, must be the subject of future research.

Notes

[1] Amongst the most important discussions of the concept are the following: Haddon R 1970 A minority in a welfare state: location of West Indians in the London housing market *New Atlantis* 2(1)

Lambert J and Filkin C 1971 *Ethnic Choice and Preference in Housing*, Final report to the SSRC, Centre for Urban and Regional Studies, Birmingham (unpublished)

Lambert J, Blackaby B and Paris C 1976 *Neighbourhood Politics and Housing Opportunities*, paper presented to the Centre for Environmental Studies Urban Sociology Conference 'Urban Change and Conflict', York University, January

Ward R 1975 Residential succession and race relations in Mossside, Manchester *PhD Thesis* University of Manchester

Pahl R 1969 *Readings in Urban Sociology* (Oxford: Pergamon)

Pahl R 1970 *Whose City?* (London: Longman)

Davis J and Taylor J 1970 Race, Community and No Conflict? *New Society* No. 406, 9 July

Bell C 1977 On housing classes *Australian and New Zealand Journal of Sociology* 13(1)

Richmond A 1973 *Migration and Race Relations in an English City: A Study in Bristol* (London: Oxford University Press)

Pickvance C 1976 *Urban Sociology: Critical Essays* (London: Tavistock)

Clarke S and Ginsborg N 1975 *The Political Enemy of Housing* paper presented to the CSE Conference, London, March

Haddon suggests that Rex's use of the concept emphasizes the type of housing actually occupied to the exclusion of access to housing. Lambert and Filkin argue that the concept rests upon the notion of a unitary scale of values which does not hold in reality. Ward, and Davis and Taylor, both emphasize that housing stress might not lead to ethnic conflict, while Davis and Taylor also place emphasis upon the profit motive amongst immigrant landlords. Richmond argues on the basis of attitude studies that Rex's implied prediction of an association between inferior housing position and racist attitudes is not borne out by observation.

Pahl restates the theory to emphasize what he calls the class of 'those who must rent' and connects this debate with the work of Manuel Castells. Pickvance suggests that Rex's use of the concept escapes some of Castell's strictures on urban sociology in general. Lambert *et al* connect their work with that of Castells by arguing that the system of housing queues is part of the ideological state apparatus which mystifies social reality. Bell, reviewing the work of Rex and Castells amongst others, asks of a system of housing class conflict, 'Who is exploiting whom?'.

The best analysis of the theoretical and methodological problems involved in the use of the concept is to be found in Ward's thesis.

Rex has replied to some of these writers in *The concept of housing class* (1971 *Race* **12** (3)), and in Sociological theory and the city (1977 *Australian and New Zealand Journal of Sociology* **13** (3)).

References

John A 1972 *Race in the Inner City* (London: Runnymede Trust)

Rex J and Moore R 1967 *Race, Community and Conflict* (London: Oxford University Press)

19 Residential Segregation in Vancouver: The Suburbs

by W Hardwick

The old suburbs

Introduction

Visitors to Vancouver are often taken to one of the vantage points where panoramic views permit an appreciation of the varied texture of the city. From Little Mountain in the geographic centre of Vancouver city, for example, the land to the west seems to be swallowed in a sea of green trees, while to the east a high density of multi-coloured roofs remind one of a northern fishing village; to the south, pretentious subdivisions with ranch homes and pastels reflect another physical urban environment. From another vista, Brockton Point in Stanley Park, a maze of high-rise apartments are reflected in the water of Coal Harbour, while to the north, tier on tier of single detached homes sit contour on contour along the foothills of the North Shore Mountains. To the east, the piers of the Burrard Inlet harbour provide a foreground of multi-storey commercial buildings. From a third point, Burnaby, along the road descending from the mountain-top site of Simon Fraser University, the rigid grid of eastern Vancouver is in striking contrast to the still incomplete landscape of Burnaby — incomplete in the sense that large parcels of undeveloped, wooded land separate subdivisions, some elegant and garish, others modest, others remnants of urban development of 50 years ago. From yet another place, the apartment towers of New Westminster, a well developed grid pattern of the city in the foreground gives way to more scattered subdivisions on the Surrey upland and to extensive industrial and agricultural land alongside the Fraser River and its delta.

Source: W Hardwick 1974 *Vancouver* (Vancouver: Collier Macmillan). This is an edited version of Chapters 5 and 6, 'Residential geography: old suburbs' (pp100–14) and 'Residential geography: the ring — new suburbs' (pp127–39).

A major sorting process took place in terms of population in the 1900s when subdividers broke the east side, south and east Vancouver, into small parcels; the southern section, including Shaughnessey, into large lots; and the west side, Point Grey, into medium-sized lots. The working classes of the day went east, the élite went south, and the middle-class went west in a pattern reminiscent of the sectoral model of urban structure. The élite and middle-classes were WASP-ish immigrants from eastern Canada and Britain who shared many values, including those evidenced in community organization and landscape development. Those who moved east and south-east were from much more diverse backgrounds. Most came to British Columbia to get a start, to get some land, and to pull themselves up by their own hard work. That, they all held in common. However, there was great variation in ethnic origins, in age, in class background, and in potential for upward social mobility and urban experience.

Beyond the old suburbs a peripheral ring of new suburbs have few of the sectoral differences found in the city. For those who chose to move beyond the city, the difference was that they were more agrarian and much less urban. Until the 1940s, many did not work in the city, but only served the city by selling agricultural products or working at resource exploitation, lumbering or fishing. Parcels of land were much larger, and except around inter-urban stations, rarely took on an urban form.

In the last 20 years, the ring of smallholdings and farms that stretches from the Fraser delta east into Surrey and Coquitlam has been the most rapidly growing area of the Vancouver region.

Social segregation had taken place in the first years of city development, contrasting the West End with Yaletown and Strathcona. The West End middle-class neighbourhood was fringed by the élite of the day occupying the amenity sites along Georgia Street West and near Stanley Park and the beaches. Working men lived to the south and east, and the ethnic groups crowded in against downtown. During the 'boom' of 1905–13, the 100 000 people who arrived in the city pushed the boundaries of settlement outward into what are now the old suburbs, leaving the West End in particular for redevelopment for multiple accommodation. Other waves of expansion followed in the 1920s and 1940s. As family groups moved to new areas, the social segregation was expanded outward into the peninsula between Burrard Inlet and the Fraser River. In the West End, a classic filtering process commenced, transferring old homes first into rooming houses and conversions, then with physical renewal as high-rise apartments. This process is manifest now in the large numbers of old and young in the core in contrast to families in the old and new suburbs.

Early history

Settlements of the older suburbs south of downtown and False Creek proceeded along five axes, each a major streetcar line. The western Fourth Avenue and Broadway lines served Kitsilano, then operated into Dunbar, and West Point Grey. To the south, the Fairview and Mount Pleasant districts were served by the 'belt line' streetcar. An extension south went to Shaughnessey. Radial lines south-east on Fraser and Main Streets extended Mount Pleasant into south Vancouver. To the south-east, the inter-urban line to New Westminster and the Kingsway streetcars provided access to a series of dispersed settlements in South Vancouver and Burnaby. To the east, along Hastings and Powell, streetcars served Grandview and Hastings East.

In many cases, settlements spilled beyond the existing neighbourhood of Vancouver. In other cases, it surrounded nodes along the transit lines, a clear example being the New Westminster inter-urban line. These local service nodes, such as were found in Cedar Cottage, Collingwood and Joyce Road areas, would serve both a small local population as well as a more rural population to the south. Where settlement spread across the civic boundary, the pattern usually was an extension of the Vancouver grid subdivision. Where it was outside, it developed its own character and orientation.

An estimated 200 people lived in the whole area south of the city in 1901. These neighbourhoods have a substantial maturity now, the product of many years of occupant concern for the residential environment. Throughout this area of some 30 square miles, the quality of housing has been continually upgraded as new generations of residents chose to buy substantial, older homes with proximity to both the work places of the inner city and to those of the suburban ring, and invested in the improvements of their homes as part of the price they were prepared to pay for locality. The deterioration of the sub-inner ring of housing and associated commercial facilities found throughout eastern and central cities of North America did not appear in Vancouver, at least not as the general pathological rule.

East–west contrasts

The old suburbs can be discussed in terms of a major east–west contrast, a historic division made manifest before 1929 in the separate municipalities of Point Grey and south Vancouver, and persisting during sequences of development and occupation that took place — up to the present time. Although the whole area south of Vancouver city was incorporated as one municipality in 1892, the social differences in residents who moved into the eastern and western sections planted the seed of the division into two separate political entities in 1908.

Point Grey, the westernmost municipality, was settled by middle-income and élite groups searching for quality urban environments. Fine houses were built along the bluffs overlooking the northern arm of the Fraser River. A number of these estates were extensive in land area and were held intact for a sufficiently long period to influence patterns of growth and change in many areas of the city's south side. The development of the estates in Point Grey followed the construction of the inter-urban railway from Vancouver out to Marpole and across the Fraser River onto and through the farm lands of the delta, to the fishing and cannery town of Steveston as well as street railways west from Kitsilano. The new transportation enabled people within these corridors quick access to the core of the city.

More important to the urban landscape of Vancouver was the opening of Shaughnessey. Prior to World War I, after several scattered attempts at anchoring an élite area for the burgeoning city, the CPR took the initiative. Shaughnessey was an elaborate subdivision of the period, with winding streets, well wooded avenues, and larger lots — an acre in size — on which people could build large formal mansions. Hycroft, often cited as the finest home of all, was built by the resident vice-president of the CPR — perhaps to symbolize the owner's confidence in the area. Standards of subdivision and house design drew upon some of the best urban design of the day.

Streets and park design were influenced by Olmstead and were characterized by paving, curbs, ornamental trees and street lighting. Many of the houses, particularly those by the architect Maclure, were of Tudor design; all went in for extensive gardens and tree planting. The formality set standards that were copied by the less wealthy and became the underpinnings of Point Grey municipal by-laws.

In adjacent areas, quality suburbs expanded, in which the neighbourhood amenities were given high priority: the streets were paved and tree-lined, the utility lines were run along back lanes, not along the main roads and the street lighting was of an ornamental nature. Shaughnessey abutted white-collar subdivisions such as Talton Place and the Second Shaughnessey further to the south.

Point Grey contrasted markedly with south Vancouver, from which Point Grey had ceded. South Vancouver was an area where working-class people took the opportunity to find comparatively cheap land on which they built homes of varying size and quality. The municipality evolved into one of neighbourly cooperation in social affairs, at a level reminiscent of the barn-raising rural tradition, an environment left only lately by many early residents. Their values included a desire for space and a high degree of privacy. These values and traditional concepts, however, remained highly personalized and did not translate readily into municipal as opposed to personal improvement. Street amenities, public works, formal planning of parks, indeed planning in any formal sense at all, were all considered frivolous extravagances compared to the practical realities of earning an improved living in a rough and ready city.

The pattern of settlement in these suburbs has an interesting difference even today. To the south of downtown Vancouver, the CPR had been granted an enormous land grant of over 5000 acres, stretching from the boundaries of the original incorporated city, around the present 16th Avenue, all the way south until it ran into the pre-empted farm land that stretched inland from the flood plain of the Fraser River Valley. In width, it stretched from Ontario Street in the east to approximately Trafalgar Street in the west. Throughout this very large area, the CPR real estate department controlled the pace of subdivision, adjusting the release of land to the construction demand, and maintaining a quite well-balanced programme of development. The consequence of this control was uniform, orderly growth over a substantial area of the city where each block was filled with houses of relatively equal size and quality, built under the same building and zoning codes.

In contrast, throughout south Vancouver and in the far western parts of Point Grey, subdivision had been on a much larger scale, with comparatively massive blocks of land being subdivided at one time. The land, however, was not taken up with the same alacrity and the pace and pattern of occupation was far from uniform. The result, as can be seen to this day, has been a mixture of homes of quite varying quality and age coexisting in the region. Often one or two houses can be dated as being built about 1912, while others stem from the 1920s and 1940s. Sometimes remnant orchards can be identified stretching through the gardens of one or two adjoining houses, reflecting the size of the original plots.

It is not unusual today to see expensive new houses crowded in between 2½-storey shingled structures dating from 1912, cottages from a decade earlier, and a row of stucco bungalows constructed in the 1920s.

Hastings East should be singled out for special comment. The Grandview and Woodlands districts of east Vancouver were integral parts of the city of Vancouver. They experienced their most rapid growth in the same years as Kitsilano, 1905–12. The residents, largely of British origin, built substantial homes on rather small plots. Most were tradesmen, in the shipping business, or shopkeepers. Most had an urban life experience prior to coming to Vancouver. More than most, many of these people were engaged in the physical construction of the city itself. Although more working class than Kitsilano, the physical structures built have more similarity to Kitsilano than to south Vancouver. The extension into Hastings East has many physical parallels to Dunbar.

By the 1920s immigrant groups which had been restricted to the margins of the core began filtering into these neighbourhoods. After World War I, Italians and Chinese in particular became significant minorities. Their penchant for land and upward economic mobility has become reflected in large capital expenditures in rebuilding old homes, often for extended family groups.

North Shore

Fortunately for the ordered development of the region, a new crossing of Burrard Inlet had been built in the late 1930s by the Guiness interests. The object of the project was to open up a vast area of hillside in west Vancouver — British Pacific Properties, the Guiness' choice for a new élite subdivision. Of course, during wartime development was very slow on the North Shore. With the end of the war, however, and particularly with the completion of education by hundreds of veterans, the flood of middle-class home-seekers switched from the old suburbs of the south to an equivalent area (in terms of distance from the core) to the north. Therefore the North Shore is introduced here, not as an outer suburb, but as another old suburb. North Vancouver city had been linked to downtown Vancouver by frequent ferry service for decades, and commuters made up a proportion of the population. The developers of the Lions Gate Bridge foresaw the hill-land as an area of upper-middle-class housing. Tolls on the bridges and infrequent and more costly public transportation were deterrents to poorer people. However, the wartime emergency saw the conversion of the North Shore shipyards into major producers of merchant ships, and much of the lowlands adjacent to the waterfront became emergency low-cost housing areas. Summer cottages along the west Vancouver beach became converted into year-round dwellings, and those who once enjoyed their morning and evening commuter ride on the passenger ferry *Hollyburn* were dragged into the new commuter system as well. Therefore, a much wider range of income groups became accommodated on the North Shore than the development of the Pacific Properties would have forecast.

Not all the North Shore developed as part of the Vancouver system. North Vancouver city continued to be the most isolated section of the North Shore from Vancouver, particularly after the ferries were abandoned. By either of the First or Second Narrows bridges, it was the most distant section from downtown. Therefore, as subdivisions for an expanding Vancouver-oriented middle class grew rapidly, the settled areas were near the bridges and less in the old city. Population expansion was rapid and names like Capilano Highlands, Delbrook, Lynn Valley and Forest Hills were added to the glossary of residential neighbourhoods.

Socially distinctive neighbourhoods

Gibson (1972), in his study of the social beliefs of

Vancouver's founding groups, identified four primary groups and demonstrated the relationships between these groups and the distinct district characteristics of the city. The dominant group that had occupied the west end of the city was called 'the eastern Canadians'. This group comprised that segment of the population associated with the arrival of the CPR, and the mercantile managerial élite. It impressed its social and political philosophy on the urban landscape of Point Grey. In contrast, a second group, comprising in part the organized labour groups, largely British working-class migrants, spread into the Mount Pleasant and south Vancouver districts, as we have already discussed.

A third group, the 'British Columbians', composed of British and American seamen, soldiers of fortune, lumbermen, and fishermen who had come to the province before the arrival of the CPR, and had found employment in the forest and construction industries, were a spent force before the suburbs developed. Although this group had capital, and engaged in the building of the city itself, it did not have the cultural background and polished business experience of the eastern Canadians. This did not, however, prevent members of the British Columbian group from contending for power in the city in opposition to the eastern Canadians. Mayor D Oppenheimer was an impressive spokesman for this group. The imprint of this group's activities, even though its identity had dissolved by about 1913, can still be seen in the landscapes of the Strathcona, Mount Pleasant and Grandview districts of the city.

The fourth group was made up of the minority ethnic populations, particularly the Asian peoples, concentrated in the inner east-side ghettos. Gibson argues that these four groups had different social beliefs, and that these differences as expressed in early years became manifest in the urban landscape throughout the city.

The morphological consequence of this segregation in population was, from the very beginning, a sectoral pattern of residence, which is still discernible in civic voting patterns, in traditional socio-economic dimensions, and even in the varying degree to which people from the different parts of the city make use of and participate in downtown activity.

The new suburbs

The peripheral ring

On the periphery of Vancouver city there is a ring of

communities which lie between 6 and 15 miles from the core, comprising a varied urban landscape. These communities have emerged recently under conditions of rapid population growth. As documented earlier, the quantity of subdivided urban land within Vancouver expanded rapidly in the first quarter of this century as the streetcar lines were driven outside the peninsular city of the nineteenth century. When land was fully utilized in the city by 1960, the population then increased rapidly in the periphery. Exceptions were New Westminster, the first city of the region, and parts of Burnaby and North Surrey across the Fraser River where, at the end of World War II, population boomed and a car-oriented area of urban sprawl evolved. This boom was curtailed when local zoning tightened and taxes started to rise sharply to pay for demanded urban services.

Much land within these municipalities was zoned for residential purposes prior to 1960, and the pace and pattern of infilling paralleled the growth of the Vancouver streetcar suburbs of the 1920s. The recent rise in numbers of people in the peripheral ring is related to the growth of economic activities there as much as to the growth in the core city itself. The construction of freeways improved access between residential, work and shopping areas within the outer municipalities themselves. Because the freeways stop at the borders of Vancouver, interaction with the core system is somewhat restricted.

At one time, peripheral living meant foregoing major shopping convenience and accepting the long journey to work in the central business district. However, in the 1960s both shopping and work became dispersed. Whereas slightly more than a quarter of the work in the metropolitan area was found in the periphery in 1955, over one-third of work was found there in 1971. Many industrial and warehousing activities moved out from the central city and most large-scale enterprises entering the region are found in this zone or beyond. The spread of people eastward made parts of Burnaby more central than the core of Vancouver to the population as a whole. Furthermore, the construction of regional shopping centres and related services contributed to the dispersion of workplaces. Also, the opening of new universities and colleges and a host of public institutions that serve the outer ring provided large numbers of professional and clerical jobs well outside the core city. Even port facilities showed patterns of dispersion. Although New Westminster has shared shipping trades for decades, it was only in the early 1970s that the

Fraser River and the offshore Roberts Bank port experienced rapid increases in tonnage handled. At Roberts Bank alone, some 4000 acres were set aside for future industrial development and the Fraser River Harbour Commission received a study indicating that several port concentrations along the main channel of the Fraser River between its mouth and New Westminster will be desirable in the next 30 years. In addition, in Port Moody and along Burrard Inlet on the eastern side of the metropolitan area, bulk loading facilities joined oil refineries as major waterfront occupants.

These outer suburbs fall into four sectors. One comprises the Fraser River delta land south of the city, areas linked to downtown Vancouver by Highway 499. It includes much of the municipalities of Richmond and Delta — an area bounded on the west by the sea, on the south by Boundary Bay, and on the east by the farms and peat bogs. The second, embracing the municipality of Burnaby and city of New Westminster, lies immediately to the east of the city of Vancouver. New Westminster has natural homogeneity, while Burnaby has close ties to Vancouver on the west and New Westminster on the east; both are older communities. The third sector, the Surrey–North Delta–White Rock area south of the Fraser River, comprises a very large area of over 100 000 residents, in part filled with subdivisions and part with smallholdings and agricultural land. Finally, east of Burnaby and New Westminster lie the burgeoning municipalities of Coquitlam, Port Coquitlam and Port Moody. The eastern edges of north Vancouver fall into the outer suburbs as well. East of Lynn Creek and in the vicinity of Deep Cove, are areas of vacant land which will become urban land soon. The rest of the North Shore is considered part of the inner system of suburbs centred on downtown Vancouver.

The south-west

In certain respects, Richmond to the south and Burnaby to the east are more tied to the city of Vancouver than to the outer fringe municipalities of Delta, Surrey and Coquitlam. Richmond comprises the major islands of the Fraser delta; it is the home of the international airport, and a whole host of industrial and agricultural activities. The municipality has five major land-use regions. Directly south of Vancouver and adjacent to the old inter-urban line is an area of smallholdings, each an acre or two, often relatively long, narrow lots. Some of these had been laid out as veterans' lands after the war; some were just subdivisions of pre-existing arms. Many of the residents grew berries, vegetables, lowers and bulbs. Some were Dutch immigrants who ook to the delta land and realized its potential. These mallholdings were rarely self-sufficient farms but, ather, were part-time ventures by families whose readwinners worked in the mills, in construction, or lsewhere within the metropolitan area.

Following World War II, and in particular after the onstruction of the Oak Street bridge between Vancouver and Richmond, the demand for land for tract ousing expanded. The smallholdings nearest Vancouver presented real problems of land assembly. Proximity to the inter-urban was no longer a critical ransportation factor; thus, tract housing leap-frogged hese areas of older smallholdings to the larger farms to he west, mostly dairy farms that had remained intact s commercial enterprises. They became natural prey o the subdividers. The farms ranged from 20 to 140 cres, appropriate sizes for land subdivision at lower ost than competing areas. These subdivisions from the econd sub-area of Richmond. Several subdivisions ttracted middle-income families — teachers, social vorkers, firemen, airport personnel — plus a whole ange of regularly employed tradesmen and service vorkers. The car was the characteristic transportation node and, of course, urban densities and better municpal control made sewers, paved streets and other urban menities a prerequisite of development.

The removal of one race track in the centre of the ubdivisions permitted the creation of Richmond 5quare, probably the best planned town centre in the whole region. Municipal, commercial and professional services are focused on this centre — a creation of the planning department of the municipality itself. Two department stores, many small specialty stores, the city hall, the school board offices, the arena, major recreational facilities and the general hospital are part of the community focus.

A third area, the eastern half of the island, was less desirable to subdividers because it is generally more inaccessible. The municipality has zoned this for agriculture and has largely been able to control the encroachment of residential land into number of social and recreational activities as a means to keep their identity. The May festival, the various championship lacrosse teams operating from Queen's Park, the 'Salmonbellies', and the Canada Games in 1973 are examples of how New Westminster has maintained its identity even though Greater Vancouver has stretched into the city itself and certainly surrounds it.

The south-east

Another interesting part of the lower mainland region is the municipality of Surrey and adjacent areas of North Delta and White Rock which forms the south-eastern quadrant of Greater Vancouver, stretching from the Fraser River in the north to Boundary Bay in the south, from the flood plain with large dairy farms on the west to Langley on the east. The central part of the municipality remains agricultural, while the north and far south are rapidly becoming urbanized. A generation ago, those areas of Surrey were dotted with smallholdings of strawberry farmers and what were known locally as stump farmers. After World War II, North Surrey became an instant suburb for New Westminster, and to a lesser degree Vancouver. It was a classic example of urban sprawl. City-type houses were built on city-size lots sprinkled about the countryside in ones and twos, little clusters here, larger developments there, mixed in with farms, smallholdings and derelict land. It was, in part, a restaging of the kind of settlement that had taken place after World War I in south Vancouver.

The difference between the two was that south Vancouver was a streetcar suburb, whereas this particular area was entirely dependent upon the car. As Jim Wilson, director of the lower mainland regional planning board stated, 'It can be best described as little bits of city in the wrong places.' Wilson and others argued that the lower mainland had limited area for development, only about 750 square miles in total, and the sprawl belt, then encompassing about 100 square miles, was too great.

In the one municipality of Surrey, the sprawl area was as large as the city of Vancouver and could accommodate, in detached houses, the growth of the whole metropolitan area for two decades. The sprawl areas were under-serviced in comparison with other urban areas, but thousands of people had gone to live in them anyway. It seemed to fulfil a valid social need. In 1961, a lower mainland planning board survey of some 200 people described the average resident: a youngish, skilled, white-collar employee below the executive professional level, with a wife and two or three children of pre-school or elementary school level, living in two- or three-bedroom infill houses that they had bought within the previous five years. Most of them had moved out of Vancouver or New Westminster where they still worked. Few came directly from the rura areas.

When asked why they had chosen to live in these fringe areas, two answers showed up: 'open surroundings, fresh air, peace and quiet' and 'it was better for the children.' It would seem from the responses that the openness-seekers got what they wanted, while those with their children's welfare in mind found drawbacks they had not bargained for. The planners pointed out that the sprawl was a costly process both in money and in land, and it must be checked if the development of the whole region was not to be seriously prejudiced. At the same time, there remained an intractable fact that the fringe areas, especially the outer fringes, provide a haven for some who cannot find acceptable housing in the city within their means. The report (*The Urban Frontier*, 1963) goes on:

Possibly the most striking thing about this is the extent to which they [suburbs] are built on illusions. Most of the residents expected open space, peace and quiet but all these vanished as the area developed. They appear to have thought they could do without urban utilities but the need for these has crept upon them unawares even though they could do without city facilities and conveniences, but found that both they and their children needed them. They presumably expected low taxes, only to find that the taxes in rapidly developing suburban areas inevitably rise, and that what they don't pay in direct taxes, have to be paid in special charges.

Behind these minor illusions, lies a great illusion, that a large number of people umbilically attached to the great metropolis can escape urban cost and condition by moving one step from it. For a small community this may be feasible. Where scores of thousands of people are involved, it is self-defeating.

These studies and comments were the basis of the adoption of the regional plan for the lower mainland in 1967 and the designation and firming up of urban areas. It is within these urban areas that more than three times as many people can be accommodated as now live in the lower mainland. It is in these areas that continued growth has taken place in Surrey. As its population has grown from 70 000 in 1961, to 96 000 in 1971, the majority of the growth has been around the town centres of Whalley and Guildford in the northern part of the municipality. In the central section around Newton, an old station on the Fraser Valley inter-urban line, a lesser development has taken place. To the south, the agricultural land had been maintained along the flood plain, with the exception of the town of Cloverdale.

Further south again is another interesting fringe area, the area of White Rock and South Surrey. Along Boundary Bay, the small resort town of White Rock had been established, consisting of a group of cottages on a hillside overlooking large sandy beaches. The area was reached by the Pacific highway, which connected Greater Vancouver with the United States to the south, and by the Great Northern Railway. The municipality

of White Rock is quite small in area and had a population of 10 200 people in 1971, an increase of some 30% in the previous five years. Many of the people moving into White Rock are older, retired people taking advantage of the micro-climate of the lower mainland which sees the southern and western extremities, having less rain and more sunshine than the city. The adjacent areas in Surrey and an area locally known as Panorama Ridge, overlooking the delta agricultural lands, are connected to the city of Vancouver by Highway 499 from the south.

The social status of these people living adjacent to Highway 499 tends to be higher than that of people found in the northern part of Surrey. There are many expensive homes on large properties taking advantage of amenity sites. The attraction of these areas (as well as Tsawwassen) to the more affluent appears, in part, to be a natural extension of the sector pattern found in Vancouver where the middle- and upper-income families live in the central west-side of the city. Although this is far to the south-east, the freeway entrance to the city of Vancouver via the Oak Street bridge goes squarely through the west-side neighbourhoods.

The eastern trio

Within the ring of new suburbs to the east of Burnaby the municipalities of Coquitlam (52 000), Port Coquitlam (19 000) and Port Moody (10 000) are growing rapidly. In Port Moody, in particular, the kinds of residential subdivisions that have taken place tend to be on amenity sites, and have attracted people with higher incomes and higher social status than some of the intervening areas in Burnaby and the eastern side of Vancouver. Although many people who are moving to the Coquitlams work in New Westminster and in the industrial areas of Burnaby, it is clear that a group of central city workers are leap-frogging the established working-class neighbourhoods of east Vancouver and Burnaby and are showing up in Port Moody and Coquitlam. The problem that many of them have, of course, is that up until August 1973 these were entirely car-oriented suburbs with no bus routes into the city. Extensive use is made of the 401 Freeway through Burnaby and the Barnett Highway as connections to the downtown area.

Nevertheless, the industrial workforce is expanding in the peripheral municipalities, with all areas except New Westminster showing actual as well as relative increases.

The ring of suburbs from Richmond to Delta, Surrey and the Coquitlams has been an area of very rapid growth in the census period 1966–71. The increase has been generally in the 50–70% range in the Coquitlams in these five years, not as fast as the municipality of Delta which had a 118% increase in population. The housing constructed in these municipalities is largely of a tract form (infilling) in many cases, the areas of smallholdings that were left after the first sprawl immediately after World War II. One of the problems that has been faced by developers is that there are very few large tracts to develop. The early subdivision of land into smallholdings meant that it was more common to have two- and five-acre plots available for sale for subdivision purposes, than perhaps 20- or 40- or even 100-acre sites which would be more advantageous to large-scale mass-produced housing. Therefore, much of the building that has taken place in these subdivisions has been of groups of four, eight or 12 houses on single streets. This, then, has not permitted some of the large-scale economies that have been present in other cities like Calgary and the peripheral areas of Toronto. Mary Hill, Glen-aire and College Park are important exceptions.

In all three areas, the south, the south-east and the east, there has been in recent years a large number of condominium town houses built at densities of 10–15 units per acre. This class of housing is still growing proportionally. In all municipal areas, there are extremely large (per capita) capital programmes under way to provide municipal services even though the developers have had to provide these within their subdivisions. The demands for new schools have to be dealt with across the board, and the need for arterial streets, primary sewage treatment, and development of community facilities such as ice rinks and swimming pools, have brought increasing pressure on the residential tax base. To some degree, the municipalities like Surrey have had modest amounts of industry to assist in the servicing of the growing population, and to prevent disproportionate sums from falling on the individual householder.

It is very clear that these areas became integral parts of the Vancouver urban system in the 1960s, and that further links between these areas and the central city are going to be critical in the immediate future. This will be manifest in plans for public transportation, in which bus services will expand into these peripheral municipalities. Vancouver is now a city region which must be analysed as a whole.

References

Gibson E M W 1972 The impact of social belief on landscape change: a geographical study of Vancouver' *PhD Dissertation* University of British Columbia

F W Howay *et al* 1942 *British Columbia and the United States* (Toronto: Ryerson Press)

Lower Mainland Regional Planning Board 1963 *The Urban Frontier* Part 1 (New Westminster, BC: LMRPB) Summary and conclusions.

20   Social Processes and Residential Structure in Eastern Europe

by R A French and F E I Hamilton

Social change in the city

The abolition of capitalism has made all urban residents economically dependent upon earned incomes from their work. Socialization of welfare facilities and the fixing of low costs of living (rents, fares, utilities) have gone far to equate opportunities at the start in the everyday lives of ordinary citizens. Thereafter, depending upon intellect or acquired skill or chance, people in cities pursue a widening variety of schooling, and occupations which are widely differentiated in incomes and status. That variation expresses 'merit' according to new national priorities and socialist needs, yielding socio-occupational stratification.

It is hard to achieve that equal start in life for all even in the longer term. East European sociologists today recognize evolving 'ensembles of systems' within their societies, there being partial invasion or complete succession of strata for classes as socialization progresses. Past class structures often survived the war, especially in pre-socialist zones of cities where populations were relatively immobile as in Prague and hundreds of smaller Czechoslovak, Hungarian or Romanian towns. In western and northern Polish cities and Bohemian rimland towns the once deeper German and non-German class divisions were replaced by a narrower and lower 'band' of classes among Polish and Czechoslovak settlers from regions further east.

Nationalization of many workers' occupations did not mean that 'all other features of their social position would disappear automatically' (Wesołowski 1966, p 174); workers continued to interact with other surviving classes and with newly emergent strata. Mental images and processes were slower to change than political, economic or material reality. Yet exposure to socialization 'decomposes' (Szczepański 1973) former status and behaviour born of capitalist–worker relations and forges new value systems which can remove high income from high prestige or political power. But 'decomposition' may be slow, especially in towns of limited change. Everywhere inherited class structures can exert strong influences on the following generation, particularly in their attitudes to education and work, and hence on emergent socio-occupational structure and stratification. Sociologists such as Wesołowski (1970), Szczepański and others in Poland, have sketched attitudes which are of profound importance in understanding the spatial patterns of social behaviour, perceptions, contacts, interaction and of residential changes in the post-war East European city. For among the once upper, middle and intelligentsia classes 'élitist attitudes, introvert concern with their own circle, snobbism and scramble after prestige . . . disdain and scorn for manual work and manual workers . . . have proved to be not only very resistant, but even very infectious, being willingly adopted by the young' (Szczepański 1973, p295).

With economic development, all East European cities have experienced social diversification. New occupations were initiated and new strata emerged, 'splitting' or 'decomposing' former classes. Rural migrants flowed in to fill new jobs or to replace townsfolk moving 'up' or 'across' the social ladder, and offspring of both rural and urban migrants began to mingle in the classroom, the dancehall or the café. While 'older' urban intelligentsia have tended to become more and more 'professional', most rural migrants have entered the factories, transport or services as unskilled manual workers. There are, however, exceptions, as ambitions are also 'infectious' among the peasantry: their children, with access to free and improved education, can

Source: Edited extract from R A French and F E I Hamilton (eds) 1979 *The Socialist City* (New York: Wiley) Ch. 10, 'Social Processes and Residential Structure,' pp275–8 and 283–90.

move into professional city jobs via universities and specialized schools. Villages are known near Warsaw, for example, whence *all* youth, including the girls, have become doctors, engineers, architects, planners or research workers since 1955 and now work in several of Poland's larger cities. No less significantly, first- or second-generation descendants of large landowners or *kulaks*, dispossessed of land by inter-war and post-war agrarian reforms, often swell the ranks of industrial managers and administrators in search of their 'lost' independence or *'sobiepaństwo'* as Kiezuń (1971, pp212–17) calls it. Thus social mobility interacts with attitudinal immobilities to shape new strata in the socialist city.

Very commonly, planned socialist industrialization has brought large-scale extractive, construction and manufacturing enterprises to 'sleepy' small- or medium-sized towns. The shorter- and long-term social consequences of these quite sudden 'shocks' to the attitudes and behaviour patterns in such cities have attracted much research, especially in Poland. Studies and syntheses of sociological investigations by Szczepański (1973), Tyszka (1970) and Zechowski (1973) yield conclusions from such cities as Legnica, Konin, Nowa Huta, Płock, Puławy and Tarnobrzeg, which are as valid elsewhere. Such cities undergo four stages of social experience, each connected with phases of project implementation: preparation, construction, activation and putting on 'full stream'. Though stages overlap in real life, each generates specific demands for workers according to skills, numbers, and hence socio-economic and spatial backgrounds. Each thus shapes social behaviour and interaction, the quality of urban life, in distinctive ways.

The first stage has least impact. Small teams of specialists usually reside in a town for short periods only. Most critical of all is the construction stage, which often requires thousands of workers, mostly male, ranging from labourers to chemical engineers drawn from local or more remote villages, small towns, regional and capital cities or from abroad. Although many workers may be 'temporary' (1–5 years), others acquire skills and eventually stay. But this stage sees social disorganization and pathology, greatest confrontation and conflict in social interaction within the towns (Ziołkowski 1967, Szczepański 1973). Traditional 'haunts', routes and routines of the townsfolk are 'invaded', 'congested' or 'dislocated', creating tensions between them and the newcomers in public places and in rented accommodation. No less, tensions in barracks and workers' dormitories emerge between the very highly paid and adaptable 'suitcase specialists' from big or foreign cities and the labourers of peasant stock confronted both by urban living at its lowest level and by their first, 'apparently' large, wage packets. The lives of urban womenfolk are transformed by the new environment of jobs, surplus men and scarcities of goods, often bringing tensions into the home. Enterprises of long-standing lose their better employees because of the higher incomes and career attractions invariably offered by new projects, altering further the daily circulation patterns and introducing instabilities into the labour force of the town's traditional functions. The 'thin end' of a broadening — if unstable — wedge of 'external' social strata penetrates even deeper to the heart of the 'internal' class structure of the town.

The third stage — production — is hardly less traumatic. Socially the newcomers and 'old timers' begin to stabilize their uneasy relationships, but new tensions emerge. Greatest pressures occur in this stage on housing, welfare services, infrastructure and consumer services (Ginsbert 1963). Although temporary workers are leaving, the permanent workforce in the project moves from its dormitories and seeks housing to buy, a room (even just a bed) to rent, in the older pre-socialist quarters, 'invading' the residential fortresses of traditional class behaviour. Or it 'queues' for the flats in new residential areas. Demand is further swollen as production requires permanent workers with new skills such as machine-minding while the city itself needs people for services, infrastructure and construction. As production approaches 'full stream' the multiplier effects on jobs and occupational strata weaken, but sooner or later they appear socially as 'marriage booms' and 'baby booms' which subsequently generate wave-like pressures through the city's medical, educational and recreational facilities. Tension and conflicts lessen, but broadly in inverse proportion to the supply of scarce housing, goods and neighbourhood services. The greater the welfare-sector and consumer-goods supplies, the quicker are the overcrowding, the congestion and the confrontation thinned out within urban space.

Not only have smaller cities experienced such processes: few larger cities have escaped them. Nevertheless Polish sociologists observe that social harmony or conflict are variable within the foregoing framework. Whether newly expanded towns or zones of long-established cities are being studied, one thing is clear. The incidence of social disorganization and pathology is inversely related to the levels of urbanization in the source regions of the migrants, and to the required 'skill levels' and scale of the new project. Thus social disorganization has been relatively high on Warsaw's east bank in Praga following large-scale industrialization in Żerań–Bródno (Polski FIAT), and in Nowa Huta or Płock, where in each case thousands of male workers have been attracted from underdeveloped agrarian eastern and south-eastern Poland. Its incidence is significantly lower in Poznań, Łódź or Gdańsk where industrial expansion has been more diversified, more regular or 'incremental', has demanded higher skills or employed more women, and drawn labour from more urbanized hinterlands. Probably much the same picture emerges from other cities in Eastern Europe.

Social change and residential areas

The 'decomposition' of classes into social strata occurs as new strata in new occupations begin to 'invade' and 'succeed' in the older, pre-socialist housing areas and so to fragment former class-differentiated zones. The old city thus gradually takes on the pattern of a socio-occupational 'mosaic'. As new residential districts are developed on the city periphery, council policies for, or the accidents of, social mixing cause a diffusive 'showering' effect of strata from the older central into the newer outer districts: people move to where flats are available in such districts, not to where they choose. Studies undertaken in the 1950s 'filmed' this process in an embryonic or transitional stage and demonstrated both continuity of 'traditional' and socially differentiated zones and change towards greater intra-zonal mixing. There is clear evidence that the latter was far more marked by the 1970s.

Socio-economic research by Pióro (1962) in Lublin and Toruń — two 'medium-sized' and less industrialized Polish towns — has shown how selected processes continued to operate in the 1950s to perpetuate pre-war spatial differentiation into dominantly professional and dominantly manual workers' areas. Indeed segregation was intensified initially as migrants from rural areas took rooms in working-class districts and as the established townsfolk, with higher skills and incomes, moved into the professionals' areas. Lublin even had a 'zone of transition' near its centre and strong spatial associations were found between social groups, housing conditions, social and biological pathology.

More striking still were such patterns in two much larger industrial cities — Łódź and Wrocław — which had inherited much nineteenth-century industrial 'fabric'. The general pattern of socio-spatial structure in Łódź has been shaped by the historic, unidirectional process of the industrial development of a capitalist city (Piotrowski 1966, p11). After 1950, planned introduction of chemicals, machinery and film-making industries, research and development to expand male employment in a predominantly textiles–manufacturing city, led to some in-migration of new strata. Yet little change occurred in the inherited social pattern. Indeed, central Łódź gained even greater distinctiveness, assuming the character of a 'small professional town' within an industrial workers' metropolis, as University and other skilled people moved in. Clearance of dreadful slums was undertaken to the north of the city centre. New residential districts built there became new ecological entities attracting many new migrants; certain pathological associations with new high-rise flats have appeared, so perpetuating the somewhat 'transitional' nature of the zone. Beyond, workers' housing estates, mixing pre-war and larger post-war housing, followed by an outer 'suburban' zone further led Piotrowski to liken Łódź to Burgess' concentric zone model.

Interviews with random families in six selected housing areas in Wrocław indicated population segregation by socio-occupational group. People with similar jobs, skills and educational backgrounds were living in similar housing conditions (Jałowiecki 1968). 'Natural areas' were also identified, giving greater credence to Piotrowski's findings in Łódź, and emphasizing continued social attitudes, values and perceptions. The pre-war socio-spatial structure of Wrocław had been reproduced — despite a high degree of war destruction and an almost complete substitution of Poles for Germans. This example serves to stress, however, the difficulties that planners and city housing officials must face if they apply the principle of minimizing the journey to work in cities with large-scale but highly differentiated capitalist heritages.

Such patterns, however, can emerge from the interaction of planning ownership restrictions on the one hand, and of freedom of movement by individuals in response to their means, motives and aspirations on the other. This is particularly true where housing is very scarce and where there are fewer restrictions on the purchase, sale or renting of privately owned premises in older city areas or of state or cooperative flats. Witkowski (1967) observed in Radom that 'the inelasticity of fixed assets and of their differentiation, especially housing, is the motive for certain social groups to aspire to occupying a higher and higher ecological position, which drives them practically to migration from older to progressively newer homes and housing districts'. As a result, weaker social groups were relegated to the worst ecological conditions. Studies of Częstochowa (Braun 1964) and Grudziadz (cited in Węcławowicz 1975) indicated similar situations. Often, conditions were worsened by the inflow of in-migrating workers into the same areas of the towns where their mates were already living, suggesting the crucial role of contact networks and information in residential choice, at least for the newcomers.

The final example from Poland relates to Płock, one of the cities subject to 'industrial shock' in the 1960s where the relatively larger scale of new, socialist, and high 'quality' growth (by comparison with Łódź, Wrocław or even Radom) produced different results. Data have been collected on occupational structure, educational levels of in-migrants and housing conditions for 45 enumeration districts. Six types of districts were discernable in the city in 1960 prior to the oil-refinery construction stage: professional professional-worker, worker, peasant-worker, peasant and mixed structures. Juxtaposition of districts with similar structures formed themselves into larger 'natural areas', indicating spatial class differentiation: the town still fossilized its social past. Between 1950 and 1960 two socio-spatial tendencies were observable: unskilled rural migrants mainly settled in existing workers' areas (as in other cities) or in the town's 'urban' fringe. *But* social levelling also resulted from the loss of elite character in old areas and some advancement of workers' areas. The major long-term impact of the oil refinery was the influx into Płock of many skilled workers. Given priority, such workers (especially those with young families) were moved into new residential districts on the periphery, leaving townsfolk and the earlier skilled 'movers' in the presocialist town. 'Decomposition' and fragmentation of the socio-spatial structure thus proceeded as further stratification of occupations and status among the townsfolk, and between them and the newcomers, has been superimposed on the old social pattern. Similar processes were observed in Prague in the 1960s (Musil 1969).

Housing problems and policies

Voluminous research in all socialist countries on commuting to expanding cities is one major index of socio-economic effects of the lags in urban housing supply. Rent and land values are irrelevant in explaining the distribution of socio-economic groups. Rents are neither differentiated with location nor with housing quality. Individual preferences interact with the housing policies that control supplies of modern flats. Priority allocation to selected groups of the new, best quality and most uniform state housing clearly restricts — on grounds of inadequate supply — the availability of such flats to other groups who, according to their considered 'lower-order' occupations or their higher income, do not have any priority. Inevitably the attention of such groups turns towards satisfying their aspirations from the pre-socialist housing stock that is usually highly differentiated in physical condition, in number and size of rooms, in fittings and in location. Since the rents for such accommodation are normally payable to the private owner-occupiers, and since the rents chargeable may vary substantially within either permissible legal or tolerated (or 'undisclosed') illegal limits, this housing 'market' situation explains some 'jockeying' among social strata for better, older housing.

Evidence suggests that social strata 'sort themselves out' among housing types and zones according to: their priority status for inexpensive state housing; their incomes which may permit them (or not) to rent or purchase better private (villa-type) housing or to become owner-occupiers of cooperative flats; and aspirations which shape their preferences. A survey of housing and social groups in Szeged by Konrad and Szelenyi (1969) observed that Hungarian housing policy — which is to ensure the right of every family to a modern, self-contained dwelling — had encouraged and facilitated a faster rate of upward filtering of lower-income groups into better housing. Typical for an historic East European city, Szeged offered five types of housing stock, differentiated by tenure and quality. Most 'desirable' were post-war state-owned flats allocated by the city council, followed by relatively expensive private villas and less expensive cooperative owner-occupier flats. In time the higher-income groups of administrators, professions and workers tended systematically to obtain this type of housing by allocation 'with the job', by purchase or by aspiration. Yet housing policy tended to neglect the most needy, so that lower-income groups aspired to expensive but more modest older property (including villas) and to either the one- and two-roomed flats or the more obsolete 'village-type' single-storey dwellings. Such aspirations for 'status-symbolic' housing seem to suggest continuities in 'pre-socialist' thought processes.

That housing *is* differentiated in quality within, and between, cities cannot be doubted. That is a legacy of the pre-socialist past and is the fault of post-war socialist planning only insofar as replacement rates of older by modern uniform housing stock has been insufficient to eliminate the significant role that the 'market' in privately owned, older dwellings plays in the social distribution of shelter. Visual evidence is enough to confirm that the two categories of poorer housing, much of it pre-dating 1918, are replicated in most pre-socialist quarters in Hungarian, Czechoslovak, Polish, Romanian, Yugoslav and Bulgarian towns. Pre-1918 and inter-war dwellings accounted for 67.8% of all housing in Czechoslovak towns in 1970 and 78% in western parts of the country (Kansky 1976), although in the Balkans the percentages are significantly lower, as in Yugoslavia where it is less than 40% of urban housing. Even in Poland, where war destroyed one-third of the city housing stock, more than 45% still pre-dates 1939.

The very considerable differentiation that the existence of such property brings to the zonal pattern in the East European city may be illustrated from the seven *dzielnice* in Warsaw (table 20.1; figure 20.1). The spatial variations in housing quality are fairly clear. Poorest by far is the 'east bank' housing in Praga Północ (including Żeran) where few dwellings in 1959 had central heating, gas supplies or bathrooms, and the lowest proportions had toilet, sewage and running water facilities: here were also the greatest proportions of pre-war housing. Such areas probably had the poorest health records in the city as the consistently higher death rates in Praga Północ (table 20.1) suggest is the case. Conditions in Praga Południe are only marginally improved by the inter-war villa-type development in Saska Kepa. Much better housing characterizes the west-bank districts, notably Śródmieście, Wola and Mokotów, which have seen large-scale rebuilding or new development schemes since 1950 and in Żoliborz, which also inherited a high standard of inter-war residential property. Nevertheless, among other factors, housing policy in Warsaw since 1950 has reduced dif-

Table 20.1.   Selected social indicators in the seven districts of Warsaw, 1960–61, 1970–71.

Indicators		Warsaw City	Districts (*dzielnice*)				Żolibórz	Praga	
			Śródmieście		Ochota			Pólnoc (N)	Poludnie (S)
				Mokotów		Wola			
Population growth (%)	1970/1	18.4	−0.2(+5.6)[1]	25.3	26.0	22.2	67.8	−4.3(+3.2)[1]	16.6
Birth rates	1960/1	12.8	11.5	12.1	11.6	13.0	12.6	13.8	13.1
	1970/1	10.4	8.5	9.9	9.8	10.2	10.4	12.3	10.3
Death rates	1960/1	6.8	6.6	5.3	6.0	5.7	5.9	7.65	6.9
	1970/1	9.0	10.5	8.0	8.4	8.3	7.6	11.1	9.1
In-migrants in population	1960/1	73.1	78.3	67.1	76.4	77.5	73.3	68.9	77.1
growth (%)	1970/1	94.3	100.0	89.5	91.8	89.8	84.6	95.4	93.9
In-migrants from rural areas (%)	1960/1	19.0	20.3	28.7	25.2	19.6	31.0	36.9	24.6
Total of all in-migrants (%)	1970/1	41.0	30.7	40.7	39.7	43.5	42.6	47.8	41.0
Average living space per capita in flats or houses (m²)	1970/1	14.2	15.9	14.6	14.1	12.8	14.0	13.6	14.1
Flats in 1960/61 with (%)									
Running water		75.0	93.9	80.4	67.9	81.8	80.4	63.6	63.0
Sewerage		75.0	93.1	79.9	68.7	80.2	79.8	60.0	64.7
Baths		51.0	73.4	67.6	50.0	48.3	66.0	22.0	38.5
Toilets		64.0	85.0	74.0	61.6	67.3	75.4	41.4	52.0
Electricity		98.0	98.4	98.2	98.9	98.4	98.8	95.9	98.9
Gas		52.6	79.0	70.0	45.0	54.8	69.0	30.0	32.0
Central heating		43.0	64.0	60.0	43.0	44.0	57.0	16.0	27.0

Sources: *Rocznik Statystyczny Warszawy* (1962, 1973).

[1] Figures in brackets indicate contrary or 'see-saw' changes 1960/1–1965/6, which would otherwise be hidden by the figures for 1960/1–1970/1.

Figure 20.1 Administrative districts in Warsaw, 1970.

ferentiation among districts, particularly in living space per capita (table 20.1) and in the average number of persons per room. In 1939 west-bank district dwellings had averaged 2 persons, east-bank dwellings 2.4 persons per room; by 1959 both had 1.6 persons per room.

The post-war challenge in housing throughout Eastern Europe has been how to use limited capital to achieve simultaneously an increase in living space per capita and an improvement in the standard of that space in the face of a rapidly rising population. Improvements have been made, but often only by retaining much substandard pre-socialist property. As this is replaced, the struggle to supply enough housing will continue. For example, in 1946 there were 1.67 persons per room in Polish dwellings and despite the construction of 4.8 million flats this density had only been lowered to 1.31 by 1970. The future plan, to reduce it to 0.80 persons per room by 1990 while replacing 20% of the entire national housing stock which is most substandard, is clearly a major challenge (Andrzejewski and Kulesza 1974).

No less a challenge comes from the spatial differentiation in housing quality between cities and within emerging urban agglomerations. Poland again offers illustrative data. Table 20.2 sets out, for urban dwellings in 1970 by voivodships, the number of persons per room, living space per capita, and the proportions

of dwellings which had piped water, a bathroom and which were self-contained (i.e. inhabited by only one family). Clearly much housing everywhere falls below the acceptable 'contemporary standard — a dwelling which is self-contained with a bathroom and central heating' (Andrzejewski and Kulesza 1974). Yet the better conditions in towns of much post-war residential construction do stand out, particularly Warsaw and towns in the southern voivodships. Elsewhere the comparative modernity of housing supply — evident in the higher percentages with piped water and bathrooms — often partially counterbalances the greater overcrowding, as in Gdańsk and Szczecin and in the cities of Poznań, Cracow and Wrocław where there are fewer self-contained flats. That almost one-half (Poznań city) to two-thirds (Koszalin) of dwellings in towns in these areas are shared by more than one family (often with in-laws) is a major index of continued overcrowding. Differences remained substantial in 1970 in the country's larger urban agglomerations. The spatial structure of housing conditions within the agglomerations is clearly dependent upon several variables. Greatest differentiation occurs within monocentric agglomerations with a large legacy of capitalist-period housing, like Wrocław or Łódź, where, using as indices the proportions of dwellings with piped water and with flush toilets and the proportion of self-contained flats, 'living conditions worsen on all counts with increasing distance from the central city to the periphery' Andrzejewski and Kulesza 1974). But in those monocentric agglomerations in which policy has attempted to 'close' the central city boundary to in-migrants, as in Warsaw, the worst living conditions occur in settlements just outside that boundary (Gliszczyński 1967). Polynuclear agglomerations, like Upper Silesia, show least variation.

Under conditions of persistent housing scarcity, Polish urban agglomerations are hardly in a position to absorb continued, let alone accelerated, migration from the countryside. Central cities still suffer from overcrowding of existing stock and, despite an expanding housing supply, will continue to do so for some years. The capacity of their 'urbanized' or 'urbanizing' hinterlands to accommodate either newcomers or central-city overspill is also severely constrained by low levels of infrastructure and provision of utilities. This raises key policy issues which are of wider significance for the future evolution of housing in the socialist city in general. In the 1980s and 1990s housing conditions will play an increasingly important role — rather than

Table 20.2.   Selected indices of housing conditions in Polish cities by voivodships in 1970[a].

Towns and cities in (voivodship)	Percentage of dwelling units			Average living space in square metres per capita	Average number of persons per room
	Self-contained	With piped water	With a bathroom		
Łódź	78.7[b]	43.3	30.2	11.8	1.42
Łódź city	78.3[b]	71.2	44.3	12.8	1.33
Warsaw city	77.2[b]	89.9[b]	75.0[b]	13.4[b]	1.24[b]
Opole	75.9[b]	83.0[b]	51.3[b]	14.9[b]	1.19[b]
Katowice	75.6[b]	81.7[b]	46.2	14.0[b]	1.25[b]
Wrocław	74.9[b]	77.0	33.4	13.4[b]	1.30[b]
Cracow	74.5[b]	80.0[b]	49.6[b]	13.2[b]	1.33
Rzeszów	74.3[b]	63.1	49.5[b]	13.2[b]	1.35
Warsaw	73.7[b]	47.9[b]	36.1	11.6	1.40
Poznań	72.2[b]	63.0	34.9	12.9[b]	1.32
Kielce	72.2[b]	58.1	44.8	11.5	1.46
Zielona Góra	72.1[b]	81.0[b]	42.7	12.9[b]	1.27
Koszalin	67.2	83.2[b]	47.3[b]	12.4	1.29[b]
Białystok	66.9	61.7	42.0	11.3	1.37
Olsztyń	66.0	87.3[b]	46.7	11.5	1.40
Lublin	65.9	60.3	44.5	11.4	1.44
Cracow city	65.6	86.1[b]	69.7[b]	13.0[b]	1.37
Gdańsk	63.0	91.4[b]	58.6[b]	12.2	1.31[b]
Bydgoszcz	62.8	73.2	39.1	12.0	1.38
Wrocław city	60.2	90.6[b]	60.8[b]	13.2[b]	1.34
Szczecin	60.0	87.4[b]	51.0[b]	12.6	1.27[b]
Poznań city	54.9	90.4[b]	60.8[b]	13.5[b]	1.30[b]
All Polish cities	71.1	75.2	48.4	12.8	1.32

[a]Cities grouped by voivodships are ranked according to the proportions of their housing units that are self-contained.
[b]Cities and voivodship groupings of cities which exceed the Polish average in quality of conditions.
Source: Andrzejewski and Kulesza (1974, pp32–40).

just the supply of jobs — in shaping the largely free choice of East Europeans to migrate from one place to another. A policy for the location of modern, attractive housing must be devised as a necessary component of a long-term national plan for the distribution of population and economic activity.

Already housing policy has been increasingly used as an instrument of economic as well as social policy (Musil 1969, Ball and Harloe 1974). Greater differentiation of socialized housing supply has been introduced in standards of space and fittings, purchase costs or rents, and speeds of 'shortening the queue' for allocation. Introduction of cooperatively owned flats is especially important. From the pessimistic viewpoint, this required the trading off of some of the longer-term quest for equal access to adequate living standards for the shorter-term necessity of narrowing the chronic housing gap. By tapping the personal savings of higher-income groups and of those who can and do travel abroad, it thus stimulates new social differentia-

tion in the city. However, cooperative blocks can be mixed with council-owned blocks to achieve 'social mixing' within neighbourhoods. There are few data on this, or indeed on the extent to which differentiation in socialized housing supply also occurs between cities. The proportion of cooperative flats in Polish towns rose from 1.5% in 1960 to about 22% in 1976; in the latter year, however, the proportion in Warsaw was almost 30%. Concentration of cooperative housing in bigger cities may be related to the greater localization there of skilled labour generally (Rajman 1972). Yet while cooperatives are successful in larger cities with housing scarcities since the local residents are willing to put their savings into them, they may not attract the necessary savings in new towns or in towns currently with poor infrastructure and located in the peripheries of major agglomerations.

On an optimistic note, the rapid increase in the purchase of cooperative flats in Poland and elsewhere suggests that more than just the professions can afford to buy them. A significant, often underrated, factor is the increased employment of women, which has doubled the number of 'breadwinners' in most urban families, and has brought the cooperative flat within purchasing range of more workers' families. Cooperatives, too, have permitted the state to concentrate its energies more than before on providing adequate modern housing for lower-income and other groups who still find cooperatives inaccessible. Thus the 1960s and 1970s have seen a more rapid 'upward filtering' of the lower-income groups into better housing. The picture, however, is far from homogeneous from city to city and there is still much evidence to imply that the unskilled rural migrant steps on to the urban housing 'ladder' on the lowest rung — by sharing a room in older urban property or by living in a workers' dormitory.

Conclusions

Further research is clearly required into the social processes shaping spatial structure and social interaction in cities of the socialist world. The limited scope and uneven coverage of empirical work as to who behaves how, and lives where — and why — in East European cities makes it unwise to generalize. This paper has relied on the findings of a fragmentary range of studies, particularly in Poland and Romania, as well as on first-hand impressions and anecdotal evidence.

First, an underlying theme which has been explored concerns the spatial aspects of relationships between (1) official public ideology and state socialist institutions and (2) private group and individual preferences and behaviour. That cities are imbedded in economies which are state-owned and more or less centrally planned and in societies in which the Communist Party is politically dominant is clear. But how is everyday urban social life affected by such institutional arrangements? What is being suggested is that the contrasts within and between socialist cities are partly a product of post-revolutionary planning but may also be due to the lag (or gap) between it and the development of socialist consciousness and behaviour. Housing and other policies are not solely determined on the basis of ideology, and furthermore such policies may well have unintended outcomes. Thus, for example, it would appear that the living conditions of the new urban working class have been substantially improved with the provision of housing estates, hospitals, higher educational places and holiday camps. On the other hand, urban society is stratified because the older middle

classes have prospered through their resilience and involvement in (though not ownership of) the political economy of the city while a new middle class of party members, bureaucrats, technocrats, managers and military personnel has emerged.

Secondly, there is the question of what criteria govern the allocation of urban services and facilities? Equality and need certainly, but to what extent are local political systems responsive to citizen preferences? Voting and pressure group activity may not be significant modes of political participation. Yet Oliver (1968) has shown that individual complaining can be effective even if the Party lays down the parameters of demand-making, and failures are often attributed to poor management and not to misconceived, centrally established priorities.

Finally, an explanation for urban residential structure has been sought in both public policies and private choices. In Hungary, for example, Konrad and Szelenyi found that both housing policies and the preferences of different housing classes resulted in neglect of those in greatest need. In Romania, socially mixed estates may well have been created by accident. Open spaces in older council estates have been infilled with blocks of flats for private ownership, flats allocated and purchased regardless of occupation or ethnic origin, and home ownership encouraged. Housing policies may have economic causes but social effects.

Identifying spatial patterns in the welfare of people who live in socialist cities may well be an arduous task, but providing adequate explanations is an even more difficult one.

References

Andrzejewski A and Kulesza H 1974 Infrastruktura mieszkaniowa i jej zróżnicowanie regionalne *Studia Komitet Przestrzennego Zagospodarowania Kraju* XLVIII, p 37, 60.

Ball M and Harloe M 1974 *Housing Policy in a Socialist Country: The Case of Poland* (London: Centre for Environmental Studies)

Braun J 1964 *Elementy Ekologii Miasta Przemysłowego* Zaklad Badań Naukowych GOP (Wrocław: PAN)

Ginsbert A 1963 O problemach komunalnych Płocka *Biblioteka Badań Regiónow Uprzemyslowianych Seria Płocka* 1

Gliszczyński F 1967 Problematyka przestrzenna sytuacju mieszkaniówej i budowniotwa mieszkaniowego Warszawy i jej strefy podmiejskiej *Studia Komitet Przestrzennego Zagospodarownia Kraju* XXI, 172pp

Jałowiecki B 1968 *Osiedle i Miasta, Studium Socjologiczno-Urbánystyczne Jednostek Mieszkaniowych Wrocławia* (Warsaw: PWN)

Kansky K J 1976 *Urbanization under Socialism: The Case of Czechoslovakia* (New York: Praeger)

Kiezuń W 1971 *Autonomizacja Jednostek Organizacyjnych z*

Patologii Organizacji (Warsaw: PWN)

Konrad G and Szelenyi I 1969 *Sociological Aspects of the Allocation of Housing* (Budapest: Sociological Research Group, Hungarian Academy of Sciences)

Musil J 1969 The development of Prague's ecological structure, in *Readings in Urban Sociology* ed R Pahl (Oxford: Pergamon)

Oliver J H 1968 Citizen demands and the Soviet political system *American Political Science Review* 63 pp465–75

Pióro Z 1962 *Ekologia Spoleczna w Urbanistyce na Przykładzie Badań Lubleskich i Toruńskich* (Warsaw: PWN)

Piotrowski W 1966 *Spoleczno-przestrzenne struktura m Łodzi: studium ekologiczne* (Wrocław: Zakład Narodowy im Ossolinskich, Polish Academy of Sciences)

Rajman J 1972 Koncentracja kadr kwalifikowanych w Polsce *Czasopismo Geograficzne* 43(1) pp 57–65

Szczepański J 1973 *Zmiany Spoleczenstwa Polskiego w Procesie Uprzemysłowienia* (Warsaw: Instytut Wydawniczy CRZZ) 307pp

Tyszka Z 1970 *Przeobrażenia Rodziny Robotniczej w Warunkach Uprzemysłowienia i Urbanizacji* (Warsaw: PWN)

Wecławowicz G 1975 Struktura Przestrzeni Społeczeno-Gospodarczej Warszawy w Latach 1931 i 1970 w Swietle Analizy Czynnikowej *Prace Geograficzne* **116**

Weolowski W 1970 *Klasy, Warstwy i Wladza* (Warsaw: PWN)

Witkowski S 1967 *Struktura Przestrzenna Miasta na Przykladzie Radomia* (Warsaw: PWN) p 155.

Zechowski Z A 1973 *Przemiany Malych Miast w Procesie Uprzemysłowienia: Studium nad Miasteczkami Powiatu Konińskiego* (Warsaw// Poznań: PWN)

Ziółkowski J (ed) 1967 *Poznań: Społeczno-przestrzenne Skutki Industrializacji* (Warsaw: PWN)

Section V
Local Government and Urban Politics

Introduction

In most advanced countries there is a separate system of local government which is formally autonomous and not under the direct control of higher levels of government. This is also the case in the three countries from which our case studies come, and in each of the cities with which we are concerned there are local (urban) governmental institutions of some importance. Of course, we should not expect urban government to take precisely the same form in Poland, Britain and Canada, but assessing the significance of the similarities and differences is a little more difficult.

Stereotypes of local government in the three countries come fairly readily to mind. In Poland one might expect the organs of local government simply to be mouthpieces through which decisions from the top, and above all from the Polish United Workers Party (PUWP, i.e. the Communist Party), are transmitted to the local areas. The task of local councils, according to such a view, would simply be to ensure the implementation of a plan whose features were decided at national level. In Britain, on the other hand, although few people would argue that our local authorities provided unequivocal examples of independence and thriving local democracy, perhaps an optimistic view would be that the balance between central control and local democracy was a reasonable one. The civil service orthodoxy holds that global controls on spending still allow flexibility at local level, even if there has been some doubt cast on that by local authority spokesmen in recent years. The existence of a multi-party system in Britain is generally held to allow greater scope for political debate and democratic control than is the case in Poland. It is possible to present different views on major issues to the voter at regular intervals. One would expect to find the greatest contrast with the apparently centralized monolith of Poland in the Canadian setting, with its federalist structure and apparently decentralized units of local government. In Vancouver not only are there regular elections but they seem to provide the greatest opportunity for individuals to have a voice since the council as a whole is elected at large by the people of Vancouver as a whole. Since the party system finds little direct expression at local level it could be argued that in Vancouver at least, it is possible to vote for the most efficient local government, and shifting political alliances may be possible on different issues.

The material included in this section supports some of these contentions and undermines others. It reinforces the dangers of taking institutional forms and the offical reasons for them at face value and helps to illustrate the strengths and weaknesses of various theoretical approaches to the study of urban politics.

The Polish case is perhaps the most interesting. Piekalkiewicz makes it quite clear that the Polish local government system cannot simply be seen as the local arm of central government or even party organization, partly because this would reduce its utility for those bodies. Although, of course, local government operates within very tight constraints it is forced to respond to locally generated pressures and is open to a range of complaints from local residents. In Cracow various professional organizations played a significant part in the 1970s in raising the issue of pollution as a local problem and placing it on the local and national political agenda towards the end of the decade.

Officially an attempt is made to consider the views of different sections of the population in the decision-making process and in local elections the list of candidates is put forward by the Front of National Unity rather than the PUWP itself. The PUWP invariably provides the majority of the candidates but two other parties, the United Peasants' Party (UPP) and the

Democratic Party (DP) are also represented. The former, as its name implies, is held to represent the interests of the peasantry and the latter is supposedly a socialist party representing intellectuals, craftsmen and other urban non-proletarian groups. It would be dangerous to exaggerate, since their representation is small and they explicitly accept the leadership of the PUWP, but there is some evidence that at local level they (particularly the DP) do provide channels for criticism of council activity.

Local government institutions also tend to have a localist orientation in the sense that their members frequently try to win greater shares of the national cake for their own areas. In Cracow this has been reflected in attempts to gain additional resources for the renovation of the old city and in the preparation of a town plan (the first in Poland) which has important resource implications at national level. Although most of the initial completion dates for various planned developments have been set back indefinitely, partly as a result of national discussions, the plan has retained its basic structure.

Piekalkiewicz argues that one of the principal tasks of Polish local government is to provide some sort of non-administrative control over the bureaucracy. This is particularly important in Poland because a number of economic and production decisions are taken at local level by representatives of local government, in marked contrast to the position in Britain and Canada where local authorities concern themselves almost entirely with consumption or service issues. Unfortunately the nature of the Polish political system itself effectively restricts the potential for providing this sort of control. The principal input from outside the council is in the form of individual complaints and inside the system there are competing bureaucracies whose main strength is that of inertia — the ability to slow down the decision-making process rather than the ability to encourage speedy action.

The concern of the national leadership with the operation of local government was expressed in a series of administrative reforms in the period 1971–75 (after the time which Piekalkiewicz is discussing). These reforms do not affect the basic arguments outlined in this paper, but they do highlight some of the problems which are perceived by the Polish leadership. One aim of the reforms was to ensure that it would be easier to make national economic policies effective locally; another that it should allow greater flexibility within budgets; a third that the administration should become

more efficient, and a fourth that clearer lines of responsibility should make it easier for councillors to monitor the activities of the administration. Piekalkiewicz outlines some of the difficulties which councils faced in his discussion of the role of advisory committees.

The main elements of the reforms were first the creation of larger local government units, including several metropolitan councils, of which Cracow is one, and secondly the transfer of administrative powers from collegial praesidiums (committees of departmental heads) to professional town managers, known as presidents in the main metropolitan areas. In principle, greater local budgetary flexibility was allowed, lines of responsibility were made clearer since one person rather than several was accountable to the council and the new strength of the president was balanced by that of the First Secretary of the local PUWP who became council leader.

The Polish system could hardly be described as a pluralist one although competing interest groups do exist. The extent to which it is even possible to talk of choices between competing élites is negligible. Nevertheless it is clear that the system depends on the involvement of many people outside the immediate party and state bureaucracy. It is not possible simply to direct. Perhaps the strongest interest group in Poland, outside the party, is the Catholic church. In Cracow it has been able to challenge state decisions and, for example, to ensure that a rather imposing church was built in the new town of Nowa Huta in spite of official opposition. It is, of course, important to avoid exaggeration since if the Polish system were able to absorb and respond to the conflicting economic, political and social pressures to which it is subject then explosions such as the wave of strikes in 1980 would not have taken place. As in other areas of Polish political life, local government leaders are caught on the horns of a dilemma since on the one hand they wish to encourage popular involvement and commitment, and on the other they cannot allow significant changes to be made to the plans they wish to implement and whose priorities are either determined nationally or appear to be technical industrial imperatives. In general, despite a limited degree of flexibility, the plans and their priorities continue to dominate.

When we turn to Newton's paper on Birmingham, some differences are immediately apparent. In particular, the impact of competitive party politics is striking. There is clearly a significant element of real or perceived electoral pressure at work and (particularly on the education issue) the impact of organized interest groups is more open and, by implication, more effective. These differences are certainly significant and cannot be ignored since the scope for local differences and open urban political activity is much greater. The mechanism by which decisions are transmitted through the system is far more authoritarian in Poland. But if we examine the two systems a little more closely then some similarities also begin to emerge.

Perhaps the most noticeable of these, and also the most superficial, is that a great deal of the work undertaken by councillors in both countries actually involves dealing with individual personal complaints and problems, particularly to do with housing. More important, however, are two carefully qualified points made by Newton which nevertheless indicate some of the limits within which local politics in Birmingham must operate. First, in some areas of council work, full-time officers will tend to have more importance in decision-making than their nominally subordinate positions might imply, since their grasp of problems and acceptable solutions is likely to be greater than that of many part-time councillors. Newton points to the importance of Manzoni for Birmingham's post-war housing programme. Nevertheless he also argues that the relationship is not entirely unequal since the political leaders within the council are also fully involved in the development of policy.

Secondly, Newton points to the overwhelming significance of 'central government on the one hand and general economic conditions on the other hand' in the determination of local policy. Events since his book was published would seem to confirm such a view as levels of government grant have moved up and (more frequently) down. The importance of such constraints is probably more obvious in the housing field where local interest groups are weak or non-existent, but even in the education field, which according to Newton conforms most closely to the pluralist model, scope for local initiative is limited once a national decision has been taken. Even within the limits set by national political and economic pressures, however, local 'pluralism' operates in a less than perfect manner. Interest groups do not start out equal. They are generated more easily within some social groups than others and their access to the ears of decision-makers will vary according to their social base. Generally, on the issues which are dealt with at local level, middle-class groups are likely to be better represented and organized than working-class groups. Thus on the issues of education

parents were generally weakly organized but they were more effectively organized in the middle-class wards and had good access to the Conservative councillors in those wards.

Even this limited degree of 'pluralism' is in marked contrast to the position in Poland. While one might deplore the way interest group politics operates in Britain since it could be argued that it tends to reinforce the position of those who already have power and privilege, the same process in Poland is less open and probably more one-sided. Similarly, Newton discusses the way in which the Birmingham Labour Party effectively began to erode the policy of the Labour group on education. It is difficult to imagine an equivalent process in Cracow. The Birmingham example indicates that local parties are not simply machines for supporting local élites: that is less clear in Poland.

It should be clear from the paper on Birmingham and the arguments above that the pluralist model is deeply flawed, at least when applied to that city. One might perhaps expect it to be more appropriate in Vancouver, where the assumptions behind the local political structures appear to be that elections operate like market decisions with equal individuals casting their votes for other individuals; national parties are not active in local politics and there is no ward structure. The growth and success of The Electors' Action Movement (TEAM) would, on the surface at least, seem to imply that when the system appears sclerotic, new coalitions of interest groups will arise to replace the old: the perfect pluralist dream with relatively few imperfections.

Ley's paper highlights the limited extent to which in practice the growth of TEAM genuinely represented a challenge to the existing élite and the reality of the change it represented. Like Newton, Ley indicates those sections of Vancouver society that are excluded from effective interest group activity, and shows the constraints within which TEAM operated. Its most ambitious project, the False Creek development, would not have been possible without a sympathetic (New Democratic Party) government at provincial level; its development control policies actually resulted in massive rises in land prices in certain areas and helped to protect the new professional élite. TEAM was an unstable coalition which rapidly shifted to the right, shedding some of its more left-wing supporters and at least temporarily allowing the old business élite (Non-Partisan Association) back in control. The lack of party or ward structure like that in Birmingham instead of providing an example of greater democratic control may actually make control (of TEAM or NPA members) more difficult since there is no clear mechanism through which supporters can be involved in the policy-making process on a regular basis. Nevertheless, attempts to re-introduce a ward structure to Vancouver have failed; in two recent referenda proposals for ward-based elections have been unsuccessful.

These papers are neither intended to show that these countries are all the same nor that they are all different. It is important in reading them to ask oneself what the important differences and similarities are and why they exist. They should help you to get a flavour of the different systems, and to remind you that in two of them market forces are the main determinants of economic reality whilst in the other the state plays the major economic part. This has important implications, since the economic situation clearly influences the scope for action in the urban context. It also has institutional side-effects since Polish local authorities are more or less integral parts of the system of economic planning with powers to make investment decisions in local industry, and both British and Canadian local authorities are almost entirely restricted to consumption issues and town planning decisions.

In this introduction, and in the papers themselves, urban politics and local politics are discussed in a relatively unproblematic way. The main issues, as we have seen, are whether pluralist models are adequate or whether other factors are not equally or more important. There has been little attempt to raise more radical questions about the role of local government in the political and economic systems, nor about the extent to which (in the West at least) urban politics can be said to be concerned with issues of 'collective consumption'. Nevertheless these issues are touched on obliquely and should be borne in mind while reading the papers. Thus the role of Polish local government in the productive system is fairly clear since it has explicit economic tasks which may sometimes conflict with its responsibilities for service provision and town planning. In Birmingham and Vancouver matters are more complicated, but the political conflicts described in the extracts are in the consumption field. In the former case, decisions on service provision depend on resource availability which, in turn, depends on the national economic situation. Challenges to decisions have tended to be more or less class-based, although with little evidence of Castells' urban social movements or anything like them. In the latter, political conflict has been between two philosophies of urban life — the 'livable city' versus the efficient city. If TEAM was initially a broad-based coalition in terms of support it was nevertheless a very narrow one in terms of programme and its hard-core support, too, was narrowly class-based. The start of the recession created almost insurmountable problems for its approach as the search for employment began to dominate over environmental issues.

Political conflict in urban areas is clearly important. There are obviously tensions and differences of interest at that level. These papers indicate some of the ways in which they show themselves, and the ways in which they are resolved in different societies.

Allan Cochrane

21 Polish Local Government: Conflicts of Interest Within the Monolith

by J Piekalkiewicz

Controlling the bureaucracy

In all modern industrial states the burgeoning bureaucracy which results from the increasing involvement of the government in the socio-economic matters is of prime concern to the political leaders — the lawgivers. It is also the whipping boy of the general public. Communists are especially sensitive to the problem of a large public administration growing out of reach of political control. Just such an independent bureaucracy played an important role in the criticism by Marx and Engels of Western liberal democracy. If it were to be proven that the bureaucracy of the socialist state, the new type of political system, is as independent and uncontrollable as that of the bourgeois state, then the socialist state would be basically no different from its predecessor criticized by Marx and Engels. It would have no right to the communist claim of superiority and uniqueness. The criticism Marx and Engels levelled against the liberal democracy would apply at least partially to the socialist state. It is ideologically vital for the communists to develop methods of public control of bureaucracy, because

The influence of the sovereign people on the activity of the state apparatus should not limit itself to the selection, control and recall of the representatives to the organs of the state power, but should embrace the whole state apparatus in its concrete, everyday activity. The cooperation of society with the state apparatus, control over it, and also initiative in relationship to its activity, is the guarantee of its correct functioning and the phenomenon of democratization of public life.[1]

Source: J Piekalkiewicz 1975 *Communist Local Government: A Study of Poland* (Columbus, OH: Ohio State University Press) pp192–204. Reprinted by permission of the Ohio University Press, Athens.

The size of the bureaucracy (or, rather, the number of specialized bureaucracies) in the communist states is much larger than in the liberal democracies, not only because of the Communist Party and the extensive state control of the social and political expressions of human behaviour, but also because of the centralized ownership, planning and administration of the economy. The very number of agencies, with their enormous staffs, all juggling and competing for power and influence, must be a nightmare to the top decision-makers. Whether the First Secretary and the top leaders of the praesidium are the actual rulers of the communist state and not the victims of a bureaucratic monster is a highly relevant question.

The top leadership has at its disposal a number of control channels over the administration — none of them completely reliable and efficient. The party, burdened with its many tasks, serves as watchdog over the activities of administration by duplicating the state administrative organs in the departments of the secretariat of the central committee and in the executive committees of the provinces and counties. The party also controls the administration by permeating it with party members, for whom the top executive offices are reserved.

The control of the legality of administrative actions, or rather, of their correspondence to the party will as expressed by the legal norms, is performed by the Office of the Procurator, which scrutinizes all activities of the state organs. The normal for all state financial supervision lies in the hands of the Supreme Control Board. The security police watch over not only political orthodoxy and purity, but also the efficiency, corruption and performance of the administration. Finally, the administration controls itself through the Council of Ministers, individual ministries and the departments of the local councils. These five channels of control should be more than ample to ensure the swift passage of commands issued by the top decision-makers and should prevent the possibility of any bureaucracy's acting in its own interest to the detriment of the efficient execution of public policies. The problem is, however, that the five agents of control are bureaucracies themselves. They are not free of their own vested interests, which may or may not be interlocked with those of the agencies under their control, but which in any case diminish their control usefulness to the top leadership.

The communist state is no less free from the necessity for independent, non-administrative control than any other modern political system. In liberal democracies this is provided by the political parties in their competition for power, and especially by the institution of the 'loyal opposition'. In the communist states the institution of the local councils is viewed as the independent agent of public control of the bureaucracy, ultimately in the interest of the top leadership of the Communist Party.

Within the structure of the national councils the most important channels of control are, to my mind, the committees.[2] Even if their participation in public policy formulation is much less effective than intended by law, the very fact that they keep under constant observation the departments of the council and other government agencies, forces the bureaucrats to exercise more caution and vigilance in the execution of their duties. Although the committees are far from able to get at the 'secrets' of the departments, the high technical qualifications of many of the committee members permit them to see beyond the official reports and, by this very fact, to upgrade the general technical performance of the administration.

The reason for the lack of truly effective control by the committees does not lie in their inability to discover faults in administrative performance, since many of them, depending on the qualifications and the zeal of their members, are perfectly capable of doing so. It lies in the deficiencies in the lines of communication between the committees and those higher authorities capable of putting pressure on the departments. The committees' advisory character prevents them from expressing their findings as direct orders to the department heads. They have to act either through the whole session of the council or through the praesidium.

The council, meeting in sessions of one day's duration a few times a year, hardly has time to consider reports of its committees. Most of the councils do not plan the committees' work and do not charge them with any specific control investigations. The praesidium, under pressure from the party, the higher praesidium and the higher departments, seldom welcomes the committees' inquiries. As far as the praesidium is concerned, the committees might produce a few embarrassing skeletons. The praesidium invites committee chairmen to its meetings if it must, but they function strictly as advisors.

The praesidium prefers to control its departments through its own members, each of whom is formally in charge of a bloc of administrative business. In this way any irregularities are kept within the close 'family' of the praesidium and are not handled by a group of outsiders, the committee members, who by virtue of their professional or political occupations might give embarrassing information to some higher authority, to the newspapers, or to the general public. It is once again the old story of the organization guarding its own secrets, defending its own cohesiveness, and presenting a unified front against outsiders. A few of the committees have greater control ability than is generally true of the majority. They have greater penetration of the administration, and their channels of communication are more open due to the inclusion in their membership of individuals who can command substantial authority stemming from their party or praesidium connections. Such committees are rather an exception, and the central leadership realizing the value of the committees' control function and their inability to perform it efficiently, presses for their greater involvement in the actual administrative processes of the department. The 1963 amendments to the 1958 statute increased considerably the committees' authority and obliged them to take more interest in the work of the departments under their supervision. The post-amendment reports of the newspapers and the evaluation of the committees' performance by Polish scholars do not indicate any considerable increase in their aggressiveness.[3]

Polish professional literature and the pronouncements of the party and government leadership constantly stress the control function of the councillors as the expression of popular socialist democracy. In reality, however, the councillor is not in a position to exercise constant control of the administration. First of all, his professional occupation permits him only a imited time for political and social work. Secondly, his authority as the representative of the people is undermined by the well-known fact that his role in public policy formulation and in personnel appointment policy is virtually nil. Thirdly, his investigation of the administration is resented by the departments as well as by the praesidium. The latter affords him no encouragement in his control function for the same reason as its resistance against the committees. He is even more of an outsider than the committee members, and he lacks their organizational and group power capacity. Finally his own role perception of himself as the nominee of the party renders unthinkable the possibility of his challenging the all-powerful state as represented by its officials. He may occasionally intervene with the administration on behalf of one of his constituents, especially if the matter is an obvious bureaucratic oversight, involves a minor official, or is exclusively technical. He will shun any question which even slightly smells of politics.

Another important feature of the council system which plays a significant role in the control function is the institution of public complaints and suggestions: 'Complaints and suggestions institute the patterns, specific to the socialist state, of social control over the activity of state organs and institutions and also the pattern of influence by citizens, social organization and press on their work.'[4] The institution of complaints and suggestions has been given a constitutional foundation. Article 73 of the constitution requires all state organs to deal with complaints 'keenly' and 'speedily' and also to punish civil servants who disregard them. The specific legal bases go back to the years 1950 and 1951.[5]

Complaints can be made concerning neglect by the state institutions and their employees of their duties and the valid interests of the citizens, violations of legality, bureaucratism and undue slowness in dealing with the citizens' business. The suggestions should concern themselves with improvement of the organization and work of the administration, enforcement of legality, protection of public property and prevention of corruption. The suggestions can also deal with the efficient supplying of the population's needs. The citizen cannot be put in any jeopardy as a result of his complaint or suggestion, providing that he acts within the limits sanctioned by law.[6] All administrative organs must counteract any attempts to prevent public criticism or to intimidate individuals lodging complaints or suggestions.

Complaints and suggestions are not constrained by any formal requirements, such as time limitation. They can be directed to any state institution and can be submitted not only by the individuals personally interested and involved in the matter, but also by other citizens, social or professional organizations, press, radio or television. The authority to review complaints and suggestions regarding the national council, the praesidium, or the department lies with the same institution in kind one step higher: e.g. for the county national council, the province council; for the county praesidium, the province praesidium; and for the county department, the province department. In the case of local enterprise under the supervision of the council, the same level in the praesidium or the department has the review authority.

The subject matter of a complaint or suggestion must be deliberated upon within two months, counting from the date of its receipt by the appropriate organ. The institution which receives a complaint or suggestion, but which has no authority to deal with it, must within seven days transmit it to the proper office. Every petitioner should be notified of the transfer and of the final decision in his case. All offices of the council must daily, in the specified hours, receive citizens with complaints and suggestions. The praesidium can also instruct the heads of its departments to see visitors on some days after normal working hours. Each institution of socialized trade, such as shops and restaurants, has a book of complaints and suggestions, and it must be displayed so that the customers can make entries. The book should be inspected by the supervisory department of the council every three days, and the matters must be treated in the same way as the formal complaints or suggestions logged with the national councils. In the praesidium the chairman himself or a designated permanent member of the praesidium receives citizens in the announced time and, at least once a week, also at night.

All complaints and suggestions are collected, grouped statistically, and reviewed every six months by the praesidium in consultation with the appropriate committees and the departments. The complaints and suggestions are one of the criteria on which the efficiency of the administration is judged. The province praesidium periodically evaluates the activity of those state institutions within the province which are not under the direct management of the councils regarding their treatment of complaints and suggestions and communicates its findings and recommendations to the higher authorities. All institutions required by law to

Table 21.1 Suggestions and demands submitted by the citizens of Grudziądz.

	Suggestions	% of total	All decisions	Favourable decisions	% of favourable decisions
Housing communal economy	352	43.7	272	166	61.0
Trade/services	89	11.0	84	29	34.5
Allocation of housing	71	8.8	. . .	. . .	. . .
Health/sanitation	65	8.1	62	26	41.9
Public order	45	5.6	45	. . .	. . .
Education/culture	38	4.7	38	. . .	. . .
Building construction/ renovation	36	4.5	36	14	38.9
Transportation/safety	24	3.0	. . .	. . .	. . .
Industry/trade	7	0.8	. . .	. . .	. . .
Referred to province or central government	30	3.7	. . .	. . .	. . .
Other	49	6.1	49	. . .	. . .
Total	806	100.0			

receive complaints and suggestions must use the material so obtained for the protection of social and individual interests, as well as for the improvement of their own administrative efficiency.[7]

The line of communication created by the institution of complaints and suggestions is without any doubt the most independent control function within the whole communist political system. Its magnitude testifies to its importance as an open channel of communication between the citizens and the state. In the course of one year the councils receive millions of complaints and suggestions.[8] The analysis of one city indicates that most of this communication is of a personal nature. In 1961 in the city of Grudziądz, the inhabitants, during their pre-election meetings and other meetings with councillors, formulated a total of 806 suggestions and demands,[9] an overwhelming number of which (87%) were in the form of claims of small groups or individuals. By far the largest category was the improvement of housing and communal economy (see table 21.1),[10] followed by the categories of trade and services, and allocation of housing. The fourth relatively large group of suggestions was in the field of health and sanitation which together accounted for 71.6% of the total number of suggestions and demands, but these matters received low priority in the councils' activities as expressed by praesidium resolutions.[11]

It is interesting to note that where data were available, there was a relatively high percentage of decisions in favour of the petitioners. This was especially true regarding the suggestions for improvement of housing and communal services (61.0%). It could be that the city fathers of Grudziądz were exceptionally civic minded, and indeed this author found a number of dedicated officials in that city's administration. On the other hand, it seems that it pays off to petition the local council; complaints or demands cannot make matters worse, and in many cases may force departments to take action and to render more favourable decisions. The whole institution of suggestions and complaints is used by the population as a last resort for applying pressure on the administration.

Yet another example draws our interest. During the pre-election period of 1965, Janusz Zarzycki, the chairman of the city council of Warsaw, instituted a new, and in many ways challenging, method of accepting complaints and suggestions by telephone. Mr Zarzycki personally listened to citizens' problems and often offered solutions or promised further action. Here is one example of a conversation:

CITIZEN—Sir, I have lived for the last six years in Marszałkowska street as a "wild" tenant.

ZARZYCKI—It is not a very nice word "wild." Judging by your voice my dear lady, you are not "wild." . . . Perhaps, let's say "illegal."

CITIZEN—Really "wild." And I had very serious problems because of it: I couldn't vote, because I was not on the roll; I couldn't enter my child into a school, because he was not registered anywhere.

ZARZYCKI—Well! All right! But why were you not registered anywhere?

CITIZEN—They didn't want to register me. Some time ago I moved illegally to this apartment. The Province Housing Committee alle cated to me a substitution apartment, I have been waiting six years for it. In the housing office [of the city council] they didn't want to talk to me because I was not registered. I only want registration, because I have the apartment.

ZARZYCKI—Where is your husband employed?

CITIZEN—In the Housing Administration.

ZARZYCKI—What? In the H.A.?! And during six years you were not able to settle this registration business? Write the whole story and send it to me please. We will try somehow to solve the problem, because it is indeed an unusual and even slightly humorous business.[12]

We admit that the selection of this conversation was made for its theatrical and tragi-comical quality, but most of the other problems were also in the nature of personal grievances. Chairman Zarzycki's exercise in 'direct democracy' is highly unusual,[13] but in any pre-election period there is a considerable increase in the complaints and suggestions submitted through the normal channels.

Both the examples of complaints and suggestions and the impressions obtained by this author in his talks with the officials and councillors indicate that most matters brought to the attention of the higher levels in the council structure are of this personal nature. What is even more, the complaints generally do not challenge the bureaucracy on the grounds of legality or propriety, although many are directed against its slowness in reaching a decision. They are, in the majority, pleas for reversal of administrative actions arrived at on the basis of existing laws and regulations. They are generally hardship cases which result from the *a priori* allocation of resources, and, as such, their control value is minimal. At best they can bring to the attention of the higher authority the lower officials' lack of aggressiveness in utilizing their own resources to solve such particulary pressing shortages as housing, supplies for population and public health services.

Of much more general value in uncovering real abuses of power, bureaucratic negligence, or waste of public property and human resources are the articles of local newspapers centred on the activities of the councils proper, the praesidia and the departments; many of the data used in this study were provided by the often frank and biting Polish press. The newspapers, employing their own investigators and utilizing the letters to the editor and the complaints and suggestions lodged with the national councils provide an important, and perhaps the most effective control function independent of the council structure. The bureaucracy is kept in tow by the knowledge that the press is encouraged by the central leadership and by the general policy of the party to attack it without mercy. This is not to say that the press is free. It is used and manipulated as the watchdog of the party, especially for the lower levels of administration. Many articles are followed by administrative action rectifying the wrong done. Many are answered by letters to the press from top local officials defending the positions taken by themselves or their subordinates. But by far the largest number of complaints and suggestions are sent not to the national councils or the newspapers, but to the local party headquarters. The citizens recognize the real power to be with the party, and they rightly assume that there will be faster action on their grievances if their petitions are lodged with the supreme centre of the decision-making process. They know the party to be capable of chastising government officials, of reversing decisions, and, on some occasions, even of violating the law or local regulations. The party is the last resort of arbitration between the population and bureaucracy, and is the most trusted control agency of the central leadership.

Some device for effective control of bureaucracy by the top leadership is essential to the maintenance of its monopoly of power, although our study of public policy formulation shows that this monopoly is not as absolute as is generally assumed. Although the several bureaucracies, considered as interest groups, cannot reverse the decisions of the central authority, they can slow down their implementation and render them ineffective in time. There are many formalized channels of control designed to prevent these occurrences. They are, however, also bureaucracies — and therefore interest groups — which may, and often do, ally themselves with the institutions under their control.

Even the party is bureaucratized, and it forms a specific interest group. In this context it becomes imperative for the top leadership to operate unstructured and independent control channels. Despite repeated efforts to achieve more effective control, however, these independent channels cannot perform a meaningful service. The council committees lack the necessary lines of communication; councillors have minute roles in public policy formulation and are only too aware of the appointive character of their jobs. They are not in a position to challenge the all-powerful state officials, who are at the same time important party leaders. The complaints and suggestions of the public seldom deal with questions specified by law — questions which would provide an effective control function. They are mostly personal pleas, designed not to criticize the administration but to extract from it certain favours. The newspapers and other media of communication remain the only truly independent channel exempt from pressure by the administration and therefore capable of fruitful criticism. For this reason they are allowed by the party more freedom of expression than any other interest group or than the society in general. They are also, however, more carefully watched and censored as to their ideological and political purity.

In conclusion, the control function of the system of national councils does not work effectively because it demands, on the one hand, free expression and criticism of the administration and, on the other, ideological and political orthodoxy and unquestionable submission to the communist monopoly of power. How is the public to know which decisions originate at the top and are therefore, by definition, outside the realm of public criticism, and those which are the product of local officials and hence free game for all? The local officials are also the dispensers of state power and the distributers of scarce resources. On both counts it is safer not to annoy them. An effective control function requires a source of power independent of the institutions it controls. With the possible exception of the media of communication, nobody in Poland at the local level can claim such a detachment.

Communication and the safety valve of pressure

The criticism of local officials by councils, the media and by the population in general is useful to the leadership for yet another reason: it provides it with a shield against the sword of public discontent. Although most of the policies originate at the top, the local officials are in the first line of attack for criticism because they themselves have to implement and enforce the decisions of the top leaders. The public is thereby prevented from placing direct blame on the central authority or on the tenets of communism. The local officials, who are part of the council structure, serve as a scapegoat for some of the misjudgment of the top communist bosses, and they can be conveniently removed from their posts in order to pacify the public wrath. This is also an effective device for the reversal of top policies when the leadership does not wish to admit that it was mistaken. Also, the semi-democratic elections of deputies to the councils and the internal elections of the executive committees, in which the electors have some, even if very limited, choice by selection from a communist-sponsored list, offer a useful

method of eliminating candidates who are most disagreeable to the population. Furthermore, the elections again give the public a feeling of participation and of identification with the council and with the officials who 'represent' the region. The people 'elect' their own local parliament and their own local government.

Public criticism provides some valuable information on the attitudes and grievances of the population. On the basis of the public's involvement in the 'direct democracy' of the national councils, the leadership at the local and the national level can adjust its manipulation instruments by shifting its policies, alternating the carrot and the stick. At the same time it does not have to compromise its ideological determination nor relinquish its monopoly of power. Because the party control the councils as well as the economy and the social and professional organizations, the communist society of today is not terrorized, but skilfully and 'gently' manipulated into acquiescence. But 'direct democracy' is not without its dangers to the communist rulers. It sometimes forces the local leaders to perform a tightrope balancing act between pressures from the top and demands from below. It often results in the heresy of 'localism', in which local officials try to obtain a bigger slice of the national cake than that allocated to them by the central authority, especially by retaining local production exclusively for local use. They may also attempt to circumvent directives of the national government in the interest of their region.

Finally, popular criticism, once permitted and encouraged to a degree, may grow unpredictably out of control and exert pressure on the central leadership itself, flooding it with the unmanageable turbulence of public dissatisfaction (the revolutions in Poland and Hungary in 1956, the 1968 events in Czechoslovakia and the 1970 workers' 'uprising' in Poland). In general, however, the skilful use of controlled popular participation and criticism within the framework of the councils provides the leadership with valuable channels of information and indoctrination. The criticism provides a safety valve for pressure, which can be loosened up or tightened according to the leadership's evaluation of the situation. Its psychological effect is to prevent desperate resorts to illegal conspiracy, since most people are not likely to risk physical repression if they can vent their dissatisfaction by verbal expression of criticism. For all these reasons the shield of the councils serves well, guarding the Olympian heights of the communist gods and their dogmas.

References and Notes

[1] A Burda 1964 *Polskie Prawo Państwowe*, as quoted by Z Izdebski, Zespoły Obywatelskie w Administracji Jako Wyraz Realizacji Konstytucyjnej Zasady Udzialu Mas w Rządzenui Państwem in *Problemy Rad Narodowych, Studia i Materiały*, No 1 (Warszawa) p56.

[2] Specialist advisory standing committees made up of councillors and co-opted specialists from outside the council [Ed].

[3] See J Piekalkiewicz 1975 *Communist Local Government* (Columbus, OH: Ohio State University Press) ch. 3, pp150-2; also, for example, see Surmaczyński *Aktywność Radnych* p15.

[4] T Bocheński and S Gebert 1966 *Zadania i Organizacja Pracy Rad Narodwych* (Warszawa) p441.

[5] The Statute of the Council of State and the Council of Ministers of December, 1950, and the Executive Regulations of the Council of Ministers of December 10, 1951, in *Monitor Polski* 1951, no. A-1, entry 1, and no. A-2, entry 16; and the Statute of the Council of Ministers, no. 151 (July 1971), in *Monitor Polski*, no. 41, entry 260.

[6] The Code of the Administrative Procedure, Art. 155.

[7] The Statute of the Council of Ministers of October 13, 1960, on the organization for acceptance and examination of complaints and suggestions *Monitor Polski* 1960, no. 80, entry 367, and Bocheński and Gebert, 1966 *Zadania i Organizacja*, pp442–3.

[8] In 1955, 1.5 million complaints and suggestions were lodged (Gebert *Zomentarz do Ustawy o Radach Narodowych* p73, note 35). The author was unable to obtain a more recent figure for the whole country. The number today, with the relaxation of police terror and with the general decentralisation of administration, is no doubt much larger than in 1955. For example, during the 1965 election campaign alone 140 000 suggestions were transmitted (Wendel and Zell *Rady Narodowe w PRL*, p26) and in the 1969 elections 104 000 (Bocheński *et al Rady Narodowe* p194).

[9] Prezydium Niejskiej Rady Narodowej w Grudziądzu *Materialy Informacyjne*, No. 1/62 (Grudziądz, 1962) p3.

[10] Compiled from *ibid* pp3–6. Grudziądz is a city of about 71 000 situated in north-central Poland.

[11] Piekalkiewicz, 1975, *op. cit.*, ch. 3, pp132–42. Another study thus groups the priorities of the suggestions: communal economy, housing, water supply, education and culture, trade and services, communication, health and agriculture (Bigo *et al Pozycja Ustrojowa* p94).

[12] Poselska 'audiencja przez telefon'—Warszawa-miasto i ludzie–Janusz Zarzycki odpowiada na pytania wyborców *Życie Warszawy* 31 May 1965.

[13] The author never heard of anyone using the same method. Mr Zarzycki should be commended for his obvious concern and also for his political flair and style. By the way, he lost his job in 1968.

22 Two Political Issues in Birmingham: Housing and Education

by K Newton

Housing

In the 22 years after 1945, 82 000 permanent dwellings were built in Birmingham, 60 000 by the corporation, 20 000 by private builders, and the remaining 2000 by housing associations. Another 42 000 were renovated and 35 000 demolished (Smith). In 1967 the council was completing houses at the rate of almost 8000 a year, and was managing to rehouse at the rate of 17 000 families a year (City of Birmingham 1967–68). With 31 506 applicants on the waiting list for corporation accommodation, the housing register was the shortest for any post-war year and considerably less than half its peak total of 1951 (Sutcliffe a). Clearly, enormous strides had been made since 1945, when it was calculated that over 100 000 houses were unfit for human habitation, or over a third of the city's entire housing stock (Smith, pp2–3). Between 1945 and 1970 the entire face of the inner city was changed beyond recognition. In place of back-to-back housing of the worst type, there are now blocks of high-rise flats, mixed development areas, an entirely new civic centre, a fully enclosed shopping precinct at the hub of the public transport system, and an inner ring road of flyovers and underpasses which feeds directly into the country's motorway system (Sutcliffe and Smith 1974).

All this is obvious to anybody who spends a few hours in Birmingham, but while this massive reconstruction was going on, the housing accounts ran into one financial crisis after another. Early in 1958, for example, the accounts gave considerable cause for

alarm and it was decided that, rather than build up a deficit, housing repairs would be cut and £200 000 transferred from the repair fund to the housing revenue account. The following year there was another deficit, and the Labour group was torn by a proposed increase in council rents in which a three-line whip was defied by five councillors, two others abstaining. In spite of rent increases, the housing accounts for 1959–60 were in trouble once more with an expected deficit of about £200 000, and in the year after that it was predicted to reach £500 000. In July 1963 the whole process was repeated again, with the housing account in such a state that urgent attention had to be given to it. Once again it was decided to increase rents and once again members of the Labour group rebelled against a three-line whip. This time the whole issue of party discipline was taken to the National Executive Committee and the events are still remembered by the local Labour Party. Housing, and especially council house rents, have raised the political temperature in the Labour group more than almost any other issue.

These two themes, one of remarkable achievement in urban renewal, and the other of depressingly chronic emergencies in the housing accounts, are different sides of the same coin. They can be understood in terms of the way in which the different component parts of the local system generate or suppress demands, the ways these demands set up complementary or opposing tensions, and the ways these tensions mould public policy which is translated into bricks and mortar, pounds and pence. The aim of this paper is twofold; the analysis of housing as a local issue will help us to understand the workings of the local political system, and the analysis of the workings of the local system will help us to

Source: K Newton 1976 *Second City Politics: Democratic Processes and Decision-making in Birmingham* (London: Oxford University Press) pp194–208. Reprinted by permission of A D Peters & Co. Ltd.

understand public policy on housing.

Starting at the most basic level, it seems that members of the general public bombard officials with a constant hail of housing questions and problems, demands and requests. Nine out of ten council members interviewed said that individual members of the general public invariably contact them on housing matters of one sort or another, and some 15 000 cases a year are passed to the local authority department via the liaison officer who has the special responsibility of linking the council with the housing management department. The department itself deals with about 200 000 enquiries a year (Royal Commission 1968), and it is small wonder, therefore, that local politicians emphasize their housing plans and proposals above almost everything else in local election campaigns. A detailed, year-by-year study of post-war elections shows that housing issues are almost as important as the general issue of rates, and that both parties are very quick indeed to make maximum political capital out of their house-building successes, just as they are even quicker to blame their failures on the national government, the bank rate, lack of building materials, labour or land (Sutcliffe b). Council members also include municipal rents among that small number of local issues which they believe have influenced their own electoral successes. There is no evidence whatsoever to suggest that housing issues have had this effect, but the error is easy to understand, for housing has been an issue in other towns and cities, and may even have had a measurable electoral impact (Hampton 1970, Bealey et al 1965). At any rate, the constant and unceasing pressure of public concern about housing helps to explain why decision-makers in the city worry and fret about their housing achievements.

There are a large number of voluntary organizations in the city which are concerned with housing, including the following:

Housing associations	48
Tenants' associations	23
Community associations	30
Residents' associations	24
Professional and trade associations and trade unions	34
Total	159

The numbers which appear in the first- or second-stage sample of voluntary organizations are too small for any generalization about the level of political activity of these organizations, but it is significant that two out of three council members were able to name at least one housing organization, and one out of three was able to name three or more. Of course, the council itself contains a high proportion of members with a direct financial interest in the housing market. In 1966 it contained six builders, eight estate agents and three property developers, and 12% of the total membership were involved in building or property interests (Morris and Newton 1970). In addition, the public works department was able to provide a list of 57 organizations which it claims to consult on planning and redevelopment matters, with the rider that it is impossible to count the local social welfare organizations which they keep in touch with since they are too numerous.

This great amount of activity and interest on housing makes it all the more remarkable that council members seem to be generally rather ignorant about one of the most basic facts of housing politics. The number of applicants on the housing register is taken as a general indicator of the success of the council in dealing with current housing problems. As one study says, the political parties are 'more sensitive to electoral pressure created by the long housing list than by the survival of the slums' (Sutcliffe c). The number on the housing register is frequently used as a political stick to beat opponents, and was the subject of debate in the council meeting which immediately preceded the interviews. The documents for the meeting give the figure as 22 000, although some members on the Labour side said that it should have been about 26 000.

With this in mind the sample of council members was asked, 'Do you happen to know how many applicants are on the waiting list for council houses at the moment?' A 'correct' answer was taken as falling within the range of more than 20 000 and less than 30 000. Almost half the answers were outside this range, with some guesses as low as 'two or three hundred' and as high as 'Oh, a couple of hundred thousand, I would say, at least' — the last being the reply of an estate agent with more than 11 years' council experience. Almost one in four were unable to give a rough estimate, even when they were pressed hard to do so. There are considerable variations within different sections of the council in the accuracy of responses. Only 42% of the Conservatives were able to give an accurate answer, compared with 73% of the Labour group, many of whom were exactly accurate. Members of the housing committee were the best informed, both

Labour members and three of the five Conservatives getting the figure exactly right.

Voting studies are fond of pointing out that the average elector is abysmally ignorant of current politics. The results given here seem to suggest that the city's political élite is also rather poorly informed about one simple fact of pressing importance. In this sense, many council members literally do not know what they are talking about.

Rather more cause for concern lies in the naive solutions which some of the respondents offered as a solution to the city's housing problem:

The best solution is the one that I myself am putting forward. National Savings, tat's the solution. Get teenagers to acquire the habit of saving so that when the time comes, there it is, the deposit for a house of their own. I've studied human nature a lot and you can take it from me, they all want their own houses. Now that, I think, is the answer to the problem. National Savings. I can't see any other solution to it. (Conservative councillor)

Oh, you know we'll have solved the problem in two or three years' time. There won't be a housing problem by 1975. (Conservative councillor)

The problem is that people are getting too particular about houses. There's plenty of houses in Chelmsley Wood, but people don't want them. Well, I say, if they turn down good, new houses their problem can't be serious. I think you have to agree that there isn't a problem. (Conservative councillor)

The solution is to give every young married couple £250 for a deposit and say to them, 'There it is, you're on your own. Go out and fend for yourself. (Conservative councillor)

Sell all council houses. That would increase the supply of houses to own, and bring the prices down. Then people could afford to buy their own houses, which is what they want. (Conservative councillor)

There is no housing problem. We're attracting ne'er-do-wells like honey attracts bees. There are too many passengers coming in from outside. You've got to put the word 'needy' back into the housing acts. Most people can afford their own houses. If you put the rents up you'd get rid of the people who are riding on our backs. (Conservative councillor)

There's only a problem for those who don't want a council house. All I know is that if a young married couple can get a flat within 12 months there can't be much of a problem. Things aren't that urgent. The problem is for those who want their own house. The council should sell off its land to private builders. We should build no more council houses for rent or for sale, and turn over land to building firms. They would solve the problem in a year. (Conservative councillor)

Stop all immigration immediately. You can never solve the housing problem with so many people coming in. (Conservative alderman)

It's caused by immigrants, but you can't say 'Stop in India or Jamaica'. Family limitation is probably the answer, but its a long-term thing because of the primitive people one's dealing with. (Labour alderman)

It's not a housing problem. It's a social problem. People have to be encouraged to buy not rent. There's a lack of individualism about now. People are wet-nursed all through their life nowadays. There's very little enterprise or independence. (Conservative alderman)

A large proportion of Conservatives, and some Labour members too, interpreted housing problems almost exclusively in terms of simple, individualistic theories of motivation and behaviour. The complexities of housing supply and demand, the availability of money, or land, and of building resources were overlooked, and the housing problem was reduced to easily understood forces. None of those quoted above, however, held any position of power. There was also a small proportion of long, careful, well informed, and thoughtful answers which, characteristically, came from the most senior and influential members of the two groups.

With these exceptions, the overall performance of council members was not at all impressive, but the reputation of some of the officers concerned with planning and housing in the city has been very considerable. Sir Herbert Manzoni, city architect and engineer from 1935 to 1963, stands out as a major influence over the physical planning and rebuilding of the city, and his predecessor had a similar reputation for power. It is difficult to underestimate Manzoni's influence at the height of his power (Sutcliffe and Smith 1974, p474), although towards the end the Labour group was taking a bigger and bigger initiative in major planning decisions. Part of Manzoni's power stemmed from the fact that he was the city architect as well as its engineer, but in May 1952 his wings were clipped somewhat by the appointment of a city architect who, in 1954, formed his own department separate from Manzoni's public works department. Before that the Conservatives had taken away some of the public works department's power by setting up new house-building committee and appointing a housing officer (Sutcliffe *b*, pp37–8, 53–4). More recently, a disagreement between the city architect and the Labour group on the division of powers between the public works and the architect's department was followed shortly afterwards by the resignation of the architect. So far as one can judge from this flimsy evidence, conflicts between officers and elected representatives have not always resulted in the victory of the officers, especially in recent years.

Yet when the separate performances of all the leading actors on the local stage have been weighed and appraised, it appears that the leading part in the city's housing drama has often been played by central government on the one hand, and by general economic conditions on the other. In fact, for all the heat and fury surrounding the house-building issue, for all the hard words in council debates and the contumely hurled by each party at the other, for all the activity of citizens' organizations, and for all the power and influence of city architects and engineers, the city's housing record is remarkable like that of other large provincial cities.

Although Birmingham's housing conditions were bad in 1945, as one might expect from any large industrial city emerging from a long war, the city was probably no worse off than others (Smith, p3). Certainly the relative position had neither improved nor deteriorated by 1951, when by most objective standards of household amenities and overcrowding, Birmingham was statistically indistinguishable from Liverpool, Manchester, Leeds, Newcastle and Sheffield (Moser and Scott 1961). The situation as revealed by the 1966 census was unchanged. One study concluded that 'just as in 1951 the Birmingham housing environment differed only in detail from other major provincial cities, so (despite improvements) by 1966 Birmingham's housing environment was still probably no better, but also probably no worse, than that of other major cities' (Smith, p18).

The city's overall record for building municipal houses between 1945 and 1966 is rather poorer than that of Leeds, Manchester, Liverpool, and England and Wales as a whole, but just as important is the fact that the year-by-year totals of completed municipal houses conforms fairly closely to the national pattern. The yearly records of house-building in Birmingham, Liverpool, Manchester, and England and Wales as a whole are all rather similar (Smith, pp2–3, 6–7). Moreover, the proportion of all new dwellings built by the corporation was similar to that of other large cities — 72% in Birmingham, 66% in Leeds and 85% in Manchester and in Liverpool (Smith, p15).

What appears to have determined the city's house-building rate more than anything else was the availability of large sites for big housing projects. With one exception, none was available between 1950 and 1962. Within a few weeks of the Labour government coming to power in 1964, sites outside the city boundaries were made available, and building rates soared to unprecedented heights a few years afterwards. A detailed study of municipal house-building sites after the war concludes that the availability of large building sites has been the dominant influences on house-building rates. Although both parties were willing and eager to build,

the land shortage prevented their success and the city's claim for overspill arrangements, new towns and boundary extensions were largely ignored by national governments (Sutcliffe a, pp59–60).

Before concluding that there is almost no room for local initiatives, three points should be made. The city had put incessant pressure on central government for large building sites to be made available, and but for this the breakthrough in building rates in the late 1960s might never have been achieved. Presumably the pressure in the city from individuals, pressure groups, and political parties was partially responsible for the energy with which council leaders pursued central government, and thus it might be argued that grass-roots pressure at the local level was eventually translated into central government action. The whole process took many, many years, and it might be said that it delivered too little and too late, but nevertheless, massive pressure at the local level does seem to have had an effect in the end.

Secondly, while the correlation of 0.60 between municipal houses completed per year in Birmingham and in England and Wales is high enough to show that Birmingham conforms fairly closely to the national pattern, this correlation leaves 64% of the variance in local housing performance unexplained. Only a comparison of municipal house-building throughout the country can hope to explain this variance. Meanwhile it is reasonable to suggest that local party and pressure group politics have something to do with it.

Thirdly, the recurrent crises with the housing revenue account might well have been avoided, or their blow softened, by large increases in municipal rents. The fact that these were not implemented says something about the politics of the Labour group. Some Labour members represented wards with a high proportion of council tenants, and another group of Labour council members felt very strongly that rents should be kept as low as possible. Between them and backed up as they were by the Trades Council and the borough Labour Party, they were able to bring a lot of weight to bear on the case against big increases. The interviews also suggest that while council members tend to be critical of residents' and tenants' associations, regarding them as a considerable nuisance, they also take good care to maintain close and good relations with these groups. In a fair proportion of cases it was clear that council members treat their tenants' associations with respect, believing that they could, if they wanted, make life very difficult for the councillor and lose him an election if it really came to the point. Once again, there is no evidence that rent increases have ever affected local election results, but the fear that they might ensures a degree of electoral accountability on the part of the city council.

There is some evidence to suggest, therefore, that the local apparatus of elections, pressure groups and parties can be used to influence housing policy within the limits set by national government and by national economic circumstances. An enormous amount of public attention and interest is given to housing — possibly more than any other area of local authority activity. Thousands of individuals take their housing problems to the department or to their councillors every week of the year, and thousands of problems are uncovered by canvassers during the campaign leading up to the May elections. The public is also organized into many voluntary associations some of which use their access to policy-makers, some of which have a good eye for publicity campaigns, some of which use their connections with the parties, and a few of which can, and have threatened with some credibility to, use electoral sanctions. All this seems to have played a part in keeping the housing issue at the front of the minds of local policy-makers over the past 30 years. Yet housing has never flared up as a controversial issue, and in this respect it forms a strong contrast with the next case study.

Education

It is said that there are really three major parties on the council — the Conservative Party, the Labour Party and the education committee. The education committee is, indeed, very special, spending in 1970–71 little short of £50 million, maintaining or assisting 500 schools, employing over 9000 teachers, and teaching 185 000 pupils. In addition, the committee has been at the centre of the most controversial political issue within living memory, with fierce battles between and within the parties. As one council member said, 'On education you've got a night of the long knives every night'. For once, local politics spilled over from the narrow confines of the council chamber right into the lap of the general public, blowing up into an angry and highly emotional affair.

Twenty-one years after the 1944 Act, education came of age as a fully fledged public controversy. For the first 20 years, it had scarcely been mentioned in election campaigns, other than in the obligatory and usually quite meaningless party slogans; the real meat of election campaigns was rates and housing (Sutcliffe b, p70). Given the low saliency of education as a political issue during this period, it is scarcely surprising that electors in England and Wales as a whole seem to know more about their local authority's responsibility for sewage and refuse collection than about its educational duties (Committee on the Management of Local Government 1967).

Before it reached the attention of the voting public however, the issue was boiling and bubbling away within the local parties, though even here it took some time to heat up. Initially, the Labour group on Birmingham council was opposed to any changes in the grammar school and eleven-plus selection system; in fact it strengthened it by increasing the number of grammar school places. Consequently, by the time the Labour group eventually decided to go comprehensive, there were so many parents and relatives with a stake in the status quo that the system proved even more difficult to change. The group had been supported by the borough party which passed a resolution in 1952 calling for an immediate increase in the number of grammar school places. Three years later the policy conference was calling for comprehensive plans, and there followed a ten-year period in which the borough party, through its main mouthpiece, the policy conference, put continual and mounting pressure upon the group to gird up its socialist loins and go comprehensive (Isaac-Henry 1970, 1972).

The group as a whole resisted this pressure, but at a cost. The comprehensive faction on the education committee grew, and in-fighting became so severe that the group leader twice replaced the committee chairman in an effort to keep the peace. The struggle seems to have produced virtually no reforms. When it finally lost power in 1960 after 13 years in office, the group had built two comprehensive schools and increased the proportion of grammar school places to over 25%. By the time it had finally decided on a comprehensive policy it had lost power to the Conservatives.

The Conservatives' handling of the issue was no more successful. In opposition they had never had to think seriously about the issue, but in 1966 they were in power and, moreover, had to respond to Circular 10/65. They revoked the Labour plan, started to draft their own, and immediately ran into a series of political squalls. The history of events within the Conservative Party is shrouded in characteristic secrecy, but informants within the group managed to leak enough information to the local press to make the outlines fairly clear. It seems that some of the alternatives considered aroused so much opposition within the group, and from the Brandwood Ward Conservative organization, that the group found itself perilously close to the Labour position of being publicly split into warring factions. The leadership could not tolerate this, so it simply took policy-making powers away from the education committee and put them into the hands of a small policy committee of group leaders, only one of whom had any social knowledge or experience of education matters. Even during their most turbulent period, the Labour group leaders would never have dared do this.

The policy committee did its work quickly but not well. It produced one plan which was promptly rejected by its own back-benchers, a revolt which is probably unprecedented in Conservative group history. From all accounts, the plan cut the number of grammar school places in the city, and Conservative councillors in the middle-class wards, which have a relatively high proportion of grammar school pupils, took fright at the idea that this would lose them their next election. Ironically, their fear had been expressed lucidly by a speaker at the Labour policy conference of 1965. 'If you are prepared to implement this [comprehensive] resolution,' he said, 'you are going to commit political suicide in the city. Every grammar school child in the city carries with him at least four to five votes' (Isaac-Henry 1970, p54). There is no telling how he arrived at his figures, but it seems the Conservatives took the message to heart, much to the chagrin of the group leaders and to the delight of the local press which printed the news under banner headlines.

The policy committee revised its plan and eventually found group backing for it. But this plan, too, was doomed from the start. It was leaked to the press by person or persons unknown before the professional associations and other interested bodies were so much as informed of its contents, let alone consulted about its acceptability. As it happened, all the associations were lukewarm about the proposals, the two largest teachers' unions in the city were downright hostile, and the NUT went so far as to break off consultations on the grounds that the plan was not even a reasonable basis for discussion. In addition, the Brandwood Conservatives were pressing even more strongly for the preservation of the grammar schools. Meanwhile, the plan was taken to the city with a series of 15 public meetings. These were well attended and, although it is difficult to

know how to assess their overall lesson, it is clear that they were often angry, resentful and bitter. One person leaving a meeting was overheard to remark: 'Well, if they're the people who run the city, God help us all!' Members of the Conservative group began to feel irate with their leaders about the way the plan had been presented to the public, and once again the group threatened to break out in public dispute.

It became clear that the proposals were surrounded by enemies on all sides, and the group leaders took the only sensible option open to them — they retreated battered and bruised by the experience. The plan, it was said, was never a plan in the first place but simply a discussion document. It was given a quiet burial soon after. In order to keep face and re-create group unity, the group leaders found a scapegoat who became the focus of the anger, frustration and bitterness which had been built up by the episode.

Various community organizations played their part in this sequence of events. There are some 66 voluntary organizations in the city concerned with education matters, but only a small handful were involved. The most important and active of these were the four teachers' associations, the National Union of Teachers, the Birmingham Association of Schoolmasters, the Joint Four, and the Head Teachers' Association. All these were involved in continuous consultation with the educational authorities, and all played a fairly direct part in influencing plans. The NUT was especially important, for with 5000 members, and very clear educational views of its own, it could not possibly be ignored. The Roman Catholic schools and the Church of England schools were also consulted although they chose, in accordance with their own national policy, not to become embroiled in local party politics and to adapt themselves as best they could to whatever plans were implemented.

Two important pressure groups operated within the party organizations. The local branch of the National Association of Labour Teachers (later the Socialist Education Association) moved a motion in favour of comprehensives at the 1953 policy conference and thereafter was instrumental in swinging the borough party away from its policy of increasing the number of grammar school places. Its role within the Labour Party should not be underestimated. The Conservative Party produced countervailing pressure from the Brandwood ward organization which acted as a focus for many who wanted to preserve the grammar schools intact. It, too, was a successful pressure group, playing a part, and probably a major part, within the Conservative group.

What was missing from the pressure group system was a really strong and effective force to express parental views. Of course, many members of the parties and groups already mentioned were parents (as the NUT was quick to point out when it was accused of packing the public meetings), but the fact remains that parents in the city were not well organized, and some sections were almost entirely unorganized. At first the only parents' organization was the Birmingham Association for Education which formed the local branch of the Confederation for the Advancement of State Education, but with barely 150 members who were internally divided it took little active part. Later it was joined by a more vigorous clutch of pressure groups, most notably the Campaign for Comprehensive Education, the South West Birmingham Association for the Advancement of State Education, and a small number of parent–teacher organizations which seemed to intervene mainly to preserve the status quo as far as their own particular school was concerned. Curiously, the 22 Old Boys' and Girls' Associations were inactive. The children themselves, of course, where wholly unorganized and unable to express any opinion.

The policy-making role of education officers seems to have been fairly minor. As in many other local education authorities, officers in the education department seem to have kept a low profile, moving in whatever direction the majority party determined.[2] In fact, within the space of only a few years, the Education Department had drawn up, or helped to draw up, a series of completely different plans, the dominant features of which were certainly determined by the elected representatives of the majority group. It is difficult to believe that the dictatorship of the official is on the march on educational matters in the city.

Finally the role of national government proved to be crucial in the whole education issue. But for Circular 10/65, the Labour group might still be in favour of grammar schools, and, but for the election of the Labour government in 1964 and 1966, the Labour group might never have lost power in the city. As in housing, the initiative and action of central government largely set the frame of reference for local policy, but there does seem to have been more room for local manoeuvre on educational matters. When forced to it by the Ministry circular, the Labour group grudgingly produced a comprehensive plan of sorts. The Conservative plans were very different, and even the most radical of them preserved the main features of selection for grammar schools. In contrast to their differences on education, the policies of the two parties on housing matters were closely similar.

Education policy-makers were caught in a classic political dilemma. Any policy was bound to find powerful enemies. The Labour group leadership did not want comprehensives until well into 1965, and consequently incurred the wrath of the borough party and the local branch of the NUT. Had it remained in power it would also have had the Minister peering suspiciously over its shoulders at its somewhat watery comprehensive plan. The Conservative group leadership did not want a comprehensive policy, but it was in favour of cutting the number of grammar school places. For this it had to deal with a recalcitrant NUT, a waspish Brandwood ward, an angry set of councillors, and an often irate general public which appeared to want many different things. The end result was an immobilist situation in which nothing was done. This was not a non-decision; it was an inability to change the status quo and, consequently, a decision which was favoured by those who wanted to preserve the grammar schools intact. Like so many other issues, the comprehensive principle is not amenable to compromise, and in these circumstances the conservatives, though not the Conservative Party, won the day.

Notes

[1] It was also pointed out by others that Chelmsley Wood rents are rather too high and that travelling distances to work are rather too far to make the estate suitable for all people.

[2] The other local authorities include Wolverhampton, Darlington, Wallasey and Liverpool, and perhaps England and Wales as a whole. See Jones (1969), Batley et al (1970), Parkinson (undated).

References

Batley R, O'Brien O and Parris H 1970 *Going Comprehensive* (London: Routledge and Kegan Paul) p72

Bealey F, Blondel J and McCann W P 1965 *Constituency Politics* (London: Faber and Faber) pp381–2

City of Birmingham 1967–68 *Abstract of Statistics No. 12*, Tables 76, 77

Committee on the Management of Local Government 1967 vol. III *The Local Government Elector* (London: HMSO) pp6–16

Hampton W 1970 *Democracy and Community* (London: Oxford University Press) pp246–77

Isaac-Henry K 1970 The politics of comprehensive education in Birmingham, 1957–1967 *M.Soc.Sci.Thesis* Birmingham University, Dept of Political Science

——1972 *South West Review of Public Administration* **11** pp29–37

Jones G 1969 *Borough Politics* (London: Macmillan)

Morris D S and Newton K 1970 Profile of a local political elite: businessmen as community decision-makers, 1838–1966 *The New Atlantis* **2** pp111–24

Moser C A and Scott W 1961 *British Towns* (London: Oliver and Boyd)

Parkinson M (undated) *Politics of Urban Education* (Liverpool: the University of Liverpool, Department of Political Theory and Institutions)

Royal Commission on Local Government in England 1968 Research Study No. 7 *Aspects of Administration in a Large Local Authority* (London: HMSO) p113

Smith R J (undated) *The Changing Housing Environment: Birmingham, 1931–1967* (Birmingham University, School of History) *History of Birmingham Research Paper No. 14*, 3

Sutcliffe A R (a) *The Production of Municipal Houses in Birmingham 1939–1966* (Birmingham University, School of History) *History of Birmingham Research Paper No. 5*, Table 2, and *Abstract of Statistics*, table 77 (undated)

—— (b) *Campaigns and Policies: Aspects of Birmingham Municipal Politics 1939–1966* (Birmingham University, School of History) *History of Birmingham Research Paper No. 15*, (undated)

—— (c) *Politics and Planning in Birmingham 1939–1966* (University of Birmingham) p24 (undated)

Sutcliffe A R and Smith R 1974 *History of Birmingham 1939–1966* (London: Oxford University Press)

23 Governing the Livable City: The Limits to Political Change in Vancouver

by D Ley

For much of its history, urban development in Vancouver has followed the categories of purposive-rational action, of the engineering mind. Vancouver was an industrial and port city from its founding in 1886 at the terminus of the Canadian Pacific Railway. While most of its immigrants were seeking a more bucolic setting than the Victorian cities of eastern North America and Europe, this did not blunt the aggressive growth of Vancouver. Vigorous port activity and a profusion of sawmills and lumber-affiliated industries were the dominant features of the 1100 industrial plants which were boasted of in a 1927 jubilee report.

The political leaders of industrial Vancouver were eminent businessmen, an élite who passed interchangeably through the Board of Trade, the major social clubs and the council chambers. Six Board of Trade presidents or vice-presidents were elected to the office of mayor between 1887 and 1914. Three-quarters of the city's mayors and nearly two-thirds of its aldermen between 1900 and 1925 were businessmen. Indeed it was only in the 1960s that this was surpassed as the occupation of the majority of newly elected council members; the newly ascendant group in the 1960s were professionals. The business elite introduced scientific management to Vancouver as they had elsewhere; the arrival of city planning in the 1920s intimated the same 'elaboration of the processes of rationalization and systematization inherent in modern science and technology' which were the *leit-motif* of scientific management

Source: D Ley 1980 Liberal ideology and the post-industrial city, reprinted by permission of *Annals of the Association of American Geographers* **70** (2) pp246–57.

(Hays 1964, Bottomley 1977). Vancouver adopted the classical progressive model of government with a non-partisan, at-large system of administration replacing the earlier ward system in 1936. The following year the Non-Partisan Association (NPA) was formed and dominated the city council until 1968; over this 30-year period 90% of its candidates were elected to political office.

It is now generally acknowledged that progressive municipal reform rationalized the appearance of a more corporate and less representative civic government. From 'the rationalization of life which came with science and technology . . . decisions arose from expert analysis and flowed from fewer and smaller centres outward to the rest of society' (Hays 1964). This American conclusion was abundantly true in western Canada, where businessmen were the typical advocates of municipal reform and where 'reform' schemes often served to reduce the franchise in favour of higher-income and propertied interests (Anderson 1979).[1] A centralized bureaucracy of experts exuded rationalism and scientific administration, for in the municipal civil service the engineering mind conveyed the dominant ideology. An article in the *Canadian Engineer* in 1923 entitled 'Reasons for town planning' emphasized the successful formula: 'Good city planning is not primarily a matter of aesthetics, but of economics. Its basic principle is to increase the working efficiency of the city' (van Nus 1979). The inevitable result of such an ideology was a convergence of political and economic interests as planning achieved little more than 'the co-ordination of the desires and development policies of private interests'. The non-partisan, corporate model of centralized municipal government promoted business rationalism both in its political theory and in its daily practice.

In Vancouver the landscape which evolved from an ideology so accommodating to business and rational performance filled in closely the development guidelines laid out in Harland Bartholomew's master-plan of 1929, a plan which the business élite had promoted, in part from a desire to stabilize land values. Bartholomew had promised that his plan would be viable until the time when Vancouver's population reached a million, a target which the metropolitan area attained in the late 1960s. But it was not simply size alone which generated a serious challenge to the ideology of non-partisan planning, but also the politicization of a new group on the urban scene. The increasing size and dispersal of the metropolitan area caused growing traffic congestion and delays, and to restore an efficient transportation network the NPA council and its technical staff approved in 1967 the first stage of a freeway system for the city. In a proposal typical of an ideology where plans came before people, efficiency before equity, and economic before social costs, the freeway alignment would have resulted in the destruction of a substantial portion of Vancouver's Chinatown. The plan, once it became known, was vigorously opposed by a coalition in which academics and architects were prominent. A few months later The Electors' Action Movement (TEAM) was founded; the counter-offensive against the engineering mind was now formalized.

Politicizing the new élite

The transition to a post-industrial society in Vancouver was accompanied by a shift from blue- to white-collar employment, and from an economy based on manufacturing to one based on services. This transition, though not complete, has been accelerating since 1960 and the emergence of a new professional, technical and administrative élite has given expression to a heightened lifestyle of consumption, and a concern with the aesthetic and the realms of human sensibility. A set of values aspiring to a higher quality of life, a livable city, could not help but breed scepticism of traditional growth, regarding it at best as banal, at worst as destructive. But the city council continued to be under the control of the NPA with their unrelenting commitment to growth and the efficient city. As late as 1971 the last NPA mayor, a millionaire property developer, boasted that 'Vancouver is the San Francisco of Canada . . . the New York. I can see it someday becoming the largest

city in Canada. Montreal and Toronto have had it' (Bottomley and Holdsworth 1974).

In 1968 the new élite was politicized with the formation of TEAM to challenge the business ideology at city hall (Miller 1975)[2]. By the early 1970s the community at large shared its social values. In 1972, for example, a random sample of 1650 adults in Greater Vancouver was polled in a survey covering a broad spectrum of attitudinal and behavioural items. One section of the questionnaire asked residents to rank in order of importance 17 urban problems covering a wide range of economic, political and social issues. The three perceived as most serious were air pollution from industry, water pollution and air pollution from private vehicles (Collins 1973). Environmental aesthetics was regarded as the most pressing urban problem. It was therefore consistent that during the same year the voters should return eight out of ten TEAM aldermen in the civic elections and Arthur Phillips, the TEAM candidate, as mayor. The livable city ideology was not only institutionalized; it was now the policy of a council majority. After 80 years of domination by businessmen, during Vancouver's ninth decade, from 1966 to 1975, nearly 70% of newly elected aldermen were professionals or semi-professionals.

TEAM in office: from ideology to practice

It is perhaps not too much of an overstatement to assert that if non-partisan management (the engineering mind) placed economics and efficiency in a privileged position while discounting aesthetics, TEAM sought to reverse the priorities when it assumed control of city hall in 1972. A more humane and aesthetic city was a primary objective especially in the critical downtown core and inner-city neighbourhoods. In the central business district the major commercial street was closed to all but public transport despite the opposition of retailers, and transformed into a landscaped pedestrian precinct; the preservation of historic buildings and of an entire district, Gastown, the core of the early city, were secured; other heritage buildings were renovated for a new performing arts centre and a separate art gallery. In the central residential neighbourhoods densities were regulated through repeated downzonings, streets were blocked to restrict commuter through-traffic, trees and shrubs were planted, and new parks were added while encroachment on existing parks was strictly prevented. Public access to the waterfront was improved and a fishermen's market was opened upon council initiative. In short, public spaces were protected, animated and humanized; a more vital and even festive ambience was sought and to some extent achieved, most notably in a series of successful annual spring and summer festivals in the parks, beaches and bays around central city, whose sponsors included the city's social planning department. All of these initiatives flowed from TEAM's policy that Vancouver should be 'a city people can live in and enjoy.' The quality of urban experience, the satisfaction of the 'higher needs' of human sensibility, became a daily preoccupation of city hall.

To such sensibilities few details were too small. Billboards were substantially reduced in number as an offence of visual pollution, while a separate by-law banned the use of advertising sandwich boards by merchants. Noise pollution was addressed in the city's first noise by-law. New urban design standards were set up with an influential design panel to vet development applications. Few options were left untried in the pursuit of the canons of good taste.

In contrast to these energetic undertakings, economics and efficiency were rarely seen as pressing concerns. Even traffic circulation, the problem *par excellence* for systems reasoning, was removed from an engineering context and interpreted instead as a human problem, the inconvenience of the journey to work, which in turn 'threaten[s] the amenity, or "livability" of the region if allowed to grow unmanaged' by unwelcome commuter intrusion on inner residential districts (Vancouver City Planning Department 1975). With a downtown office boom and 8000 new jobs a year being created in the early 1970s, there was no need for an employment strategy; TEAM concurred with a regional plan to decentralize jobs to suburban town centres in order to relieve the 'congestion stresses' of commuting. Only in the recession of the late 1970s with unacceptably high vacancy rates in the overbuilt core was this strategy quesioned. But even then TEAM was selective of its new employers. In a speech to the Vancouver Real Estate Board in 1977 Mayor Volrich noted 'that we can easily identify financial institutions as being a very desirable kind of business to encourage, and technological industries and many other "clean" industries.'[3] White-collar employment would be welcomed, but not polluting industries. While park acreage has increased substantially, 400 acres of industrial land was rezoned to other uses between 1968 and 1976. By the latter date park acreage in Vancouver covered an area 25% larger than industrial land use.

These land-use changes were reflections of an ideology that was believed to be disinterested and favouring broader public interest. Certainly TEAM did not see itself as a pro-development lobby. Its position towards traditional unchecked growth was unreservedly hostile, and towards entrepreneurial interests equivocal at best. From the beginning, one of its populist objectives had been the containment of the development industry and its aggressive power plays. The planning director, a TEAM appointee, consistently supported citizens rather than business interests in rezoning controversies; he resisted granting a redevelopment permit to one proposed residential tower in a high-amenity central location on the grounds of its being 'unneighbourly' in its intrusion on existing properties, a social criterion unthinkable before earlier NPA councils. The assault on high-density living and particularly high-rise developments was conducted with vigour, and in four years the council had achieved residential downzonings in every major apartment district in the city. In almost every instance the downzonings were supported by local citizens' groups and opposed by the land development industry. Nor were downtown commercial interests more successful in gaining council backing; repeatedly their viewpoint was rebuffed at public meetings in the council chamber.[4]

Linked to its coolness toward entrepreneurial interests was TEAM's policy of open government, in marked contrast to the highly centralized and secretive decision-making of the non-partisan era. Numerous practical steps were taken to heighten public awareness of civic issues, to disseminate information, and to draw citizens into the process of public decision-making. The most controversial element of TEAM's populism was its advocacy of representative government. This included a commitment to some form of electoral reform leading to partial ward representation, though in two separate plebiscites (in 1973 and 1978) a proposal for a partial ward system failed to receive substantial endorsement from the electorate. This initiative for representative government was thereby thwarted by local residents, leaving Vancouver the only major Canadian city with a totally at-large council. Success was equally frustrated with the other major political reform, decentralized local area planning. Participation has always been an important springboard of TEAM policy; in its 1976 paper on planning and development policy, for example, the first of eight points was 'to encourage participation in the planning process of persons and organizations', while a later item was 'to give to the occupants of neighbourhoods as strong a voice as possible' in formulating neighbourhood policies and by-laws. But after some difficult early experiences in the implementation of local area planning, TEAM aldermen withdrew from their initial strong endorsement to a more limited model of consultation (Hardwick and Hardwick 1974).

The redevelopment of False Creek

The False Creek redevelopment is perhaps the most dramatic landscape metaphor of liberal ideology, of the land-use implications of the transition from industrial to post-industrial society, from an ethic of growth and the production of goods to an ethic of amenity and the consumption of services. False Creek was a major industrial site in the zone in transition adjoining the downtown core, covering 500 acres of land on each side of a tidal inlet. It included sawmills and other lumber-related industries, metalworking, marine industries, and on its northern side a large railyard. By the late 1960s leases on a number of the industrial sites were near expiry and the NPA council determined to continue to plan for False Creek as an industrial area.

In contrast TEAM development policy in 1968 included an innovative proposal to transform False Creek 'from purely industrial use to a combination of residential, recreational and "clean" industrial uses.' By 1972 TEAM was looking forward to False Creek as 'inner-city living at its best,' while 'the waterfront should be a continuous system of parks and marinas for all the people to enjoy.'[6] The False Creek redevelopment was to be the largest inner-city project undertaken in Canada, covering an area larger than the existing downtown, and housing when completed up to 30 000 people. It provided a perfect *tabula rasa* for the realization of liberal ideology, 'a beautiful addition to Canada's most beautiful city'; it would be, of course, 'a place for people' (False Creek Development Group 1977). This transition is the more remarkable in as much as 10 years earlier False Creek had been described as 'a garbage dump, a sewer outlet for the city of Vancouver. It is, first and foremost, the industrial heart of the city' (Fukui 1968). In the process, as was so often the case with TEAM urban strategy, social and aesthetic priorities eclipsed economic reasoning. In the opinion of the most detailed review of the False Creek project: 'rather remarkably, the general objective of creating a quality, livable environment seems to have taken a distinct priority for some time over any of the financial aspects of redevelopment' (Rodger 1976). This was for a redevelopment whose first 50-acre phase alone was estimated to have a capital cost of over $57 million.

False Creek is a microcosm of the livable city vision. The objective advertised in 1974 was for design teams to develop workable proposals to 'reflect [TEAM's] False Creek policies, provide excitement and innovation, quality, a high degree of livability, be acceptable to the potential residents and the general public and be a practical concept in economic terms' (Rodger 1976). False Creek was envisaged as a quality environment, set up from the beginning as a 'livable community,' a development committed to heighten the urban experience of residents. That experience was to have both physical and social components, as many of TEAM's urban strategies were given landscape expression. The car was to be relegated to peripheral and underground locations, while the curving interior streets would be pedestrian precincts; a fundamental policy was that False Creek would be 'a non-automobile orientated environment' (Rodger 1976). A new bus service would be introduced and the development would face not the land but the water, where a sea wall would provide a continuous pedestrian, jogging and bicycle route. Jane Jacobs' views on the advantages of mixed land use were firmly taken up: 'The most important message from my experience is: create diversity, don't segregate functions, and provide lots of reasons for lots of people to converge and use spaces' (Hardwick 1974, see also Rodger 1976).[7] Diversity was to extend to house types, which would include low-rise and high-rise blocks, townhouses and houseboats, and also to improve architectural design and materials. False Creek was a conscious reaction against unimaginative urban design, while keeping densities substantially below conventional inner-city standards. Parks and landscaping were important design features, and included in the first phase of development a 16-acre park, a waterfall and lake, a garden of native plants, and a 60-foot wide landscaped pedestrian overpass, broader than a normal residential street. Aesthetics were reflected in the quality and diversity of construction materials, extensive design features to control noise pollution, and the height and arrangement of buildings which were located to optimize views of the mountains, waterfront and the downtown skyline.[8]

More significant yet were the social components of design. In 1968 TEAM's policy on public housing had been critical of the traditional 'low income housing ghetto . . . TEAM believes public housing which segregates people does not work.' The most dramatic component of the vision for False Creek was to be social mixing of lifestyles, income groups and tenure types. The 865 units of the first phase were to include housing for families, couples, the elderly and singles; the income mix was to reflect the metropolitan area with approximately one-third low-income, one-third middle-income, and one-third high-income groups; tenure types included substantial proportions of subsidized rentals, cooperatives and market condominiums. The cooperative sponsors included service clubs, an ethnic association, a physically handicapped society and a floating homes society; False Creek was to celebrate plurality. Liberal ideology could not have been more explicit: 'Communities which offer little social and physical diversity are unhealthy . . . health in any form is invariably connected to diversity' (Rodger 1976). Yet for diversity to be expressed a supportive milieu was necessary 'to support rather than destroy the vast mosaic of subcultures' (Rodger, p9). The design solution was for small circular enclaves to be constructed to shelter homogeneity within a broader development of heterogeneous enclaves. This strategy would also aid in creating a sense of neighbourhood or resident identity and control, regarded as important features of livability. Nothing was left to chance; even street names would evoke continuity rather than transience with names like Foundry Quay and Sawyer's Lane sustaining a theme of False Creek's industrial and maritime heritage.

The management of the redevelopment was equally innovative. Public participation and consultation were continuous; indeed it was negative public response to council and planning department proposals in 1968 and 1969 which gave momentum to TEAM's redevelopment strategy. A citizens' advisory panel was set up and the public response from 1200 questionnaires was an ingredient of the final design decisions. Senior levels of government showed an unusually creative response to the challenges False Creek presented to conventional forms of administration. Finally, the project sought out creative and innovative design strategies. The design team utilized Christopher Alexander's pattern language (a qualitative programme of systematized intuition) for design and planning. Pattern language, devised at Berkeley and Oregon over the past decade, followed principles of use-based design not previously used in a major Canadian development (Alexander 1977). The planning ideas of liberal social scientists including Herbert Gans and particularly Jane Jacobs were promoted by the academics on the city council. TEAM's leadership was critical, but it was part of a broader social movement, a tide of changing social values which shaped the design principles in 1970, and brought TEAM to power in 1972 to implement them. False Creek is a product of 'positive public reaction . . . political dynamism and professional innovation' (Rodger 1976). It is a landscape testimony to a social movement advocating pluralism and the virtues of self-actualization in the residential environment, while pursuing the canons of good taste.

Critique: liberal ideology in retrospect

The False Creek redevelopment represented the major achievement of livable city planning, demonstrating what could be accomplished on public land by creative political initiatives. Market interests were laggardly in their contribution; major developers refused to become involved and mortgage lenders were slow to participate. But this vacuum was filled by support from the housing departments of senior governments. During the critical 1972–75 period the provincial government was controlled by the sympathetic left of centre New Democratic Party. At the federal level because False Creek fell within the constituency of a senior Liberal minister it received priority attention in Ottawa. Subsequent proposals for Granville Island, an area of federally owned land in False Creek, have shown a common development philosophy between the ideology of TEAM and federal liberalism.[9]

However, where its control was more limited and constraints were greater, planning was far less successful, particularly in the private housing market. The promotion of the culture of consumption, the quality of urban life, had unfortunate side-effects. In an era when amenity was a significant factor not only of personal migration but also of industrial and office location, TEAM's livable city strategy helped to inflate housing demand pressures in the city centre while, at the same time, its development policies and those of the provincial and federal governments contributed to limit the supply.[10] Property owners and developers capitalized on this bottleneck and land prices sky-rocketed; from 1972 to 1974 during the tenure of the first TEAM majority council, Vancouver house prices doubled. In contesting the city efficient, TEAM had not inaugurated the age of urban equity; indeed in the private land market liberal ideology promoted a new if unintended élitism.

These relationships may be illustrated briefly by three examples where TEAM policy precipitated undesirable social consequences. Its plan to beautify Granville Street, the main downtown shopping avenue, and transform it to a pedestrian mall was at first resisted by a number of shopkeepers. Their resistance was justified, for soon after the facelift landlords raised store rents substantially and a number of small retailers were forced to relocate. A second issue was TEAM's support for the development of a 55-acre botanical garden on the site of a former golf course in Vancouver's most prestigious residential district. In 1977 the park lost $340 000; if houses compatible with the neighbourhood's tone had been built, they would have contributed $600 000 to the city in taxes. Finally, the False Creek redevelopment itself has had external effects which have removed low- and middle-income housing in the adjacent neighbourhood of the Fairview Slopes. This district contained modest and in some instances dilapidated housing for the workers who had previously manned the industries along the Creek below. But the redevelopment of False Creek had replaced a noxious area by a highly desirable one, and the old residences of the Fairview Slopes were demolished and replaced by expensive town-houses. In each instance an action stemming from liberal ideology disfavoured a vulnerable income group and favoured the more privileged.

The unintended élitism of livable city policies pointed to the biased distribution of TEAM's power base and the interests it represented. In no civic election did TEAM alderman candidates win half of the popular vote. The remainder of the vote was divided between the conservative Non-Partisan Association and the Committee of Progressive Electors (COPE), a left-wing party also founded in 1968. TEAM policies aggravated the constituencies of both of its rivals. The NPA represented business interests and conservative groups among the lower middle class and elderly; as an essentially free-enterprise party it reacted against TEAM's active intervention in urban issues and particularly its slighting of the business lobby. COPE represented poorer segments of the working-class immigrant community and tenants; these groups were critical of TEAM's social policies, claiming that insufficient attention was paid to housing and welfare problems.

With TEAM's energetic programme for urban development impinging on the interests and convictions of the other involved parties, the decade 1968–78 was politically volatile. Between 1973 and 1975 alone,

98 land-use conflicts were reported in the city's major newspaper, and in only 10 of these was a majority of the TEAM-controlled council aligned with the business lobby. On the other hand, however, TEAM's activism in issues was geographically localized. While council policies initiated 15 conflicts in western planning districts, its electoral source of strength, it initiated only three conflicts in the working-class eastern districts. Inevitably, COPE sympathizers charged TEAM with an élitist programme neglectful of the needs of the underprivileged. Those charges had some substance. In the field of housing, rental vacancy rates were extremely low, affordable housing was scarce, and by 1978, 25% of the city's households were spending excessive amounts (over 30% of income) on shelter. Such failings of the livable city ideology eventually led to the dismembering of TEAM as two of its aldermen concerned with welfare and housing issues left the party in protest against the low priority these problems received. But by the mid-1970s TEAM nonetheless remained more liberal than the population at large over social questions; in 1976 the electorate turned down a five-year capital budget for a variety of programmes, including subsidized housing. Indeed TEAM's collapse was confirmed in its 1978 convention when party members urged more liberal policies upon their elected representatives; two more TEAM council members, perceiving the conservative shift in the electorate, resigned and fought the 1978 civic election as quasi-NPA candidates. The tensions inherent in a reform coalition, the retirement of a number of leading figures, and the changed circumstances of the late 1970s all led to TEAM's fracturing as a discrete reform movement.

The shift to the right in the electorate indicated by the rejection of the 1976 capital budget favoured the fiscally conservative NPA. Just as a surge of reform sentiment had endorsed TEAM's vision of the livable city in the early 1970s, so a popular conservative movement in 1978 contributed to its downfall. The spectre of expensive government during an economic downturn challenged vulnerable members of the middle and lower middle classes. The threat to consumption standards reinstated a concern with growth and fiscal conservatism by government. In 1974 one of TEAM's aldermen had embroidered its expensive urban programme with the hope that Vancouver might 'grow' from the third largest to the tenth largest Canadian city! By the late 1970s neither the expense of the urban programme nor the qualitative definition of growth it presented satisfied a majority of voters.

A livable city ideology and an ideology of equity are only coincidental in special cases where economic strength is assured, public intervention is active, and private interests are constrained. The severity of these requirements suggests that the ideologies will often be incompatible. In free-market conditions an urban strategy favouring a high level of consumption with style will only serve to attract the wealthy and penalize social groups with limited market power. The solution would appear to be countervailing intervention by government, but this solution may in turn alienate business interests and vulnerable middle-class groups, especially as inflationary demand pressures raise costs and taxes (including housing costs and the costs of public services). Moreover, the growth of government bureaucracy may have its own shortcomings. In addition to the sense of alienation often accompanying 'big' government there is also the perception of decreasing economic efficiency, leading to the fear of a further reduction in personal consumption standards, and translated predictably into a political movement for free enterprise. A critical factor then becomes the strength of the economy, for it is during an economic downturn that tensions and vulnerabilities are bared, and the legitimacy of government policy is challenged. The harmonizing of goals of efficiency, equity and the quality of life are profound problems of national administration; it is not surprising that they reappear to present a crisis of management in the post-industrial city.

Notes

[1] On money by-laws the Edmonton reform model allowed large property owners as many as four votes. In western Canada 'the reform model of urban government was anti-democratic in the extreme' (Anderson 1979).

[2] Besides TEAM the Committee of Progressive Electors (COPE) was formed in 1968 as a progressive workers' party (Miller 1975).

[3] Mayor Volrich, speech to the Vancouver Real Estate Board, 19 October 1977.

[4] For example, the downtown retail lobby was frustrated by the council over issues of commercial tax levies, downtown traffic plans, and by council support for competing retail development outside the central business district.

[5] Among the reforms leading to more open government were the holding of council meetings at more convenient hours, the publication of aldermen's voting patterns, the dissemination of public information magazines by the planning and social planning departments, and the advertising of development permit applications to aid community awareness of potential land-use changes.

[6] *Vancouver Province* 5 October 1972.

[7] Hardwick (1974, p205), an urban geographer, was the foremost

TEAM alderman from 1968 to his retirement from the council in 1974. He is widely regarded as one of the major architects of the False Creek redevelopment project (see Rodger 1976).

[8] The preference for quality materials was illustrated by the decision to surface the pedestrian areas with quartzite, which is expensive to maintain and costs four times greater than concrete and ten times greater than asphalt.

[9] Granville Island is to change from 'an industrial site to a predominantly "people-place" . . . a place of "recreation" in the fullest sense.' With mixed uses such as open space, an experimental theatre, an art college, etc (Vancouver Planning Department *The Redevelopment of Granville Island* 1977). Symptomatically, the proposal has been opposed by downtown businessmen (*Vancouver Sun*, 17 March 1978).

[10] The details of the housing market and government intervention are complicated, but briefly we might note the effects of municipal downzonings and development delays, a provincial rent freeze, and the federal removal of tax concessions on apartment development.

References

Alexander C 1977 *A Pattern Language* (New York: Oxford University Press)

Anderson J 1979 The municipal government reform movement in Western Canada 1880–1920, in *The Usable Urban Past: Planning and Politics in the Modern Canadian City* eds A Artibise and G Stelter (Toronto: Macmillan) pp73–111

Bottomley J 1977 Experience, ideology and the landscape: the business community, urban reform and the establishment of town planning in Vancouver, BC, 1900–1940 *PhD Dissertation* University of British Columbia (unpublished)

Bottomley J and Holdsworth D 1974 A consideration of attitudes underlying community involvement with civic issues, in *Community Participation and the Spatial Order of the City* ed D Ley (Vancouver: Tantalus) B C Geographical Series No. 19, pp59–74

Collins J 1973 *Urban Priorities and Attitudes: Socio-economic and Lifestyle Determinants* Vancouver Urban Futures Project Report No. 6 (Vancouver: University of British Columbia, Dept of Geography)

False Creek Development Group 1977 *False Creek: South Shore* (Vancouver: City Planning Dept)

Fukui J 1968 *A Background Report on False Creek for the Vancouver Board of Trade* Vancouver

Hardwick W and Hardwick D 1974 Civic government: corporate, consultative or participatory? in *Community Participation and the Spatial Order of the City* ed D Ley (Vancouver: Tantalus) B C Geographical Series No. 19, pp89–95

Hays S 1964 The politics of reform in municipal government in the progressive era *Pacific Northwest Quarterly* 55 pp157–69

Miller F 1975 Vancouver civic political parties: developing a model of party system change and stabilization *B C Studies* 25, pp3–31

Rodger R 1976 *Creating a Livable Inner City Community* (Vancouver: Ministry of State for Urban Affairs and City Planning Dept, False Creek Development Group) pp8–32

Vancouver City Planning Dept 1975 *Employment Growth in Vancouver*

van Nus W 1979 Towards the city efficient: the theory and practice of zoning, in *The Usable Urban Past: Planning and Politics in the Modern Canadian City* eds A Artibise and G Stelter (Toronto: Macmillan) pp226–46

Section VI
The Power of Planning

Introduction

The major factor behind the choice of a North American and an East European city to complement the British case study was that of obtaining as wide a spectrum as possible in terms of the power of planning and state intervention and the free rein of market forces. On the surface at least, it is a commonly held belief that most North American cities have little in the way of planning powers, the pattern of development being largely determined by the market in its search for greater profitability. Conversely, East European cities are commonly believed to exhibit all the characteristics of a strongly centralized planning system operating within the context of a planned economy.

One of the aims of the course, and this Reader, is to see to what extent these perceived differences hold up in reality and, conversely, to examine the extent to which planning and state intervention do exercise a major role in North America and the extent to which market or quasi-market forces exert an influence in Eastern Europe. Put another way, we are concerned to discover whether the power of the market and the power of planning are as dominant as they are often alleged to be. In the case of Britain, and Birmingham in particular, we are motivated to assess the relationship between planning and the market in a so-called 'mixed' or social democratic society.

Turning first to Birmingham, in David Saunder's paper the problems of planning in a mixed economy at once become apparent. As Saunders observes (p177) 'The West Midlands conurbation entered the 1950s with a planning strategy based largely on the philosophy of containing urban growth within the then existing urban limits, and assumed that the main problem to be handled was the redevelopment of the high density inner areas rather than overall population growth.' Unfortunately, as Saunders points out, it was becoming increasingly clear by the mid-1950s that the assumptions on which the regional plan had been based

were crumbling. Continuing in-migration and an acceleration of the rate of natural population increase combined with the growing need for additional land if Birmingham were to maintain its massive urban redevelopment programme, all combined to put increasing pressure on the boundaries. In 1959 and again in the mid-1960s Birmingham applied for substantial boundary extensions. The first, at Wythall in Worcestershire for 2500 acres, was defeated after a major battle, but the second at Chelmsley Wood to the east in Warwickshire was successful and Chelmsley Wood was rapidly developed between 1967 and 1969.

Other plans followed, notably the West Midlands Study in 1965, the West Midlands Economic Planning Council Study in 1967, the West Midlands Regional Study in 1971, and the Joint Monitoring Steering Group in 1976, along with a series of structure plans from 1973–75, all of which were trying to take account of and plan for the changing circumstances and conflicts within the area.

Saunders concludes that enormous changes have occurred in the West Midlands since 1950, some because of planning, and others in spite of it. He credits planning with major achievements such as the redevelopment of inner Birmingham, and the inner ring road, commenting that as a result, Birmingham has witnessed probably a greater change in its physical environment and its housing stock 'than any comparable city of its size in the UK over the same period.' Nonetheless, Saunders adds that the West Midlands experience also demonstrates that 'whilst planning policies can be effective negative instruments of control, their ability to bring about development in the locations preferred by the approved plans has been variable . . . the strength of the forces which planning was grappling with was often under-estimated.' The confidence of the planners in the early 1940s and '50s has given way, says Saunders, 'to the pragmatism and incrementalism of the mid-1970s.' The planning vocabulary, suggests Saunders, is now full of words such as uncertainty, flexibility, robustness, monitoring, etc, and it is now reluctantly recognized, that 'planning can no longer prescribe in detail and must learn to live with uncertainty and with contemporary economic and social realities and pressures.'

What then have the fortunes of planning been and what are they likely to be in Vancouver? On the evidence of the two articles selected, it must be said that the answer is, not unexpectedly, less, although not entirely negligible. As the paper by Gertler and Crowley shows, regional planning certainly takes place, currently through the Greater Vancouver Regional District (GVRD) and previously through the Lower Mainland Planning Board. The major problem faced in Vancouver is that of managing growth. In the 20 years 1951–71 the Vancouver metropolitan area experienced a very high rate of growth, half of which stemmed from in-migration, the result being a population in excess of one million. Gertler and Crowley discuss the GVRDs plan to try (a) to control in-migration and (b) to direct and channel new growth through the strategy of regional town centres. The plan itself is elegant but, as Gertler and Crowley rightly ask, 'While the rationale for a programme of regional town centres is compelling, the inescapable question arises: Can it be done?' The answer is essentially that it would first require a major strengthening of existing planning arrangements, and second, it depends on the attractiveness and acceptability of the scheme to market forces. Planning in Canada would seem to be effective to the extent that it is congruent with market forces. This is particularly well shown in the second paper on Vancouver.

John Weaver's paper sets out to examine the relationships between the property industry and land-use controls, particularly where Harland Bartholomew's master-plan and zoning by-laws of 1929 are concerned. Weaver shows in his admirably well researched and argued paper that from the beginning of the century the nascent property industry had begun to recognize the value and desirability of protecting sites against non-conforming land-use encroachments. The first manifestation of this desire to minimize 'negative environmental externalities' was that of restrictive covenants but these only protected the developers' own land and not the surrounding areas. The city council used their discretion in applying their fire and health regulations to complement private covenants, but there were already pressures from the property industry for rational land use. As Weaver observes, 'No business

suffers a free market which introduces too much uncertainty', and it was the desire to reduce this uncertainty which was the motive force for land-use controls. Initially, the ratepayers' association, often backed by real-estate interests, pressed for informal zoning, but the threats to property values as Vancouver matured, and the demands of middle-class home-buyers became stronger.

The property industry's main interest in regulating land use was to enhance and protect property values and when Harland Bartholomew was brought in to prepare a master-plan in 1926, they ensured that they played a major role in the formulation of a plan which satisfied their interests. Similarly, they were instrumental in pressing for alterations to the zoning laws where they were felt necessary. Weaver concludes that Vancouver's experience with land-use controls 'supports a view of urban affairs which maintains that socio-economic forces . . . overpowered the goals of reformers or experts who aspired to shape the city.' Weaver asks whether planning, assuming it was desirable, could have been applied in a community which respected property rights and had influential pressure groups dedicated to their defence. In Vancouver, as elsewhere in advanced capitalist societies, Weaver argues that 'businessmen have defined the instruments of land-use control and directed their outcome.' Whatever the divergent intellectual or legal traditions in American and Canadian urban planning, the economic imperatives in both countries have presented similar and overruling considerations.

Turning to Poland, it would appear that the power of planning, certainly that of spatial or land-use planning, is not as great as might have been supposed. The Soviet model of national and regional economic planning was adopted in Poland in 1949 and until 1961 local physical planning had little more than advisory powers regarding the siting of new developments. The power of central investors was virtually absolute until 1961 when negative powers over development were granted to physical planners. From then until 1972 there was little real coordination of economic and physical or land-use planning as the two sets of plans were drawn up separately. So too, the central state investors still had considerable latitude in selecting regions and cities for developments, and no national spatial plan existed until 1972.

The result was that as a consequence of the uncertainty and economic constraints of central economic planning, land use in cities has been inefficient. As

Hamilton observes: 'excessively empty spaces lie between those projects which have fallen short of their original planned size or which have been 'temporarily' abandoned . . . increasing congestion [also] occurs where projects have exceeded their initial predicted scales.' Thus, taking the example of Nowa Huta, the steelworks has expanded constantly from a planned capacity of 1 million tons p.a. to 11 million tons at present with consequent results upon the growth of the adjacent new town. Allied to these problems, individual investors have rarely informed the relevant city council of their plans until a specific site was required. In consequence both housing and facility provision has posed problems as has the physical coordination of investment programmes. Thus despite the absence of a free market in land, in many ways town planners in Poland have faced rather similar problems of control to those in the West. The reason would seem to have been the fact that large central state investors have behaved, in relation to local planners, as large investors and developers have done in the West. If anything, Polish town planners would seem to have had less control until 1972 owing to the primacy accorded to national economic planning and, subsequently, greater coordinating powers were given to the local administration. Nonetheless, they are still faced with the difficulty of adopting local plans whilst implementing the national economic plan.

If any generalization can be drawn perhaps it is that economic power, be it private or public, dominates the power of planning in both East and West. This would appear to be borne out by several references in Danuta Jachniak-Ganguly's paper. She notes that industrial developers tended to choose locations 'for their direct economic significance to the developers regardless of their detrimental influence on the environment.' Fortunately, in the case of the 'pollution-free zone' west of Cracow designated in the regional plan, the planning applications could be rejected, as they could for noxious industries seeking to locate in Cracow itself. Thus, even where the power of refusal exists it is apparent that many enterprises make planning applications based solely on their own economic considerations, ignoring wider social costs, even though they may be production target-oriented and not profit-oriented as in the West.

Chris Hamnett

Reference

Hamilton F E I 1979 Spatial structure in East European cities in R A French and F E I Hamilton (eds) *The Socialist City* (New York: Wiley) Ch 9, p204

The Changing Planning Framework in the West Midlands

by D L Saunders

Introduction

The West Midlands conurbation entered the 1950s with a planning strategy based largely on the philosophy of containing urban growth within the then existing urban limits, and assumed that the main problem to be handled was the redevelopment of the high-density inner areas rather than overall population growth. However, this strategy for the conurbation owed as much, if not more, to the general planning consensus of the late 1940s — which favoured containment — as to any comprehensive objective assessment of the particular needs and circumstances of the West Midlands conurbation. The recommendations of the Abercrombie–Jackson plan for the West Midlands itself owed much to the Abercrombie plan for Greater London, and it is symptomatic of the plan's genesis that the authors argued against peripheral development because it would 'lead towards conditions which are known to call for drastic action in the case of London' (Abercrombie and Jackson 1948). From the Barlow Commission's Report on, through the wartime and immediate post-war series of reports and legislation dealing with town and country planning, new towns, land values and the inter-regional distribution of industrial employment, the problems of London were a major formative influence on this emergent group of national, strategic planning policies and tools.

There is a particular case for regretting the ready adoption of the Abercrombie–Jackson plan for the West Midlands conurbation since an alternative strategy had been put forward in *Conurbation* (West Midlands Group 1948). The basic philosophies of these two documents were not dissimilar, both reflecting the national consensus about urban containment as they did, but whereas Abercrombie and Jackson saw overspill as the inevitable counterpart to their philosophy of containment, *Conurbation* argued that the housing needs of the conurbation could be met through imaginative planning, and determined action within its existing boundaries. *Conurbation* was especially concerned with the treatment of derelict land — one tenth of the land in the Black Country was identified as derelict, i.e. spoiled by extractive industry, industrial waste and derelict buildings — and argued that this and other waste and unused land provided a major land resource for producing better living conditions inside the conurbation. *Conurbation* therefore favoured a strategy of settlements within a sea of green space, while Abercrombie and Jackson were emphasizing the need to define the urban limits of the conurbation by means of a green belt with provision for overspill in and dispersal to selected areas beyond. But, curiously perhaps, and unlike the plan for Greater London, no new towns were proposed for the West Midlands. It was assumed that sufficient capacity could be provided in places just beyond the conurbation, like Bromsgrove, Cannock and Coventry and Tamworth, to cater for the expected housing needs of the conurbation. The difference of emphasis and philosophy between *Conurbation* and the Abercrombie–Jackson plan was to be a continuing element in the West Midlands planning scene for the next quarter of a century, and the structure plans of the mid-70s still contained powerful echoes of that earlier debate.

The Minister of Town and Country Planning eventually endorsed the Abercrombie–Jackson plan and the West Midlands entered the 1950s with its first officially approved regional plan, which predicted and provided for the decentralization of over a quarter of a million people from the conurbation in the 14 years of the plan.

Source: F Joyce (ed) 1977 *Metropolitan Development and Change: The West Midlands — A Policy Review* (London: Saxon House) pp36–49.

The 1950s

By the early 1950s Birmingham's urban redevelopment programme was getting into full swing. Although Birmingham had lost some houses through enemy action during the war, its greatest problem by far was its legacy of high densities and slum housing in the inner areas. Consequently, Birmingham, ahead of the rest of the country, seized eagerly the new tools forged by wartime and post-war planning legislation and five comprehensive redevelopment areas were identified, covering nearly 1400 acres. A typical plan for one of these comprehensive redevelopment areas involved halving the population in the area, a fivefold increase in the school acreage, a tenfold increase in public open space, while maintaining the industrial acreage at about its previous level. Redevelopment was therefore intended to transform the living conditions of the inner area and provide for the first time in such areas a comprehensive package of better housing, better schools and community facilities, some much-needed open space, while maintaining industrial activities in the area.

Birmingham's policy on densities was to aim for 120–175 persons per acre in the inner residential zone, and 50 persons per acre in the outer zone. These densities represented a considerable reduction on the historic densities in the inner zone which had neared 200 persons per acre, and were a major factor in Birmingham's need for additional land. The first slums had been pulled down in 1948 and by the early 1950s Birmingham was rehousing 1000 families a year from its redevelopment areas.

The early 1950s also saw a change of emphasis in central government's approach to the promotion of overspill, with the passing of the Town Development Act (TDA) in 1952, which can be interpreted as a moderating move, lessening the emphasis on the new town programme of the former government. However, true to form, Birmingham immediately started discussions with Staffordshire with a view to negotiating town development schemes, but progress was slow and can in part be attributed to the fact that whereas new towns were centrally financed with an appointed corporation to purchase land — at preferential prices — the TDA schemes required inter-authority agreement and the central government financial input was modest. However, by 1957 Birmingham had negotiated 10 overspill agreements, although only a handful of houses had been built. Meanwhile, the process of urban redevelopment was continuing apace in Birmingham and generating a strong demand for additional land.

By the mid-1950s it was becoming increasingly clear that the assumptions on which the regional plan had been based were crumbling. *Conurbation* had not provided for a continuing high rate of in-migration and the Abercrombie–Jackson plan had not allowed for an acceleration in the rate of natural increase which set in around 1955 and so, by the mid to later 1950s, the quantitative basis of the regional strategy was increasingly in question. To these demographic factors was added Birmingham's growing fear that it could not maintain its urban redevelopment programme without additional land on which to locate the displaced population from the redevelopment areas. Furthermore, insufficient resources were made available to finance a land reclamation programme on an adequate scale in the Black Country. This combination of factors fuelled the new towns' cause and pressure was put on members of parliament, resolutions were passed by the city council and pressure groups formed, all advocating the case for new towns to provide the necessary relief to the conurbation's growing problems.

In the midst of this increasing turbulence the government introduced a circular which can be seen in many ways as nailing the final plank into the Barlow Reith/Abercrombie–Jackson platform, namely the introduction of statutory powers for the creation and confirmation of green belts. Although green belts had figured in the Abercrombie plans for both London and Birmingham, it was only in 1955 that the concept was given statutory backing. The counties surrounding the Birmingham and Black Country conurbations took up the 1955 circular with enthusiasm and within a few years submissions had been made for a statutory green belt encircling the conurbation, which became a powerful planning tool, even though it was many years later before those submissions were given final ministerial approval.

In March 1959 Birmingham submitted a proposal for a boundary extension covering 2432 acres in an area to the south-east of the city at Wythall in Worcestershire. This was to produce one of the major set-piece battles on the post-war West Midlands planning scene whose echoes can still be heard. Birmingham's contention was that while some of its population pressure — predominantly that resulting from the faster than expected increases in both total population and household formation — could reasonably be expected to 'overspill' new capacity provided in the ring of towns beyond the green belt, it was unreasonable and unrealistic to expect the population displaced by the redevelopment of Birmingham's inner areas to move to such locations. These people were seen as Birmingham citizens for whom Birmingham must make provision, and by the late 1950s Birmingham had concluded that such provision could only be made by a boundary extension. The ensuing public inquiry saw a major confrontation between Birmingham's aspirations and the philosophy of the surrounding counties, and the difficulty in disentangling planning considerations from political considerations illustrated the way in which a planning concept, the green belt, had become inextricably linked with political and inter-authority boundary considerations.

The outcome of the Wythall inquiry was a virtually complete victory for Worcestershire who had opposed Birmingham, with only a slight hint that some limited development at Wythall might eventually be allowed if all other efforts at providing for Birmingham's housing needs were to fail.

The 1950s therefore represent a significant transitional period between the confident assumptions and expectations of what could be achieved through the regional plan and the realization by the end of the decade that the overspill component of that strategy had been insufficient and not made fully operational at a time when the scale of the conurbation housing problems was demonstrably increasing.

The 1960s

Calculations of overspill were now being revised upwards and by 1961 the West Midlands New Towns Society argued that there would be a need over the next two decades for overspill provision for upwards of 300 000 people. By 1962 the fruits of Birmingham's overspill agreements numbered some 1600 houses and even if all the Town Development Act agreements negotiated by Birmingham could be fully implemented, the problem was outstripping the provision negotiated.

Dawley in the older industrial centre of Shropshire was designated as a new town in January 1963 to receive overspill from the conurbation, and its target was to grow from 35 000 to 90 000 by 1980. In 1964 Redditch, almost due south of Birmingham, was designated as a new town, with a plan to grow from 32 000 population at the time of designation to 70 000 by 1980.

Simultaneous work by the West Midlands Study (an official exercise initiated by central government) and

by a group of academics led by David Eversley, produced a further upward revision of the overspill estimate for the conurbation, and in 1965 it was calculated that, allowing for natural growth of population, some net inward migration and slum clearance, the conurbation would need some 340 000 additional dwellings, of which 170 000 would have to be provided in overspill locations. Meanwhile Birmingham had made a further major bid for additional capacity beyond its boundary, this time at Chelmsley Wood to the east of the city in Warwickshire, for a development similar in scale to that proposed earlier for Wythall, and this time Birmingham was successful. In the event, Birmingham developed the Chelmsley Wood site at an extremely rapid rate and between 1967 and 1969 some 10 000 houses were completed there.

The return of regional planning

No systematic monitoring of the Abercrombie–Jackson plan had taken place in the region, and it had been left to individual authorities, academics and concerned individuals to watch the emerging situation in the conurbation.

The initiation of regional studies in several regions in the early 1960s, the setting up of the Department of Economic Affairs and of the Regional Economic Planning Boards and Councils in 1964 can be seen as the turning point in central government's re-engagement in the systematic assessment of regional strategic planning problems. The West Midlands Study, published in 1965 (Department of Economic Affairs 1965) went on from its overspill calculations to pose three strategic alternatives:

(a) peripheral expansion with some incursions into the green belt;

(b) close-in satellites such as Stafford, Lichfield and Tamworth within commuting reach of the conurbation; or

(c) longer distance overspill schemes beyond commuting range.

With the formation of the West Midlands Economic Planning Council in 1964 there was formed for the first time a grouping of industrialists, local government officers and members, trade unionists, academics and others concerned with the interest of the region, charged with the responsibility of producing a planning strategy for the region. Their document entitled *The West Midlands: Patterns of Growth* (West Midlands Economic Planning Council 1967) worked on the latest calculations of overspill but its philosophy had echoes of the 1940s with references to the 'social and economic threat' of a growing conurbation, and they underwrote overspill policies with the recommendation that industrial mobility — which they recognized as the key factor in any successful overspill policy — should be stimulated by incentives to encourage firms to move to overspill sites. In the event this suggestion conflicted with the inter-regional policy of the Board of Trade and was rejected. The Planning Council's locational strategy involved growth outwards along five corridors; north-west to include Dawley; northwards to north Staffordshire; north-east to Burton-on-Trent; southwards to Redditch; and south-westwards into Worcestershire.

The government's response to the Planning Council's strategy mentioned the intention to enlarge Dawley new town to include Wellington and Oakengates, and in due course Telford new town was designated in December 1968, with a planned increase of population from 73 000 at designation date to 220 000 by 1991. The government's response also referred to the need for a planning study in depth of the conurbation and the area around it, so that the scale, timing and possibilities of accommodating population could be fully examined. In the course of discussions between Birmingham and Worcestershire about overspill provision it was proposed that there should be a series of negotiations between the city and the surrounding counties. With the formation of the West Midlands Planning Authorities' Conference, the local authorities proposed that they should undertake a full study of the conurbation and the region, and in 1967 the study was launched, with some central government technical participation, but with control of the study in the hands of the local authorities.

The 1970s

In 1971 the Regional Study reported with a document entitled *A Developing Strategy for the West Midlands* (West Midlands Regional Study 1971). This contained proposals for the periods to 1981 and 2001 which included a considerable amount of long-distance dispersal as well as some close-in development in Warwickshire, following a sub-regional study of Coventry, Solihull and Warwickshire. Meanwhile, the Economic Planning Council had published its own economic appraisal of the region (West Midlands Economic Planning Council 1971) which examined in depth the structure and performance of the regional economy, and concluded from a number of indicators that there was cause for concern about the future prospects of the regional economy and that economic and industrial considerations should figure more prominently in strategic planning for the region.

The Secretary of State for the Environment in January 1974 replied to the Chairman of the West Midlands Planning Authorities' Conference accepting with modifications and reservations the various submissions made by WMPAC and the regional offices of central government departments. These documents, together with the Secretary of State's letter of January 1974 constituted a new regional strategy. This new strategy was essentially an attempt to strike a realistic balance between the views of WMPAC, the EPC and central government. In the process a fairly generous view was taken of likely overspill from the conurbation and the resultant strategy, expressed in a series of zones radiating outwards from the conurbation, included some significant new peripheral development in the Solihull area and at Sutton Coldfield, it endorsed the existing expansion schemes at Tamworth and Redditch, paved the way for new strategic provision in the Kidderminster area, and endorsed the principle of additional provision to the north and west of the conurbation but left the details of this to the structure plans. For the rest of the region the new strategy allowed for growth in a number of towns on the assumption that they were self-dependent and not primarily related to the conurbation. An important part of the concordat of January 1974 was the agreement that regional strategic monitoring should be undertaken jointly by WMPAC and central government working together in partnership. So after 24 years, the West Midlands could again claim an up-to-date government-endorsed regional strategy in operation.

The agreement to monitor the regional strategy on a joint basis was put into immediate effect and reports were produced in the autumn of 1975 and the autumn of 1976. In the autumn 1976 Joint Monitoring Report (Joint Monitoring Steering Group 1976), it was concluded that the regional outlook had changed in several significant ways since the original strategy package, culminating in the Secretary of State's letter of January 1974, had been constructed:

(a) Total regional population growth will be much less than previously assumed.
(b) The growth of households is continuing.
(c) Overspill from the urban centre may be less than previously estimated.

(d) Industrial mobility will be less than previously anticipated.

(e) Both personal and resource costs of commuting are more significant than they used to be.

(f) Employment growth in both manufacturing industry and services will be lower than previously anticipated.

(g) Public expenditure levels will be lower than previously anticipated.

(g) Public expenditure levels will be lower than previously anticipated and resource constraints may have an important influence on development.

(h) There is an increasing awareness of the social and economic problems of urban areas and particularly inner areas.

The report went on to argue that 'these changes cannot be ignored and it is therefore proposed to up-date the existing strategy with a view to producing towards the end of 1977 a document for submission to Ministers, West Midlands Planning Authorities' Conference and the Economic Planning Council which will take these changes on board and provide the basis for the rolling forward of the up-dated strategy.' So one of the early fruits of the joint monitoring system was the important recognition of the way in which the major assumptions and variables in the regional strategy calculation had changed during the early 1970s, that something of a watershed in the region's development had occurred in the late 1960s and early 1970s and that some of the key variables had changed to a very significant extent over a very short period.

In mid-1977 the regional strategy was therefore again under active consideration with a view to updating the strategy settlement of January 1974 and rolling forward the period of the strategy from 1986 to 1991. Perhaps the most significant difference compared to the previous strategic exercises in the region was that the current reconsideration was undertaken on a joint basis between central government departments and the West Midlands Planning Authorities' Conference, and with the active support of the Economic Planning Council, whereas all the previous regional and conurbation exercises had been largely unilateral exercises undertaken by one or other of those parties.

Structure plans

The West Midlands planning authorities were among the first in the country to take up the new development plan legislation enacted in the early 1970s. This provided for a distinction between structure plans which were to indicate broad land use and transport policies and proposals for future development, leaving detailed map-based plans to a separate and distinct local plan stage. Before the reorganization of local government

took effect on 1 April 1974, structure plans had been submitted for all of the region except Shropshire county and Worcester city. As was pointed out above, one of the reasons for attempting to get an agreed new strategy for the region in the early 1970s was the need to provide an up-to-date regional context for the forthcoming structure plans. In the event, the plans submitted were not entirely compatible with the strategy as determined in January 1974, and there were a number of regional issues raised by the county and county borough structure plans. Following submission, a series of five examinations in public took place starting in autumn 1973 (the Coventry, Warwickshire and Solihull structure plans) and finishing in spring 1975 (the six conurbation structure plans — Birmingham, Solihull, Sandwell, Warley, Dudley and Wolverhampton).

Although there were considerable variations in the character and content of the structure plans submitted, each of them considered the main variables against which the future planning of their area should be considered and questions of housing need, overspill, industrial growth and industrial mobility figured prominently in both the submissions and at the examinations in public. In addition to these predictable issues the new legislation required an explicit consideration of the resource and expenditure implications of the planning policies and proposals under consideration, and regard to the social impact of the structure plans. Therefore, while the examinations in public often contained strong echoes of the earlier strategic battles between the urban areas and the counties, they also contained important new elements which widened the debate and added important new dimensions to the problems and issues under examination. Many of these plans were prepared rapidly against a deadline set by the date for local government reorganization, and undoubtedly there is room for further development and improvement of structure planning in the West Midlands region, but to have produced such a comprehensive coverage so far ahead of the rest of the country was a major achievement.

Perhaps one of the most important documents to be produced in the course of this first wave of structure planning in the West Midlands was the report of the panel set up to examine the six conurbation county borough structure plans. This represents something of a milestone in conurbation planning in the West Midlands. One of the major tasks of the examining panel for the six county borough structure plans covering the conurbation was to weld these separate plans into something approaching a single whole. In the course of this the examining panel naturally had regard to wider metropolitan and regional strategic considerations, and some indication of the range of issues which they had to consider is given in the following quotation from their report to the Secretary of State: 'We can appreciate Staffordshire County Council's reasons for wishing to oppose any higher level of close-in development: the need to control the form that expansion of the conurbation will take; the preservation of the rural character of some areas on the periphery; the opportunities for recreational development may be lost and the resources already committed to development elsewhere. However, we also recognize the force of the arguments put by WMCC [West Midlands County Council] and the Metropolitan Boroughs; above all, that if there are insufficient mobile jobs there is no point in moving people a long way from their current place of employment and probably away from their friends and relations. We therefore believe that peripheral and close-in development will have an important role in meeting the needs of the area over the next few years' (Department of the Environment 1976). In particular, the panel drew attention to the urgent short-term problems of the conurbation: 'Finally we emphasize that the need is at its greatest now. Even though it may not be possible to achieve all the aims by 1986, much will no doubt have been done by that time. In particular, if the national and regional birth rate does not begin to rise again substantially, the pressure which an increasing population has placed upon conurbation housing and planning authorities for many years should begin to ease towards the end of the plan period. But that date is a long time off for somebody who is homeless or living in totally unsatisfactory conditions. To help them every effort must be made to achieve the housing programme for the next few years. We therefore urge that it should be a general policy that priority be given to the development of those areas of land, whether within the Six Plans Area or outside at places not too far from where people work, which are suitable for housing and where the necessary infrastructure is already present or can be provided quickly. In this way the problems and the misery which are hidden behind the statistics in this and the other Chapters of our Report may be relieved for as many as possible as soon as possible.' The panel estimated a housing deficit in the West Midlands conurbation of 44 000–65 000 households for the period 1971–86.

The Examining Panel attached especial importance to industrial and employment considerations: 'We see the conurbation Structure Plans as providing primarily for industry that must remain at or near its original location if at all possible. Unless firms in such a position can be provided with suitable sites near their original location they will either give up all thoughts of expansion or, if forced to move, will all too probably go out of business. It is therefore, in our view, not a question of depriving the outer areas of the region of industry, but rather of giving conurbation industry a suitable environment in which to prosper.'

In many ways anticipating the initiative which the Secretary of State for the Environment was later to take in respect of inner-city problems, the panel recognized the importance of local authority policies in the regeneration of industry in inner city areas and they welcomed the policy of fostering industrial nursery estates and factories and the encouragement of employment opportunities for women located near to their homes, making it easier for them to take up jobs. The panel went on to argue: 'We consider that particular attention should be given to the problems of areas suffering from poor general environment and poor housing, areas where there is often a high proportion of unskilled workers with low mobility. Geographically, such areas will normally correspond with the inner ring areas in Birmingham, but similarly deprived areas are found in parts of the Black Country.'

One of the most interesting sections of the report of the Examination in Public concerns the treatment of social considerations in the structure plans. The panel argued that social considerations should be an integral part of the structure plans for the area and that the social consequences of policies in structure plans should be taken into account from the early stages of structure plan preparation. The panel took a look at the housing and employment policies with special reference to their effect on particular groups, such as single young people and immigrant groups and particular areas within the conurbation. The main conclusions of the panel, having looked at the social aspect of the policies and proposals, was that although a concern for social factors had been implicit in many of the policies and general proposals, the consequences had not been clearly set out. However, they emphasized the role of the structure plans in supporting the concept of a community of communities and they endorsed the greater emphasis given to the renewal and improvement of existing housing which they believed would help reduce the disruption of communities caused by redevelopment. While recognizing that much of the action in the disadvantaged areas would have to be tackled through local plans and under housing legislation they recommended that a general policy should be incorporated in each plan to discriminate positively in favour of socially disadvantaged areas in the formulation of detailed land-use policies and the distribution of resources.

Conclusions and current planning issues

Since 1950 there have been enormous changes in the West Midlands brought about in part through the operation of planning policies conceived in the late 1940s and in part despite those policies. Some of the key assumptions on which the strategic planning policies applied to the conurbation were based proved to be unsound, and the strength of the forces with which planning policies were grappling was often underestimated. Since the late 1940s it has been demonstrated that while planning policies can be effective as negative instruments of control, their ability to bring about development in the locations preferred by approved plans has been variable. However, this does not detract from the major achievements which can be credited to planning policies in the conurbation over this period. Top of the list must come the dramatic scale of urban redevelopment in Birmingham. By the early 1970s the five redevelopment areas were virtually completed, an inner ring road had been built which encircled the central business district, and as a result, Birmingham witnessed probably a greater change in its physical environment, its housing stock and its urban lifestyle than any comparable city of its size in the UK over the same period. All this was made possible by the new tools of planning forged in the '40s and wielded enthusiastically by the city of Birmingham in the '50s and '60s. As the recent official history of Birmingham concludes: 'In 1939 it was still possible for an outsider to be indifferent to Birmingham: in 1970 it could not fail to provoke a thrill or perhaps a shudder among all who beheld it' (Sutcliffe and Smith 1974). In the Black Country the pace of change was much slower and more incremental utilizing in the process at least some of the more readily usable derelict land.

Throughout the major part of this period, the industrial prosperity of the conurbation and the region could be taken for granted. The planning issue was essentially seen as one of controlling a dynamic industrial situation. In more recent times this basic assumption has been questioned, and one of the issues of greatest current concern in the region is whether the change in the relative economic fortunes of the West Midlands compared to other regions and the country as a whole will be of a short-term nature or whether it indicates a more significant longer-term change. The conurbation is heavily dependent on the metal industries in general, and the vehicle industry in particular, and is therefore very sensitive to the fortunes of those industries and the policies applied to them by central government. The planning authorities have responded to this situation by recognizing the importance of nurturing the industry that is in the conurbation, and there is evidence that policies towards non-conforming industry are changing and that there will be far less wholesale clearance of industry within the conurbation and that the key consideration will be whether particular industries are 'bad neighbours'. This represents a significant shift of emphasis from earlier policies which generally assumed that the close juxtaposition of industry and housing was environmentally unacceptable. The historic example of the Black Country, with its loosely connected scatter of industrial villages and towns, may provide a model for the policies towards industry in urban areas which will be operating in the coming decades although some of the traditional Black Country industries, e.g. foundries, would come in the 'bad neighbour' category.

Since the first strategy for the region in the late 1940s, it can be said that the problems to which both *Conurbation* and Abercrombie–Jackson addressed themselves had not been solved by the end of their plan period. This was partly because the scale and character of the problem grew and changed during the period, but also because the adopted policies turned out to be partial and insufficiently related to the real problems. The series of border battles on the periphery of the conurbation were indicative, not only of a clash of philosphies between the urban areas and the counties, but that the approved Abercrombie–Jackson had been incomplete and, unlike its Greater London parent, had not included a sufficient programme of planned overspill to enable the basic containment concept to become operational. The end result, therefore, was in theory a strategy of containment but increasingly in practice a pragmatic combination of limited (belated) overspill into new and expanded towns, plus, on grounds of expediency, as well as for social and economic reasons, some substantial development in selected peripheral locations.

Perhaps the greatest cause for regret is that one of the concepts integral to *Conurbation*, the utilization of the substantial areas of derelict and waste land which existed within the conurbation, was not vigorously followed through. This cause tended to languish during most of the quarter century and there was no sustained reclamation programme on a sufficient scale to help offset the growing land hunger which increasingly dominated the rest of the conurbation. The problems of land reclamation are considerable, but with the benefit of experience elsewhere during the period, there is increasing indication that the importance of this land resource has now been recognized and that policies and plans will be devised to utilize this resource to the benefit of the conurbation as a whole.

The period under review has witnessed the arrival, the departure and subsequent return of regional planning as a structured activity. There is now a general acceptance that some sort of regional overview of the conurbation in its regional setting is essential and there is now mutual agreement that the responsibility for a regional strategy must be shared between central government and the local authorities, together with the Economic Planning Council.[1] Hopefully, the next quarter of a century will start with an updated regional strategy for the West Midlands. Central government has strengthened its regional presence, local government has established effective operational regional machinery, and the two are now working jointly on updating the strategy. The regional dimension to both central and local government looks to be rather deeper rooted in 1977 than events have shown it to have been in 1950.

The experience of the West Midlands with the package of planning policies constructed in the late 1940s and operated from the 1950s, bears strong witness to the need to relate policies to the circumstances of the area in question and the danger of importing policies conceived for other areas with problems which looked superficially similar. Conurbation strategies need to be just as much tailored to the needs and problems of the individual conurbation as do the plans for villages and smaller areas. The different emphases now being adopted in the current generation of regional strategies and conurbation structure plans is a reassuring indication that this lesson too has been learned.

The current concern with the future of our cities and especially of the inner areas of our major cities cannot be divorced from the planning policies and the strategic concepts which have been operated in the region since the 1950s. Although our understanding of cause and effect relationships is still incomplete, planning policies of one sort and another cannot be absolved from some responsibility for the problems in our inner areas. This current concern is reinforcing the emphasis that was deliberately written in to the new planning system that structural policies should have regard to social, economic and resources aspects. Although this undoubtedly makes forward planning a more complex and difficult activity, perhaps it was the omission of these elements from early post-war planning that produced an outcome which Peter Hall graphically summarized in the following words: 'It certainly was not the intention of (the founding fathers of the planning system) that people should live cramped lives in homes destined for premature slumdom, far from urban services or jobs; or that city dwellers should live in blank cliffs of flats, far from the ground without access to play space for their children. Somewhere along the way a great ideal was lost, a system distorted, and the great mass of the people betrayed' (Hall *et al* 1973).

Although there are some similarities between the mid-1970s and the early 1950s, such as a very low expectation of overall population growth and tight limits on public expenditure, in most other respects attitudes are very different. The confidence of the planners of the 1940s and early 1950s gave way to the pragmatism and incrementalism of the mid 1970s. The planning vocabulary is now full of words such as uncertainty, flexibility, robustness, monitoring, etc. It is now recognized, perhaps reluctantly and belatedly, that planning can no longer prescribe in detail and must learn to live with uncertainty and with contemporary economic and social realities and pressures. But perhaps the biggest challenge left over is how to reconcile this new-found pragmatic, incremental approach towards change with the same quality of conviction and concern for the human lot which underpinned the first post-war efforts at strategic planning. If the aim is no longer to build the new Jerusalem, the task of present and future planning strategies should still be to make the conurbation 'a more attractive and efficient place' (West Midlands Group 1948).

Note
[1] Saunders' optimism has been overtaken by harsher historical experiences. Economic Planning Councils have now been abolished and regional plans reduced to almost irrelevant statements of good intent (Eds).

References

Abercrombie P and Jackson H 1948 *The West Midlands Plan* (Ministry of Town and Country Planning, London: HMSO)

Department of Economic Affairs (1965) *The West Midlands: A Regional Study* (London: HMSO)

Department of the Environment 1976 Examination in Public of the Structure Plans for Birmingham, Dudley, Walsall, Warley, West Bromwich and Wolverhampton. Report of the Panel.

Hall P *et al* 1973 *The Containment of Urban England* (London: Allen and Unwin)

Joint Monitoring Steering Group 1976 *A Developing Strategy for the West Midlands, Second Annual Report* (Department of the Environment and West Midlands Planning Authorities Conference)

Sutcliffe A and Smith R 1974 *Birmingham 1939–70* (London: Oxford University Press)

West Midlands Economic Planning Council 1967 *West Midlands: Patterns of Growth* (London: HMSO)

—— 1971 *The West Midlands: An Economic Appraisal* (London: HMSO)

West Midlands Group 1948 *Conurbation* (London: Architectural Press)

West Midlands Regional Study 1971 *A Developing Strategy for the West Midlands* (West Midlands Planning Authorities' Conference, Birmingham)

25 A Strategy for Deconcentration: Regional Town Centres, Vancouver District

by L Gertler and R Crowley

Introduction

In the two decades 1951–71, the Vancouver metropolitan area experienced a very high rate of growth (averaging about 4% annually), and in the process acquired a population of over a million. While currently the population increase has moderated a little, projections of growth indicate an annual rate from 2.5 to 3.5%, which in either case would produce a metropolitan population well over two million by 2001. Much of the growth is attributable to Vancouver's attraction for people moving in from other parts of the country or other countries. With about 9.5% of the total population of the 22 census metropolitan areas, Vancouver attracted over 26% of those immigrants destined for metropolitan places outside Ontario in the five years 1966–71, and about 21% of total net domestic migration. Internal migration in that period accounted for over half of Vancouver's growth and close to one-third of those originated in rural counties within British Columbia. Vancouver is a strong magnet for people and it is not very likely that the 'tap' can be turned off very quickly, nor very much.

This situation was reviewed by the planners of the Greater Vancouver Regional District (GVRD) and they put forward (March 1975) a set of 'proposals to manage the growth of Greater Vancouver' (see figure 25.1). These represented a double-barrelled strategy (1) to work with federal and provincial governments to influence immigration and other factors which affect population growth, and (2) to direct and channel new growth

Source: Len Gertler and Ron Crowley 1977 *Changing Canadian Cities: The Next 25 years* Ch.4, pp174–82. Reprinted by permission of the Canadian Publishers, McLelland and Stewart Limited, Toronto.

'so as to maintain or enhance the livability of the region.' One of the key features of that strategy was the concept of regional town centres, a tactic of general interest for two main reasons. It was central to achieving a radical change in the balance of employment between Vancouver, particularly the downtown, and outlying areas, which otherwise would be predominantly dormitory in function. The concept matured to the point where a specific method of implementation — an 'action program' — was spelled out. These aspects should be of interest to other metropolitan areas like Toronto, Montreal and Edmonton, which are equally preoccupied with the management of growth.

The basis of the concept

A number of considerations have come together to produce the concept of the regional town centre. One consideration is the pressure on downtown Vancouver. This arises from the persisting build-up of jobs and structures in the small peninsula that contains the downtown area. Behind the city's mushrooming Manhattan image are such indices of concentration as 62% of the region's total employment (1971); 60% of rentable office space (1973); 65% of office space under construction (1973) and 50–60% of office space in the planning stage (1973). The area is also the setting for some of the region's major cultural facilities: theatres, museums, art galleries, as well as interesting restaurants and fashionable shops.

The critical evaluation of this trend raises concern about the impact on the physical environment and metropolitan transportation movements. About 40% of downtown Vancouver would have to be torn down and

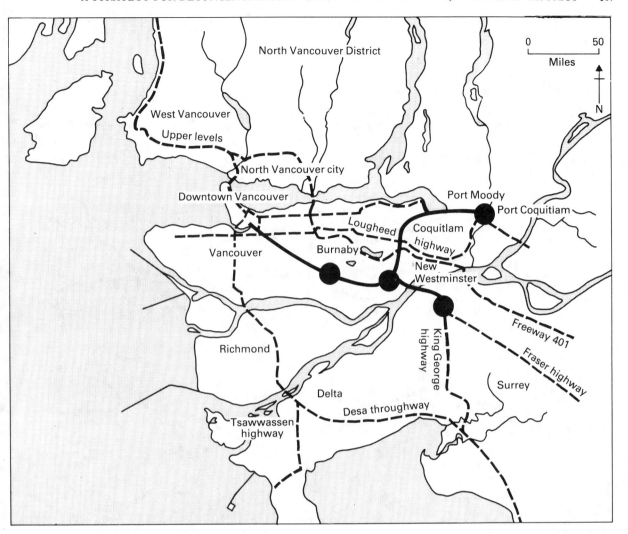

Figure 25.1 Growth management strategy: Lower Mainland, British Columbia. (Note: the strategy proposes to start four regional town centres by 1986.) Sorce: *The Livable Region 1976/1986 Proposals to Manage the Growth of Greater Vancouver* (Vancouver: Greater Vancouver Regional District) 1975, p18.

rebuilt to accommodate this proportion of growth to 1996; and development would have to assume an increasingly concentrated high-rise form. Access to the downtown core, which is feasible only by means of a relatively few arteries and bridges, would become progressively aggravated because of the regional distribution of jobs and houses associated with the pattern of centre dominance. The balance of residential growth has shifted decidedly towards suburban locations north, south and east of the city of Vancouver. Ratios of jobs to resident workers of 1 to 1.7 for the North Shore, and 1 to 1.8 for the north-east sector and northern Delta Surrey (figure 25.2) mean heavy cross-town journey-to-work traffic and mounting pressures on the downtown itself for car space — particularly as only 10% of daily trips in the region are made on public transport. Neighbourhoods along the major transportation channels also experience increased environmental disruption.

A second consideration underlying the 'regional town centres' proposal arises from the desire to improve existing town centres in the outlying municipalities. These vary in size from under 50 000 square feet of commercial floor space in Port Moody (White Rock South Surrey) to huge centres with 800 000 to 1 000 000 square feet in the facilities at

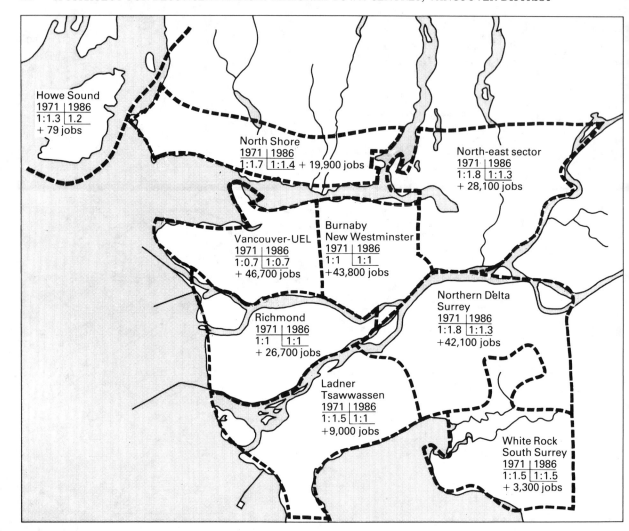

Figure 25.2 Ratio of jobs to resident workers in sub-regional areas: Lower Mainland, British Columbia. (Note: A ratio of 1:1 means the number of jobs in the area is equal to the number of workers living there. A ratio of 1:2 means there is an imbalance: only one job available for every two workers living in the area. (The North Shore at 1:1.7 is close to this.) Comparing the 1971 and 1986 ratios for each area shows how much they propose to improve this balance by 1986. Also shown is the actual number of new jobs to be created by 1986. Source: *The Livable Region 1976/1986 Proposals to Manage the Growth of Greater Vancouver* (Vancouver: Greater Vancouver Regional District) 1975, p15.

Lougheed (Burnaby), and Park Royal (North Shore). Some of these are very big developments considering that typically the central business district of a medium-sized Ontario city of 100 000+ population has about 500 000 square feet. But size apart, all of these are essentially shopping centres, and not town centres in the sense of focal points that provide the range of services required by most communities. As such, they have some serious limitations. They may offer a choice of half a dozen shoe stores but no library or medical clinic or good hotel. There may be a lot of relatively unskilled service jobs in retail establishments, but very little professional and administrative employment in offices. Both of these conditions spell heavy dependence of the city's residents on one or two more fully developed centres such as the downtown areas in Vancouver and New Westminster, and all that implies in the way of the costs and stresses of cross-town urban traffic.

Features of regional town centres

The response to these circumstances that has emerged from the livable region programme is a proposal to transform some of the existing centres into the focal points of communities that each serve a minimum of 100 000–150 000 people. These centres would be sufficiently large and diversified to play a 'specific role in bringing jobs, leisure and education nearer to home by attracting activities that would otherwise continue to locate in Vancouver.' Certain minimum size requirements are suggested: 7000–10 000 jobs; 700 000 square feet of retail space; 1 000 000 square feet of office space; theatres for stage performances with seating capacity up to 500; and up to 3000 dwellings mixed into each centre. The critical transformation as far as activities are concerned is in the arithmetic of the three basic components: shopping, offices, and other commercial and leisure activities. The ratios of shopping to offices to leisure and other commercial activities have to be changed from the typical mix in existing centres of 4:3:1 to a future ratio of 4:6:2. The balance must shift from shopping to personal and professional services, to offices, and to such leisure facilities as swimming pools and theatres.

Turning shopping centres into regional town centres requires the right mix and balance of activities — but much more than that. The concept implies certain design features: an intimate human scale; pedestrian orientation; separation of cars and people, consumer and delivery/maintenance circulation; effective public transportation access; and the expression of the unique attributes of each location.

These are elements which in themselves do not assure success. They are important for the principle they suggest: attraction to people. The alchemy of design links the local and regional roles of such centres. Only by giving intrinsic satisfaction to residents in the surrounding communities can regional town centres help relieve the pressure on downtown Vancouver and attain a better regional balance of jobs to population.

Priority locations, transportation links and centre functions

Applying the tests of need and feasibility the planners of the Vancouver district identified four priority locations: in New Westminster, Burnaby, the north-east sector and Surrey (see figure 25.1). In the latter two areas there will be a large gap between planned residential growth and local employment unless strong regional town centres are created. And the policy statement anticipates that beyond 1986 such centres will be crucial to sustain a pattern of decentralized metropolitan growth within an arc of about 25 miles from downtown Vancouver.

The creation of regional town centres is strongly linked in the regional growth strategy with a certain approach to urban transportation. The basic policy asserted is that the transportation system has to be moved from its overwhelming focus on downtown Vancouver to a system which satisfies two other requirements: the access of employees and clientele to regional town centres, and the linking of centre to centre. 'A transportation plan that improves the local accessibility of centres to the communities they serve, and links them with each other across the region, can encourage centre development.'

While the rationale for a programme of regional town centres is compelling, the inescapable question arises: Can it be done? The regional planners in Vancouver have taken a hard look at this question. They have studied the locational preferences and tendencies of centre-oriented activities. It was discovered, through a survey of corporations, that particular functions depend strongly on the milieu of the major urban core, while others have a weaker affinity. In the first category are head office administration, marketing and finance functions. In the second are such activities as research and development; some computer-related operations such as credit accounting, airline reservation systems and forest resource inventorying; and certain businesses with marketing operations that are not highly dependent on downtown promotion such as utility and resource companies, liquor and food processors, as well as new companies not yet enmeshed in a web of downtown contacts.

In addition, some kinds of public sector and community functions can play a critical role in the process of centre development as well as providing the necessary balance and variety of facilities. Federal and provincial government offices are both comparatively flexible in locational requirements and in the decade to 1986 could be a substantial decentralizing force. They will account for about 25% of the total new office space. And developments related to government offices (private projects following government, and supporting businesses and services) could constitute an important indirect employment and development stimulus. Similarly, recreational and cultural functions, ranging from sports arenas to arts and crafts studios, are presently underdeveloped and provide a lot of scope for centre development. Per capita public expenditure on such activities, which show a range in existing municipalities of $10 (West Vancouver) to $1 (Coquitlam), indicate that most of the area's potential regional centres have nowhere to go but up.

The action programme

While the GVRD regional studies have indicated the conditions favourable to the attainment of regional town centres, such places will not develop without a regional strategy to coax and push the identified prospects into reality. The strategy assumes the form of an 'action programme' with four major features: joint planning, the reservation of sites, land assembly, and a development management process. While these are expressed in terms that apply to the conditions and institutions of Vancouver and British Columbia, there are certain general features that can be identified. The programme is of interest as a demonstration of how municipalities and regional agencies can play a constructive role in the urban development process.

The *planning* aspects involve both a number of formal steps to establish the concept of regional town centres as official policy, and certain processes to ensure the effective implementation of that policy. Thus, under British Columbia legislation, a plan for each proposed centre would be incorporated in the appropriate municipal by-laws as an official community plan, and the entire set of centres would be incorporated in the official regional plan.

The GVRD would serve as the agency for the broad direction of a regional programme, evolved through the interplay of local, regional and provincial interests. For each regional town centre, joint planning and administration would be assumed by a development corporation. The regional planning functions would include (1) a coordinated servicing programme which identified the government agencies responsible for roads, public transportation, parking, utilities and community facilities, as well as the costs and schedules for construction; and (2) a five-year programme, updated annually, which would combine the servicing programme for each regional town centre with the region-wide programme — including costs, schedules

and revenue allocations — for urban service and utility improvements and public land acquisition.

In the period before the planning mechanisms are fully effective steps would be taken to *reserve* sites for the priority centres and linking transportation corridors. The instruments used would be a combination of official plan and zoning amendments, and public purchase of land at market value less speculative increases. The latter would require new legislation.

Total land requirements would be substantial and beyond the normal capacity of municipal budgets. Some extraordinary measures would have to be taken to ensure the required scale of public *land assembly*. One possibility is the establishment of a revolving fund, supported by the municipalities and the province. The operative principle would be to generate revenues from the initial capital outlays (through the sale or preferably lease of centre lands) and to plough gains back into the development of successive centres.

The development corporation set up for each centre would be mainly responsible for the *development management process*, including site reservation, land assembly, the staged planning of the centre, and the coordination of public and private inputs. The corporation, financed by the revolving fund, would include provincial, municipal and GVRD representation on its board of directors; it would also have an advisory community and business group. To be effective the corporation would have to be backed up by regional city policy and programmes that actively support regional decentralization of office employment. Some of the mechanisms for achieving this would include agreed targets, development control, and programmes of monitoring and information to assure that targets are met and not exceeded in the downtown area, and developers are made aware of opportunities in the regional town centres.

The concept of regional town centres is of interest in itself as a development feature, but it has greatest significance in a discussion of urban patterns as a tactic in a broad strategy to create a decentralized form of metropolitan growth. It is a solidly developed, creative response to some of the characteristic problems of metropolitan growth. Its full demonstration will be eagerly awaited and observed.

26 The Property Industry and Land-use Controls: The Vancouver Experience, 1910–45

by John C Weaver

A city's land-use patterns derive some of their form from its topography. An urban site brings with it peculiar attributes — heights of land, vistas, ravines and marshes. These can affect the timing of land development as well as the economic and social characteristics of property.[1] Although cities have unique features related to site, men, ideas, and capital have been exceedingly influential and have acted in a similar fashion from place to place. By the early twentieth century, the residential choice offered by streetcars, the infant discipline of urban planning, and the emerging real estate profession were sorting out land uses into more clearly defined spatial arrangements. Vancouver shared fully in these experiences so that, in spite of a singular location, its land-use history has familiar events and themes.[2]

In the early 1920s, Vancouver and neighbouring municipalities on British Columbia's lower mainland abounded with talk of urban planning (figure 26.1). Unlike the monumental aims of the 'city beautiful' movement which left Vancouver with a park fountain and with blueprints by English planner Thomas Mawson, the revived planning interest had a pragmatic focus keyed to basic concerns of important pressure groups. The Vancouver Planning and Beautification Association of 1914 had hoped to establish an alluring setting for the surge of tourists expected when the Panama Canal opened, but the supporters of planning in the 1920s accented health, traffic flows and, above all, the protection of property values.

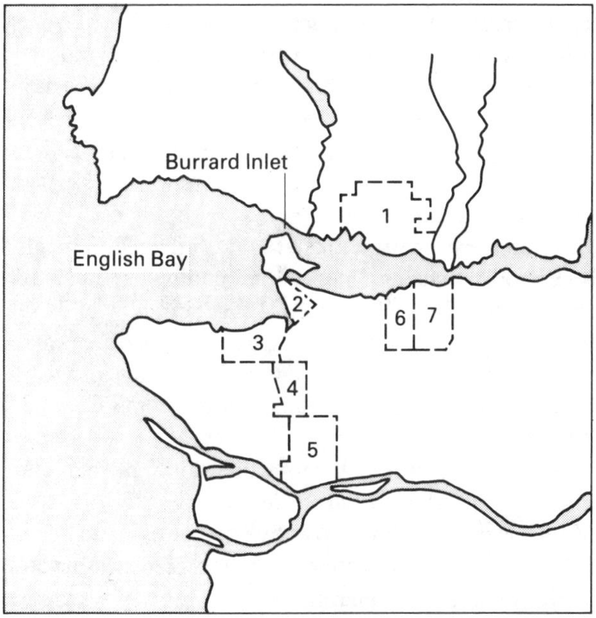

Source: John C Weaver 1979 *Plan Canada* **19**(3) Sep–Dec, pp211–25. Reproduced by permission of the Canadian Institute of Planners.

Figure 26.1 Vancouver and neighbouring municipalities. 1 North Vancouver; 2 West End; 3 Kitsilano; 4 Shaughnessy Heights; 5 Eburne; 6 Grandview; 7 Hastings Townsite.

Between 1918 and 1925, a series of businessmen's luncheons and an array of special civic committees built up a momentum that resulted in Vancouver becoming the first major Canadian city with comprehensive zoning. The present analysis of a specific theme — regulation of land use — presents Vancouver's experience as an illustration of a one-sided mingling of real estate interests and planning concepts common to other cities.

The property industry, 1900–20

The turn of the century brought a transition of Canadian urban development procedures. Land auctions passed from favour as sales were increasingly handled by a nascent real estate profession. As well, the restrictive covenant came into wider use.[3] In an active real estate market with competing land developments, it was recognized as advantageous to be able to protect lots against non-conforming encroachments that might upset potential buyers. This protective impulse of suburban developers, however, did not characterize all realtors. For example, some real estate professionals regarded health and building codes as vital aids that helped to support property values, but tenement managers chafed at what they deemed civic oppression. Preferring quick sales, promoters of many instant suburban tracts that flourished during the boom years before World War I had little interest in land use controls. However, there were some subdivision developers interested in controls. As one realtor said 'the strongest point that any real estate man had in making a sale in Shaughnessy Heights was the restriction on residential property.'

Given the concern with status, as reflected in neighbourhood character, covenants could be arranged which specifically excluded 'undesirables' and set minimum house values. As equity, covenants became solidly entrenched in Canadian property law and were only overthrown by the Canadian Supreme Court in 1951.[4]

Between the circumstances which could be regulated and those which could not, there existed a critical area of uncertainty presided over by city council and, more directly, the civic bureaucracy: building inspectors and health officials. Covenants, after all, only protected a developer's land and not the surrounding area. The decision to locate a new isolation hospital, a baseball park, or simply the issuing of a permit for a gas works, garage, Chinese laundry, or tenement could depress neighbouring land values. Random land use policy was inimical to certain types of suburban development and, until the passage of town planning acts, Vancouver and other cities used considerable discretion in applying their fire and health regulations so that they might complement private covenants. No business suffers a free market which introduces too much uncertainty, hence elements in Vancouver's property industry exerted pressure for rational land use well before the introduction of zoning. The problem with relying upon the existing jurisdiction of fire and health codes was

that unwarranted actions in their name were being defeated in the courts. In implementing covenants and seeking regulated conditions on the fringes of their property holdings, developers fulfilled the logic of the market as they sought to comply with middle class taste. In addition to market place indications of homebuyer preferences, there was a specific forum for a mutual shaping of attitudes, namely the ratepayers' association. Even in the nascent stage of these residential areas, a defensive mentality found expression through the associations. In late 1911, the Kitsilano ratepayers joined other associations from wards 3, 4, 5 and 6 in requesting that the building inspector prevent the erection of Chinese laundries 'in the midst of a quiet respectable residential neighborhood.'

The exercise in informal zoning — a process which grew out of prejudice, the concerns of realtors and ratepayer associations, and which rested on public safety codes and licensing procedures — merits description. Tenements and cabins in Chinatown became, by mutual consent of the Police Commission, Mayor and most aldermen, the locale for the seaport's houses of ill-fame. Better they stay in one area than disperse. Drugs, prostitution, poverty and Orientals clustered on the same streets. It was only natural that to the clerks, managers and professionals who flocked towards the security, status and greenery of the suburbs, the Chinatown blight was pathogenic. Its first symptom came in the guise of a Chinese laundry. Those suburban petitions, which called for the building inspector to refuse laundry permits in suburbs, ultimately prompted a by-law restricting their location on the pretext that the dirty laundry presented a health problem. The health threat only seemed to apply to the suburbs. Public safety provided a fictitious cover for another occasional segregating device, the fire zone. Fire zones had been derived from a real concern with fire protection, but they had additional implications. When a non-Asiatic business applied to Vancouver's building inspector to permit an exemption from the regulations of fire limit number 3, a favourable decision followed. After all, admitted the inspector, the fire zone was established to deter the type of buildings 'which it was contemplated that Chinamen would erect.' The restriction had kept them out; the belief that Chinatown would expand in the direction of this area was 'a prediction which was not fulfilled.' Now the standard could be adjusted. It is useful to recall, in comparison, that one element in New York's move toward land controls was pressure from the Fifth

Avenue Association to prevent expansion of the Jewish garment lofts.[5]

Support for segregated land use did not entirely stem from racial prejudice. Individuals in all classes sensed economic threats due to uncontrolled use of neighbouring property.

The list of threats to property values grew as Vancouver matured and the expectations of home-buyers became more discriminating. A boom town could tolerate random features and a certain mingling of peoples, but not an established city with middle-class aspirations for order and status. Furthermore, after World War I, new commercial and light industrial activities which were deemed objectionable, began to crop up in the suburbs; petrol filling stations being considered a pervasive threat. Still, racial prejudice which had found expression in violence and provincial legislation directed against Orientals remained a feature of Vancouver in the 1920s.[6] Apartment houses, which some apprehensive home-owners felt would cater to European immigrants, encroached on suburban Kitsilano. Since an Italian contractor had purchased land for apartment construction, owners of nearby lots were 'afraid that if these buildings are permitted, we shall have in our midst a colony of Italians or other undesirable people.' Individually and through ratepayers' associations, homeowners and developers demanded protection. In some instances, they turned to the traditional expedient of appeals to the building inspector or medical health officer, but planning was increasingly recognized as a more complete remedy. The civic pressure groups which represented property owners consequently joined more idealistic individuals in lobbying for a British Columbia town planning act and a Vancouver plan. Convinced of the practical advantages of planning, the Board of Trade's Civic Bureau passed a motion as early as January 1918, calling for a town planning act in the name of 'proper living conditions, greater industrial efficiency, and more economical methods of land use.'

From that point until passage of a town planning act in December 1925, the Board of Trade sent letters and delegations to the provincial government.

The property industry's relatively new and positive interest in regulating land use to enhance and protect property values actually overturned earlier apprehension. In 1912, at the peak of a real estate boom, a journalist who prepared a series of articles on the need for planning suburban development practically lost his position 'owing to the ire he aroused among the real estate men who were very extensive advertisers.' A shift from hostility to endorsement was a certain clue— something was afoot. Real estate interests, seeing the advantage of capturing planning, not only advocated planning but were careful to place members on the key committees and commissions.

The planners, 1920–30

Real estate interests and the local architects and engineers in the Town Planning Institute were not the sole participants in Vancouver's adoption of land-use controls. Planners of international renown arrived with different approaches to shaping cities. In the 1920s the young planning profession included men with assorted training and ideological commitments. Two distinct trends — personified by Thomas Adams and Harland Bartholomew — found their way into Vancouver. Adams, a product of the British town planning and garden city movements, had campaigned across Canada for provincial town planning acts during his tenure as the town planning adviser to the Canadian Conservation Commission. During one of several visits to Vancouver, Adams presented a speech espousing his planning principles. They were not at all in harmony with the aims of the property industry. Asserting that town planning gave 'stability to real estate values' — a welcome statement— he proceeded to recommend that the municipality retain 'half of the increased value of any property by reason of benefits accruing to such property' due to planning improvements in the neighbourhood. Adams also proposed that there should be 'power to acquire land compulsorily without cumbersome process of arbitration; and to acquire land in excess of the amount needed to widen a street . . . and to re-sell such land after the improvement is made.' Finally, he recommended that authority be granted to 'rectify or alter existing subdivisons.'

Adams zealously worked for town planning acts across Canada. He undertook this as a mission. However, when the Vancouver Town Planning Commission sought an adviser to draft a master-plan and zoning by-law, they turned to a businessman. Hired in 1926, Harland Bartholomew approached planning as a consulting professional. The dapper resident of St Louis symbolized both the urban vitality and the materialism of the 1920s. Dashing about the continent in pursuit of commissions, with an itinerary prepared one year in advance and arranging well publicized visits to urban centres, Batholomew was an aggressive man of affairs.

His crisp correspondence with Vancouver conveyed an icy professional confidence, almost a distant omniscience with a keen interest in every detail of his company's fees and expense accounts. His fieldmen collected information and drafted plans according to 'universal' land-use formulae, while Bartholomew moved on to other cities arranging future contracts. Adams had offered the paternalism of garden city-style social reform; Bartholomew brought deportment appropriate in a business culture. He appreciated better than Adams that planners needed to be politic. Commenting on Adams' early draft for a British Columbia town planning act, Bartholomew wrote that 'too much regulation . . . is usually susceptible to general criticism, I am a very strong believer in the promotion and execution of city plans through the education of the public.'

Drifting away from the reform goals of securing sanitary housing for working men and strong civic planning powers to achieve social goals, concerns of activists in the early town planning movement, Bartholomew and Associates did have a commitment to rational, even allegedly scientific, formulae of efficient land use. The firm adhered, for example, to a ratio of commercial to residential space in residential areas, maintaining that it facilitated convenient shopping.

Paradoxically, strong challenges were soon thrown at Bartholomew from those pressure groups which had endorsed 'town planning' at the end of the war and through the early 1920s. The relatively open and searching attitude of the business community and property industry had receded virtually in proportion to the return of good times. By 1926–29, when Bartholomew and Associates arrived, 'things were on the move.' In 1920, the economy and the movement of property had long been depressed; six years later commerce and population growth had rebounded. With a vital economy, there resumed conversion of property from single-family residential use into apartments; commercial and industrial sites were expanded as well. Attempts by the Vancouver Town Planning Commission and Bartholomew to inaugurate an interim zoning by-law and to fashion a definitive zoning by-law came at the very moment of major transitions. The outcry from the property industry was immediate and, at times, chaotic. In addition to the altered economic climate, another consideration helps to explain the *volte face*. Not until there had been contact with planners did the business community fully appreciate all that planning implied. The very act of seriously looking into the

future of property opened up uncertainty and stimulated public discussions that inevitably led to anxiety and bickering. At this stage, bargaining and the power of special interests were to become established as essential elements in the zoning procedures.[7]

The bargaining process, 1925–45

Controversies about zoning designations in the West End and Kitsilano districts illustrate the nature of interests which had been stirred up. The history of property development in the West End commenced in 1885 when owners of property in the townsite to the east induced the Canadian Pacific Railway (CPR) to select their community as the western terminal for the transcontinental. As part of the arrangement, the property owners granted parcels of land in the unsettled West End to the railway company which promoted the lots as a high-status residential development. The shrewd land department of the CPR after it had disposed of its West End lots, opened up huge landholdings to the south. The key promotional tactic consisted of laying out a new exclusive area — Shaughnessy Heights. By 1910, a transformation of the West End was well under way with older homes being disposed of in favour of relocation in Shaughnessy Heights. Changes in the West End slowed after the economic collapse of 1913, but they resumed in the 1920s with homes being carved up for boarding houses or torn down for apartment buildings.[8]

In the midst of the renewed shift, the Vancouver Town Planning Commission announced that apartment construction in the West End would be frozen, claiming that apartment blocks would detract from a bucolic entrance to Stanley Park. This was one of several episodes where the Commission took a hard line approach because of a commitment to aesthetic planning ideals. However, the majority of land owners favoured conversion. Some wanted out at a profit in order to resettle in a more fashionable area; a few widows wished to dispose of large family homes and felt that apartment development presented just the opportunity for realizing a sound price; a number of realtors, needless to say, already had assembled property for local and eastern investors eager to erect apartment buildings. A few petitions supported the freeze, but a cross-check using assessment rolls verified that 'a clear majority' of *bona fide* land-owners favoured no zoning controls. What is more, the politically influential had an interest in encouraging West End apartment construction. Member of Parliament H H Stevens held lots for speculation as did Sir Charles Tupper, son of a former Prime Minister of Canada.

Individual property owners, realtors and developers disputed the interim zoning designations in the West End and the Associated Property Owners supported the complaints. The APO had kept a wary eye on all features of the permanent zoning document as it evolved. Representing major business and realty concerns and overlapping in membership with the Vancouver Real Estate Exchange, the organization was a major conservative force in civic affairs, scrutinizing civic expenditures and attacking proposals to extend the municipal franchise to tenants.

Just as it once had campaigned for a town planning act, the APO supported the concept of zoning. What kept the APO interested were reassuring responses to inquiries made in other cities. From the city planning engineer of Los Angeles came confirmation in 1928 that zoning 'had a great effect in stabilizing property values.' Nonetheless, the APO did not swing behind zoning with naive enthusiasm. The time had arrived for a hard struggle to capture planning to serve realty interests and the APO was the prime force in that campaign, a fact recognized by civic authorities. Thus all drafts of the zoning by-law were sent to the APO in advance of their presentation to city council. Elected civic officials fell into line whenever the APO indicated displeasure with some portion of the drafts presented by the Town Planning Commission. The APO knew where and how to argue its case and apply pressure. Their standard tactic was to claim that a certain measure would have, in their expert opinion, an adverse reaction on property assessments and hence on tax revenue. With the APO involved, the realty campaign succeeded in the West End where areas in dispute ultimately were zoned to permit apartments. Something of a repetition of these events occurred in the mid-1960s when a controversial rezoning permitted high-rise blocks in the scenic West End.

The West End controversy of the 1920s galvanized members of the property industry. Too many had committed themselves to the land conversion process in this area to allow meddling by an earnest element in the Town Planning Commission. The situation in suburban Kitsilano presented a contrast as it demonstrated how in certain circumstances the property industry could break into factions, though it continued to be influential. A relatively new suburban area, bordered on the east by the factories, warehouses, and tenements of Fairview and on the west by the prosperous residential community of Point Grey, it had attracted tremendous speculative and construction activity. Due to its ambiguous location, the expectations of interested parties were not homogeneous. Some entrepreneurs specialized in apartment blocks; others concentrated on new homes. The character of the area had not yet been established so that neither the planners nor the pressure groups could assert clear opinions. Instead, the planning process opened itself to an avalanche of petitions from individual parties, each argument inflated with the sweet rhetoric of community welfare. An apartment contractor accented the need for decent high-density housing. One property holder who favoured apartment construction even claimed that Vancouver's warm climate would attract wealthy tourists and 'persons in poor health.' Thus, provision should be made for accommodation like 'scores of seaside cities in England.' From a major contractor of single-family dwellings came a familiar argument that apartments would shatter the serenity and community cohesion. The final zoning by-law reflected the clash of real estate interests rather than any certain principles of land use or any precise guidance from the APO.

Points of friction during the framing of a zoning by-law did not always involve residential property. Shipping and industrial interests complained that the planners had failed to provide sufficient districts for their expansion. The APO took up their cause and, in case anyone had missed the message about the short life of 'city beautiful', made this statement:

We are all in favour of a beautiful city, but this enviable position cannot, in our opinion, be attained without the wealth introduced by the development of sufficient industries in the city to maintain it. Most of the large industries that may be induced to establish themselves in Vancouver would, no doubt, do so with a view of manufacturing for export, hence the majority of these concerns would require water frontage for loading freighters.

It was not that the APO represented manufacturers, rather it calculated that aesthetics might impede waterfront development and slow the growth of tax assessments. With many of the APO members involved in property development and others holding downtown commercial property, the organization had a strong motive for keeping assessments rising. A slow-down struck at booster claims of city growth and implied a heavier tax burden for property owners. Rising assessments were central to the property industry even more than to home-owners because the latter could fight rising taxes by moving against civic expenditures on servicing speculative tracts. In this instance as in others, APO protests reached the Town Planning Commission which in turn recommended that Bartholomew and Associates 'take cognizance of the requirements of some of the larger industries' and sketch in modifications; Bartholomew complied.

In each of the above episodes the shape of zoning reflected an assortment of pressures. There was diversity, but the range of participants was actually quite limited. Beyond the obvious significance of the APO, there was the fact that tenants, small businessmen, and employees were not generally involved. Public hearings brought out 'concerned citizens' — usually carrying the protest of a group with a profound economic interest.

The scuttling of rigid controls began with the demise of Adams' recommendations and appeared in alterations to the planning map before the passing of the zoning by-law. Whatever one might think of the issues involved — strong cases can be made for both sides — the manner of resolution was indicative of an undemocratic strain in North American urban affairs. An important question embracing the public interest, the public purse, and property rights had been resolved by an appointed Commission meeting with special interest groups.[9]

From 1930 to 1933, the *Annual Reports of the Town Planning Commission* recorded protests against an easy granting of zoning alterations. Several Commission members retained a commitment to the integrity of a zoning man. The property industry responded by by-passing the Town Planning Commission, using the Zoning By-law Board of Appeal, and by going directly to city council. Under sustained political pressure and adverse publicity, the Commission's concern about too much flexibility soon withered. The *Annual Report, 1934* as if to mark recantation, printed a favourable reference to an anti-zoning pamphlet prepared by a real estate agent on behalf of the Los Angeles Chamber of Commerce and entitled *Zoned into Oblivion*. Concurrently, the Vancouver Zoning By-law Board of Appeal announced that it had begun to relax its provisions. A full explanation followed in the *Annual Report, 1935*.

The present period of economic distress is reflected in the number of applications requesting changes in the zoning classification from a residential or apartment district to a commercial district. The tendency on the part of owners to endeavour to secure immediate gain by having their property zoned as a business district is much the same as in the past four or five years. . . . The Zoning By-law Board of Appeal has been able . . . to give a considerable amount of relief during these times by the relaxations of the provisions of the Zoning By-laws, within its powers without amendments having to be made in the By-law.

The significance of the reversal was all too apparent to the Town Planning Institute's member on the Town Planning Commission. Arthur G Smith resigned early in 1934 'depressed by the idea that we were, as a Commission, not accomplishing as much as we might have done.' The new appointee, E G Baynes, had been 'a pioneer building contractor.'

It is apparent from the economic argument advanced in 1935 that pressure group activity was vital to, but not the sole basis for, a relaxation of zoning. Depression circumstances, after all, seemed to call for extraordinary measures. The exceptional situations were frequent and altered some of the features of the zoning map. From depression, Vancouver shifted into a wartime boom complete with jerry-built characteristics common to other North American cities having military personnel and war industries. Requirements for wartime housing were answered in part by a special federal government order permitting conversion of single-family homes into boarding and apartment houses. In 1944, a concerned alderman described what this meant in terms of the original concept of zoning, alleging that the Appeals Board had 'practically nullified the operation of the By-law':

The large map I have in my office is studded with hundreds of pins with heads of different colours indicating where duplex dwellings have been permitted in single-family dwelling zones. . . . Some of the pins on this map are so close together that they are almost on top of one another. . . . We do not like to see the nice districts slipping into what might be termed depressed areas; we do not like to see our home districts being exploited, mostly by newcomers, by having certain houses in them used for commercial purposes. . . . We feel definitely that the members of the Zoning By-law Board of Appeal have not stood up to their responsibilities.

Peace brought forth a new rationale for departures from zoning by-laws. 'Commercial and industrial interests were looking forward to their post-war activities' and they felt restricted by the existing by-laws.

Conclusions

Given perpetual bargaining and concessions to economic circumstances, the impact of a zoning map on a city is bound to be less than dramatic. A question raised by planning historian and early critic of zoning, John Reps, is most appropriate. Reps, writing in 1955, wondered whether the discretionary powers of Boards of Zoning Appeals constituted a 'safety valve or leak in the boiler.'[10] Reps and others, without benefit of internal correspondence which so clearly indicates a real estate connection in the formulation of land use controls, concluded from published reports that appeal boards had been 'generous with their special favours.'[11] Moreover, the original zoning map itself was hardly a document calculated to mould new spatial arrangements. Suburban covenants, the price of land, topography, and the location of industries and railways had sorted out basic land use traits which the zoning by-laws confirmed. Truly formative planning implied an active rôle for planning idealists and professionals. These individuals, however, had little to do with the ultimate application of land use controls. Adams was shunned. The APO scotched the aims of planners on the Town Planning Commission. Bartholomew, the adroit businessman closing one of nearly one hundred contracts, had mastered compromise. Thus zoning with bargaining — planning's pale imitation — was what Vancouver settled upon and it showed no capacity to affect major natural land use determinants like the ones described by the Grandview Chamber of Commerce.

The land-selling activities of the CPR, the erecting of the new university buildings, loan company policy, the construction programmes of the B.C. Electric, the B.C. Telephone Company and of the city itself in providing adequate services for the rapidly shifting population has decided for all time the section to be most favoured for residential purposes.

The process has been a cumulative one. The shift of population made the Burrard Street Bridge necessary, traffic adjustments followed, and these in turn were followed by business and private enterprise . . . in the less-favoured districts deterioration was permitted to make very considerable inroads. . . . And we say further that the Town Planning Commission has acquiesced in all this or, to regard the matter in its most favourable light, merely remained aloof.

On the other hand, zoning did reinforce the tendency toward single-family dwelling neighbourhoods.[12] All together, Vancouver's experience with land use controls, at least up to the end of World War II, supported a view of urban affairs which maintained that socio-economic forces — exogenous pressures as well as internal power relationships — overpowered the goals of reformers or experts who aspired to shape the city. A disillusioned supporter of town planning who wrote despairingly to the Vancouver Town Planning Commission about 'the impossibility of ideal town planning under the capitalist regime' had raised a fundamental issue. Could substantial urban planning, assuming that

it was desirable, have been applied in a community which respected property rights and had influential pressure groups dedicated to their defence?

Indeed, the historical perspective does introduce an unsettling evaluation as to where professional planners and idealists have fitted into civic affairs. Even before Reps noted problems, political scientist Robert Walker warned of difficulties that confronted planners, but he remained an optimist trusting the political system. 'With time,' he wrote, 'we can expect to see planners providing more effective leadership in making planning an effective function of government.'[13] To make planning work, the politician 'must be sold in the first instance.'[14] This line of reasoning and the belief that planners could effect changes by entering the administrative apparatus and honing political skills take as their premise the belief that urban affairs are rooted in an open political process, that able marshalling of information and access to the politicians are intrinsic to success at city hall. The historical record should introduce doubts. In Vancouver, and surely elsewhere in advanced capitalist societies, businessmen have defined the instruments of land use control and directed their outcome. Whatever the divergent intellectual or legal traditions in American and Canadian urban planning, the economic imperatives in both countries have presented similar and overruling considerations.

In light of this, a conclusion that extends beyond an historical sketch is in order. If planners deem certain objectives as desirable, then one recommendation is to consider how planning aims affect the property industry and how economic inducements built into a scheme might buy support from the property industry. This piecemeal approach that 'sups with the devil' is likely to become bogged down in pressure group negotiations where the resources and influence of the property industry are particularly effective. That is one lesson of the Vancouver experience. Another approach is activist urban planning, meaning the promotion of social goals and disclosure about the key features of the property industry. Whatever the emphasis, both tactical and activist planning require knowledge about financial institutions, the many elements of the real estate profession, and the use by both of law and government. In some small way, the Vancouver civic records may assist urbanists in arriving at generalizations about the private and public institutions that frame land-use decisions.

Notes

[1] Peter Goheen 1970 *Victorian Toronto, 1850 to 1900*, The University of Chicago Department of Geography *Research Paper No. 127*, (Chicago: Department of Geography, University of Chicago); Kathleen Neils Conzen 1975 Patterns of residence in early Milwaukee, in *The New Urban History: Quantitative Explorations by American Historians* ed Leo F Schnore (Princeton University Press); Peter O Muller 1977 The evolution of American suburbs: a geographical interpretation, in *Urbanism Past and Present*.

[2] Walter G Hardwick 1974 *Vancouver* (Don Mills: Collier-Macmillan) pp 27–30; W G Hardwick and J Lewis Robinson 1973 *British Columbia: One Hundred Years of Geographical Change* (Vancouver: Talonwoods) pp23–8; 52–5.

[3] Very little has been written about land development and covenants in urban Canada. See John C Weaver, From land assembly to social maturity: The suburban life-cycle of Westdale, 1911–1951, *Histoire Sociale*. Also see Michael Doucet 1977 Building the Victorian city: the process of land development in Hamilton, Ontario, 1784–1881 (unpublished dissertation, University of Toronto). For a legal history of covenants of various types in the United States see Normal Williams Jr 1955 Planning laws and democratic living *Law and Contemporary Problems* 20 pp336–8.

[4] John C Weaver From land assembly to social maturity, pp29–30; *Canada Law Reports: The Supreme and Exchequer Courts of Canada*, Part 1 (Ottawa: King's Printer) pp64–80.

[5] S J Makielski Jr 1966 *The Politics of Zoning: The New York Experience:* (New York: Columbia University Press) pp11–13.

[6] For a brief account, see Stephen M Beckow 1974 *Keeping British Columbia White* in *Canada's Visual History Series I* (Ottawa: National Museum of Man). The legal question of excluding Orientals from trade and commerce by denying licences is thoroughly discussed in Patricia E Roy 1975 Protecting their pocketbooks and preserving their race: white merchants and oriental competition, in *Cities in the West* ed A R McCormack and Ian Macpherson (Ottawa: National Museum of Man). Unlike licences, however, covenants were based in the laws of equity and were not on the same weak legal footing as exclusion by denial of civic licences.

[7] Discussions of this bargaining feature in other cities are to be found in the following studies: Richard Babcock 1966 *The Zoning Game* (Madison: University of Wisconsin Press); S J Makielski Jr 1966 *The Politics of Zoning: The New York Experience* (New York: Columbia University Press); Bernard H Siegan 1972 *Land Use Without Zoning* (Toronto: Heath).

[8] I am indebted to Norbert MacDonald of the University of British Columbia for the details of the scheming. Professor MacDonald is completing a study of the CPR and early Vancouver. Also see Daniel Wood 1976 The West End, in *The Vancouver Book* ed Chuck Davis, Marilyn Sacks, and Daniel Wood (Vancouver: Douglas).

[9] Concerning the general comment about decision-making in urban affairs see Samuel P Hays 1964 The politics of reform in municipal government in the Progressive era, *Pacific Northwest Quarterly*, vol. LV. The Canadian experience is outlined in John C Weaver 1975 Elitism and the corporate ideal: businessmen and boosters in Canadian civic reform, 1890–1920, *Cities in the West* (Ottawa: National Museum of Man). The corporate and non-partisan nature of Vancouver civic politics is briefly discussed in Hardwick, *Vancouver, op. cit.*, pp30–1. For the membership of Planning Commissions across the United States, see Charles M Haar 1955 The master-plan: an impermanent constitution, *Law and Contemporary Problems*, vol. xx pp336–8.

[10] John Reps 1955 Discretionary power of the Board of Zoning Appeals *Law and Contemporary Problems* vol. xx, p281. This was one of the Reps' earliest criticisms. Also see Reps' Requiem for zoning, *Planning 1964* (Chicago: American Society of Planning Officials).

[11] For the quotation see Reps, Discretionary power, *op.cit.* p297. A similar attack and call for revision appeared in William Weismantel 1969 Administrative discretion in zoning 1969 *Harvard Law Review*.

[12] Hardwick *Vancouver op. cit.*, p27; Deryck Holdsworth 1977 House and home in Vancouver: images of west coast urbanism, 1886–1929, in *The Canadian City* eds A Stelter and Alan F J Artibise (Toronto: McClelland and Stewart) p205. A defence of residential protection by zoning appears in Zoning: what's the good of it? *ASPO Newsletter*, vol. xxx, July–August 1964.

[13] Robert A Walker 1950 The implementation of planning measures *Journal of the American Institute of Planners* vol. xvi p125.

[14] *Ibid* p123.

A Regional Plan in Practice: The Example of Cracow

by D Jachniak-Ganguly

This paper analyses the operation and methodology of regional plans and their importance as a tool of land management. Regional plans are long-term economic and spatial plans, general and strategic in character. They set out the long-range aims of regional development and the spatial profile of the region's economy to which all other kinds of plan must be subordinated.

Since the 1961 Spatial Planning Act, regional plans have served a number of functions as a policy framework, i.e. to help state authorities prepare the national perspective plan; to help regional authorities control and administer centrally governed elements of the regional economy as well as those subordinated to the people's councils; and to help local authorities set their own objectives for administrative and economic activities in their own areas within the framework of the plan.

The Cracow region has been chosen as an example because of its interest from the viewpoint of regional spatial planning. It has areas of outstanding natural beauty, structural differences in the economy, diverse spatial composition, a high rate of economic growth and has shown rapid changes in land-use patterns. The administrative authorities in the Cracow region were responsible for about 30% of production, 30% of expenditure on investments and 65% of fixed material assets. The central administration, which was subordinated not to the regional authorities but to the ministries and nationwide institutions, supervised the rest. The regional authorities, however, could exert influence on the administrative class by way of the 'standard coordination' carried out:

(i) economic plans: the economic objectives are

implemented through successive five-year plans,

(ii) location decisions: arrived at on the basis of regional plans,

(iii) local plans: more detailed analyses for the location of particular projects.

Implementation of the regional plan

Based on the estimated potential growth of regional income, the plan defined detailed objectives set out in terms of the balance of regional economic trends, and the efficient location of production and national services. On the basis of various studies, particularly those of raw materials, demographic phenomena and future investment policy of the region, the plans defined optimal development criteria for the various sectors that constituted the regional economy and which influenced the volume of income.

Significant structural changes in the economy were planned in the course of regional development over the period 1960–80, as illustrated in terms of employment in table 27.1.

Investments were to be directed to specific areas, and these changes had direct spatial implications. The con-

Table 27.1. Planned structural changes in employment 1960–80 (percentages).

Employment sector	1960	1980
Agriculture and forestry	51.3	26.4
Mining, manufacturing industries and handicrafts	21.9	30.3
Construction industry	6.7	9.6
Transport and communication	4.1	6.4
Trade	4.3	7.9
Other services and industries	11.7	19.4
Total employment	100.0	100.0

Source: D Jachniak-Ganguly 1978 Administration and spatial planning as tools of land management in Poland, *CES Occasional Papers No. 4* (Centre for Environmental Studies).

ditions of development differed and have therefore resulted in differentiated yet interlinked zones of various key industries at various stages of development. The Cracow region was divided into the city of Cracow and three other zones on the basis of availability of mineral and agricultural raw materials, types of soil, manpower and recreational facilities.

Zone A (industrial) — predominantly for industrial production as there existed the conditions for its development. Industrial investment projects were designed to use raw materials and manpower available in the region as a whole.

Zone B (agricultural)— predominantly for agricultural production on fertile soil, its production matched to the needs of the population of the whole region.

Zone C (recreational)— comprising mountainous areas unsuitable for industry or agriculture, but suitable for the development of recreational facilities. The supply of these services in this zone exceeded the needs of the region, but policies were developed in cooperation with the central authorities to develop these facilities for the country as a whole.

Based on the division of the region into functional zones, and in accordance with the objectives of regional planning, the authorities in their successive five-year economic plans tried to secure for their regions the largest number of investments to be made by the central authorities. Before allocating such investments the Central Planning Commission had to be satisfied that the programme proposed was based on the regional plan. They also issued decisions on the location of investments under their own control. The location and description of investments were not precisely given in the five-year plans, but details were added and their effectiveness evaluated more precisely during the technical documentation. In the Cracow region, with its comparatively favourable resource base in terms of heavy industry (necessary for the development of other branches of industry), advantageous conditions existed for investment in chemical and metallurgical industries, the generation of electric power, and machine tools.

A very important incentive which the Cracow regional authorities were able to offer in their 1966–70 plan for the location of industrial investment, was a comparatively large increase in manpower, revealed by demographic studies. In accordance with the plan, the development of industry was one of the main objectives of socio-economic development, and in Cracow this was to be based on the production of raw steel at the

Lenin foundry and on the aluminium works in Skawina. One reason for setting up a complex in Cracow was the accumulated scientific and research potential, as well as highly skilled personnel in the city. An industrial complex producing consumer goods was also to be set up to serve in a complementary capacity.

Investment in the local food-processing, construction and manufacturing industries was provided by the regional authorities to meet local needs under local control taking into account increased consumption of goods as specified in the regional plan, and to meet the needs of key industries for ancillary products to complement the main production. Agricultural investments were principally provided by regional authorities and private farmers. Regional funds were mainly directed to infrastructural objectives such as irrigation, electrification and the provision of agricultural technical equipment. Recreational investment projects were planned in areas of natural beauty, attractive to the population of the whole country, with the finance for the bigger projects coming from central government.

The choice of locations was sometimes controversial due to the tendency on the part of a number of the investing enterprises to stick to traditional industrial areas, where concentration was already excessive, and to the bigger towns, or to areas where projects came into conflict either with recreational facilities (water and air pollution) or with agricultural policy (water supplies and resources of manpower). Infrastructural investments scheduled in these five-year plans were concerned mainly with transport and electricity, and were located where it was felt that basic investment would result in the growth of regional income. The regional plan laid the foundations for infrastructural improvement designed to encourage secondary investment. In this particular case it provided a new railway line across suitable areas for industry; large investment for the modernization of roads in areas promising the most effective expansion of agricultural production; and new roads along the highest mountain chain, the Tatras, to enable institutions from other regions of Poland to build recreation centres.

The regional plan, which indicated the proportion of the regional income to be allocated to meeting the needs of the growing population, stimulated migration between regions, and thus became instrumental in raising average personal incomes. In the Cracow region, for instance, there was overpopulation in rural areas, and consecutive plans encouraged the employment of these people in bordering areas of Silesia where there was a labour shortage. Regional planning was of even greater significance in equalizing standards of personal incomes. For instance, during the preparation of the Cracow regional plan, studies revealed differences in personal incomes. The findings suggested to the authorities the need to create more jobs and thus absorb excess manpower e.g. projects for industry, intensification of farming, concentration of service facilities of national significance, etc. However, the possibilities of increasing jobs in any given area were limited, since the plan favoured the migration of excess labour to territories with shortages.

Special attention was also given to the careful planning of service facilities to maintain a balance within the economic development of the region, and to meet the needs of the population. Studies showed that in industrialized regions there was a tendency towards the development of industry in advance of service facilities, which sometimes led to a decline in services, such as housing and social services in industrial towns. These imbalances occurred over longer periods than those covered by the five-year plans. In determining the relative growth of service facilities required in towns over the next 20 years, the aim was to reduce the imbalances within the horizons of the five-year plans. In the Cracow region, for instance, sub-regional community projects (water and sewage systems, roads) were started in the Olkusz area in 1961–65 because considerable investment in the zinc industry, which required a number of new residential quarters, had been planned for 1966–70. Planned investments were brought forward to coordinate the rate of investment in housing, trade and other social projects with industrial development.

Economic development, and particularly the industrialization of a region, is often accompanied by a deterioration of the environment. Preservation of the ecology constituted one of the chief objectives of the regional plan, but this was sometimes in conflict with other economic and social objectives, and the regional plan was also the vehicle for the resolution of these conflicts. As the policy instrument for the balanced development of the region it was able to encourage the preservation of favourable environmental conditions in the region. Location approvals for the construction of tar and benzole processing plants, coal oxidation plants and coke plants within the municipality of Cracow or its vicinity were withheld. Due to noxious waste produced by these plants, approval for sites near to Cracow

would have led to a further deterioration in the natural environment of the city. For similar reasons, a site within Cracow was refused for leather reworking and tanning plants (the restitution of a number of small tanneries was refused but, due to the need to provide employment for the existing qualified labour force, an alternative location was found some way away from the city). The proposal to locate a large sand and gravel mining plant within the city caused great controversy, but in view of the great demand its site was approved on condition that after the excavation was finished the whole area would be reclaimed for recreational purposes. In certain cases alternative locations were proposed either because other uses of particular plots of land were foreseen, or because of the necessity to go ahead with the project. In applications for new sites, particularly for industry, developers were often reluctant to invest in expensive equipment to reduce harmful effects of industrial waste. Sites were often chosen for their direct economic significance to the developers, regardless of their detrimental effects on the environment. Therefore, regional plans were a necessary instrument for the authorities to further their policy of preserving the ecological balance. For instance, because of the prevailing westerly winds, an isolation zone 20 km west of Cracow had been introduced in the regional plan to protect the city against air pollution. In the following five-year plan and in other projects, several attempts were made to get permission to construct factories, work coal mines, etc, in this isolation zone, but the regional authorities were able to reject those that would have an adverse effect on the environment of Cracow.

The plan was an instrument in the spatial coordination of investment projects for development. For example, the plan reserved land in the western zone of the industrial area on which, exclusively, plants for the exploitation of the local coal and zinc deposits could be sited, as other industries would hamper the exploitation of these raw materials. Naturally, industries connected with the use of these materials tend to initiate the concentration process and to attract industries that do not directly utilize them.

Regional strategic planning also serves to reconcile potentially conflicting planning objectives. If state policy resulted in specific regional problems these could be tackled at a local level and more relevant regional policies formulated. An example of such a conflict was that posed by the location of constructional facilities. These are investments strictly connected with towns and, as such, must be located in their close vicinity. But since the state's policy foresaw only minimal alternative use of agricultural land or other reserves of potential investment areas there were many cases of the dispersal of constructional facilities away from Cracow, either to the suburbs or to the other towns of the voivodship. A similar problem was posed by the location of warehouse facilities for industry, trade, transportation bases, etc.

Thus one of the elements in the development of a region's productive capacity is spatial harmony. The regional plan included projects which delineated zones of differentiated utilization and of networks which constituted a synthesis of economic and non-economic factors. In effect, the plan attempted to provide a rational balance of land uses, a sensible division of territory into zones, correct spatial schemes for office buildings, services and recreational facilities, as well as the best transportation system linking them.

The plan designated areas for new residential settlements and recreation facilities, in such a way that they would be least exposed to the harmful effects of industrial activity, and at the same time be within convenient commuting distance. The links between the three zones of Cracow were to be provided by an existing railway network and by a partly existing and partly projected network of roads.

It may be said therefore that the regional plan for the Cracow region was a complex long-term plan for the coordinated and balanced development of the region in time and space. Its general aims were the growth in regional income, the encouragement of suitable industrial investment, the provision of adequate infrastructure, and protection of the environment. It also included detailed objectives to be achieved in the short and medium term rather than in the long term. Communal social investment control and labour mobility are examples of these.

Analysis of the more important locations in Cracow and its surroundings, 1961–75

Policy-makers took into account regional objectives in deciding on general location decisions for the proposed industrial plants, such as steel production (rolling and cutting plants) and construction and machine industries in the Cracow area (e.g. Myslenice, Sulkowice, Bochnia, Wadowice and Kety). Branches of metal, machine and the electro-technical industries were located in the old Cracow region, especially its southern part with its large reserves of labour and industrial land.

A number of permits had been given for the location of food-processing plants (based on local produce), and chemical plants (based on local minerals — rock salt and rock minerals), although in the latter case a limiting factor was the protection of the environment and of agricultural lands. The concentration of industry in various centres foreseen in the regional and local plans, according to their nature and functions, was used as the guiding principle in location decisions. New industrial sites were approved in the municipality of Cracow bearing in mind the need for decentralization, and preferential treatment was given to the development of modern industries which utilized accumulated scientific and research potential.

It would therefore seem that the location policy of the state in the period in question followed the basic directions of the economy and land utilization set out in regional and local plans. It should be noted, however, that in spite of the plans, transformation of the functional and spatial structure of individual settlement units in the voivodship was not achieved. This was the result of, among others, a lack of adequate coordination between spatial utilization plans of the study area and development programmes of branches which are divisions of the national economy with limited powers of investment.

Section VII
State Intervention

Introduction

An understanding of the role of the state is central to any analysis of modern society. The extent of state intervention not only varies between different countries but even the ways that state intervention is interpreted are different in different societies. The significance of this can be seen in the three cases we have chosen. Thus, in Britain we are able to ask what state intervention is intended to achieve, and to examine the tension between state spending intended to encourage profitable production and state spending whose main purpose is the subsidization of consumption or the provision of services. In Poland, on the other hand, such a question would be almost meaningless. It would have to be turned on its head and raised in a different form: it is not a question of explaining why the state intervenes but rather of asking why in certain areas of economic and social activity it attempts to copy market mechanisms. Finally, in the Canadian context, the question must be posed rather differently again, since it is necessary to explain why state intervention into the operation of the market is relatively limited and why there is a greater concern to operate a system of market-based incentives.

The classic image of state intervention is the British one, since the concept seems to imply both a relatively strong state and reasonably strong private sector. Thus the idea of state intervention usually goes along with the idea of the mixed economy — something which is neither wholly capitalist, nor wholly socialist. The state is assumed in some way to be above society and above the economy, able to intervene to correct mistakes and, if necessary, to take over functions not adequately provided by the private sector.

This approach to state intervention is directly challenged in the paper by Cochrane and Dicker below which argues first that traditional local authority intervention, for example through planning policies, has been of marginal relevance to the inner cities and secondly that current inner-city policies and programmes are unlikely to succeed. Its discussion of the early stages of the inner city policy in the mid-1970s indicates some of the problems associated with the naive view of state intervention outlined above. In particular the extract makes two points — first that the resources being allocated to revitalizing Britain's inner cities are completely inadequate for the task in hand, and secondly that the bulk of state investment is still directed towards activities which are likely to continue the process of industrial movement out of the inner areas. At the same time as the inner-city programmes were launched the state was also attempting to encourage industry to modernize and raise productivity with the help of grants and other financial assistance. Despite changes of policy at government level there can be little doubt that the balance remains the same and insofar as firms do attempt to rationalize and re-equip it is unlikely that they will choose to do so in the cramped surroundings of the inner cities.

A discussion of government policies towards the inner city and the context within which they have developed serves to highlight the dilemmas of state intervention in a capitalist or mixed economy. It raises the issue of whether the main purpose of such intervention is to encourage the rationalization of industry in such a way that productivity levels can be increased and profit rates improved, or whether it is primarily oriented towards the provision of services for the working population. Where there is some conflict between the two possible aims of state intervention it is necessary to ask which will tend to dominate.

On the basis of the experience of Saltley in Birmingham, the answer is relatively clear although in other cases the balance could be different. The state has encouraged the process of economic rationalization and economic decline and this seems unlikely to change, particularly in the BL plants. Inner-city policy itself not only takes a rather secondary role but, on the basis of this paper, would appear to have little more than an ideological function — in other words, it helps to provide some legitimacy to the political system without offering fundamental change or basic improvement. Certainly some houses have been improved and some new employment has been created, but the process of house improvement (of urban renewal) has been cheaper for the council than old-style redevelopment and has helped to provide accommodation for a large pool of low-paid and, increasingly, unemployed labour, while the employment created has been negligible compared to that lost in major state-assisted closures. To put it crudely, it could be argued that Britain's inner-city policies are intended to stop the natives getting restless, to plug up some gaps temporarily and to make the run-down more acceptable.

The situation in Poland raises quite different questions. In principle the economy is state-run and managed and the internal market (except in agriculture) is residual. The state makes the basic economic decisions so that it is hardly appropriate to examine state intervention as such since there is no strong private market (at least in the urban areas) into which the state can intervene. Nevertheless, it is possible and important to raise two related points about state activity and the market in Poland. First, it is useful to assess the extent to which market forces still exist in Poland and the extent to which the state itself attempts to manage and use market and market-type methods. Secondly, given that extensive state intervention is generally held to encourage greater equality, it is appropriate to ask how the provision of services by the state actually operates in practice. The two papers below help to answer these questions.

The paper by Ball and Harloe shows the ways in which state housing policy has increasingly moved away from the provision of heavily subsidized state housing to the growth of cooperatives and state lending. The limited stock of state housing goes either to the very poor or to key skilled and administrative workers, and the bulk of the population live in cooperatives. A surprisingly high proportion of dwellings are also owner-occupied and, although to some extent this reflects old ownership patterns, over 10% of new housing in Cracow is being built for owner-occupation. The introduction of cooperatives and rationing by price within them, however, is certainly the most significant element in Poland's housing policy and is likely to encourage an increased degree of social segregation. It may also (following the Western model of a property-owning democracy) be expected to encourage some additional commitment to the system, or at any rate to a stable society, since it implies that accommodation is in some sense owned by the occupier.

The form of housing provision then can, in one way or another, although probably not as clearly as in the West, be expected to encourage division rather than equality. The extract from Fiszman's article reinforces the argument that the pattern of state spending in Poland should not necessarily be expected to bring greater equality and social justice. Whilst the educational system provides greater opportunities than in the past, its privileges are unequally distributed, so that rural areas in particular (but also small towns in some parts of the country) remain poorly served. This means, of course, that the families of small farmers are unlikely to escape successfully from their background, despite the claims of the government. Education may actually act as a barrier to advancement — as a hurdle which some can clear more easily than others — rather than a gateway to success. According to Fiszman it is increasingly becoming a means of protecting the new élite, and the grandiose promises of universal education are not being met. The early class-based quotas for admission to higher education are increasingly being ignored as education becomes a passport to well paid employment.

Despite these arguments, however, it should be remembered that there have been major programmes of state spending on urban projects in Poland. The high-rise 'suburbs' of most Polish cities, the development of several new towns (including Nowa Huta) and the provision of the associated urban infrastructure should be enough to indicate that. Without Poland's particular state socialist structure it is difficult to believe that these developments, which have changed the face of major cities such as Cracow, would have taken place. Following the line of argument developed in discussing the Birmingham paper, however, it is important to note that social spending (for example, on housing or education) has generally taken second place to state spending on industrial investment. The argument has been that if production and productivity can be increased then ultimately living standards too can be improved. To a large extent economic planners in the East have taken Western models and aimed to emulate them on the basis of large-scale investment. This has meant that limited resources have been available for social spending. This means in turn that, despite major differences in approach, priorities in state spending have often been similar in the two systems.

This is partly the result of deliberate policy decisions, such as a commitment to accept many of the practices adopted in the Soviet Union; to some extent it stems from the need to support a rather bloated bureaucratic apparatus; and most significantly it stems from the problems of trying to develop within the constraints of a world market. Poland depends on the world market for many of its commodities — in particular for advanced machinery — and it has gone into massive debt with Western (capitalist) banks in order to pay for its industrialization with foreign plant and machinery. A significant number of Poland's new industries rely on license deals with companies such as Fiat, which have supplied (at a price) the necessary engineering and technical knowledge to build a car factory whose products are already beginning to clog up Poland's inadequate urban road system. Since Poland has one of the highest levels of international debt of any country in the world its own state planning depends often on decisions of Western banks and Western companies.

Poland's basic economic problems provide an important justification for some of the policies outlined above. Thus the shift away from state subsidies in housing is explicitly seen as a means of encouraging consumers to pay more for services so that a greater proportion of state funds can be invested in industry and the inability of the Polish state to provide the education system to which it aspires reflects similar financial constraints. In a sense, therefore, spending programmes in Poland are paradoxically not only a reflection of independently determined state polices, but also of the intervention of market forces at national level.

In turning finally to the experience of low-income housing in Canada, it is perhaps first noticeable that there seem to be shared assumptions at some very basic level about state intervention in Britain and Poland which do not exist in Canada. In both Britain and Poland (despite changes of government in the former) the state still tends to be identified as providing solutions to a wide range of social and economic ills. In a sense state intervention is unproblematic. If a problem has been identified the state is expected to intervene to do something about it. In Canada matters are approached rather differently.

The fourth paper comes from a report prepared for the Canadian government-sponsored Central Mortgage and Housing Corporation but which was finally published independently because the Corporation seemed reluctant to circulate it more widely. In it Dennis and Fish discuss the problems of providing adequate housing for low-income groups and critically assess the state's attempts to assist in the process. In particular, they note the state's unwillingness to intervene in areas of private provision, despite the well documented failings of the housing market, and the reluctance of state agencies to undertake any coherent plan for housing. Public housing is provided only for the poorest members of society and any suggestions that housing policy might be tied into a wider system of economic and social planning is, of course, excluded.

Nevertheless, it would be a mistake to imagine that the state of federal, provincial and municipal levels is not in practice heavily involved in providing grants, subsidies and services in the housing field. Dennis and Fish make it clear that there is a wide range of spending programmes, even if the dominant view appears to be that only minimal state intervention is acceptable or necessary. In Vancouver the main area of political debate was not about the need for subsidies or particular spending programmes, but about the extent to which the regulation of private economic activity and private development might be expected either to make the city a more pleasant place in which to live or, on the other hand, reduce its attractiveness to employers and thus reduce employment opportunities and prosperity. But this debate and the apparently dominant view should not allow us to miss some of the realities of state intervention. State spending is significant and is often essential if major urban development or redevelopment schemes are to get under way. Simply because the state's role is often hidden in partnership and cooperative ventures does not make it any less significant. But it does perhaps make clearer the extent to which the state actually assists and takes an explicitly secondary position to actors in the private economy, making it possible for developers to operate profitably. Whilst the Canadian state is often central to development schemes (for example, to redevelop the docks in Vancouver), it generally operates as part of a partnership with private concerns or (as in the case of the False Creek development discussed by Ley in paper 23) operates as a sort of safety net for private concerns by guaranteeing certain developments.

One common theme can be drawn out of all these extracts, namely that the state does not simply intervene in the urban system from some altruistic point of view. In none of the three countries is there a neutral body called the state floating in the ethereal mists of objectivity above society, watching for problems and intervening to correct them. Almost always the actions of the state and its various component parts can best be understood in terms of the particular needs and stresses of the economic and social system within which they operate. Indeed, the state's officials are always getting their hands dirty and taking sides in the conflicts which carry on down below, and in each country the sides they take tend to reflect the economic priorities identified by the owners and managers of industry and commerce. This in turn can have dramatic effects on urban living since, as we have seen, it may encourage inner-city economic decline, or result in increased housing costs and less housing construction, or reduce access to other collective facilities such as education. But this emphasizes another aspect of the activities of the state and its agencies, namely the extent to which intervention helps to legitimate the operations of the system which it serves, even to those who have little power within it. In Poland the legitimation process is the least effective, since the failure of the apparently all powerful state to live up to its promises can and has had dramatic and destabilizing effects, exemplified in the strikes and political upheavals of 1980–81. But even there the state is forced to attempt to carry out a delicate balancing act, between economic priorities, external pressures (for example, from the Soviet Union), and political concessions, particularly in the form of consumer goods (such as cars and housing) or services (such as education). The balance in Britain and Canada is less delicate and choices are not so stark, but they are being made all the time.

Allan Cochrane

28 Renewing the Inner City? Government Priorities in Practice in Birmingham

by A Cochrane and R Dicker

Local authorities have sometimes been blamed for the employment problems of the inner city. In particular, the whole structure of town planning and redevelopment has been criticized for making life difficult for small firms, and for removing them entirely in cases of large-scale redevelopment. It has recently become fashionable to argue that less care should be taken in identifying 'non-conforming' uses in areas zoned as residential. It is feared that such concerns may otherwise simply close down and move away.

This may even happen to some extent, but most of the relevant studies have indicated that the difficulty of getting planning approval is not a major cause of closure, even for small firms. Indeed, in Saltley, the lack of a strict application of zoning and the avoidance of any harsh discipline on certain small and unsightly employers has caused a great deal of unpleasantness for local residents without significantly increasing employment levels. At least one among the undisciplined sprawl of car dismantlers along Bordesley Green Road has even been allowed to occupy land without holding a lease to it, yet the planning department acknowledges that the operations being carried out may be hazardous to others.

The small employers in Saltley are not harassed by the planning department but even if they were, that would provide no explanation for the rundown since the war. The small firms in the area are not closing down on any scale — if anything there are more employers of less than 20 today than there were in the past.

The old sites are being taken over by firms, not always small in themselves, but employing small numbers.

The scrap yards are one example of this, but so too are the trading estates, the cement works in Adderley Road South, and tenants of Saltley Mill and others. The closure of one British Leyland or one Metro–Cammell factory accounts for lost jobs at a level greater than the total employed in the area by firms employing less than 50 workers each. Even the rundown at British Rail locally would need the opening of over 20 such firms to compensate and if all the jobs lost by major employers were taken into account, hundreds of new small businesses would have to be opened.

It is common for many politicians to bemoan the decline of small firms, and to lay a great part of the blame for inner-city unemployment on this; perhaps they feel that they can do something at that level. Meanwhile, minor changes by large firms have earth-shattering effects locally, and that is the main problem.

Many of the same arguments apply to the problems allegedly created by redevelopment policies. Since there has hardly been any redevelopment in Saltley, however, it has obviously not been responsible for the loss of jobs. That the area still has enormous problems shows, therefore, that redevelopment is probably not as important a factor as is sometimes argued, even elsewhere.

In general, it should be clear that the actions of the local authority are not the most important when it comes to causing the problems of industrial decay. They may, however, be able to do something to stop it or limit it. In general, the powers of local councils are permissive rather than initiatory. They can make facilities available, but they cannot ensure that they are

Source: Birmingham Community Development Project 1977 *Final Report No. 2* Workers on the Scrap-heap (Social Evaluation Unit, University of Oxford) pp42–52.

used. They have even less power than the exponents of regional policy, which comes out very clearly in the field of industrial policy, with one or two exceptions.

The most common operation for councils in the economic field is the use of advertising and promotion of their own areas, accompanied by lists of sites, factories and available land. Both the city of Birmingham, through the estates officer, and the West Midlands county council, through its industrial information service, have promotional agencies, which regularly advertise to attract industry.

The city of Birmingham uses the slogan *The City at the Centre*, while the county council calls the area *Businessland UK*. Both agencies provide a central pool of information on the availability of land and premises, in cooperation with surveyors, estate agents and other bodies, as well as other expert advice on IDCs (industrial development certificates), planning regulations and so on. Any enquiries are in the end passed on to the relevant estate agent.

At a more dynamic level, both councils have offered industrial land and the county council has been involved in the reclamation of industrial land. In December 1974 the then leader of the council pledged support for British Leyland in the local evening paper, and said that the council was prepared to supply industrial land if that was what the combine wanted. He also added that the city's educational establishments could provide training facilities if there was a shortage of properly trained workers.

In some cases, the city council has offered and supplied industrial premises as well as land for building on. The redevelopment of the jewellery quarter resulted in the building of two flatted factories in the 1950s, and some industrial conversions were completed in the 1960s. Property awaiting demolition has also been let on short-term leases.

No one would disagree with all this in so far as it actually provides more jobs or saves old ones, but it cannot do so on any great scale. It assumes that there is a demand for industrial space in the cities, and that the main problem is that the buyers or potential buyers do not know it is there. That may be true in marginal cases, but if it is true for Birmingham, then it is also true for Newcastle, Manchester, Liverpool and Glasgow.

If all the various cities advertise then the amount coming to Birmingham will not alter significantly, and the amount coming to the inner areas will alter still less. The prime sites will be sought out, not the less popular ones. Indeed, once the advertising gets under way, it is difficult to see who will benefit overall, except the advertising trade and the new breed of industrial development officer which is arriving. Soon all the major urban areas will be running fast to stay still, or to drift slowly downwards, and the new industrial centres will continue to grow, in so far as there is any growth at all.

It is also possible in some very special circumstances for the councils to get involved in setting up their own concerns. In Birmingham, there is a long, if chequered, tradition of municipal enterprise, stretching back to Joseph Chamberlain in the nineteenth century. Although it is difficult to imagine the present Conservative group emulating their great predecessor, as they seem to be against any expansion of municipal enterprise, the Labour group then controlling the county council did attempt to launch an abortive bill in 1975 which would have made such enterprise easier in the West Midlands. It failed to pass through the House of Commons.

There was, however, a substantial degree of agreement between both parties on the building of the National Exhibition Centre at Bickenhill, just outside Birmingham. Birmingham council was instrumental in getting this centre off the ground and although it was not the only argument involved, one of the most important was that the centre would generate employment in the region.

As Clive Wilkinson (then the leader of the district council) put it in *Brum Bugle:*

First and foremost, the NEC itself will provide an enormous number of jobs in constructional and maintenance work. There will be a host of allied jobs created in the display and exhibition fields, in transport, and in freight and packaging work.

There should also be plenty of business for hotels, restaurants and nightclubs. These should provide a host of new jobs for the people of the Birmingham conurbation. The city has been heavily dependent upon manufacturing, particularly in metal trades, so this is an important factor.

What I also hope the NEC will do is act as a magnet to attract business firms to the city. The NEC will pull thousands of international visitors to Birmingham, many of them prominent industrialists. This may lead firms to consider setting up offices and factories in the Birmingham area.

One source estimated that with this in mind, the district council put £20 million into the NEC, with the hope that the centre would become profitable in the 1980s (by 1983 in the latest estimate). Although it is too soon to decide how successful the NEC has been, and is likely to be in time, one indication of its initial impact can be seen in an estimate (in the *Financial Times* 5/7/76) that even before the centre was completed, the number of hotel beds within 20 miles of the city had been multiplied by six to about 14 000.

Again, however, although it may be unkind to dismiss the importance of the NEC for the inner cities, we should remember that it is serviced by the whole of the West Midlands, and its biggest employment impact is likely to be on the Solihull area which is closest to it, to which industry, offices and warehouses are already moving. If anything, the NEC actually reinforces the trend away from the inner city. In so far as it has a direct employment impact on the inner city of Birmingham, it is likely to be minimal, and will simply increase the number of poorly paid service jobs available.

Although there may be a need to end the city's reliance on manufacturing industry, a shift to the notoriously badly paid hotel trade is hardly much of an improvement. At a time when there is little or no investment being carried on, the NEC's ability to act as a magnet for business firms must remain open to question, particularly when many visitors will travel from London and return to it at night. Again, even if they are attracted, and all they need is such a marginal push to invest in the West Midlands, why should they choose to do so in the inner cities? At best they will simply be used, as they are now, as places for the poorly paid to live, before travelling to work for one of the NEC's offshoots.

It is significant that the NEC was developed by the council, because it shows the possibility of more direct involvement in the economy. It does not just have to sit back and hope for things to happen, but can actually get involved in making them happen. Although the NEC itself is a logical extension to the council's usual role as a provider of services, it also presents the real possibility of a different approach. Such programmes as local authorities do launch are, of course, to be welcomed if they provide any employment or reclaim any land or property. But, however much it is talked around or however many cheap plans are produced, the solutions mean large-scale public spending. No juggling with corporate management schemes, self-help schemes, planning policies and information services can hide that.

One of the dangers of the present policies and policy instruments available to councils is that in attempting to solve problems without spending much money, they will actually solve nothing but still spend too much in their own terms. The cheapest way of attempting to solve inner city or other economic problems of the conurbations is to provide promotional facilities — to advertise cities; to advertise industrial locations; and to provide an advice service.

It is well nigh impossible to achieve the aim of spreading unemployment and other industrial problems more evenly across the country by using these methods, working as they do against major rationalizing and centralizing economic factors. All they are likely to do is increase the cynicism with which local politicians and local initiatives are seen.

Central government policies and proposals

Recently, the problem of the inner cities has attracted more and more attention. In the inter-war years, as unemployment mounted, the problem of the regions was taken up by government. Today the inner cities play a similar role. As unemployment rises some areas are bound to be hit particularly hard, and because governments usually feel they can do little about the overall problem (indeed, they may even tacitly encourage increased unemployment by some of their policies) they attempt instead to spread the load of suffering more evenly. They try to alleviate the problems where they appear at their sharpest.

It is, therefore, not surprising that many of the early arguments about regional policy are being repeated again today in the context of the inner cities. The continued existence of huge regional imbalances should warn us against putting too much faith in the same old nostrums being brought in.

In June 1977 the Department of the Environment issued a White Paper entitled *Policy for the Inner Cities*, based to a large extent on the reports of the DOE-sponsored Inner Area Studies. The White Paper stated that:

The Government believe that the time has now come to give the inner areas an explicit priority in social and economic policy, even at a time of particular stringency in public resources.

A cynic might argue that a policy for the inner city has been developed now, precisely because of 'particular stringency in public resources'. It is after all, cheaper to try to improve some inner areas than to provide work for all those who are unemployed. It is cheaper to go for urban renewal than for redevelopment.

Nonetheless, the problem was a real one and the government's arguments and proposals were important. In the summary of the Liverpool Inner Area

Study final report, the problem was posed very clearly. The authors asked: 'To what extent does the decline of a particular inner city reflect social and economic changes, to be reversed only at very high cost, or is it at least in part the consequence of government action which could be more easily changed?' The White Paper answered as follows:

Some of the changes which have taken place are due to social and economic forces which could be reversed only with great difficulty or at unacceptable cost. But some of the movement of jobs and people has been facilitated by policies aimed at reducing the overcrowding of the older parts of the cities. In the post-war years this was an essential part of public policy, but in most cities it has largely been achieved. It should be possible now to change the thrust of the policies which have assisted large-scale decentralization and in course of time to stem the decline, achieve a more balanced structure of jobs and population within our cities, and create healthier local economics.

The White Paper tried to lay down guidelines to achieve this changed thrust. Although these proposals were concerned with a very wide range of policies for the inner city, because the point was forcefully and correctly made that a comprehensive approach was needed, the remainder of this paper will be concerned only with the narrowly economic ones because they are central to the White Paper.

The Department of the Environment laid great emphasis on the economic side because, 'The relief of unemployment and the provision of decent jobs with good wages would go a long way towards dealing with poverty and raising morale.'

Not all of us will be surprised at the view that poor people do not earn very much and many do not have decent jobs, but it is perhaps important that the department has recognized it, and that the problem of urban deprivation is no longer seen simply as one caused by the individual inadequacies of inner-city dwellers, to be solved by better social services and community provisions. Such ideas still sometimes creep into the text but the overwhelming emphasis is different. The poverty of the inner city, it is now generally agreed, has been imposed on its residents, not caused by them.

The suggested programmes were based heavily on working with the relevant local authorities. The overall ethos of the suggestions can be summed up in the quote: 'Local authorities with inner area problems will need to be entrepreneurial in the attraction of industry and commerce.'

Unfortunately, not only cities with inner-city problems look for mobile industry and try to retain existing firms. All of them feel the pinch of recession. Others are likely to be more successful entrepreneurs — they have something better to offer. In any case, at a time of public stringency, there is not a great deal of industry about to be entrepreneurial with. They will be fighting over scraps, and even within their own council districts and counties, there will be strong pressures from non-inner city areas for their standards also to be maintained and improved.

The involvement of the government does bring a new dimension even to the role of the councils, however. The White Paper argued that most of the necessary expenditure would have to come out of the main programmes of central and local government, with a changed emphasis towards the inner areas ('The rate support grant will remain the principal source of financial assistance to local authorities'), but it also suggested giving the local authorities more power to assist industry, and promised some greater financial aid from an increased urban programme (up from £30 million to £125 million (1977–8 prices)).

Any additional funds for the inner areas of our cities are to be welcomed, as are plans to clear and develop derelict and semi-derelict land. The incentives being offered, however, will not bring the industry flooding back, or retain the present employers. While it may be true of some inner areas that the main employers are small firms who are handicapped by out-dated premises which need relatively minor improvements, that is not the case in Saltley, where large employers have closed down, and private development has built the industrial estates, probably on a bigger scale than councils would have done even with government aid.

This has not even begun to solve the problems, and it has created some more of its own. Saltley is by no means the worst of the inner-city areas in Birmingham and no doubt has far less poverty than is to be found in Liverpool and Glasgow, but it has faced serious decline and will face still more, although many of the government's suggestions are already being carried out in practice by private enterprise. If the government began to reclaim and develop the hundreds of vacant acres of land left in the area around Saltley, owned by the Gas Board, British Rail, and even the district council, it is difficult to see who would fill it. Both government and council are reliant on bodies whose actions they cannot control and whose behaviour they can only guess at and attempt to influence.

Although in the 1977 White Paper scheme the main emphasis was put on the actions of the local authority, central government also became involved. The

Department of Industry built advance factories in inner areas and encouraged firms to go to such areas. Inner London and Inner Birmingham took precedence, after the assisted areas, for IDCs, ahead of new and expanding towns. The Location of Offices Bureau gave particular attention to the promotion of office employment in inner urban areas. Whatever forms of job creation are developed, priority will go to the inner cities.

On almost every question ranging from industrial policies to education, social services and housing, central government will try to add an inner-area component.

Much of this is to be welcomed, as long as it does not simply penalize residents of the new towns (many of which have their own problems), the peripheral council estates, and the suburbs while adding nothing to the inner city. How far an inner city component can or will be given to the various functional aspects of central government remains to be seen, but one is entitled to be sceptical. The sudden discovery of the inner city may simply indicate how easily it could be forgotten in the future. The impact of the schemes central government proposes will be small. Changes in IDC policies are unlikely to have much impact. In 1971–75 not one IDC was refused in the Washwood Heath or Small Heath employment exchange areas. Whether the Department of Industry or the council builds advance factories and industrial estates will make little difference: tenants are needed to fill them. The vision of the inner city as a forest of small factories and industrial estates cannot be maintained, if Saltley's experience is anything to go by.

As far as office development is concerned, there is no reason why new offices should be built in the inner city of Birmingham, at a time when there is already a great deal of vacant property in the city centre and elsewhere. (In May 1976 a planner's report on the city centre estimated that the surplus of office space in the central core could be 25% and in the area around it 30%, if planning consents already agreed were implemented.)

Finally, if job creation is to be helpful to the inner areas, then the jobs must be well paid, useful and long term. As long as job creation schemes depend solely on the young with a few underpaid supervisors, are mainly concerned with the equivalent of charity work, and cannot last more than 12 months, their contribution will be negligible and even counter-productive as they breed cynicism and demoralization.

At present, Saltley is particularly well provided with job creation schemes — it has had two, more than most

other comparable areas of the city. They also employ a relatively large number of workers for such schemes, but that still only amounts to less than 20 temporary employees. Not surprisingly, many people view the schemes as little more than political window-dressing for the government.

It is all very well for the government to talk of the need for a unified approach to the problems of the inner city and to talk of the mismatch between the skills of the population and the type of jobs available to residents as they did in the 1977 White Paper. But it is surely hardly surprising that poorer, less skilled people live in areas where the housing is cheaper and more easily available. While the government is saying all this its own industrial policy is helping to push the inner areas deeper into trouble. The policy encourages the building of larger, integrated plants which are bound to be away from the inner city.

Perhaps that is why the emphasis in much of the writing on inner cities is always on small firms — the large ones are already spoken for. The success of the government's industrial strategy depends on firms like BL concentrating in large modern complexes, like the new Rover plant in Solihull, built with the help of government money at the cost of about one quarter of the total money to be available each year through the new urban programme. And the new programme money is to be spread very wide, and only partly on industrial development.

The question that has to be answered is not only whether the forces affecting employment in the inner city are so great that they can only be reversed at high cost, but also whether governments (of whatever political complexion) are more concerned to assist these forces — to help modernize British industry — or to resist them and try to hold back these forces.

The first part of the question has to be answered 'Yes'. The answer to the second part is less clear. Governments seem to want to have it both ways, but the overwhelming emphasis of policy since the war, and particularly since the 1960s has been towards helping industry, nationalized and private, either to move from high-cost, outdated factories (usually in inner or older urban areas) to new plants on greenfield sites, or to modernize and increase productivity on the older sites, thus also employing fewer workers.

For all its suggested improvements *Policy for the Inner Cities* does not suggest an alternative. Indeed some of the grants suggested may unwittingly have the same effect as other state aid to industry, as increased investment reduces employment and employers in old property move to the more modern advance factories.

Conclusions

No doubt we shall be criticized for not providing any answers, and for not coming up with any proposals which the government or civil servants can implement to solve the problems of the inner city and older urban areas, but we believe that it is impossible to do so along conventional lines. Our analysis should indicate that the problem is not one of a lack of community involvement or a lack of voluntary organizations. It is not a problem which can be solved by the residents of the area pulling themselves up by the bootstraps in an orgy of self-help and community associations.

We do not believe, for example, that new town policy has resulted in the run-down of the inner city. In essence such a policy does not differ from the original development of our decaying cities, whose present inner cities were originally built to house the labour for the first greenfield sites. The main difference is that in the nineteenth and early twentieth centuries this could be done by private enterprise (by Lord Norton in Saltley) while today the state has to do the work.

Nor do we believe that local planning policy and redevelopment programmes have been a major force in industrial decay. While it may have helped to close down a few back-street factories, the derelict and vacant sites which overwhelm areas like Saltley and on which all local authorities would like industry to develop are a clear sign of how much more important other factors must be.

Our understanding of inner-city industrial decline identifies it as an essential part of present economic development, rather than as an aberration. Indeed, it could be argued that if British industry is to rebuild itself on a profitable basis then inner-city decline must accelerate.

Such an approach has, at least, the advantages of consistency, and it does not pretend that significant changes are possible on the basis of minor shifts in resources or planning policies. Recently it has become fashionable again to call for these. The Inner Area Studies have with one voice called for more resources to be devoted to the inner areas, and the Department of the Environment, with the assistance of grandiose 'Save Our Cities' conferences sponsored by the Calouste Gulbenkian Foundation and *The Sunday Times*, has made it clear that resources are to be shifted

to the inner cities, and that more attention is to be paid to them. Every policy is to have an inner-city component. In the 1980s the problems of unemployment and vandalism in the new towns, which stagnation is bound to bring and already has brought in several cases, will result in a transfer of resources back, as the switchback of government policy is ridden and reallocation is presented yet again as a great panacea.

Three basic approaches can be adopted. The first is to take up the permissive position of allowing change to happen as a result of economic development, and even to encourage it through government policies. Although it was never clearly articulated, and no one thought of the inner cities while economic policy was being made, this is a reasonable outline of what governments since the war have done (or have tried to do) in practice.

It might be accompanied by attempts to clear up the resulting mess via redevelopment policies and even policies which actively encourage industry to move. In the inner city context the argument would be that the quicker the decay takes place, the less time local residents have to suffer conditions they don't like. In Britain's case, however, all such policies have meant is continuing decline for the inner cities, and no alternative coming from the growth that we are still waiting for.

The second approach is to accept that change is happening, but to alleviate its worst effects. If challenged, this might be the approach which the government identified itself with, although this is by no means clear through all the rhetoric about revitalizing the inner cities. The fact is that economic stagnation has not only brought new town development to a halt, but has also stopped any chance of redevelopment.

It is perhaps not surprising that the discovery that there was no money left to pay for big rehousing schemes was accompanied by the discovery that the old communities in the inner cities still had some life in them and could be propped up instead of being demolished. The attempts to knock the rough edges off the process of decay have generally failed because they were seen as ways of saving money rather than as parts of a wider plan. Certainly the brave new world of urban renewal is already looking tarnished and all the sound and fury from the Association of Metropolitan Authorities and the Department of the Environment does not look likely to change that.

One of the most striking facts about the inner area problem in its rediscovered form, is that no one seems to talk of the reason for its existence, and no one seems to admit that the proposals put forward for solving it are going to make very little difference. Certainly, no one could oppose the reclamation of derelict land; the building of flatted factories or even the encouragement of small firms, but neither should anyone imagine that such policies will make much difference.

If our politicians and pundits could be honest for a moment, then the reality of the inner city would present itself differently — at best it provides an area of cheap housing in which poorly paid groups like immigrants can live, and at worst it is simply rows of boarded-up terraced houses. Of course, it is better to improve housing than to do nothing, but we should be clear that unless this is done on a large and consistent scale, it will simply create more problems as residents fail to meet the high cost necessary.

If the inner cities are not to decay, in terms of employment, housing and environment, then a thoroughgoing programme of public works is essential. No half-hearted maintenance of slums will do. Land must be reclaimed and developed for housing, industry or leisure. A planned programme of house improvement is needed — not on the piecemeal basis of small jobbers presenting enormous estimates to poorly paid residents, but on the basis of a properly organized municipal programme of direct works. Otherwise some streets will be half-finished, and others will just be left to rot.

Many local residents simply cannot afford to pay for improvements. That is what poverty and unemployment means. But this takes us far away from the ideas of patching up and making do. It is not possible to get real improvements for Saltley simply by extending job creation or urban renewal schemes. In practice it would involve an enormous battle particularly when one of the main arguments for urban renewal at the moment is that it's cheaper than redevelopment.

Finally, the third approach is for the state to intervene more actively in the economic sphere to direct industry, combining this with policies to improve the living conditions in our Victorian heritage and to improve access to work outside the city. This, too, would imply huge upheaval in policies.

One variant of this approach might be similar to that suggested by Stuart Holland in his work on regional problems. He suggested that the National Enterprise Board should take equity shares in major British companies to ensure that they direct investment to depressed areas, yet are strong enough to survive competition with the multinationals. This, of course, would require investment which went far beyond the limits already allowed for the National Enterprise Board.

Many would argue that such an approach does not go far enough, and for that reason is utopian. It leaves the government to direct the economy from a position of weakness — always in a minority — and would result in the companies with National Enterprise Board shares accepting the pressures of the market. The argument centres around how best to plan and control the economy to ensure an expansion of production and employment and to improve the situation of those who live in areas like those we have described.

A whole series of questions is raised once matters are seen in this way, ranging from the practicalities of take over, to how the industries should be run and which industries should be involved. We soon move away from local issues to issues of national economic policy — to why British industry is in the state it is, and how the overall situation can be changed.

Clearly, if this third approach is taken, it is not a question simply of presenting proposals for grants under urban aid or any other element of the urban programme. Instead, it requires a wide-ranging political debate. Indeed, whichever of the three approaches is taken, a political decision is being taken, however much it is concealed by attempts to cover it with the mantle of objective truth.

The indications are that the 'debate' about the inner city will be discussed in terms far removed from the overall economic and political background. There will be a transfer of resources, from the new towns, a grant to the building industry, the construction of a few advance factory units and trading estates, a large number of conferences and a great deal of concern. Every step will be portrayed as a solution and no thought will be given to the contradictory policies being carried out by other government departments. That is what the bright ideas of the past will amount to.

References

Holland S 1976 *The Regional Problem* (London: Macmillan)
Holland S 1976 *Capital Versus the Regions* (London: Macmillan)

29   Housing in Poland

by M Ball and M Harloe

Perhaps the most interesting questions about current Polish housing policies concern their effects on the distribution of housing opportunities and costs. It seems highly likely that the present policies will reduce or even reverse the equalizing tendencies apparent in many aspects of the first period of Polish post-war housing policy.

At the most general level, if an increasing proportion of housing is financed by individual means and the range of choice of housing and amenities available widened, income differentials will be reflected in differentials in access to housing and in the quality of housing obtained. It seems that, as a consequence, socio-economic differences will be reflected in physical differences in types of housing consumed and Polish cities may develop 'high-status' and 'low-status' areas — as in capitalist cities. We were told that some sort of social differentiation of cooperatives appears to be occurring anyway, although the difference between rural and urban origin, as well as socio-economic position, appears to be a significant factor causing segregation. There have been severe problems in some new housing areas with regard to social integration. Social integration was clearly one of the ideals of the first post-war housing policy. Some Polish sociologists have suggested that the problems can only be solved by a switch to smaller, more socially, economically, and culturally homogeneous cooperatives. The difficulty is that such an approach would clearly increase differentiation. In summary, the new policies seem likely to increase variation in the housing consumption of social groups, which were present even before these new policies emerged.[1]

The incidence of housing costs appears to be largely unrelated to income. Initially, under the policy of low-rental state housing for all, there was no attempt to make richer people pay more. However, state housing is now reserved for 'key workers' and the very poor. The maximum qualifying income for state housing is now 1000 zloty per month, which excludes most households from state housing; in September 1972 only 4.8% of those working in the socialized sector earned 1200 zloty per month or less.[2] In effect, the vast majority have to apply for cooperative housing which is far more costly — here the only subsidies available are connected with the savings schemes and with the rate of repayment of debt. Neither of these subsidies do anything which is particularly and specifically directed at giving more help to low-income families; indeed, provision which gives substantial remission of debt to those who pay off their credit fastest clearly helps those with the highest incomes most. Similar provisions aid wealthier owner-occupiers.[3]

Meanwhile, state housing will in future (apart from a small section of the very poor) cater mainly for 'key' industrial and professional workers, who are likely to be relatively highly paid in order to induce them into their 'key' occupations or professions, but who will be protected from paying anything near the true level of cost of the housing they occupy. State rents cover current maintenance only (major repairs, etc, are met by the state), whereas cooperative rents cover all costs, i.e. repayment of credit, repairs and management. The housing costs of individuals in tenant cooperatives are on average two or three times that of those in state housing. Individuals in owner-cooperatives pay two to four times the amount paid by those in state housing.

The new housing policies therefore seem not only to be increasing inequalities in access to housing and in the distribution of space and amenities, but also increasing inequalities in the pattern of housing costs which are not deliberately related to income and tend to be regressive.[4] It is interesting to note that no emphasis appears to be placed on the effect of economic policies

Source: M Ball and M Harloe 1974 Housing policy in a socialist country: the case of Poland *Centre for Environmental Studies Research Paper No. 8* pp47–51.

on the distribution of income. A change to a system which uses economic incentives inevitably increases the range of incomes. In housing, where this increasing differentiation of income has been accompanied by greater reliance on individual finance, consumption differences between income groups must be becoming increasingly apparent. Many of these effects are now being discussed in Poland although policy modifications — such as a new rent policy linking rents to incomes and aid for low-income families, young couples, the aged, and large families[5] — are not yet forthcoming; indeed the whole trend of policy seems to be to increase rather than reduce housing differentials. Some effects of the new policies as they affect one group of those in acute need in Poland, young couples, have been studied in detail. A series of papers published in 1966[6] drew attention to the heavy financial burden that the need to apply for cooperative housing put on many young couples and the benefit that the better qualified obtained. Surveys in Warsaw and Wrocław in 1963 showed that 60–70% of the young couples interviewed were only eligible for cooperative housing. While waiting and saving for this they lived in poor conditions — one-third of those in Warsaw and a quarter of those in Wrocław were found to live apart and only 4% in Warsaw and 10% in Wrocław lived in non-shared dwellings. Two years later substantial numbers still had to live apart with only a small minority living in non-shared dwellings. It is significant that those who lived in the better housing conditions also possessed better jobs and education qualifications.

Apart from the effects of current policies that we have already discussed, there is one further possibility inherent in the move to a more market-oriented housing system which emphasizes and encourages ownership. It is that investment in housing by owner-occupiers could provide the base for the accumulation of property and wealth, a development which would obviously be at variance with the growth of a socialist society.

There is an open market in the sale of private houses but a number of constraints lead to a tendency for price stability at a level approximately equal to the construction costs of new houses. Unfortunately no data are available to verify this assertion, but examination of the constraints operating at present in the private housing market tend to justify it. The housing shortage means that few transactions of individual houses take place. Most individual housing in rural areas is associated with peasant holdings[7] in which the overall selling price is more related to the productivity of the holding than to housing. In urban areas the situation is obviously more complex. The state's credit policy limits the possibility of price increases as it fixes a price for individual housing, 3000 zloty per m² in the 1971—75 plan, on which its credit lending rules are based. As there are no large individual concentrations of wealth in Poland, this credit policy has a long-run stabilizing effect on house prices. However, 40% of the new construction of urban individual housing is undertaken without the use of credit which would seem to militate against this credit policy. But much of this consists of households who construct their dwellings themselves, over a number of years. Second homes in the country are becoming increasingly fashionable and in this submarket where location becomes very important the market price can be very high. Apart from this small sector the general feeling is that the price of individual one-family housing is reasonably constant and that increments in personal wealth cannot be derived by owner-occupiers from transactions in the housing market. Whether this situation will continue in the future, as the housing shortage eases and incomes rise, must be open to doubt, however.

To summarize, present developments in Poland's housing policies seem to be leading to a degree of increase in socio-economic inequalities, to an extent which we are unable to quantify. Furthermore, the relationship is probably a dual one; inequalities in socio-economic status are reflected in housing inequalities. We have seen that some of these differences are historical, or at least predate the present policies. But it has been observed in countries where the market dominates housing provision that when housing production rises the poorer tend not to benefit as the richer families consume more, absorbing much of the increase. After the war Poland tried to prevent this by the reorganization of its housing market. It will be interesting to see the extent to which it reappears as a consequence of the (albeit limited and partial) return to a system of housing provision which has many features akin to that of a capitalist society.[8]

Notes and References

[1] In 1963 workers' families had 10.2 m² of dwelling space per head on average, whereas administrative employees' families had 13.0 m² and those of technical staff 13.2 m² per head. *The place of housing expenditure in the total consumption of the population*, A A Nevitt 1967 *The Economic Problems of Housing* (London: Macmillan) p166.

[2] *Petit annuaire statistique de la Pologne* 1973 (Warsaw: Central

Statistical Office) p264, table 8.

[3] For example, owner cooperatives get a 40% credit reduction if their loan is repaid in one year, 30% if repaid in 5 years and 20% if repaid in 10 years.

[4] A full documentation of the regressive nature of housing finance and whether and to what extent it is a part of a general regressive distribution of socio-economic opportunities, would require far more information than we have available.

[5] Suggested, for example, by Andrzejewski *et al* 1971 *The Role of Housing in View of the Changing Economic Structure of the Country* in *Housing Problems* (Warsaw) pp20–1.

[6] *Spoleczno-ekonomiczne problemy wyzu demograficznego* 1969 (Warsaw) reviewed in *Housing Problems* 1971 (Warsaw) pp181–4.

[7] Only members of the Peasant's Union may purchase agricultural land.

[8] Compare, for example, British and Polish public housing policies or American and Polish policies for the finance of owner-occupied housing. Comparison of the comments of Donnison, regarding the existence of owner-occupation in Eastern Europe in the early 1960s, with our argument about the effects of the new housing policies is interesting: 'The spread of owner-occupation may be objectionable if it leads to an unduly wasteful use of land and housing space; if it creates, or reinforces class division and the educational and social handicaps typical of socially segregated neighbourhoods, if it leads to a wasteful or unfair distribution of public funds through the provision of tax reliefs, grants, and subsidies that are concentrated on wealthier sections of the population, and if it distracts attention and resources from the needs of the old, the young and the transient for whom this form of tenure may not be appropriate. But these are not inevitable features of a housing market in which a large proportion of people own their own homes and it is difficult to conceive of any valid objection to home ownership in itself and for its own sake.' (D V Donnison 1967 *The Government of Housing* (Harmondsworth: Penguin) p148.)

30

Education and Social Mobility in People's Poland

by J R Fiszman

The official Polish literature makes frequent claims of big strides in the area of education as compared to the state of affairs which prevailed during the inter-war period. The network of kindergartens, for example, has grown from 1506 during the school year 1938–39, the last year of pre-People's Poland, to 7950 in 1966–67. The number of institutions of higher learning has increased during the same period from 32 to 76. However, the number of *lycea* of general education has increased only by 77, from 789 in 1938–39 to 866 in 1966–67, and the total number of elementary schools has actually decreased, from 28 921 in 1938–39 to 26 564 in 1966–67. The increase in kindergartens and the decline in elementary schools can be explained in terms of the still-felt repercussions of the population slaughter in World War II, boundary changes, urbanization, the increased absorption of women into the labour force, etc. Having given up the predominantly rural areas of the east and having gained, instead, the urbanized areas of the west which were under German administration before World War II, the Poles supposedly were able to cut back the number of elementary schools (especially rural) and replace them with more centrally located facilities. However, between 1938–39 and 1966–67 the elementary school population grew by 563 550 pupils (from 4 963 500 to 5 527 050) and the secondary school population by 88 506 (from 234 200 to 322 706). The largest student body increase was registered by the vocational school system: from 227 632 in 1938–39 to 1 629 180 in 1966–67, an increase of 1 401 548.

As a result of the inability of the building enterprises to meet the plan for 1966, many school construction projects were postponed for the following year. Consequently, 11 new school buildings were erected in Warsaw during 1967 — seven elementary schools, three vocational schools and one special school. Nevertheless, construction continues to lag behind the plans. The addition — as a result of the school reform — of an eighth grade to the 'complete' elementary schools placed a special burden on that educational level, taxing the existing plants and affecting the work of the teachers. As in the past, rural schools suffered the most. One provincial school official pointed out to this author in the course of an interview that as a result of the school reform and the addition of an extra grade to each school at least 31 additional classrooms were needed in his county (*powiat*) at a time when each school suffered from a classroom deficit predating even the reform. He said:

We were told the situation can be improved only through the exercise of local initiative, that we should not look to the central authorities for help because in Warsaw they have their hands full. However, our district (*województwo*) National Council did not plan for the need and did not appropriate the necessary funds. You see, Warsaw makes plans but these do not sift down to the local organs. Since 1961 the Education Department of our county (*powiat*) National Council has its own building crew since it was difficult to make any headway with the normal construction enterprises. Yet this building crew planned for 1966 only alterations, routine painting jobs, minor improvements in the existing facilities, but not the construction of new ones. And this in the Millennium Year when all the talk is about school contruction.

Q. What could be done?

A. We are trying but, frankly, it is like beating your head against the wall. We hope to arouse people in the county, to generate public discussion on the problem — then maybe someone will move.

Part, but only part, of the difficulty is that the centrally based Fund for the Construction of School Buildings and Dormitories (*Społeczny Fundusz Budowy Szkół i Internatów*) will cover only 60% of the cost of construct-

Source: J R Fiszman 1971 Education and social mobility in Peoples Poland *The Polish Review* **16** (3). Reprinted in B L Faber (ed.) 1976 *The Social Structure of Eastern Europe* (Praeger) pp93–100, 106–9. Reprinted by permission of The Polish Review.

ing new school facilities, the remaining 40% of the cost to be derived from locally generated funds — funds to be obtained through special drives such as that launched nationally for '1000 New Schools for the 1000th Anniversary' or from the income of locally based industry. It is also the responsibility of the local authorities, the local national councils, to set the educational building goals for the areas within their respective jurisdiction and to create the funds to meet a substantial portion of the operating expenses. However, the sources from which some local councils could raise the necessary funds are rather limited, and, consequently, they turn to the councils of higher administrative level, shifting the burden of responsibility upward. The problem is, of course, less acute in the economically wealthier regions such as Silesia (the political base of a former first secretary of the PUWP, Edward Gierek), but in the areas of chronic economic depression (as in the *województwo* of Białystok or in the eastern parts of Warsaw *województwo*) the matter of providing 40% of the necessary funds takes on dramatic proportions indeed. Moreover, because of the inability of the various construction and maintenance enterprises to fulfil their job contracts on schedule, local authorities find themselves unable to draw up firm financing plans at the beginning of the fiscal year, to allocate necessary funds for new projects, since they find themselves having to draw from the current budget for work undertaken in previous years but completed only presently. Even within metropolitan Warsaw, which is divided into city precincts (*dzielnice*) with corresponding *dzielnicowe* national councils, certain precincts more than others must rely on the all-city council which, in turn, finds it difficult to budget all the programmes undertaken. However, Warsaw is in the fortunate position of having the central authorities located with the city and of having well established links to the government ministries and the party leadership.

Other localities within the Warsaw area are less fortunate however. For example, the county (*powiat*) of Grodzisk Mazowiecki within the Warsaw area has 53 elementary schools of which only 7 were able to add the required eighth grade in 1966–67 to bring them up to 'complete' status. Of the 53 schools, nine are located in towns and 44 in fair-sized villages. However, most of the school buildings are in various states of disrepair: seven structures need major alterations and additions, and 40 were listed as in need of 'routine' repair work such as roofing improvements, installation and water

pipes, toilets, heating facilities, etc. For 1966–67 the county had 500 000 zlotys allocated for capital school improvement and 220 000 for 'routine' repair and maintenance work. The county authorities of Grodzisk Mazowiecki were thus more sympathetic to the needs of education than were similar authorities elsewhere. However, in meeting their plans — for which funds were allocated — they met head on with the usual obstacle: to find a building enterprise which would undertake the jobs and, once undertaken, be able to complete the work on schedule. In principle, municipal or state building enterprises should assume the responsibilities of constructing public structures (such as school buildings) and capital improvements. But these enterprises must show a degree of economic self sufficiency, and in order to keep a labour force on its books it must produce at year's end a bonus which can be shared by its employees. Consequently, the municipal and state construction enterprises would rather undertake the building of income-producing structures such as apartment houses and industrial plants which would yield a premium upon completion. Also, schools habitually have a lower priority than buildings for governmental administration and, as a result, those responsible for school construction and maintenance must turn to independent construction cooperatives or private entrepreneurs which, however, have a lower priority in securing building materials than the municipally or state-owned enterprises and also have greater difficulties in attracting skilled labour (because of the fringe benefits available to those employed in the publicly owned firms). Moreover, most of the work required by the schools involves repairs, and since the cooperatives and private contractors find these types of jobs less profitable than outright construction, they are reluctant to bid for them. There is not much profit for a private entrepreneur in a repair job for which he may receive from the county 15 000 zlotys and for which, in addition to labour, he must supply hard-to-obtain and expensive material. For the opening of school year 1966–67, the *powiat* was hoping to have two new school buildings of six rooms each, additional school office space, badly needed workshops, plus a teachers' apartment housing project to accommodate the expected influx of 40 new teachers to whom housing had been promised. However, by the end of June, 1966, none of the projected new structures, additions, or repairs were even near completion and the nervous school authorities were making plans to rent private homes and farm dwellings as temporary living quarters for teachers and for classrooms. According to the Warsaw *województwo* school curator a similar situation obtained in all *powiats* of the Warsaw area.

Less dramatic than the lack of adequate school buildings and facilities, but no less detrimental to educational goals and no less annoying to the educator who feels frustrated and abandoned to his own devices, is the matter of the scarcity or poor quality of instructional materials.

The absence of pencils, chalk, notebooks, an adequate number of textbooks, stencils, typewriters and paper, for instance, can drive a teacher to despair. During the school year 1966–67 only every third student in Polish elementary schools could boast possession of a required atlas.

On the secondary school level, although the situation appeared to be less desperate, it still was not good enough to assure every *lyceum* student his own atlas. Although new sets of textbooks were to appear for the newly established eighth grades of elementary schools, these were not produced in time nor were they issued in adequate numbers to fill the need.

In the process of obtaining an education and utilizing the educational opportunities available, the rural areas and economically poor provinces are being left behind much because a great deal of the responsibility for providing educational facilities is left to local initiative and resources, which are simply not equipped for the task either in terms of the local economy or because of the lack of an appropriate cultural and educational tradition. As a consequence, higher educational opportunities and consequently greater social and occupational opportunities, remain — as they always have been in Poland — the reserve of citizens of the large metropolitan areas or of members of those social classes and groups which have traditionally held education in high esteem. The son of a peasant, for example, must simply try harder, show greater perseverance, diligence, stubbornness, and intelligence in order to achieve in and through education the same benefits as fall to the son of city-based intelligentsia parents who tried less hard, demonstrated much less perseverance and diligence, and whose tests indicate a lower intelligence level. Thus, while educational opportunities have become more available and more widespread than they were before the establishment of People's Poland, as well as more 'democratized' inasmuch as they do not by legal devices or through political decisions consciously discriminate against certain groups of the population (as they did against ethnic and religious minorities

during the inter-war period), the educational opportunities still remain far from being equally distributed because much within the system, the manner in which it functions, and much within the particular cultural tradition and heritage is stacked against those of lower-class background and against the rural areas in general.

While the student population in the secondary schools of general education has increased twentyfold — much because of the variety of opportunities open to general education *lycea* graduates and because of the traditional élitist stamp borne by these schools — the vocational school population has increased less than eightfold: from 7000 during 1937–38 to 50 000 in 1965. The comparatively lower increase in the vocational school population occurred in the face of exhortation to the youth to become trade-oriented, to think in terms of future employment possibilities and incentives, and to try to adjust their training to the needs of the economy, in the face of industrial and technological expansion and the stress on the values of a new industrial culture, and, finally, despite the fact that by 1962–63 the authorities had put into operation in Warsaw *województwo* 107 basic vocational schools and 96 *technikums* and vocational secondary schools in order to back up the 'polytechnic push.' Thus, as in other areas, here too the plans and designs of the political system met head on with ingrained cultural and community values and norms.

Conclusions

Many of the officially sponsored systemic values find their existence in People's Poland, as elsewhere, only in the realm of oratory and on the symbolic level. Thus, there is a great deal of talk about work and efficiency, of rational planning and secularization, of socialism and the classless society, of the importance of education if stated goals and objectives are to be achieved. However, oratory constitutes one level of behaviour and practice another, often without apparent relationship between the two. Carefully drawn development plans often leave no mark in reality and the plans which are realized frequently bear no relationship to officially stated goals and sometimes result in practices which are counterproductive to the formally stated objectives. Rigid social stratification continues and is perpetuated because — despite the oratory on the importance of education as a big 'social leveller,' as the only rational vehicle for individual advancement — education remains a low-priority item in the allocation of total resources, and educational opportunities are unequally distributed among the various sectors of society thus continuing old status distinctions. For, despite its low priority in terms of resource allocation, education is indeed a mark of status, along with family background and socio-economic position as it affects one's ability to pursue the 'good life'. The educational structure itself is highly differentiated, with lines of demarcation between various levels and types of education, with obstacles erected at crucial points of the individual's educational career — and the net result is a perpetuation of many of the old divisions along traditional lines of class, status, and prestige. People's Poland is very much a class-conscious society despite declarations to the contrary and despite an official ideology which posits classlessness as an ideal. If the lines of social status and prestige do not correspond to income levels, such lack of relationship is not new to this culture whose élite was traditionally drawn from an impoverished gentry class which shared with the Marxist a common disdain for profit and money-making. Those of high income in People's Poland — the private entrepreneurs (that is, independent artisans or merchants) and private farmers — never enjoyed high social prestige. It is interesting to note here that even some segments of the bureaucracy or the military whose salaried incomes are above average lack prestige because they have been recruited — or are perceived as having been recruited — from the traditionally lower classes. Such traditional socio-cultural pulls lead the Pole to prefer a classical and humanistic education over a technical and vocational one, thus further frustrating official goals and systemic plans relative to industrialization and technological advancement.

Yet, as indicated, although education is held in high esteem and is perceived as a vehicle to higher status and prestige, low priority is given to investments in education generally. Such low priority is the product not only of conscious systemic decisions resultant from various economic and political pressures — in the face of limited resources — but, in a way, also in response to broad community demands which, ultimately, value the availability of consumer goods, housing, and the material aspects of the 'good life' above education. In fact, the very promises and hopes generated by ideology have whetted appetites for tangible betterment, especially among the lower socio-economic classes. As does the system, members of these classes find themselves facing a dilemma: while aspiring toward education they lack the tradition of paying for it; having emerged from economic deprivation, still in the midst of relative poverty (if compared to other European political systems), having emerged from a destructive war and five years of occupation, the hunger for material goods carries the quality of impatience.

Although the system stresses centralized authority and central planning, much of the responsibility for financing education falls on the local authorities whose abilities to plan and operate are limited (or enhanced) by the type of economy prevalent within the area. As a result, industrial regions are placed in an advantageous position vis à vis areas of primarily agricultural or small craft economies. But, again, although industry provides the ability to pay for education, the tendency remains to seek traditional types of education which often have little relationship to immediate industrial needs. These aspirations characterize not only the traditional élite youth but also the youth of provincial towns and villages who continue to associate social status with gentry models and achievements. The institutions of secondary and higher education, unable to accommodate all seekers of a traditional type of humanistic or classical education, are forced to favour youth of superior educational background — that is, usually youth of the traditionally upper classes and the big cities — leaving provincial and rural youth not infrequently feeling frustrated and stranded. Yet, it is precisely from among the provincial working class and peasantry that the system seeks its support, in behalf of whose interests it legitimizes its rule and whose youth it professes to favour. To be sure, efforts are periodically made to encourage sons and daughters of the working class and peasantry to continue the process of education; and certain preferences are being given to youth of these backgrounds (such as special entrance credits, preferential quotas, priority in dormitory allocation and stipends, etc). However, such administrative measures are not quite able to solve the basic problems on a truly mass scale nor do they subsequently radically alter the existing status and class differentiations.

Many, especially among leading members of the Polish academic community, not infrequently stress the importance of equalizing both the quantity and quality of post-elementary education so as to decrease the 'cultural persecution' of students from rural and small town environments.[1] Some speak hopefully of, at the minimum, an eventual universalization of secondary education. However, those who criticize existing conditions or who propose the most radical structural reforms of the educational system are not in decision-making positions, regardless of their own social status and prestige. The hitherto introduced school reforms have not really addressed themselves to the problems which produce or perpetuate existing social inequalities. Although a network of adult education facilities, for example, was established, there continues to be a lack of meaningful programme — meaningful in the sense of providing tangible career benefits, a second chance, as it were — of education for adults and 'late bloomers', many of whom are discouraged by the system from repeating an examination once taken and failed. The system of rigorous examinations at each consecutive step of the educational ladder, the difficulties encountered in entering a university or a higher professional training institution — and given the prevailing patterns of prestige and status attached to education and membership in a profession — only serve to perpetuate a system which is highly stratified and structured along lines of class and status, the official ideology notwithstanding.

Note

[1] Sentiments reflecting the need for greater support of the school system, understanding of teachers, as well as the need for greater equality in the distribution of the cultural and national resources were voiced especially vigorously during the Second Day of the Congress of Polish Culture which took place in Warsaw during October 1966. Too late to have any effect on the educational reforms which were already being instituted at the time, many of the statements made during the Congress were critical of the reform measures, especially of educational plans which avoided tackling some of the basic philosophical and organizational assumptions of the Polish educational system. Among the most active participants in the debate were professors Jan Szczepański (sociology), Jan Zygmunt Jakubowski (history) and Zdzisław Rajewski (archaeology). Professor Szczepański expressed during the debate (and in numerous conversations with this author) the belief that Polish secondary education must become universal within the next ten years or so since otherwise it will merely perpetuate existing élitist patterns. For reports on the Congress debate see *Polityka*, weekly (Warsaw) **X** (45) p505, 5 November 1966, p1, and *Życie Warszawy*, daily (Warsaw) 10 October 1966, p1.

31

Low-income Housing, the Market and the State in Canada

by M Dennis and S Fish

Housing policy in Canada has been directed solely at starts. Its aim has been to increase the total stock of 'decent, safe and sanitary accommodation' to the point where there is sufficient adequate housing for all Canadians, demolishing substandard housing and replacing it wherever necessary.

Little or no concern has been shown for the distribution of either the newly produced or existing stock; the price of that stock and the ability of consumers (low-income consumers in particular) to afford it; the environmental quality of new housing produced; the condition of the existing stock, except for 'slum housing' which would have to be destroyed and replaced; the right to free and dignified use by the consumer of his home.

Instead reliance has been placed on the market to allocate the stock, set the price, determine the level of quality, and the protection of the position of the low-income tenant has been left to the provinces. The only minor shift which has occurred has been the expansion of the public and low-rental housing programme, and a lesser attempt at assisted home ownership. Within these programmes the emphasis has been very much on quantity rather than quality; units produced constituted only a minute portion of the total housing stock (some 2%) and came nowhere near meeting the need. The vast majority of low-income households have been left to the vagaries of the market.

The public–private dichotomy

A dichotomy has developed since the end of World War II, despite recommendations to the contrary. For example, in 1935 a report warned:[1]

Source: M Dennis and S Fish 1972 *Programs in Search of a Policy: Low-income Housing in Canada* (Toronto: Hakkert) pp 1–26.

The formation, institution and pursuit of a policy of adequate housing should be accepted as a social responsibility . . . There is no apparent prospect of the low rental housing need being met through unaided private enterprise building for profit . . .

In 1964, the theme recurred:[2]

A constant claim of the proponents of 'pure' private enterprise that it could solve the housing problem should be considered against the evidence of an historic ineffectiveness . . . Private enterprise seems to be at its most dynamic level when protected by extensive loan guarantees and substantial borrower's equity and when properties are all sited in a bustling urban market.

In 1971 it was again pointed out:[3]

The recognition of access to housing as a universal right implies a direct intervention by the State throughout that industry which, even today, depends almost entirely on free enterprise. Just as universal rights to education and welfare meant that the State had to assume responsibility in those sectors in place of free enterprise, then equally the recognition of access to housing as a universal right implies a similar direct intervention in the field of housing services.

Politicians and senior civil servants have consistently taken an opposite tack. In 1949 the Prime Minister stated:[4]

While we hope that as much of our new housing as possible can be provided through private and local enterprise, we recognize that privately initiated housing may have to be supplemented and stimulated by even further government support for low rental housing.

The Minister responsible for housing put the matter even more strongly in 1956:[5]

It was the government's view, which I have stated publicly on a number of occasions, that we would be justified in using public funds for housing only where private enterprise fails to meet the need.

A clear statement of federal policy on the matter was that of the then Minister, in May 1969:[6]

We must, therefore, not only improve the operation of private markets in order to accelerate the total output of housing, but we must also stimulate the provision of modest accommodation for low-income people, augmenting it, if necessary, with what may be regarded as non-market devices in order to get a higher yield of new units out of the nation's housing efforts.

The refusal to act stemmed from an almost religious belief in the private market as the only fair and efficient mechanism for distributing society's resources. Even the social housing programmes, which received much publicity, were an afterthought, an appendage to the unguided, uncontrolled market system. No effort was made to plan for them, to determine the type, extent, location and magnitude of need; that would have necessitated greater efforts, increased intervention, more interference with the private production process.

The only 'planning' for housing has been done by financial officials, who have used housing as a short-term stabilization tool. That overriding concern has been entrenched in housing policy. Nowhere was it clearer than in the constant reference to housing starts. Housing starts are an indicator of economic activity. Housing completions are the additions to the housing stock available to serve consumers, but they are seldom referred to. Emphasis on aggregate goals, economic activity and private market decisions also explain the sacrifice of quality for quantity. Housing is an artifact, a product, a manufactured good. It is not viewed as a package of services, nor as a place where people live. Once the start has commenced, concern ends. Subsequent management and maintenance are irrelevant. Locational factors such as neighbourhood context, community services and facilities, and even interrelationships between units produced are ignored. Design is a secondary consideration, as are the rights of the user with respect to the good produced and its producer.

With the growth in social housing activity there are faint signs of change, but inroads against the dominant production mentality are slow.

The housing problem

For some years, federal policy makers have been concerned with whether there is a housing crisis or a housing problem or no problem at all. The most recent verdict is that there is no immediate housing problem, that there is an income problem for low-income families likely to be displaced by redevelopment and unable to find satisfactory alternative accommodation and that policies restricting the development of raw land for housing may lead to a housing crisis in the future.[7] That position should be compared with the one taken by the Murray study in 1964.[8]

Aside from its physical qualities, a sizeable segment of Canadian housing is economically troubled . . . The new housing production, whether for ownership or for rental, is completely out of reach of something better than one-third and something less than one-half of the population. The existing housing stock is almost equally inaccessible because of the combined effects of high prices and inadequate financing terms.

The situation has not improved. In 1967 approximately 400 000 low-income households spent on average in excess of 40% of their incomes on shelter alone. When household operation, telephone, furnishings and equipment are added, the percentage is more than 50. 800 000 low-income households spent on average in excess of 25% of income on shelter alone, and 1 200 000 spent on average in excess of 20% of their incomes on shelter.

Somewhere between half a million and one million buildings (with the available data no better guess can be made) probably require rehabilitation simply to bring them up to the standard of decent, safe and sanitary accommodation. They either lack heating, plumbing and electrical systems or have faulty ones or are in need of structural repairs. Perhaps a third to a half of these units are in rural areas and small towns where the annual cost of shelter may not be a problem, but incomes are too low to permit the necessary investment to upgrade the housing.

About a million low-income households are tenants and that number is likely to increase by more than 50% over the next decade. These tenants are not only plagued by high shelter-to-income ratios and poor physical conditions, but also do not have the security of tenure and the freedom to use their homes in a reasonable fashion that low-income owners possess. Most of them are on month to month leases and are subject to arbitrary control by their landlords. Although there have been improvements in provincial landlord and tenant legislation, landlords' attitudes have not changed and a precarious economic position and sense of powerlessness prevent the poor from asserting the rights which they do have.

The majority of low-income households are located in city centres or in rural areas where community services and facilities are lacking. In cities, they are frequently located in industrial or commercial areas where noise and air pollution are high. Newer government low-income programmes have located them on the fringes of developing areas which are devoid of community facilities.

Equal access to decent housing

That is the rough picture, in absolute numbers. The relative position is even worse. If one compares the shelter-to-income ratio for the bottom 20% of the income distribution with that of the average family, the bottom group spend twice as great a proportion of their income for shelter. When the comparison is made with the top quintile, the bottom group spend $2\frac{1}{2}$ times as much. If one looks at renting households only, the situation is even worse, with the bottom 20% spending three times the proportion which the top group spends.

Similarly, the poor are much more likely to live in older housing which is in need of structural repairs or lacks essential plumbing or heating facilities. In 1961, those in the bottom quintile were three times as likely as the average household to be living in a unit in need of major repair and eight times as likely as the top quintile. They were almost twice as likely as the average, and almost four times as likely as the top quintile to lack adequate heating systems.

Housing and poverty

Housing poverty is partly a function of low incomes. It is also a result (as are the low incomes themselves) of having the status of a poor person. Societal attitudes ensure that the rewards go to the producers, to those who make the economy grow. Those who cannot or can no longer produce (the elderly, handicapped, single-parent families, rural families) get the residue after the producers have been rewarded.

To a considerable extent this results from the shared attitudes of public decision-makers and producers. Equally important is the unequal access of the poor to the decision-making process. Public agencies — particularly housing agencies — provide limited information about policies and practices, except to producers who are actively sought out for participation and voluntarily supplied with information.

Middle and upper income consumers are only beginning to organize themselves to participate in housing decisions. Better education, superior financial and technical resources, available time, and social-psychological characteristics are far more likely to result in quickly organized, independent initiative activity by them. The poor are not accustomed to exercising control over their own lives and are far more likely to feel a sense of powerlessness in the face of public decisions.

The production of adequate housing

Housing built during the 1960s tended towards higher densities, a limited range of standardized accommodation, reduced variety, limited common facilities and a segregation of unit types. That built in the early 1970s was largely the same kind of housing as that produced at the beginning of the period. New low-income housing resembled that built for any other sector of the population made cheap by tight costs, reduction in size, and poor sites.

In all housing, the form of the dwelling units is determined by the economics of building, rather than by user needs. The user is fitted into what can be built. Federal policy has promoted the construction of low-density suburban homes, neglecting the development of alternate forms of higher-density urban housing. Little attempt is made by the builders and no attempt by the central mortgage and housing corporation (CMHC)[9] to determine user response to the existing models. CMHC's residential standards have had limited effect on housing form. Their function has been to regulate and prevent blatant defects, rather than promote improvement and innovation. The review procedures are essentially policing actions.

The building industry will not substantially improve its product or innovate without government intervention. Building firms are becoming larger and more bureaucratic. Their primary concern is the development and marketing of land. The profits made on the construction side are minimal, land profits are high. The developer attempts to contain costs by standardizing the product and producing housing which simply meets the administrative requirements of the lenders and the rigid planning requirements of municipalities, and thereby allows him to make his land profits as quickly and on as large a scale as possible.

The real capacity to innovate is found in the subcontractors who do the actual construction. The majority of large builders now subcontract out more than three-quarters of the work done; subcontractors are becoming increasingly more productive, but are not growing in size. Contractual arrangements leave them completely dependent on the builder-developer and prevent the harnessing of their innovative capacities.

State programmes

The present method of dealing with low-income housing problems consists of three programmes: a public housing programme, with deep operating subsidies, run on a shared cost basis; an entrepreneurial and non-profit low-rental housing programme, with preferred lending rates and virtually break even, controlled rentals; and a variety of assisted home ownership programmes, provincial and federal.

Public housing

This is the only programme serving the lowest income group. The federal government provides subsidies through CMHC to provinces and municipalities prepared to develop public housing. We recommend the abandonment of the programme, at least in its present form, for the following reasons.

1   New housing produced solely for the poor carries an inevitable stigma, given existing social values. This is seen in the attitudes of tenants, surrounding neighbours, programme administrators and politicians.

2   The programme involves very deep subsidies. 1970 subsidy levels were approximately $1000 per unit and by the end of the decade, if they grew at *half* the present rate, would be $2500 per unit.

3   Cost considerations limit the number of units produced. At present production levels there would be 250 000 units available by the end of the decade. There are presently about 1.2 million low-income households paying in excess of 20% of their incomes for shelter. By the end of the decade, the number will be closer to 2 million. If production were increased by 250% to 50 000 units per year, only one-quarter of the need would be met with subsidies of approximately $1.25 billion per year.

4   Cost factors also limit decisions on location and design. Public housing sites are frequently marginal and corners are often cut on construction to hold down costs. The result is the production of less than satisfactory living environments which will be with us for a considerable period of time.

5   Decisions regarding need are taken by public intermediaries, not by the housing consumer. The intervention of public middlemen means that the most serious need is frequently excluded. For example:

The bulk of the units have gone to the Province of Ontario, which is best able to afford the cost-shared subsidies.

Only 14% of units have gone into urban centres from 1000 to 30 000 in size, which have one-third of the urban population.

Virtually none have gone into rural areas.

Some municipalities refuse to accept public housing or request only token amounts.

Most provinces have limits, explicit or implicit, on the number of welfare families which can be admitted to any project. Other examples of 'creaming' (i.e. selecting more desirable, less problematic families) can be found.

6   Despite federal initiatives aimed at improving public housing management, there has been little progress in this field over the last several years. The societal and administrative attitudes noted above impede the development of skilled, sensitive management.

Entrepreneurial full recovery housing

Under schemes of this sort loans are made available at preferred lending rates to private builders to build housing for low-income families at below market rental. In 1964, dissatisfied with the results of the programme, CMHC in effect shut it down. In 1968 the programme was restored, but the same problems have returned to haunt it. They include:

1   poor, marginal locations;

2   inadequate site planning and facilities;

3   a propensity for one- and two-bedroom, high-rise units in what is nominally a family housing programme;

4   under-utilization of approximately one-third of all units, and 'creaming' out of undesirable tenants;

5   increased income limits. In its early years, the programme was competitive with public housing. Today the programme starts where public housing leaves off. The result is a substantial gap in the groups which can be served by the two programmes.

6   heavy-handed management over which the federal government exercises no control;

7   funding at a level which does not begin to meet the need;

8   a big-city bias, similar to that found in the public housing programme. Only 9% of all units have gone into centres of less than 25 000 people.

Non-profit housing

The non-profit housing programme has funded, for the most part, municipalities and service clubs providing housing for senior citizens. The expectation of the federal government was that the provincial governments would make capital cost contributions and the municipalities might provide land more cheaply and/or tax abatements. Without that further assistance the programme cannot serve the really low-income elderly. As the federal government makes no contribution towards subsidies for non-profit housing, the provinces are now moving towards use of cost-shared public housing for elderly persons. Non-profit operators of senior citizens' housing are subject to criticism from the elderly for charging more for the units than public housing does. Similar problems of location, design, etc, exist in this programme, but are easier to solve in some cases, because municipalities, churches, etc, supply better sites, and because high-rise, high-density projects can be employed. Little research has been done on the suitability of very high-density projects for the elderly.

In the last several years, attempts have been made by non-profit groups to use the programme to provide housing for families and unattached individuals (both single and middle-aged). The response of the federal government have been hesitant and uncertain.

Assisted home ownership
The federal government steadfastly avoided involvement in programmes to assist low-income households to own homes until the late 1960s, although its lending programmes have long shown a bias towards ownership for the upper half of the income band.

Federal opposition to assisted home ownership has rested on considerations of cost, protection of the activities of private lenders and an unwillingness to subsidize the acquisition of assets by low-income consumers (as distinct from high-income producers).

A number of provinces initiated programmes aimed at the lower middle and middle-income groups. The latter, confronted with rapid price inflation, found themselves unable to afford new housing. In most provinces, provincial efforts were a response to the resultant pressures.

To its credit, the federal government, in its $200 million programme, aimed at a lower-income group, in effect the top half of those eligible for public housing. The results parallel those in the entrepreneurial full recovery rental programme:

1 Reduced costs resulted from substantially reduced quality. In a number of cases corners were cut, units were finished poorly, space standards were reduced drastically, project amenities were minimal.

2 Locations were poor, on the fringes of cities.

3 Purchasers were small, young, upwardly mobile families who probably could have afforded to buy in a couple of years at any rate.

4 Income levels were frequently revised upwards, as builders claimed to be unable to produce or find purchasers at lower levels.

5 Almost all units were produced in major centres, because of the emphasis on the need for a large volume of starts in a short period of time.

Cooperative housing
The Curtis Committee Report in 1944 pointed to the European experience and clearly anticipated a substantial cooperative housing effort. During the 1950s the federal housing agency supported the activities of building cooperatives, self-help groups which built single-family dwellings for individual ownership. No support was given to continuing cooperatives, non-profit groups which wanted to build multiple projects to be owned collectively and rented to individuals. They were denied preferred lending rates under the full recovery section of the Act on the basis that they were really developing a form of home ownership. There was concern that loans to them would open the door to claims for preferred lending rates by individual home owners.

Legislative provisions requiring that the corporation be satisfied that at least 80% of the units in the project will be occupied by members of the cooperative have been interpreted to mean that no advances can be made on loan commitments until 50% of the members have been signed up as shareholders and accepted as borrowers. Difficulty in meeting this requirement virtually precluded the development of cooperative housing.

Opposition to cooperative housing within the corporation has arisen because of basic philosophical differences. This is best seen in the statement of one of the corporation's policy advisers.[10]

Home is a very private thing and anything to do with one's own private affairs is best kept independent and separate from the friendly contact with neighbours . . . I can't think of anything more likely to jeopardize this kind of stability of family life than becoming involved in a venture of cooperative housing.

That attitude continues to prevail despite the recent development, supported by CMHC, of condominium housing, which mixes home ownership with an interdependent, high-density lifestyle.

The corporation has funded a national Cooperative Housing Foundation and then left it to the cooperatives to stand or fall on the rules of the marketplace. It refused to change its general policies adopted in the late 1950s.

Cooperative housing associations have developed at the provincial level, with assistance from the provinces, and at the project level with help from labour unions, cooperative financial institutions and churches. With changes in programme requirements and real governmental support, the prospects for production at a meaningful level are quite good.

Rehabilitation

The federal government's initial policy prescription for deteriorated housing was clearance and replacement. Under pressure from the households to be cleared and displaced, this changed to an emphasis on partial clearance, together with rehabilitation and conservation of existing dwellings. Very little rehabilitation was carried out under urban renewal schemes before that programme was shut down. For improvement in urban housing, reliance was placed on guaranteed home improvement loans by banks. These served the middle income group and have fallen off drastically in the last decade.

CMHC lacks the legislative tools to tackle the rehabilitation problem. It was not until 1969 that it was empowered to lend directly for home improvements under the NHA (National Housing Act). No loans have been made specifically for home improvements (as distinct from improvements made when an existing unit is acquired) under the 1969 changes.

Even under that legislation it cannot lend at interest rates below its own borrowing rate nor make grants to low-income households. Experience has shown that these households cannot afford to and will not incur further debt to upgrade their housing.

While the corporation put forward specific proposals in 1965 and 1968 to deal with the housing problems of rural families no action has been taken on them. The only rural rehabilitation today results from grants under the Canada Assistance Plan and the FRED programme in Prince Edward Island. Yet one-third of the units needing rehabilitation are in rural areas.

Conclusions

Canada has had social housing programmes on its statute books for over 30 years but it is only since the mid-1960s that they have had life breathed into them. Until then, complete reliance was placed on an assisted free market to produce enough adequate new housing that there would ultimately be sufficient decent dwelling units for all Canadians. When it finally became apparent that decent housing simply would not filter down to those at the bottom quickly enough (if ever), social housing programmes received greater funding.

Faith in aggregate goals and private production and operation of housing remained paramount. Social housing only amounted to some 15–20% of total annual construction and to an annual increment in the total stock of 0.7% in 1969–72. Government intervention was carefully segregated from overall market operations. The philosophy of minimal intervention at the tail end of that market has assured the failure of new production programmes and has caused the defects discussed previously.

New and radical solutions need not be developed to deal with low-income housing. Very few new proposals are put forward in this study. The necessary changes have been recommended time and time again over the last three decades. For example, in 1944, the Curtis Committee recommended that the government plan for the necessary volume of production for the next five years, to be distributed evenly over each third of the income distribution, that public non-profit or cooperative housing production be relied upon to meet the needs of the bottom third, and that steps be taken to improve housing conditions in rural areas and city centres.

Cooperative housing

The Curtis Committee Report in 1944 pointed to the European experience and clearly anticipated a substantial cooperative housing effort. During the 1950s the federal housing agency supported the activities of building cooperatives, self-help groups which built single-family dwellings for individual ownership. No support was given to continuing cooperatives, non-profit groups which wanted to build multiple projects to be owned collectively and rented to individuals. They were denied preferred lending rates under the full recovery section of the Act on the basis that they were really developing a form of home ownership. There was concern that loans to them would open the door to claims for preferred lending rates by individual home owners.

Legislative provisions requiring that the corporation be satisfied that at least 80% of the units in the project will be occupied by members of the cooperative have been interpreted to mean that no advances can be made on loan commitments until 50% of the members have been signed up as shareholders and accepted as borrowers. Difficulty in meeting this requirement virtually precluded the development of cooperative housing.

Opposition to cooperative housing within the corporation has arisen because of basic philosophical differences. This is best seen in the statement of one of the corporation's policy advisers.[10]

Home is a very private thing and anything to do with one's own private affairs is best kept independent and separate from the friendly contact with neighbours . . . I can't think of anything more likely to jeopardize this kind of stability of family life than becoming involved in a venture of cooperative housing.

That attitude continues to prevail despite the recent development, supported by CMHC, of condominium housing, which mixes home ownership with an interdependent, high-density lifestyle.

The corporation has funded a national Cooperative Housing Foundation and then left it to the cooperatives to stand or fall on the rules of the marketplace. It refused to change its general policies adopted in the late 1950s.

Cooperative housing associations have developed at the provincial level, with assistance from the provinces, and at the project level with help from labour unions, cooperative financial institutions and churches. With changes in programme requirements and real governmental support, the prospects for production at a meaningful level are quite good.

Rehabilitation

The federal government's initial policy prescription for deteriorated housing was clearance and replacement. Under pressure from the households to be cleared and displaced, this changed to an emphasis on partial clearance, together with rehabilitation and conservation of existing dwellings. Very little rehabilitation was carried out under urban renewal schemes before that programme was shut down. For improvement in urban housing, reliance was placed on guaranteed home improvement loans by banks. These served the middle income group and have fallen off drastically in the last decade.

CMHC lacks the legislative tools to tackle the rehabilitation problem. It was not until 1969 that it was empowered to lend directly for home improvements under the NHA. No loans have been made specifically for home improvements (as distinct from improvements made when an existing unit is acquired) under the 1969 changes.

Even under that legislation it cannot lend at interest rates below its own borrowing rate nor make grants to low-income households. Experience has shown that these households cannot afford to and will not incur further debt to upgrade their housing.

While the corporation put forward specific proposals in 1965 and 1968 to deal with the housing problems of rural families no action has been taken on them. The only rural rehabilitation today results from grants under the Canada Assistance Plan and the FRED programme in Prince Edward Island. Yet one-third of the units needing rehabilitation are in rural areas.

Conclusions

Canada has had social housing programmes on its statute books for over 30 years but it is only since the mid-1960s that they have had life breathed into them. Until then, complete reliance was placed on an assisted free market to produce enough adequate new housing that there would ultimately be sufficient decent dwelling units for all Canadians. When it finally became apparent that decent housing simply would not filter down to those at the bottom quickly enough (if ever), social housing programmes received greater funding.

Faith in aggregate goals and private production and operation of housing remained paramount. Social housing only amounted to some 15–20% of total annual construction and to an annual increment in the total stock of 0.7% in 1969–72. Government intervention was carefully segregated from overall market operations. The philosophy of minimal intervention at the tail end of that market has assured the failure of new production programmes and has caused the defects discussed previously.

New and radical solutions need not be developed to deal with low-income housing. Very few new proposals are put forward in this study. The necessary changes have been recommended time and time again over the last three decades. For example, in 1944, the Curtis Committee recommended that the government plan for the necessary volume of production for the next five years, to be distributed evenly over each third of the income distribution, that public non-profit or cooperative housing production be relied upon to meet the needs of the bottom third, and that steps be taken to improve housing conditions in rural areas and city centres.

In 1964 the Murray report recommended the production over the next 20 years of 2 million units of either public housing or full recovery housing for the bottom 40% of the income band, the promotion of cooperative and non-profit housing, the development of a federal housing department which could take the lead in comprehensive planning for housing.

In 1965 the advisory group of CMHC made a number of progressive recommendations. These included: assisting home ownership through long-term low-interest loans in rural areas; abandonment of the entrepreneurial limited dividend housing programme; 100% loans coupled with capital grants for housing to be provided by non-profit corporations; assumption by the federal government of an increased share of public housing subsidies; grants in aid for the establishment and organization of non-profit housing agencies; grants for rehabilitation in rural areas, economically depressed regions and fringe urban areas; the grouping, in one division of the corporation, of responsibility for all low-income housing programmes, public and private.

In 1969 the Hellyer Task Force recommended: that all urban residential land be developed and marketed by municipalities and that federal loans be made for that purpose; that social housing programmes only for the poor be terminated; that subsidies be paid to people, rather than attached to buildings; and that cooperative and non-profit housing programmes be expanded.

Real progress has not been retarded by an absence of ideas or understanding but by an unwillingness to act, to come to grips with the problem and to attack it systematically and comprehensively. Governments must be prepared to establish the goal of decent housing for all Canadians at a price which they can afford and make whatever changes are necessary in the mechanisms for producing, maintaining and distributing housing to see that that goal is met.

The simple fact that the majority of the poor will live in existing older housing must be accepted. Then the problems which that situation presents for them must be analysed and attacked. Separate policies must be developed to cover their difficulties in respect of income, housing price, housing quality and community services and facilities. They must be developed within the context of a plan to deal with national housing requirements and the cost, quality and distribution of all housing, both new units produced and the existing stock.

In closing, we note that the source of Canada's weak, low-income housing policy over the last two decades has been the lack of political leadership. At both the federal and provincial levels, autonomous crown corporations were created and left to their own devices. No attempts have been made to define national or provincial housing goals. Worse yet, repeated pressure by CMHC for an expanded social housing programme, over a ten-year period from 1956 to 1966 was resisted by the federal cabinet and its senior policy advisers. During that period the corporation advocated an increase in the volume of low-income housing produced, increasing the share of subsidies borne by the federal government, the establishment of a substantial non-profit housing sector, devolution of authority to provinces and municipalities and a number of other recommendations.

Faced with continuous opposition, it appears to have abandoned its initiative position. This has occurred at a time when there has been a substantial increase in low-income housing produced. Faced with both quantitative and qualitative changes in the nature of the problems confronting them, neither the federal nor provincial governments have put themselves in a position to do strong, strategic, anticipatory planning.

To reach such a position the fiction must be rejected that housing decisions centre on what are essentially technical, banking issues. The issues of who gets what, where, when and how are political. We recommend that at both the federal and provincial levels social housing should be a departmental responsibility. (That recommendation was made by the Glassco Commission in 1963, the Ontario Association of Housing Authorities in 1964, and by the Hellyer Task Force in 1969.) Greater political involvement than a periodic check into the affairs of a crown corporation is required.

References and Notes

[1] *Report of the Special Parliamentary Committee on Housing* 1935 (Ottawa).

[2] *Good Housing for Canadians* 1964 A Study by the Ontario Association of Housing Authorities (Toronto) p50.

[3] *Rapport de la Commission d'Enquête sur la Santé et le Bien-Etre Social* 1971 (Gouvernement du Quebec) Vol. 1, pp184–5.

[4] *Speech*, Prime Minister Louis St Laurent, April 1949.

[5] *Letter* from Minister to President, CMHC, 8 June 1956.

[6] *Notes for Statement on Bill C-192* R.K. Andras, House of Commons, May 1969.

[7] *Urban Problems and Prospects* 1971 Res. Monograph 2, Housing in Canada, (Ottawa: CMHC) p19.

[8] *Good Housing for Canadians*, op. cit. p58.

[9] CMHC was set up as an autonomous crown corporation by the federal government in 1946. Its first main task was to provide rental housing for returning war veterans, but this was gradually disposed of, mainly to the occupiers, in the post-war period. More recently the corporation's main activities have been to lend to middle- and upper-class families to finance owner-occupation and to act as banker to the provincial housing corporations which manage most public housing. It has increasingly lent money to assist in the provision of low-income housing (Eds).

[10] CMHC *Memorandum* 11 October 1963.

Author Index

Bold type indicates main references. Page numbers in italic refer to figures and tables.

Subject Index

List of units in the Open University Course, Urban Change and Conflict